INSTITUTIONS
&
PUBLIC LAW

TEACHING TEXTS IN LAW AND POLITICS

David A. Schultz
General Editor

Vol. 40

PETER LANG
New York • Washington, D.C./Baltimore • Bern
Frankfurt am Main • Berlin • Brussels • Vienna • Oxford

INSTITUTIONS & PUBLIC LAW

Comparative Approaches

TOM GINSBURG & ROBERT A. KAGAN, EDITORS

PETER LANG
New York • Washington, D.C./Baltimore • Bern
Frankfurt am Main • Berlin • Brussels • Vienna • Oxford

Library of Congress Cataloging-in-Publication Data

Institutions and public law: comparative approaches /
edited by Tom Ginsburg, Robert A. Kagan.
p. cm. — (Teaching texts in law and politics; v. 40)
Includes bibliographical references.
I. Public law. 2. Judicial power. 3. Political questions and judicial power.
I. Ginsburg, Tom. II. Kagan, Robert A. III. Series.
K3150.I57   342—dc22   2004022830
ISBN 0-8204-7477-0
ISSN 1083-3447

Bibliographic information published by **Die Deutsche Bibliothek.**
Die Deutsche Bibliothek lists this publication in the "Deutsche
Nationalbibliografie"; detailed bibliographic data is available
on the Internet at http://dnb.ddb.de/.

Cover image from clipart.com
Cover design by Joni Holst

The paper in this book meets the guidelines for permanence and durability
of the Committee on Production Guidelines for Book Longevity
of the Council of Library Resources.

© 2005 Peter Lang Publishing, Inc., New York
275 Seventh Avenue, 28th Floor, New York, NY 10001
www.peterlangusa.com

Printed in the United States of America

For Martin Shapiro

Table of Contents

Introduction

Institutionalist Approaches
to Courts as Political Actors

Tom Ginsburg
Robert A. Kagan

The essays in this book lie at the confluence of two recent trends in political science scholarship on public law. One is the approach to public law known as the "new institutionalism," which emerged in the 1990s in the United States as a challenge to the dominant behavioralist approaches to courts.[1] The other trend is the broadening outward of work on law and courts beyond the United States. Recent years have seen increasing scholarly attention to the European Court of Justice (ECJ) and its role in European integration, as well as a number of studies of national courts in other regions of the world (e.g., Goldstein 2001; Stone Sweet 1992, 2000; Widner 2001). Together these two trends constitute a broad scholarly agenda, one that puts politics and the relationships between courts and other branches of government more firmly at the center of the study of law in political science. That agenda is reflected in the range of work here.

This introduction traces the links between institutional analysis and the comparative work on courts. It argues that the institutional approaches represented in this volume offer the most promising set of tools for students of law and courts in an increasingly transnational and comparative context.

I.

Institutionalism is a broad term that reflects a range of approaches rather than a single paradigm. In the economic and political science traditions, institutionalism refers to that strain of rational-actor approaches that takes institutional structures seriously, rather than focusing on the particular individual agent alone. In the sociological tradition, on the other hand, institutions are sources of constraint that frame preferences, define roles, and constitute the structures within which individual agents operate (Koelbe 1995; Gillman and Clayton, 1998a, 6–7; Smith 1988, 90; Powell and Dimaggio 1991). What these various approaches have in common is a focus not on the behavior or preferences of individuals but rather on the structures that constrain and empower them. Institutions are more than the sum of the individuals that make them up.

In the study of law and courts, institutionalism has two broad strands reflecting these different methodological approaches. The rationalist strand uses positive political theory to model the position of a court within its political environment or the aggregation of preferences among the judges. This approach traces how the court and its members seek to accomplish exogenously defined preferences in an instrumental manner. The second strand is more constructivist, and seeks to understand how institutions shape preference formation (e.g., Gillman 1998). Practitioners of this approach typically adopt a historical perspective, tracing how institutions evolve over time. Key junctures of institutional change help frame decisions at later times in a path-dependent process (Steinmo et al. 1992).

These various institutionalist approaches share a view that understanding law and courts as political institutions requires attention to questions beyond how judges make decisions or how judicial preferences are aggregated on high courts. A comprehensive understanding of courts also requires attention to the political dynamics that shape their design and authority, defining their role in the broader political system. It must examine norms, structures and processes within which judges do their work and which therefore shape their incentives. Courts are not merely epiphenomenal sites for aggregation of political preferences, but complex institutions whose internal structures and external context matter for outcomes, and those outcomes help shape contests for power in other government institutions as well.

The institutionalist approach contrasts with the dominant attitudinal paradigm in public law scholarship in the United States, and the relative merits of these approaches have been debated in earlier work.[2] Attitudinalism focuses on judicial behavior, viewing judges as essentially politicians in robes, whose primary motivation is the maximization of their own policy preferences, and who are only weakly constrained, at best, by judicial precedents, principles and norms of consistency. Institutionalism, on the other hand, starts with the observation that courts are agencies of government, and ought to be understood, in Martin Shapiro's phrase which serves as the title of one of Shep Melnick's essays in this volume, as "one government agency among many" (Shapiro 1964a, 15). This simple observation gives rise to several crucial implications that form the overarching themes of these essays.

First, courts, like other government agencies, exercise power. They not only decide the fate of litigants but make policy, seeking to affect the behavior of governmental officials, business corporations, and large groups of citizens. To do so, courts, like other governmental officials, constantly need to bolster their political legitimacy, so that their decisions will evoke consent and compliance rather than opposition and resistance. The pursuit of legitimacy, however, constrains the behavior of judges, just as it constrains presidents and prime ministers.

Second, if courts are political like other government agencies, they will interact with other agencies in a dynamic process, and will be subject to the similar external pressures of ideas, ideology and politics. To understand courts, therefore, scholars must attend not only to the ideologies and votes of individual judges but to the institutional interactions between courts and the ideas that flow from the legal academy and political journalists, as well as judicial interactions with other actors in the political system.[3] Thus institutionalist scholars have observed that judges, like other politicians, often do not do what is dictated by principle but what which is politically possible. They must act strategically, for their decisions, if sufficiently controversial, may be overruled by legislatures, be circumvented by governmental officials, or even trigger political retaliation against the court itself (Murphy 1964; Barnes 2004; Epstein, Knight and Shvetsova 2001).

Third, courts are a *particular* kind of government agency, seeking legitimacy in distinctive ways. Judges wear robes (and in some countries, wigs). In common law systems, they write lengthy opinions. Their rulings purport to be dictated by preexisting law, not public opinion or the decision-makers' policy preferences. The fact that American courts are not organized in the same way as, for example, the forestry department, committees of Congress, or the Federal Reserve System, is crucial for understanding how courts operate, why they produce the outcomes they do, and how they interact with other institutions in the political system. In Herbert Kritzer's (2003, 409) words, "[c]ourts legislate, but that does not make them legislatures; courts administer, but that does not make them administrators." The way in which courts operate matters for understanding how courts affect the policy process—and the limits on that influence.

Together, these three points lead to a fourth implication of the institutional approach. Because courts are a particular type of institution embedded in larger political structures, the reach of law and courts is not presumed, but is itself a target of inquiry. In this sense, the institutional approach contrasts with traditional legal analysis, which tends to take the boundaries of the legal universe as given, and proceeds immediately to normative questions about the content of the law. Recognizing the whole domain of law and courts, institutional analysis raises new questions: What are the conditions under which law and courts are potent as a mechanism of social ordering? When and why does judicial power and authority wax and wane? What explains the increasing "judicialization of politics," a phenomenon that has gone well beyond the United States and Western Europe, to include countries in the former Soviet Union, Asia, Africa and Latin America, as well as a growing number of international regimes (Tate and Vallinder 1995; Epp 1998; Ginsburg 2003). Answering such questions requires a comparative approach, one which examines when and how law and courts matter across a range of different national, institutional and political contexts.

The institutional approach, moreover, facilitates comparative analysis by providing a set of analytical lenses that operate across nations and legal traditions. While comparative legal scholars historically have attributed variation to difference between the mode of thought of "the civil law tradition" (Merryman 1984) versus the "common law tradition," institutional scholars see variation as stemming from different incentives presented to judges by different political contexts and governmental structures. Hence institutionalists are well-positioned to observe and explain non-incremental *change* in law and courts, such as the sudden rise of active constitutional courts in countries with no such legal tradition, such as Korea and Taiwan (Ginsburg 2003), or the way that European judges, after appointment to the European Court of Justice, abandoned the restraints of their civil law training to become bold legal policymakers (Stone Sweet 2004).

II.

The essays in this volume were written during an era of rapid legal change. Throughout the world, law's empire has been expanding, intensifying its penetration of social, political and economic life (Galanter 1992; Kagan, Garth and Sarat 2002). There is talk of the globalization of law (Shapiro, 1993). European legal scholars write of the increasing "juridification" of labor relations, social welfare administration, and land use (Teubner 1987). The World Bank and the International Monetary Fund (IMF) condition loans on recipient nations' willingness to strengthen the rule of law. Scholars also now write about the "Americanization" of European law (Wiegand 1996)

and "The Globalization of American Law" (Kelemen and Sibbitt 2004)—
shorthand for a style of governance, which one of us has dubbed "adversarial
legalism," featuring lawyer-dominated litigation and frequent use of courts to
challenge governmental and corporate actions (Kagan 2001). Similarly,
books are written with titles like *The Global Expansion of Judicial Power*
(Tate and Vallinder 1995). Indeed, granting high courts constitutional powers
to review and reverse executive and legislative acts seems to have become a
necessary symbol of governmental reliability and of a nation's entitlement to
a respectable place in the international community (Ginsburg 2003, 1–23).

The growth of law and judicial authority begs for explanations.
Institutional scholars might put the question this way: Why should political
leaders—those who have the power to rule—surrender more and more
decisional (and hence policymaking) authority to judges? Why should they
subject themselves to the risk of lawsuits that challenge their decisions and
constrain their actions? Scholars who emphasize the role of ideas in history
might attribute such developments to both elite and mass revulsion against
the horrors and injustices of authoritarian rule, and hence to widespread
popular demand for democracy, the rule of law and justice. In long-
established democracies, the growth of law might be attributed to popular
demands for a greater measure of security and equality of treatment in a
richer, more rapidly changing, technologically sophisticated world (Friedman
1985; Kagan 1995).

Democracy and the rule of law, however, need not result in a substantial
political or *policymaking* role for courts and litigation. In some post-
authoritarian, democratizing regimes, newly empowered high courts have
been reluctant to exercise their powers assertively (Couso, this volume) or
have done some only in some policy areas, for fear of provoking retaliation
by political leaders (Epstein, Knight and Shvetsova 2001). Some actually do
provoke political retaliation and end up backing off (Silverstein 2003;
Moustafa 2003). In democracies with a strong tradition of judicial
independence, some democratic governments have responded to public
demands in ways other than expanding litigation and judicial policymaking.
British judges, for example, are trained to apply existing law in a formal
manner, not to serve as social problem-solvers (Atiyah and Summers 1987).
In strong welfare states, compensation for injuries is handled primarily
through social insurance systems, and judge-made tort law is not a salient
factor (Schwartz 1991). Regulatory agencies in Japan and Germany
emphasize government-business cooperation and informal "administrative
guidance," with a limited role for judicial review (Kagan 2001, chap. 9). In
Japan (Upham 1987; Tanase 1990), the Netherlands (Blankenburg 1994) and

Great Britain (Kritzer 1996) disputes are channeled to informal administrative tribunals rather than to courts. The upshot is that establishing and maintaining courts that use their law-interpreting powers to make policy, that can and do overrule the acts of elected legislatures and parliaments, represents a political choice that requires more specific explanations. Institutional analysis points to a number of different scenarios, based on the structure of political power, that lead to a larger role for law and courts.

Political Insurance/ "Hegemonic Preservation"

Rational choice institutional scholars are inclined to seek explanations in the situation-specific, self-interested motives of the powerful. They note that as political and economic conditions change, political leaders may view the surrender of some power to law and courts as a way of enhancing their own security and legitimacy. Some scholars, for example, attribute political leaders' decisions to empower courts and judges to the politicians' desire to reduce political uncertainty. When currently dominant leaders sense that they may be displaced in the next election, it makes sense for them to lock their preferred policies into law, or better yet, into difficult-to-change constitutional provisions; the next step is to empower the courts to enforce those rules should the successor politicians seek to change policy course. Ginsburg (2003) calls this the "insurance theory" of the institution of judicial review; Hirschl (2004) labels it the "hegemonic preservation" theory.

The political uncertainty that is at the heart of the insurance theory is magnified, of course, when political power is divided among two or more political parties. Dominant political factions which control all the commanding heights of governmental power marginalize courts as policymakers. They rule by informal pressure, less by law and lawsuits. Fragmented power, however, increases the current government's risk of opposition or displacement, inviting them to rely on detailed laws, litigation, and courts to entrench their policy preferences.

Separation of Powers/Divided Government

Fragmentation of political authority contributes to the growth and exercise of judicial power in other ways as well. Consider, for example, the United States, with its separation of powers (at both the state and federal level) between the elected executive and a separately elected bicameral legislature.

In such systems, political authority may be divided between two parties, one controlling the executive, the other one or both chambers of the legislature. With power thus divided—as has often occurred at the federal level in the United States since the late 1960s—legislative party leaders may fear that an ideologically hostile chief executive (and the bureaucracies he controls) will not energetically implement the legislature's policy preferences, even when embodied in legislation. Under such circumstances, legislatures are inclined to empower the intended beneficiaries of statutes to challenge bureaucratic inaction in court (Melnick 1992), or grant beneficiaries the legal right to file lawsuits against corporations or local government bodies who violate the statutes, thereby bypassing the bureaucracy. Thus, legislation enacted in periods of divided government often expands the power of the courts to review governmental action (or inaction) (Kagan 2001, chap. 3; Kelemen and Sibbitt 2004, 109–10).

From the standpoint of courts, fragmented and divided government makes it more difficult for politicians who dislike a judicial decision to enact a law overriding that decision. In such systems, therefore, judges have more degrees of freedom in interpreting the law to make new policy (Atiyah and Summers 1987). Courts also have less fear of a political backlash when political parties are not very disciplined and cohesive (as in the United States), for that kind of political fragmentation too makes it more difficult for political leaders to pass override legislation. Thus, it is not surprising that courts in political systems like the United Kingdom—that is, with a parliamentary form of government and (at any one time) a single dominant, disciplined party—tend to be more cautious policymakers than American courts (Atiyah and Summers 1987; Cooter and Ginsburg 1996).

Policing Federalism

Fragmentation of governmental power along another structural dimension—a geographic one, as in federal systems—also contributes to the establishment of judicial power and the growth of politics-by-litigation. Martin Shapiro and Alec Stone Sweet (2002) point out that when separate governments form federalist political systems, each may fear that others will manage to unfairly seize political or economic advantages, or that the central government will erode their autonomy. Hence federal constitutions often grant considerable powers to courts to enforce the constitutional commitment to abide by common rules and to umpire jurisdictional disputes between the central government and the subnational regional governments. This dynamic, so prominent in the history of the U.S. Supreme Court, has been replicated in recent decades by the ECJ in the European Union (EU).

Policy Change in Federal Systems

Federalism encourages litigation in another way, as well. Courts provide a low-cost mechanism for enforcing the central government's values and laws without unduly expanding the central government bureaucracy; the key is to provide private actors legal rights and incentives to bring lawsuits against businesses and local governmental bodies that are violating the central government's rules and regulations. Thus, one would expect judicial action to increase rapidly when the central government steps up its rate of lawmaking, and particularly when the central government, in doing so, is seeking to impose new norms on recalcitrant subnational cultures. Thus, in the United States in the 1960s, in the absence of an effective national ministry of justice, American federal courts reinterpreted the U.S. Constitution to elaborate new controls on evidence-gathering and treatment of criminal suspects by local police departments. Beginning about 1970, federal courts (pushed by lawsuits and appeals filed by private environmental advocacy groups) became crucial actors in the implementation of federal environmental statutes that crimped corporate and local governments' economic development plans (Kagan 2001).

Economic Liberalization

Some scholars have pointed to one other factor as an engine of judicialization of politics: economic liberalization (Kelemen and Sibbitt 2004). The United States has long been an exemplar of a system with high levels of judicial activity and power. This is partly because the U.S. has had high marks on all the dimensions of political fragmentation mentioned above. But another reason, one might argue, derives from the organization of the American political economy. American capitalism has long been more decentralized and competitive that most European market-oriented economies. American markets less often have been dominated by cartels, huge banks, or nationalized companies. Many vital services—telecommunications, electricity, health care, working class housing, transportation systems, financial services—have been provided to a much greater extent by privately owned companies rather than government monopolies. Compared to most European economies, therefore, there have been fewer institutions that can informally contain conflict among businesses, punish misbehavior, or forestall insolvency. Regulation of commercial relations in the United States, accordingly, has been left more fully to the realms of contract law, private litigation, common law policymaking by courts, and more legalistic modes of regulation. In recent decades, as globalization has intensified competitiveness of markets, the rate of litigation among businesses has increased, further drawing courts into a policy-making role (Kagan 1997).

In recent years, many other nations have adopted "neo-liberal" policies—privatizing government monopolies, contracting out services to private companies, and lowering restrictions on competition—in sum, starting to look a bit more like the U.S. political economy. Freer markets, Steven Vogel (1996) found, generate demands for more legalistic modes of regulation, since informal, hierarchical means of control are no longer adequate. Meanwhile, the ECJ is confronted with a steady diet of cases concerning the rules of fair competition and elimination of non-tariff barriers, propelling it into the realm of EU-wide policymaking. By formulating the "direct effect' doctrine, it has invited private interests to bring cases based on EU law into member state courts, expanding their role in governance as well (Stone Sweet, this volume; Alter 2003).

These scenarios or potential explanations are all evident in the essays in this volume. The essays provide no definitive theory, but they push the search for understanding of the reach of law and the behavior of legal institutions further and in new directions, while also providing a sampling of institutional modes of public law analysis.

III.

The chapters in this volume are organized into three sections—work on politics, law and courts in the United States, in the EU, and in other regions. First, however, Shep Melnick's first essay completes the introduction to the institutional approach through a focus on one crucial scholar, Martin Shapiro, in whose honor many of these essays were written. Shapiro's work has received increasing attention as "Anticipating the New Institutionalism" (Kritzer 2003) and "Progenitor and Provocateur" (Gillman 2004). Melnick's essay situates Shapiro within the broader milieu of American scholarship, noting how Shapiro steered a course between traditional legal formalism and the narrow attitudinalism that has been so prominent in the field. He focuses on Shapiro's move of treating courts as political agencies of American government, interacting with other agencies and affecting policy.

The power of courts to participate in governance depends first of all on what kinds of disputes they get to decide, or as lawyers put it, on what cases fall within the courts' jurisdiction. In two essays on the role of the federal judiciary in the United States, Howard Gillman and Shep Melnick both focus on the seemingly arcane details of the law governing the jurisdiction of the federal courts—illustrating how expansions and contractions in jurisdiction often reflect fundamental political struggles. In federal systems, as suggested above, courts are drawn into play to enforce the boundaries of the relative power of state versus the central government. But as Gillman and Melnick both teach us, decisions about jurisdiction also are often about conflicting policy preferences or views of good governance.

Gillman's account of the expansion of the jurisdiction of U.S. federal courts in the decades after the Civil War illustrates one of the previously mentioned pathways to a greater judicial role in politics: political leaders, particularly in a politically fragmented system, use the courts to advance their policy agenda. In the 1870s and 1980s, Gillman shows, the Republican Party's agenda was economic nationalism. They wanted to help build a strong nationwide corporate industrial economy—unhindered by populist-inspired, anti-corporate regulation that Democratic state and local governments might be inclined to adopt. Moreover, as in the previously mentioned "political insurance" scenario, they feared the Democrats might take both the presidency and the Congress. Even when in 1872, the Republicans held the White House and the Senate, they lacked the political dominance (and perhaps the Constitutional authority) to enact laws that would displace or block the local regulation that would frustrate their policy agenda. The solution they adopted was to authorize the federal courts to decide lawsuits by regulated businesses that charged that local regulations or laws violated the Commerce Clause of the U.S. Constitution, or the fourteenth Amendment's Due Process Clause. Late nineteenth-century Republicans, in other words, favored policy implementation via adversarial legalism. Their post-Civil War laws—along with their assiduous efforts to staff the federal bench with pro-business Republican judges—laid the foundation for the famous "*Lochner* era" Supreme Court jurisprudence. But by expanding federal court jurisdiction, they inadvertently established the judicial structure that liberals resorted to for a more recent expansion of adversarial legalism in the 1960s and 1970s, when a Democratic Congress passed legislation giving private lawyers incentives to sue corporations (and conservative state and local governments) in federal courts for violating national environmental and anti-discrimination laws.

Shep Melnick picks up the story in the latter part of the twentieth century. He describes the post-1970 growth of litigation against state and local governments in federal courts, forcing them to comply with enforcing federal anti-discrimination, labor, and social welfare program regulations. against state and local governments. Again, the key to that expansion of judicial governance was fragmentation of power. Politicians in Washington, while happy to take credit for announcing new social regulations and benefit programs, lacked the political unity to construct or fund federal bureaucracies that could implement those programs effectively. The solution, as in the 1870s, was to authorize lawsuits against the regulated entities by interested private parties.

Melnick's essay goes on, however, to illustrate another tenet of institutional analysis of courts. As Shapiro repeatedly has emphasized, if political authorities want credit for establishing *credible and reliable* courts and legal institutions, they must grant those institutions a visible measure of independence. Once so empowered, however, judges tend to adopt minds of their own. Melnick describes how in the 1990s a cluster of conservative Supreme Court justices, the "Federalism Five," pursued a political vision of their own, interpreting the Constitution and federal statutes so as to restrict federal courts' ability to entertain private lawsuits against state and local governments. These conservative justices alone, without pressure from interest groups or Republican Party leaders, have sought, however incrementally, to *reduce* the scope of adversarial legalism and federal judicial power. Yet the Court majority, Melnick notes, has acted strategically in this regard, picking and choosing its restrictions—so that its rulings have not triggered significant political opposition (beyond the outraged law professors who write in law journals).

In the EU, another federal system, the ECJ has been the primary agent of legalization, as analyzed in Alec Stone Sweet's essay. This is a striking development in terms of legal tradition, as suggested earlier, for unlike the United States, Western European member states, with their parliamentary systems of government, disciplined political parties, and a general view of judiciaries as bureaucratic law-appliers, traditionally had not invited litigation and judicial policymaking as modes of political action. But the fragmentation of power in the governance of the EU—particularly the need for unanimity for important policymaking in the European Commission and the Council of Europe—opened up a policy space that the ECJ gradually saw it could fill, transforming the constitutional character of the Union. The ECJ, like the U.S. Supreme Court in the era discussed in Gillman's essay, first used its authority to strike down regulations that interfered with the freedom of interstate commerce. Later (like the U.S. Supreme Court in the Warren Court era), it became a key policymaker on social issues as well as the core agenda of economic integration. "Today," Stone Sweet's essay asserts, "the ECJ has no rival as the most effective supranational judicial body in the history of the world; on any dimension, it compares favorably with the most powerful constitutional courts anywhere."

Stone Sweet's essay lays out the institutional logic of the growth of the ECJ's power. And he shows how particular institutional features, such as the preliminary reference procedure and the development of a robust doctrine of precedent, expanded the power of the ECJ systematically over time. Overall, the story Stone Sweet tells supports a confluence of several of the scenarios of judicial power mentioned earlier. The ECJ's rise exemplifies the institutional logic of courts as necessary umpires in a tentatively unified federal system; the logic of courts as powerful actors in a political regime in which power is fragmented among several institutions; and the logic of courts as policy-elaborators in federal regimes attempting to make substantial policy change—in this case, largely a neoliberal, trade-promoting policy agenda.

Both Carol Harlow and Paul Craig remind us that there is more to public law than litigation and judicial decision making, and that courts must be viewed in the context of other lawmaking and governance institutions. Harlow's piece explores the evolution of the administrative law of the EU. With a more fragmented institutional power structure, the EU differs from the unitary structures of European member states, and this has gradually created incentives for the substitution of the concept of "governance" for "government" in EU administrative law. The American experience provides a point of comparison, for the EU institutional structure she describes has some resemblance to the institutional environment of American independent regulatory agencies, with multiple principals seeking to influence policy. But the EU has a greater "democratic deficit" because of the historical absence of parliamentary supervision or an elected executive, and in fact relies heavily on national experts in amorphous "policy networks" and the so-called "comitology" process to define rules and standards.

This fragmented policy environment would seem to invite courts to emerge as important supervisors of European administration, and Harlow documents the growing role of the ECJ and the Court of First Instance in imposing procedural requirements. But the Courts have declined to follow an "American" approach of expanding standing so that courts themselves become a political arena of pluralist conflict or negotiation. This seems to be an instance wherein the European courts have not resolved what their role should be, or the extent to which they wish to insert themselves into day-to-day policymaking, notwithstanding their power to do so. Her contribution reminds us of the importance of ideas about government and democracy that shape judges' and adminisitrators' conceptions of their proper roles.

Craig's chapter covers similar terrain from a different vantage point. Community administration, he argues, has become constitutionalized through the adoption of the new Financial Regulation. He traces in rich detail the emergence and evolution of the Regulation against the background of inter-institutional dynamics within the Community, notably those leading to the fall of the Santer Commission and its aftermath. The new structure relies on a separation of policymaking and implementation, recalling Harlow's classic model of administration. Within the ever-expanding realm of policy implementation, however, the Community devolves authority to line organizations, including Member State agencies and European organizations within and outside the formal community structure, that are actually involved in the program in question. The story is one of a generalized dynamic that occurs when public agencies contract implementing functions to private organizations. Craig also evaluates the role of law in the evolution of the Common Agricultural Policy, noting institutional dynamics that led to structural over-expenditure and inadequate controls. In the stories of both the Common Agricultural Policy and Financial Regulation, the pressures for legalization and enhanced controls resulted rather directly from perceived defects in earlier institutional structures. Yet judicial review, while important, was far from the only legal solution to the problem. Courts appear as one alternative monitoring regime among many to the institutional problems of Community administration.

As dramatic as the European story of the emergence of judicial power has been, the development of courts as important political institutions in new democracies around the world has been more surprising. In many such environments, there is no tradition of autonomous courts constraining politics, and threats of authoritarian reversal may limit the role of the judiciary. At the same time, two developments have led to the expansion of judicial power in many democratizing societies: the shift toward neoliberal policies, with an emphasis on entrenched property rights, and the worldwide rise of a human rights agenda. In some circumstances, both departing authoritarians who seek to preserve property rights and new democrats interested in human rights can agree on courts as an important overseer of government. But judicial capacity to carry this double burden depends on both the willingness of other political institutions to tolerate the judicial role and the courts' own ability to effectively maintain an image of neutrality.

Javiar Couso's chapter discusses the development of judicial independence in Latin America, focusing especially on the case of Chile. Growing legalization in Latin America has not produced effective results in part because of the lack of institutional structures to effectively guarantee judicial autonomy. Through a careful historical analysis, Couso finds that a strong legislative branch may be a precondition of judicial independence in Latin America, to counterbalance the dominant power of the executive.

Tom Ginsburg's chapter discusses powers of constitutional courts beyond the paradigm function of constitutional judicial review. Constitutional courts in new democracies have been given jurisdiction over a wide array of political disputes far afield from their traditional role, including deciding electoral disputes, challenges to sitting political officials, and drafting legislation. The story is one of expanding jurisdiction of ostensibly neutral courts to areas beyond their traditional role, and no doubt is a sign of the success of legalization around the world. But these powers lead the court into explicitly political terrain, with possible consequences for judicial autonomy and the image of neutrality that is so important to courts as institutions.

In the late nineteenth-century United States and in the EU, we have seen, proponents of neo-liberal or efficiency-enhancing policy changes relied on judges to nullify regulatory legislation and regulatory agency rules that operate as non-tariff protectionist measures or otherwise fail the judges' economic efficiency tests. An analogous contemporary way of imposing such supra-democratic constraints on regulation, Bronwen Morgan's chapter argues, is not to use courts—which like the U.S. Supreme Court since the 1930s, may become reluctant to make such judgments. Instead, neoliberal political leaders vest "meta-agencies" with powers to subject legislation and regulations to cost-benefit analysis. Using the example of regulatory reform in Australia, Morgan outlines the powers and court-like processes in these extrajudicial institutions. The chapter argues that the increasing prominence of economic review of legislation reflects a species of legality, institutionalizing an emergent "rule of economics" that shares characteristics of the rule of law. Her work is at the cutting edge of institutionalist scholarship, going beyond law and courts to quasi-legal processes that are increasingly important in the global economy.

Together, these chapters provide a nuanced set of responses to the three core questions of institutionalist scholarship: How do courts affect governance in the political system? What is distinctive about courts and their mode of policymaking? And what is the reach of law?

One further theme runs through the papers, and that is the work of Martin Shapiro, whose final chapter provides an overview of the field of comparative public law. Most of the chapters in this volume were presented at a conference in honor of Shapiro's work, at Berkeley in March 2003. As perhaps the foremost political scientist working on law and courts of his generation, Shapiro has profoundly shaped the study of public law in the United States and Europe. His early work on constitutional and administrative law in the United States has been highly influential. As Herbert Kritzer noted, even though the term is seldom used, Shapiro's "political jurisprudence" has triumphed (Kritzer 2003, 407). His work on Europe played a major role in shaping that field. In the comparative area, Shapiro's book *Courts* (1981a) was described by Dan and Sam Krislov as "the most significant single contribution in the field" of public law in political science (Krislov and Krislov 1996). But they also noted that his influence has been limited, since it is hard to follow work whose method is vast erudition and bold thinking. All of the authors here acknowledge our intellectual debts to these qualities of Shapiro's work, even if we do not exhibit them in the same degrees.

For a number of years, Shapiro has urged scholars of law and courts to move down and out: down from an excessive focus on the Supreme Court, and away from a narrow focus on the United States. His chapter and many of the other essays here illustrate the extent to which his advice has been heeded.

16 *Ginsburg and Kagan*

Notes

The editors would like to thank Rosann Greenspan, Assistant Director of the Center for Law and Society, for her role in organizing the conference on the work of Martin Shapiro; Alexandra Huneus of the Jurisprudence and Social Policy Program, Corey Tellez of the University of Illinois College of Law and Zoë Ginsburg for editorial assistance; and James Pfander and Gordon Silverstein for helpful editorial suggestions.

Chapter Two was originally published as *How Political Parties Can Use the Courts to Advance Their Agendas: Federal Courts in the United States, 1875–1891*, American Political Science Review 96: 511–524 (Sept. 2002). Chapter Three appeared in revised form in Craig Parsons, ed. *Evolving Federalisms: The Intergovernmental Balance of Power in America and Europe* (Syracuse, NY: Campbell Public Affairs Institute, 2003). Chapter Four is based on Alec Stone Sweet's *The Judicial Construction of Europe*, published by Oxford University Press in 2004. Thanks to the publishers for permission to use this material.

[1]   The evolution of the new institutionalism and its relationship with the "old" institutionalism is traced in Clayton (1998) and Kritzer (2003).

[2]   The most prominent attitudinalists are Jeffrey Segal and Harold Spaeth (see Segal and Spaeth 1993). For earlier accounts of the debates among these approaches, see especially Gillman and Clayton (1998a; 1998b), Segal (1997), and Whittington (2000).

[3]   One stream of comparative work on courts is beginning to apply the 'separation of powers' games that model intergovernmental interactions to context outside the United States (see Epstein, Knight and Shvetsova 2001).

I. The American Context

...

1.

"One Government Agency Among Many": The Political Juris-Prudence (sic) of Martin Shapiro

R. Shep Melnick

All the contributors to this volume have been trained or inspired by Martin Shapiro. Since the early 1960s Shapiro has been the dominant figure in the public law subfield of political science. Yet as the reader of this volume will soon discover, it is difficult to identify a school of thought one could call "Shapiroism." To a large extent this is a reflection of the man's intellectual curiosity and breadth of view. Rather than drilling his students in the proper methods for studying law and courts, he has directed their attention to new questions and unexplored territory. Underlying his writing is a fierce resistance to the reductionism and specialization that so often lie at the heart of the gangs of academia. His books and articles display an encyclopedic knowledge of subjects as varied as labor and antitrust law, Supreme Court doctrines on freedom of speech, the bureaucratic pathologies of the Patent Office, reapportionment and gerrymandering, the evolution of common law courts in England, the problem of appeal in the courts of Islam, economic regulation in the EU, and torts in civil law countries. At the same time Shapiro has demonstrated an uncanny ability to make complex matters understandable and to pluck fundamental political issues from a morass of convoluted legal analysis. If Shapiroism involves combining sophisticated doctrinal analysis with such extensive knowledge of politics and policy, one might justifiably conclude that only Martin Shapiro is capable of being a Shapiroite.

To complicate matters further, Shapiro's work does not fit within our familiar methodological and ideological pigeonholes. One prominent division within public law pits those who do quantitative work (behavioralists, attitudinalists and rational choicers) against those who study the history and nuances of judicial doctrine. Shapiro is an outspoken empiricist, a steadfast critic of political scientists who aspire to become "little law professors." Yet he rarely does quantitative work, and years ago he identified serious flaws in the analysis of those who claim that judicial decisions are nothing more than political attitudes wrapped in fancy legal lingo. His writing is full of painstaking doctrinal analysis. For example, the first chapter of *Who Guards the Guardians* is devoted to showing how one strand of moral philosophy, "post-consequentialism," has influenced the development of administrative law. For Shapiro, political analysis is not a substitute for careful examination of legal doctrines, but an exploration one can begin only after mastering the details of legal reasoning.

Shapiro is also hard to categorize politically. Most public law scholars can readily be pegged as either critics or defenders of the Warren Court, advocates of judicial activism or judicial restraint. Not Shapiro. For nearly forty years Shapiro has argued that Supreme Court decisions are inevitably and inherently political. The arguments for judicial modesty advanced by Learned Hand and Felix Frankfurter, he maintains, are ultimately untenable. But if Shapiro is a critic of the Warren Court's leading critics, neither is he a fan of the judicial activism of the post-1954 era. For complicated reasons (which I hope to illuminate in the final section of this essay), Shapiro has remained an admirer of Hand and Frankfurter and a Warren Court skeptic. This unusual combination of political positions has endeared him to neither liberals nor conservatives.

This chapter seeks to identify the central and distinctive themes in Shapiro's vast work of law and courts. I should be candid about my reasons for doing so: I believe that political science as a discipline has ignored or forgotten many of the important lessons Shapiro has tried to teach us about studying the role of the courts within the broader political system. No one reads *The Supreme Court and Administrative Agencies* anymore, and that is a shame. A new generation of graduate students needs to go back and read his case studies on patent, tax, antitrust, labor law, energy and transportation policy, and reapportionment and congressional investigations in order to see what it means to do "political jurisprudence" with depth and flair. They need to read *Who Guards the Guardians* to understand what "institutional analysis" really entails. It may be true, as Herbert Kritzer wrote in a recent article, that Shapiro's work "anticipates" the "historical institutionalism" that became fashionable within political science in the 1990s (Kritzer 2003). But this is like saying that the Republicanism of Abraham Lincoln "anticipated" the Republicanism of Ulysses S. Grant. Kritzer's essay helps us see what public law scholars have learned from Shapiro; I hope to point out a few things they have forgotten.

Political Jurisprudence, Institutional Wing

In one of his first and best known essays, Shapiro wrote,

> The core of political jurisprudence is a vision of courts as political agencies and judges as political actors. Any given court is thus seen as a part of the institutional structure of American government basically similar to such other agencies as the ICC the House Rules Committee, the Bureau of the Budget, the city council of Omaha, the Forestry Service, and the Strategic Air Command. . . . In short, the attempt is to intellectually integrate the judicial system into the matrix of government and politics in which it actually operates and to examine courts and judges as participants in the political process. (1964b, 296–97)

Judges are political actors not because they collect government paychecks, but because they exercise discretion in making and applying legal rules. The premise that "judges make rather than discover law" is one that political jurisprudence "shares with all modern thinking about law." This raises the obvious question of how "political jurisprudence" differs from other forms of contemporary thinking about law and courts, particularly the legal realism that dominates law schools.

Over the years, Shapiro has had an occasional good word to say about law professors, but has repeatedly warned political scientists to resist the temptation to imitate their better-paid colleagues. In part, this reflects his sage advice that political scientists should recognize their comparative advantage—above all familiarity with non-judicial actors and institutions—rather than become second-rate legal craftsmen and brief-writers. More importantly, however loudly law professors may proclaim their adherence to legal realism, most law professors have compelling professional and personal reasons for maintaining the myth of the unambiguously correct court decision. Law professors need to teach students how to make convincing legal arguments. Moreover, the law professor "knows that what he teaches concerning the nature of law and courts today will determine the attitude and actions of the next generation of the bench and the bar" (Shapiro 1963b, 589–90). Preserving the legitimacy of judicial institutions requires submerging the essential truth of political jurisprudence since "in nearly all societies, courts gain their legitimacy and the consequent consent to their judgments by pretending that they discover the single correct outcome to every law suit" (Shapiro 1988a, 227). Political scientists are free from the obligation to preserve this noble lie primarily because we so rarely have any effect on public opinion or the institutions we study (Shapiro 1963b, 589). Impotence has its own charm: An honorable political scientist could, for example, write an essay entitled "Judges as Liars" (Shapiro 1994).

Much more disturbing than the law professor's effort to preserve judicial myths is the professional advocate's uncanny ability to convince himself that the correct interpretation of law and precedent is the one that corresponds to the policies that he favors outside the courtroom. Shapiro has never embraced "value free" social science, but he believes that political scientists have a calling higher than skillfully producing briefs on behalf of their favorite clients. Despite his at times cynical tone, Shapiro remains devoted to "the scientific ethic of truth telling, rather than the advocacy ethic of making the best case for your side" (1989b, 99–100). In short, law professors have a strong incentive to disguise judicial choice; political scientists have a responsibility to identify it. Law professors have a tendency to focus narrowly on the issues before the court; political science should focus on what these particular legal disputes tell us about the nature of the political system as a whole.

From the beginning, Shapiro has described himself as a member of the "institutional wing" of the new political jurisprudence. Like many "institutionalists" of the 1950s and 1960s, he understood that he was doing something different from the "behavioralists," but did not feel compelled to spell out in detail the nature of his alternative. Both *Law and Politics in the Supreme Court* and the "Political Jurisprudence" article contain brief, but devastating critiques of behavioral research that are as potent today as they were forty years ago (Shapiro 1964a, 34–41; 1964b, 326–40). Shapiro showed that much of this work was tautological: It attributed votes to attitudes, but discovered attitudes primarily by looking at votes. It not only excluded from analysis those unanimous decisions that are most likely to reflect non-attitudinal factors, but also ignored the inconvenient fact that the swing justices who decide many cases have the most weakly defined political views. To make matters worse, their attitudinalists' quantitative analysis was heavily dependent on the traditional legal analysis they so disparage. (More on this below.) Most importantly, these models attempt to explain only how Supreme Court justices vote, not what they say in their opinions. As Shapiro convincingly demonstrates in his many case studies, it is the opinions not the votes "which provide the constraining directions to the public and private decision makers who determine the ninety-nine percent of conduct that never reaches the courts" (Shapiro 1968, 39). Of course, none of this seems to have fazed the attitudinalists, who have their story and are sticking to it.

Given the amount of energy many academics devote to internecine warfare, it is notable that after this initial critique Shapiro never devoted much attention to his disagreement with the behavioral wing of political jurisprudence. After all, in an important respect, the attitudinalists were correct: the Warren Court "was engaged in a consistent and comprehensive constitutionalization of the New Deal's fundamental vision of social justice" (Shapiro 1983a). The main problem with attitudinalists is that they are so intent upon producing a simple theory with quantifiable measures that they ignore the diversity and complexity of the issues that come to court, the multiplicity of judges' goals, and the subtleties of communications among judges and between them and repeat players.

But what does it mean to be an "institutionalist?" Shapiro's most sustained examination of courts as institutions came in his magisterial 1981 work, *Courts: A Comparative and Political Analysis*. This book is first and foremost an attack on the conventional legal understanding of the prototype of courts. Independence, adversarialness, decisions according to preexisting rules, and winner-take-all decisions, he argues, are not essential elements of courts. Not only do courts vary enormously from regime to regime, but they are always in part an instrument for the exertion of sovereign power: "To the extent that the judge employs preexisting rules not shaped by the parties themselves [i.e., virtually always], he acts not independently but as a servant of the regime, imposing its interests on the parties to the litigation" (Shapiro 1981a, 28). Rather than focusing on the inherent nature of courts as judicial institutions, Shapiro examines how political battles shape judicial institutions and how these institutions both serve the needs and limit the power of other political actors. What is most evident in this book is not how institutions shape politics, but how politics shapes institutions.

With one exception. All courts face a common, chronic problem: they gain their legitimacy in large part from their role as impartial arbiters of the concrete controversies that are brought before them by private parties. But the more the role of the judge is institutionalized and the more the judge follows pre-established law, the more likely it is that the loser will question the impartiality of the judge (whom he did not chose) and the law (which was established by others, often those in a far-away capital). The judge-plaintiff-defendant triad "involves a basic instability, paradox, or dialectic that accounts for a large proportion of the scholarly quarrels over the nature of courts and the political difficulties that courts encounter in the real world:" the moment an "impartial" judge decides a case, the loser will be inclined to interpret the situation as "two against one" (Shapiro 1981a, 2). The central feature of courts as institutions—indeed the only characteristic common to all courts—is the difficulty they face in preserving the legitimacy of the triad. In Shapiro's words,

> The basic social logic, or perceived legitimacy, of courts rests on the mutual consent of two persons in conflict to refer that conflict to a third for resolution. The basic

logic is threatened by the substitution of office and law for mutual consent, both
because one of the two parties may perceive the third as the ally of his enemy, and
because a third interest that of the regime, is introduced.... Thus, while the triadic
mode of conflict resolution is nearly universal, courts remain problematical in the
sense that considerable tension invariably exists between their fundamental claims
to legitimacy and their actual operation. (1981a, 36–37)

Institutional analysis of courts, then, involves understanding how courts play
their lawmaking and social control functions while preserving their ability to
induce losers to comply with their orders. Such institutional analysis does
not provide us with a theory of the judicial process, but only identifies a
perennial political problem that regimes handle in widely varying ways.

In order to get a better handle on the distinctive features of Shapiro's
"institutional wing" of political jurisprudence, it may be useful to step back
from the abstractions we academics throw around with such abandon, and
remember that Shapiro was trained as a student of American politics, not a
"judicial specialist." Very early in his career he was distressed by the
parochialism of the public law subfield. A distinctive feature of his work on
American government is that he pays as much attention to administrative
agencies, congressional committees, interest groups, and electoral systems as
to courts. Shapiro did not reduce these non-judicial actors to stick figures—
as contemporary students of the "separation of powers game" are wont to do
(literally). Promising to "integrate the judicial system into the matrix of
government and politics in which it actually operates" sounds like the
vacuous boilerplate that many of us include in our grant applications. What is
most remarkable about Shapiro's work is that he actually does it.

Having studied policymaking in Congress and the executive, Shapiro
became an astute observer of the ways various institutional settings shape
and channel political activity. As Lyndon Johnson's career demonstrates, it
takes different skills to be a successful president than to be a successful
Senate majority leader. The House Rules Committee's tasks, norms and
recruitment patterns differ significantly from those of the House Education
and Labor Committee. It is hard to read Shapiro's case studies on tax law and
conclude that federal judges, the commissioner of the IRS, and members of
the Ways and Means Committee all think about tax issues in the same way
(Shapiro 1964a, chap. 4). Judges put their jobs in danger by taking calls from
politicians and the parties before them; political executives put their jobs in
danger by refusing to engage in such ex parte communication. As Shapiro
noted,

The study of things political is, to be sure, partially aimed at exposing similarities
between various political actors and institutions, but surely it is also aimed at

discovering differences.... If I say that Al Capone and FDR were both politicians, I am not saying that the President was a gangster. (1964b, 317)

A few years later he offered a different comparison:

[I]t is not enough to say that the Pope and the President are both politicians. It is the task of students of politics to systematically describe both the similarities and differences between the various phenomena he labels political.... More awareness of the difference between various kinds of politicians might make it clear that in calling a judge a politician we do not necessarily mean that he kisses babies and worries about voters back home. (Shapiro 1968, 15)

Following Aristotle, Shapiro places political man somewhere between the godly Pope and the beastly Capone. Describing exactly where and what difference this makes is an important part of the job of an observant political scientist.

In legal studies, it is commonplace to compare judges with legislators. Traditionalists warn that unelected courts should not become "super-legislatures" and that judges should not "legislate from the bench." Attitudinalists reply, "Don't be naïve, they do it all the time." Shapiro, in contrast, offers the enormously useful advice that we should pay particular attention to the similarities between courts and bureaucracies (1968, 17–18, 44–45; 1981a, 20–28, 49–56; 1964b, 306, 319–24). Both courts and bureaucracies are hierarchical organizations for which the problems of coordination, uniformity and compliance by lower level operators are of critical importance. Both are expected to obey written rules, to follow established procedure, to document their decisions, and to avoid personal favoritism. At the federal level, both judges and administrators are appointed officials who are exceedingly difficult to fire. Perhaps most importantly, Shapiro argues, courts and agencies are both "subordinate, supplemental lawmakers" engaged in incremental decision making. The more we learn about administrative decision making, the more it looks like the technique of stare decisis (Shapiro 1968, chap. 1). In *Courts*, Shapiro adds that "in a startling number of instances" judges and administrators are not only the same person, but "a person who draws little or no distinction between administering and judging" (1981a, 20).

One of the chief advantages of thinking about the similarities between judicial and bureaucratic hierarchies is that it forces us to examine how those at the top (e.g., justices on the U.S. Supreme Court) try to induce those below them (e.g., federal circuit and district court judges, state courts, and a wide array of federal, state, and local administrators) to comply with their commands. Of the hundreds of thousands of federal court rulings, millions of state court decisions, and untold number of administrative determinations issued each year, the Supreme Court scrutinizes only about one hundred. Appellate courts have a peculiar mechanism for ensuring compliance by lower courts: They wait for formal appeals from those wealthy or angry enough to challenge the initial determination. Needless to say, appellate courts do not investigate random samples of lower court decisions, nor do they ask for elaborate statistical reports or conduct surprise inspections—the stock in trade of administrative agencies.

Within this context, the Supreme Court (or even a circuit court) cannot hope to control the discretion of lower court judges merely by deciding discrete "cases and controversies." Rather, it must use these "cases and controversies" as an opportunity to issue the elaborate instructions-cum-decision we call a judicial opinion. Ambiguities in these instructions will seriously weaken hierarchical control. Justices who are unable to explain what "desegregation" means are unlikely to desegregate many schools. Those who cannot define "pornography" but only "know it when they see it" are destined either to watch a lot of movies or to delegate policymaking to lower court judges (Shapiro 1964a). Allegedly hard-headed political realists who dismiss judicial doctrine as mere smokescreens are themselves naïve about the problem of hierarchical control.

A comparison of courts and agencies also highlights the fact that those at the top are likely to be nearly as interested in organizational maintenance as in "policymaking." Most political executives find (with disappointment) that they spend far more time defending their agencies, pleading for resources, mediating internal disputes, and maintaining morale than in making policy determinations (Kaufman 1981, chap. 2; Wilson 1989, chaps. 10–11). It should not come as a surprise to us, then, that the U.S. Supreme Court frequently decides cases not because the justices have strong policy preferences, but because they think it is important to reduce inter-circuit conflicts, to rein in particularly unruly judges, and to keep the judicial trains running on time (Perry 1991). Just as political executives will battle to protect bureaucratic "turf," appellate judges will struggle to limit the autonomy of specialized courts and agencies. The Supreme Court often looks for ways to promote consistency among courts and cooperation between state and federal officials without getting too mired in the complex (and often deadly boring) details of each statute and program (Shapiro 1964a). Justices who expect lower court judges to respect Supreme Court precedent must be wary of openly ignoring precedent themselves; for if lower court judges believe everything is up for grabs in the Supreme Court, then voluntary compliance with past decisions is likely to decline. In short, like administrators, judges manage complex institutions as well as make public policy.

There remains, of course, a major difference between administrators and judges: the former are primarily specialists, the latter generalists (Shapiro 1968, 52–54). Ideally this means that judges avoid parochialism and clientelism, maintaining an open mind and a broad point of view. But it also raises the specter of judicial incompetence and dilettantism. As Donald Horowitz has put it, "That judges are generalists means, above all, that they lack information and may also lack the experience and skill to interpret such information as they may receive.... Judges are thus likely to be doubly uninformed, on particulars and on context" (Horowitz 1976, 31). In this sense, judges reviewing administrative agencies or hearing "mass toxic tort" cases are in a position similar to presidents supervising the military, congressional committees overseeing complex regulatory programs, or political executives trying to manage large departments. All these generalists must search for ways to monitor and guide hordes of specialists without throwing a monkey wrench into a process they only vaguely understand.

In short, Shapiro's "institutional wing" of political jurisprudence combines the central postulate that judges make political choices with an appreciation for the ways in which different institutions face distinctive tasks, incentives, expectations, organizational maintenance imperatives, and compliance problems. We can learn a great deal about the operation of courts by thinking about them as bureaucratic organizations. But we also must bear in mind that (at least in the United States) courts are staffed by generalists rather than specialists, and that they must cope with the fundamental conflict between the basis of their legitimacy (the impartial third leg of the triad) and the reality that they are in part an instrument of sovereign power. All this helps us understand what sort of "governmental agency" courts—or rather, American federal district courts, Texas courts or French courts—are. But it does not bring us yet to Shapiro's central concern, understanding "the nature of the Court as one governmental agency among many" (1964a, 6). Given how often Shapiro repeats this phrase it is incumbent upon us to be clear about what this entails.

Taking the Policy Perspective Seriously

In "Political Jurisprudence," Shapiro claimed that while the behavioral wing of the new jurisprudence "raises the most hackles," the institutional wing, "in a fundamental sense," is "the most radical" because it "breaks down any remaining barriers between law and politics" (Shapiro 1964b, 307). What is in fact most radical about Shapiro's approach is that it requires us to abandon traditional legal categories and to expand enormously the scope of our inquiry. The heart of Shapiro's argument is that the courts are usually one small part of a much larger policymaking process. In order to understand their role we must range backward and forward in time, understanding both the underlying policy debate and the patterns of interaction among a wide array of actors. Since issues, participants, and patterns differ from one policy arena to another, conducting detailed case studies becomes the order of the day. Anyone who has taken the time to read Shapiro's case studies on labor, tax, antitrust, and patent law, transportation and energy regulation, congressional investigations, and reapportionment can see that this requires immersion in very complicated matters.

Over the years nothing has provoked Shapiro's ire more than the constricted focus of most public law scholarship. Centuries ago in common law countries, it might have made sense to equate "law" with the rulings of courts. Then came two of the most important developments of the nineteenth and twentieth centuries: statutification and bureaucratization. For some time now, Parliament, Congress, state legislatures, and city councils have had the nasty habit of enacting laws of their own. Since the New Deal, administrative agencies have been churning out legally binding commands called regulations, administrative orders and the like. Much of what federal courts do today is interpret and enforce statutes; approve, disapprove, enforce, extend, or circumscribe agency rules; and serve as referee for a wide variety of state, federal, and local lawmakers. Increasingly, this is true of state courts as well. Even areas that used to be considered pure constitutional law—civil rights, religious liberty, habeas corpus, federalism—now involve large doses of statutory interpretation. No matter what area of the law one examines, the courts are usually adding, subtracting or otherwise modifying something done by another branch or level of government. These other branches and levels frequently react to the courts, and another round begins. Staring at only one short segment of the story line is unlikely to teach us much about the nature of politics or policymaking.

Scholarly efforts to restrict the scope of judicial studies produce glaring anomalies. Consider, for example, Jeffrey Segal and Harold Spaeth's "attitudinal model," which claims to explain justices' voting patterns in terms of their "policy preferences," but quickly returns to conventional legal analysis. Segal and Spaeth dismiss judges' arguments about institutional roles and judicial restraint as "simply bunkum" (1993, 236). To them, Felix

Frankfurter, the patron saint of judicial modesty, was nothing but a pious hypocrite who

> used judicial restraint solely to rationalize his substantive policy preferences, which, in his case, were those of a staunch economic conservative: pro-business and anti-union. He supported state regulation of labor because the states' regulations opposed labor. He refused to support their business regulations, as well as federal agency regulation, because these decisions were predominately economically liberal. (Segal and Spaeth 1993)

Leaving aside the curious question of how a trusted advisor to President Franklin Delano Roosevelt became so hostile to the New Deal, it is clear that for Segal and Spaeth policy preferences, not institutional norms, drive Court decisions.

It comes as something as a surprise, then, to learn a few pages later that liberal and conservative justices have divergent views on both federalism and the power of the courts—the very shams Segal and Spaeth had so fervently dismissed. In describing their categories of "liberal" and "conservative" outcomes, they write,

> In judicial power, a 'liberal'—more accurately, a judicial activist as opposed to judicial restraintist—supports the exercise of judicial power, including review of administrative agency action. In federalism, a liberal vote supports national supremacy—that is, is a pro-national and anti-state. (Segal and Spaeth 1993, 243)

These are the categories they use in their extensive quantitative analysis (Segal and Spaeth 1993, 256–60). One might have thought that liberal justices would support state governments when it would help their cause (e.g., when progressive states try to set environmental standards higher than those established by the federal government; or when the Florida Supreme Court mandates a counting process that appears to help the Democratic candidate) and would oppose judicial review of agency action when it threatens their cause (e.g., when Republican appointees on the D.C. Circuit take a "hard look" at OSHA rules issued by the Clinton Administration). But apparently not: liberals just like centralized government and judicial activism. Except when they don't.

What is going on here? Why can't Segal and Spaeth stick by their cynical, policy-preference, anti-legal bunkum guns? What is going on is that the Supreme Court, like most courts, issues at least two types of decisions, plus a large number that fall between the two extremes. In a few decisions, they try to establish a relatively clear substantive legal policy. (Whether or not they succeed, of course, is another matter—and a highly significant one at that.) *Roe v. Wade* announced a trimester framework for regulating abortions.[1] *Loving v. Virginia* made interracial marriage legal.[2] Fourth Amendment cases tell police and prosecutors what they must do in order to be sure that a conviction will hold up on appeal. It is not hard to give each of these rulings the equivalent of an ADA or COPE rating.

Many more Supreme Court cases, though, revolve around the authority and procedures of various units of government. The particular parties and even the particular program or statute directly involved in the case may be tangential. What really counts is what the Court has said about the operation of various public institutions. When must the courts of one state accept the determinations of the courts of another state? Does extensive federal regulation of an industry bar state courts from hearing tort and contract claims against the regulated companies? When can federal courts decide issues involving interpretation of state law? Should circuit court judges defer to trial court judges on the qualifications of expert witnesses?[3] It might be possible to estimate the likely policy consequences of some of these decisions. But this would require that the observer (and, presumably, the justices themselves) to know a great deal about this area of the law and the government institutions involved. Moreover, it is likely that the policy consequences will be uneven, varying from program to program (e.g., helping business in economic regulation, hurting business in social regulation), from state to state (e.g., helping liberals in California and conservatives in Texas), and from time to time (empowering first liberal Clinton appointees and then conservative Bush appointees). No matter how determined and policy-driven its members, a court that decides fewer than a hundred cases per year will not be able to fine-tune its institutional rules in order to get exactly the policies favored by the majority.

Consider *Chevron v. NRDC*, one of the most important Supreme Court decisions of the past quarter century.[4] In this case, environmental groups lost; industry and Environmental Protection Agency won. Conservative, right? But the lenient judicial review of agency action established by Chevron frequently insulates the decisions of program advocates within federal agencies from probing review by conservative judges appointed by Presidents Ronald Reagan and George Bush. That is, unless the political appointees of Republican presidents were actually calling the shots and Carter appointees dominated the D.C. Circuit panel hearing the case. But what about review of decisions made during the Clinton Administration? Now consider the Supreme Court's decision in 2000 not to apply Chevron deference to agency rules and interpretations that have not gone through the notice-and-comment rulemaking process.[5] Segal and Spaeth's coding rules require us to categorize them as "liberal" since they increase judicial oversight of agency action. Yet, in the that case, Justice Clarence Thomas wrote the opinion, while Justices John Paul Stevens, Stephen Breyer and Ruth Bader Ginsburg dissented. Obviously, the attitudinal model has difficulty handling these issues of institutional authority.

In short, most Supreme Court opinions are about the rules of political engagement. Everyone knows that these rules will have policy consequences, but no one can be sure what these consequences will be. Judges are inevitably guided not just by their "policy preferences," but by their "own analyses of how the political system operates" (Shapiro 1964a, 330). Political jurisprudence inevitably involves institutional analysis because institutional analysis is central to the reasoning of judges.

In the case studies he wrote in the 1960s as well as in his 1988 book *Who Guards the Guardians?* Shapiro traces the subtle interplay of judges' policy preferences and their institutional analysis. In the concluding chapter of *Law and Politics in the Supreme Court* he notes,

> Justices are highly aware of the constant and intimate relationships between themselves and other government agencies and that they create both substantive and procedural law that seeks to acknowledge the complex patterns of power and capacity in which the Court operates. Much of the legal performance of the Supreme Court that seems unclear, illogical, or contradictory when examined in strictly legal terms comes into focus under policy analysis. (Shapiro 1964a, 331)

For example, the Supreme Court's vacillating and inconsistent decisions on labor practices and tax policy become more understandable once one sees that the Court was trying to keep a hand in these complex matters without getting too involved "in the minutiae of fact-finding and interpretation" by the National Labor Relations Board and Internal Revenue Service (Shapiro 1964a, 126). In labor law, Shapiro found, the Court generally succeeded; in tax law, it failed. Since court decisions rest on judges' political and institutional analysis and not just on their policy preferences, it is quite possible that they will make mistakes. Often these miscalculations will be called to their attention in later cases, providing them with an opportunity to adjust their doctrines and to rethink their assumptions. Thus, one cannot understand how court doctrines evolve without considering their consequences outside the courtroom.

Fitting the courts into the broad sweep of policymaking is the central goal of political jurisprudence. It is difficult to convey in an essay such as this the comprehensiveness and subtlety of *Who Guards the Guardians?* and the case studies Shapiro wrote in the 1960s. Since I want to give the reader some idea of what is involved in this sort of political analysis, I offer the following rules of thumb for the political jurisprudence that I have gleaned from Shapiro's work.

First, as Shapiro's study of labor law demonstrates, the political jurisprudence must abandon traditional legal categories—particularly the misleading distinction between constitutional and non-constitutional cases—and examine all court decisions affecting a particular policy or agency. In doing so he might unexpectedly discover, for example, that the First Amendment was "initially used by the Court as a tool for coordinating federal and state labor policy" (Shapiro 1964a, 82). To take another example, in the late 1960s and early 1970s, constitutional law and statutory interpretation were two tactics in the Court's effort to reform welfare. Statutory interpretation proved a more powerful tool for achieving the goals laid out most clearly in the Court's constitutional opinions (Melnick 1994, chap. 4.) Moreover, since the judiciary's contribution to policymaking often is "not made by sweeping judicial gestures, but by the patterns and over-all effects of numerous decisions, none of which is individually very striking" (Shapiro 1964a, 41), one must look well beyond the well-known, well-argued leading cases. This means that the public law scholar must become familiar with a large number of complicated Supreme Court and lower court opinions usually read only by labor lawyers, patent lawyers, tax lawyers, environmental lawyers, legal services attorneys, and other specialists.

Second, the investigator must understand the underlying policy issues and dilemmas facing legislators, administrators and judges. For example, antitrust law seems to require judges to criminalize normally acceptable business practices when those practices prove unusually successful (Shapiro 1964a, 269–78). Judges and regulators must sometimes choose between maximizing the extent of competition and the number of competitors, between protecting small producers and maximizing consumer welfare. Similarly, in reapportionment cases judges implicitly chose among competing models of representation (Shapiro 1964a, 216–52; Bybee 1998). Patent law tries to establish property rights in ideas, creating a host of paradoxes and difficulties (Shapiro 1968, 47–55). In the 1950s, Congress expected the Federal Power Commission (FPC) to control natural gas prices and prevent curtailment of service, but gave the FPC direct control only over pipelines (Shapiro 1968, 233–42). Disability benefit determinations—whether announced by administrators or judges—involve highly subjective judgments rather than clear medical findings (Stone 1984). Legal doctrines may reflect judges' efforts to acknowledge these complexities—or to avoid them altogether. The student of political jurisprudence must also consider how liberal and conservative positions on policy issues shift over time. For example, the New Deal liberals supported price and entry regulation, but by the 1970s, disillusioned liberals (led by activist judges) were calling for deregulation (Derthick and Quirk 1985, 39–57). One cannot hope to understand the courts' role in policymaking without understanding the broader dimensions of the policy debate.

Third, political jurisprudence involves placing court action within "the everyday world of bargaining, persuasion, concession, and compromise which is central to an understanding of the actual process of American politics" (Shapiro 1968, 271). Judges seldom have either the first word (since they are usually interpreting or enforcing statutes or regulations) or the last word (since legislators and administrators can often refine, amend, overturn, or ignore court decisions). This means public law scholars pay most attention to such things as agencies' standard operating procedures and incentives for settling disputes (Shapiro 1968, 185–99; 1964b, 99–126); conflict between state and federal regulators (Shapiro 1964a, 77–99); the role of committee staff in writing legislation (Shapiro 1968, 204–13); compromises and inconsistencies in complex statutes (Shapiro 1968, 233–57; 1988c, 79–94); legislative attempts to overturn court decisions, to restrict litigation, and/or to expand upon judicial initiatives (Shapiro 1968, 204–16; Melnick 1994, 238–44, 256–64; Burke 2002; Barnes 2004); efforts by Congress, agencies, and lower courts to evade court rulings (Fisher 1984; Derthick 1990, chap. 7; Melnick 1994, 172–75); and mutual augmentation of regulation by courts and administrative agencies (Halpern 1995, chap. 3; Davies 2002). Shapiro points out that public law's fixation on constitutional law has overstated inter-branch conflict and ignored the extent of cooperation. One might add that it also tends to overstate the extent of intra-branch unity. What might look like healthy judicial-administrative cooperation to lower court judges and bureaucrats might strike presidents and the Supreme Court as pathological collusion (Shapiro 1981b, 151–57; Melnick 1985, 653).

Fourth, court decisions affect public policy not just by changing "law on the books," but by shifting the incentives of potential litigants and intervenors. For example, the major effect of the Supreme Court's decisions on patents was to make patent-holders more reluctant to bring infringement suits against those who have used their "invention." The good news was that this counteracted the Patent Office's bureaucratic bias in favor of granting patents; the bad news was that this often allowed infringers with deep pockets to overpower inventors with shallow pockets (Shapiro 1968, 200–03). The greatest significance of a court decision might lie in the leverage it provides the winners in legislative and administrative forums (Melnick 1994,

217–21, chap. 7; Taylor 1984) or in the opportunities it creates for a group to appeal to its constituency and negotiate with its adversaries (McCann 1994; Kagan and Axelrad 2000). Political jurisprudence must include examination of the shifting litigational strategies of key players as well as the bargaining that takes place "within the shadow of the law."

Fifth, judges usually face a steady stream of cases on a particular topic, allowing them to engage in a dialogue with other actors and to learn from their experience. Smart judges will be cautious about committing themselves to a rigid position until they have seen a number of cases. They will try to nudge Congress or an agency in a particular direction to see what kind of response they get. But to the extent judges rely on subtle hints or broad themes rather than per se rules, they run the risk of being ignored (Shapiro 1968, 164–84 and 242–49). Litigation is an iterative process in which judges must navigate between arrogance and impotence.

Sixth, one cannot expect that judges will play the same role in every policy arena. The Supreme Court may be

> a policy leader, as in the antitrust area, or it may retreat from policymaking, as it does in the tax field. It may face such a relatively simple task in political analysis as assessing the function of Congressional investigations or the immensely complex one of deciding how to alter the geographic bases of representation. It may brush aside other agencies' findings of fact as it tends to do in antitrust cases, or it may seek to leave fact-finding entirely to another agency like the N.L.R.B. In some instances, it develops strong doctrinal positions like those of legislative purpose and presumption. In others, the gift cases in the tax area, for instance, it resolutely refuses to have any doctrine at all. (Shapiro 1964a, 328)

Relations between the courts and Congress may depend on the nature of the committee with jurisdiction over the issue at hand (Melnick 1994, 264–69; Barnes 2004). Federal judges might be less willing to defer to state officials than to federal administrators (Melnick 1994, 245–49). The number and variety of litigants is likely to depend on the program's distribution of costs and benefits. Well-known political science classifications of policy arenas may help us understand these variations—but only after we have done the difficult work of collecting detailed case studies.

Part of the appeal of both traditional legal analysis and the behavioral wing of "political jurisprudence," is that they comfortably narrow the range of material to study. The former focuses almost entirely on appellate decisions. The latter says, "Don't worry about complex legal doctrines, just code the outcome." Shapiro's brand of political jurisprudence, in contrast, commands us to look at virtually everything—legal doctrine, voting patterns, administrative behavior, congressional coalitions, lower court compliance with appellate decisions, interest group activity, shifting intellectual trends—you name it, he has studied it. At least for the young scholar it culminates in case studies—"mere journalism" according to many within the discipline—rather than simple arguments about correlation and causation. All that work, and still no hope of an article in a peer-reviewed professional journal. Like socialism, radical Shapiroism may take too many evenings.

Incrementalism, Rationalism and the Art of Governing

In many respects, Martin Shapiro is an unreconstructed pluralist. In the United States policy emerges incrementally through the mutual adjustment of separated institutions sharing power. The fragmented American political system produces satisfactory public policy despite the fact that this policy was not the result of anyone's conscious design. Following David Truman's lead, Shapiro adds the courts to Charles Lindblom's image of "muddling through," Aaron Wildavsky's description of strategic bargaining over budget increments, Herbert Simon's understanding of "satisficing," and Richard Cyert and James March's emphasis on standard operating procedures, rules of thumb, and feedback (Truman 1951, chap. 15; Lindblom 1959; Wildavsky 1964; Simon 1976; Cyert and March 1963). Adding the courts to this mix transforms the old "iron triangle" into the new "iron quadrangle" (Shapiro 1981b, 151–53). Although pluralism has often been denounced as inherently conservative or even reactionary, Shapiro used it to defend the modest activism of the early Warren Court. As long as judges limit themselves to "small-step change" and allowed legislators and administrators to engage in incremental adjustment as well, there would be little to fear from the political activity of the courts. Shapiro hinted that the real danger would come either from judicial capitulation to politically insulated specialized agencies or from judicial insistence that theirs was the one true way. His refusal to portray the Warren Court either as a hero or villain flowed from his recognition that the Court remained but "one government agency among many"—and before 1964, a relatively cautious one at that.

As usual, Minerva's owl flew at dusk. Just as graduate students were rushing out to buy *The Supreme Court and Administrative Agencies*, pluralism and incrementalism were going out of fashion in academia and on the D.C. Circuit. The academic critique is well known to most political scientists. The way in which this critique influenced judges and administrative law has been explained in detail by none other than Martin Shapiro. Twenty years after *The Supreme Court and Administrative*

Agencies, Shapiro provided a three-pronged intellectual, legal and political explanation for the replacement of incrementalism with "synopticism"— which he defined as "a process that gathers all the facts, considers all alternative policies and all the possible consequences of each, and chooses those policies with the highest probability of achieving agreed goals at least cost"—as the guiding idea of administrative law (1988c, 15). The political science of one generation, he claimed, is the administrative law of the next. Unfortunately, his previous claim about the impotence of political science professors had proved inaccurate.

The changes in administrative law Shapiro describes in *Who Guards the Guardians?* were part of a broader shift in the federal courts' confidence in achieving large-scale policy change and their receptivity to innovative legal doctrines. Among the best examples of this shift are *Reynolds v. Sims*[6] and *Lucas v. Colorado*,[7] the two big reapportionment cases announced in 1964, shortly after publication of Law and Politics in the Supreme Court. Over the next few years the Court applied the "sixth grade arithmetic" of one person, one vote with increasing rigidity. In his lengthy chapter on reapportionment in *Law and Politics*, Shapiro cheered both the Court's rejection of the "political questions" doctrine in *Baker v. Carr*[8] and its willingness to reform badly mal-apportioned state legislatures. But he also warned against application of a simplistic equal-population principle that recognized neither the complexities of representation nor the courts' responsibility to reflect "the American balance between Madisonian and populistic democracy" (Shapiro 1964a, 248). According to Shapiro, the expectation that the Court must act on the basis of "neutral principles" is doubly dangerous: Usually it relegates the Court to utter passivity, but once the Court believes it has discovered a "neutral principle" it will throw caution to the wind, solving "problems with a sledge hammer rather than with the scalpel that is actually required" (1964a, 248). He suggested that after putting the issue on the political front burner, the Court would have been wise to step back and see what others could come up with. Reading the one person, one vote writing on the wall, though, Shapiro predicted that

> the result of the Court's new ruling in terms of real political equality will be largely random.…Viewed as an attempt actively to contribute to greater political equality in the U.S., rather than simply as a philosophical editorial, the Court's new position is little more than a random stab. (1964a, 249)

Looking back over nearly forty years of reapportionment litigation, there is good reason to believe that Shapiro got it right.

Shapiro recognized that judges would at times be tempted to offer sweeping pronouncements and to attempt to solve grave social problems by themselves. And he predicted that when they tried to do so, things would usually turn out badly. Clear standards and principles, he warned, "have a certain 'damn the torpedoes quality....Standing on principle, in international, barroom, and legislative-judicial relations is likely to lead to a fight" (Shapiro 1963b, 602).   When judges insist that courts rely on abstract principles rather than on prudence, they will usually err either by trying to do too little (the Supreme Court of the 1940s and 1950s) or too much (the Supreme Court of the 1960s and 1970s).

The themes of judicial overreaching and excessive reliance on abstract principles is at the center of Shapiro's work on administrative law. The first half of *Who Guards the Guardians?* is devoted to an elegant explanation of why the federal courts demanded that administrative agencies replace the old pluralism and incrementalism with the new synopticism. The second half explains why the courts did not in fact produce more rational policymaking, but instead created a more dishonest and politically insulated bureaucracy. The courts seriously overestimated both the prospects for synopticism and their ability to remake administrative agencies. Within agencies, technical expertise and rational decision-making did not replace "muddling through," "satisficing," bargaining, and partisanship. Administrative discretion simply went underground. Agencies had no choice but to lie about how they came to their decisions. This had the unfortunate and unintended consequence of making it harder for political executives, members of Congress, and reviewing judges to understand what administrators were doing.

> There is, then, a sense in which we now have the worst of all possible worlds. The courts force the agencies to disguise the crucial elements of their decisions, which are really prudential and actually could be understood and reviewed by judges representing the lay public. By requiring the agencies to present these decisions as if they were rationalist, technical, and synoptic, the courts drive the very prudential decisions that ought to be out front and subject to public and judicial scrutiny under a technological smoke screen. So what we get is secret prudence unguarded by anyone. (Shapiro 1988c, 156)

Call it the revenge of incrementalism.

For reasons explained at the beginning of this paper, Shapiro generally avoids telling judges how they should decide cases. But on one constitutional issue, partisan gerrymandering, he offered a glimpse at the type of advice he would offer members of the Court. Intervening to prevent partisan gerrymandering, he points out, is incompatible with the formal, individualistic reasoning underlying *Reynolds v. Sims* and its progeny.

Moreover, there is no judicially manageable standard for identifying partisan gerrymandering. But anyone who thinks that lack of precedent or lack of standards is sufficient to deter American judges from tackling a problem like partisan gerrymandering is seriously mistaken. In *Brown v. Board of Education*,[9] the Court could offer neither convincing precedents nor manageable standards for defining desegregation. The same was true for *Baker v. Carr* and mal-apportionment. But neither case was wrongly decided. Emphasizing a point he had frequently made in the past, Shapiro explained that judges

> are often in a position to identity a wrong without being able to define the right. Finding themselves in this position, they are ethically entitled to, and in fact do, intervene against the wrong. The same point is made in a policy-making context by the whole body of writing about incremental decision making and satisficing. Individual and organizational decision makers often do, and indeed often must, move away from a wrong position without being able to specify precisely what ideal position they are moving toward. (1985, 228)

The problem was not that the courts started the reapportionment revolution or contributed to the civil rights revolution—for that they are to be admired—but that they later thought they could define and complete them both.

Shapiro offers the Court a prudential argument for why it should avoid the partisan gerrymandering thicket. Once the Court starts down that path, he maintains, there are only "two plausible battle scenarios. The first results in a war of attrition with casualties too high for the Court to accept. The other results in nuclear disaster" (Shapiro 1985, 252). If the Court decides cases on an ad hoc basis, identifying gerrymandering according to Justice Stewart's know-it-when-you-see-it rationale, the Court will face a never-ending series of cases, each provoking a hail of complaints about the Court's partisanship. The Court will be forced either to give up or to find a simple, understandable, seemingly neutral principle for resolving cases. That standard will inevitably be proportional representation: It is both "easy to calculate" and "obviously democratic to the naïve." But adopting proportional representation as the standard for evaluating districting is a dreadful idea. Shapiro's conclusion on this score follows from his "appreciation of how wonderful, mysterious, and unique is the American system of relatively stable, two-party democracy" and a well-grounded suspicion that proportional representation undermines stable two-party systems (Shapiro 1985, 255). In short, "[i]f it works, don't fix it." Prudent judges should avoid fundamentally changing "the most successful democratic political system that the world has ever known without having any idea what they have done or whether the system can survive it" (Shapiro 1985, 255–56).

Shapiro is a rare specimen among students of public law: a Burkean who distrusts "rationalist visions" and who denies that either judges or administrators can govern through the application of abstract rules and principles. He is usually inclined to adopt the point of view of the "prudentialist" for whom "each [governmental] decision is tailor-made to the past, present, and future of the particular situation rather than logically derived from a preexisting general rule" (1988c, 216). That general rules are usually insufficient and occasionally dangerous is a theme that has run throughout Shapiro's work for decades (1961; 1963a; 1964a, chap. 5). When he says that judges are political and that judges are often unprincipled, he means this as a compliment.

Shapiro's understanding of the role prudence and principle play in politics—judicial and otherwise—sheds light on his position on the relationship between political theory and empirical studies of law and courts. In his well-known exchange with Rogers Smith and Sotirios Barber, Shapiro wrote, "Before public law political scientists begin worrying about RORTY, they might begin worrying about NEPA and OSHA" (1989b, 101). One might be tempted to dismiss such a statement as a manifestation of the parochialism of contemporary social science if it were not for the fact that Shapiro himself has written extensively about the way in which the thinking of Rorty and other "post-consequentialists" have significantly altered legal doctrine (1988c, chap. 1). No one is more attentive to (and appalled by) the way intellectual fashions shape judicial thinking than he. In his 1989 essay, Shapiro bases his characteristically contrarian views about Rorty and OSHA on a comparative advantage argument: those who study courts will not be as good at moral philosophy as those who do it full time; better that they devote their attention to what they know best. While that might be good career-counseling advice, it does not really address the arguments of Smith and others about the wisdom of combining two parts of political analysis which were only recently pulled asunder. Why should an aspiring public law scholar do what Shapiro says (worry about OSHA instead of Rorty) rather than what he does (show how Rorty influences judicial review of OSHA)?

I think the deeper insight behind Shapiro's advice—an insight that has guided virtually all his research and writing—is his appreciation of the extent to which one cannot govern on the basis of general rules and abstract principles. Academics—law professors, political scientists, English professors, you name it—love to dwell in the world of abstraction. What characterizes most academics today is that they have never done anything or run anything outside an academic department. They lack experience, particularly the experience of governing. Such experience is almost always humbling. It teaches us that the world is extraordinarily complex. It teaches us that many people disagree with us. It teaches us that there are great limits on our ability to have things turn out as we wish. It teaches us that we can learn from the advice and experience of others. It teaches us that it is very hard to make things better, but remarkably easy to make things worse. On top of this, it reminds us that governing—whether in the form of judging, executing, or legislating—involves the use of coercion. A courtroom is not a seminar room; no one loses his life, his property, or his children when the bell rings.

Indeed, the peculiar experience of most academics, especially those specializing in moral philosophy, Shapiro warns, tends to make them particularly dangerous as advisors to judicial princes (either in the form of law clerks, authors of law review articles, or teachers at big-name law schools) or, God forbid, judicial princes themselves. From law professors, both on the left and the right, students learn to view legislators, administrators and actual citizens (as opposed to that abstract entity, "the people") with contempt. They learn that law embodies morality and that judges enunciate the highest aspirations of a nation. Over the course of the past century, elite's opinions in general and legal elites in particular, have transformed the judge from "industrial idiot" to "post-industrial hero" (Shapiro 1983a). Convincing law students, bar leaders and judges that their political prejudices should guide the nation is about as difficult as convincing voters that what the nation really needs is another big tax cut. It is hard to imagine a more reckless political education: "As recent experience reminds us, prophets armed are dangerous people" (Shapiro 1989a, 1589).

Reading the work of Shapiro or engaging in the type of research he recommends, provides a much different sort of political education. By placing us in the middle of complex, sprawling, never-ending policy controversies, it offers vicarious experience in governing. Shapiro does not hesitate to point out the foibles and parochialism of legislators and administrators, but he also explains the value of the distinctive perspective and intelligence they bring to bear on political issues. He illustrates the severe constraints on judges' ability to direct policy. He points out that judges, legislators and administrators are all particularly likely to produce a raft of unexpected and unwanted consequences when they engage in big-step, as opposed to incremental, change. He teaches respect for the logic of "the multi-decision-maker process which is the central feature of American government and politics" (Shapiro 1968, 90).

The reader might assume (as I once did) that the brash young proponent of "political jurisprudence" who attacked then-dominant ideas about judicial modesty, neutral principles and political questions slowly became more conservative as he aged and as the Warren Court became more adventuresome. There is nothing wrong with that. As the saying goes, the only thing more ridiculous than a young conservative is an old radical. But those who take the time to read Shapiro's early work carefully will discover that he did not in fact change his tune.

His early writing was in part an attempt to reconcile his enormous respect for Learned Hand, Felix Frankfurter and Alexander Bickel, with his unwillingness to accept the line they tried to draw between law and politics. In the preface to his first book, Shapiro wrote,

> The one truly moving episode of my graduate education was hearing Learned Hand deliver the Holmes Lectures, and my thinking about the Supreme Court has been largely an attempt to grapple with the ideas of Hand, Justice Frankfurter, and Professor Wechsler. It is the proper job of a preface to thank those who have helped the author, and my first thanks must surely go to the intellectual leaders who created a body of thought about the Court that I view as fundamentally incorrect and immensely challenging. (1964b, vii)

He devoted several law review articles to this dialogue with Hand, Frankfurter and Wechsler, concluding that their doctrines deserve respect as "maxims of prudence" and "good practical advice," but not as "abstract truths and moral imperatives" or "philosophic universals" (Shapiro 1963b, 604). Years later, he struck a similar chord in arguing that Robert Bork's originalism

> is really dominated not by loyalty to the framers but by a consciousness of the ambiguities and difficulties of political life....Bork's proclaimed desire to stick with the framers' intention is an awkward attempt to construct a positive rational for a negative and prudential message. Judges ought not to attempt making policy that has wide ramifications because policymaking is difficult and big policy changes are particularly risky. (Shapiro 1989a, 1572)

Because Bork dressed up his compelling political arguments in unconvincing "myths of framers' intentions," he made it too easy for legal scholars to ignore his warnings. The moral is that one cannot improve political jurisprudence by denying that it exists.

In his policy studies, Shapiro rarely devotes much attention to a particular judge nor does he offer much praise for those he names. A notable exception is his extended discussion of Learned Hand's patent decisions, which Shapiro explained, showed how "the most challenging and fascinating judicial mind of the twentieth century" managed to reconcile his progressive impulses in public policy with his extreme version of judicial modesty (1968, 216–20). The key, Shapiro indicated, was making small changes in existing policy that counteracted the biases of other institutions and helped others actors think more clearly and fully about the underlying issues. This required respect for the other branches, a thorough understanding of policy issues, and a tentativeness that avoided brash declarations and per se rules. This was judicial politics at its best.

Shapiro feared not only that the form of modesty espoused by Hand and Frankfurter was intellectually untenable, but also that it led to judicial passivity in the face of such obvious injustices as racial segregation and hideously mal-apportioned legislatures. More subtly it threatened to produce judicial surrender to bureaucratic "specialists without spirit, sensualists without heart" (Weber 1958, 182). Our political system needs to incorporate judges' sense of injustice as well as the common sense and breadth of view they bring to their oversight of policy specialists. But no one should underestimate the difficulty or the danger of the undertaking. If law is part of politics, then judging is part of governing, and judging well requires statesmanship. I doubt that Martin Shapiro would ever use the term "statesmanship." But when all is said and done, that is what he teaches.

Notes

[1] 410 U.S. 113 (1973).

[2] 388 U.S. 1 (1967).

[3] *Baker v. General Motors*, 522 U.S. 222 (1998); *AT&T v. Central Office Telephone*, 524 U.S. 214 (1998); *Chicago v. Int'l College of Surgeons*, 522 U.S. 156 (1997); *General Electric v. Joiner*, 522 U.S. 136 (1997). All these cases come from a single term of the Supreme Court.

[4] 467 U.S. 837 (1984).

[5] *Christensen v. Harris County*, 529 U.S. 576 (2000).

[6] 377 U.S. 533 (1964).

[7] 377 U.S. 713 (1964).

[8] 369 U.S. 186 (1962).

[9] 347 U.S. 483 (1954).

2.

How Political Parties Can Use the Courts to Advance Their Agendas: Federal Courts in the United States, 1875–1891

Howard Gillman

The history of the relations between Congress and the Supreme Court during the twenty-five years following the Civil War is most telling proof that the various organs of government are not mechanically set apart from each other.... The practical workings of the Supreme Court in the scheme of our national life may be as decisively determined by the extent of appellate jurisdiction allotted to it by Congress, the issues open on review, the range of jurisdiction of the inferior courts, and the machinery available for the disposition of business, as by the learning and outlook of the Justices, the quality and the training of the bar.

Frankfurter and Landis (1928, 86)

Introduction: Explaining Expansions of Judicial Power

This chapter offers a case study in American political development—the dramatic and controversial expansion of federal judicial power in the late nineteenth century—in order to illuminate two seemingly unrelated questions of general interest to political scientists: What tools are available to party leaders who seek to institutionalize their substantive policy agendas or insulate them from electoral politics? How do we account for expansions of judicial power?

Exploring the relationship between these questions requires an integration of two relatively distinct traditions of political science research. The first tradition focuses on the motives and methods behind the creation or empowerment of potentially autonomous policymaking institutions by legislators or other power-holders who have a presumptive interest in maintaining tighter control of policy. The literature on this question typically looks at the origins of bureaucratic agencies or regulatory commissions, at decisions to delegate powers to such executive or quasi-executive bodies, and at the process by which oversight or control of these institutions is maintained. Studies have attributed institutional empowerment to a variety of political motivations including a desire to shift decision making responsibility on issues that elected officials consider politically sensitive, enhance credible commitments to favored constituencies, reduce cycling effects or decision-making costs, and protect favored policies against reversal (for an overview, see Voigt and Salzberger 2002).

The second research tradition looks at expansions of judicial power (see Tate and Vallinder 1995). Many scholars who have examined this topic have tended to attribute judicial empowerment to factors other than the short-term, self-interest of elected power holders acting on the basis of conventional political agendas.T[1] Many constitutional historians and law professors often take a law- or court-centered view and discuss judicial power as if it was a by-product of essentially legal choices that relatively independent judges make about the proper scope of their own authority. Other legalist interpretations suggest that nations may simply reach a point at a certain stage of their development when they begin to appreciate the system-wide advantages of the judiciary's enforcement of agreed-upon rules (Stein 1980). Some scholars who have studied the European Court of Justice (ECJ) have argued that the expanding role of the ECJ is a product of the efforts of various supranational and subnational actors pursuing their shared self-interests (e.g., Burley and Mattli 1993; Stone Sweet and Brunell 1998a). Others have treated judicial empowerment as reflecting a more general interest in promoting "rule of law" governance, dispute resolution or consensus politics (e.g., Elster and Slagstad 1988; Stone Sweet 1999; Tsebelis 1995). Relatedly, rational choice scholars have attempted to explain expansions of judicial authority in terms of establishing efficient mechanisms for the maintenance of investor security (e.g., Olson 1993; Weingast 1997, 1993), the oversight of bureaucracy (e.g., McCubbins, Noll and Weingast 1987), and the desire to maintain policy stability in competitive party systems (Ramseyer 1994).

Unlike most of these accounts of judicial empowerment, I argue that the expansion of federal judicial power in the late nineteenth century is best understood as the sort of familiar partisan or programmatic entrenchment that we frequently associate with legislative delegations to executive or quasi-executive agencies. In this case, however, the institutional beneficiaries of this entrenchment were courts rather than agencies or commissions.

It is generally acknowledged that federal judicial power in the United States, and the power of the Supreme Court in particular, expanded toward the end of the nineteenth century. A system of lower federal courts that at mid-century was understaffed and underpaid, lacking in courtroom facilities (and thus was often forced to rent space from state governments), that attracted men of little prominence, and had only limited jurisdiction had become by century's end a real third branch of government, with expanded personnel, a new layer of appellate courts, and dramatically broader jurisdiction (Hall 1973, 29–87, Purcell 1999, 687). A Supreme Court that only fleetingly, and insecurely, exercised power at the beginning of the nineteenth century, and that had undermined its reputation and authority among many former supporters with the *Dred Scott* decision in 1857, began after the Civil War to strike down laws with greater regularity and to involve itself in more significant national policy disputes (Graber 1998a, 1999; Griffin 1996, 97). The Chase Court voided at least eight federal laws between 1865 and 1874; another eight were struck down by the Waite Court up through 1888. An important troika of cases by the Fuller Court in 1895— on the Sherman Anti-Trust Act, the Income Tax, and the use of labor injunction—drew critical attention in the 1896 Populist and Democratic Platforms (Westin 1953). While the pre-Civil War Court struck down state laws at a rate of less than one a year (forty-one laws through 1864), the Chase, Waite, and Fuller Courts established a rate of around three laws a year between 1864 and 1895 (Epstein et al. 1994, 96–110). By the 1890s, a "muted fury" toward federal courts had already begun to build among those who felt the need to resist what had become a bastion of conservative policymaking (Ross 1994). Some prominent legal scholars also felt compelled to advise federal judges of the virtues of restraint (Thayer 1893).

In accounting for this expansion it has been common for scholars to argue that judicial activism was initiated by conservative judges who objected to the regulatory policies being pursued by other branches of government, with the goal of either constraining progressive legislation or (more generally) imposing conservative values on an increasingly tumultuous industrial order. Some versions of this argument assume a class-conscious and coordinated response by the bench and bar (e.g., Jacobs 1954; Paul 1960; Twiss 1942); others focus more simply on individual judges pursuing their policy preferences (Segal and Spaeth 1993, 304–05). Either way, the explanations assume that judicial power is best seen as arising in opposition to conventional political power in a zero-sum battle of control over policymaking; in other words, an expansion of judicial power is treated as inconsistent with the preferences of legislators. On the basis of this assumption some normative constitutional theorists have even depicted these late nineteenth century developments as the moment when the judiciary began illegitimately to assert unprecedented policymaking claims against the elected branches, thus giving birth to the modern preoccupation with "judicial supremacy" or the "countermajoritarian difficulty" (e.g., B. Friedman 1998, 2001; Haines 1932; Jackson 1941).

However, there are good reasons for thinking that late nineteenth-century developments are best viewed as "politically-inspired" rather than "court-inspired" (see Sunkin 1994). As I will demonstrate, much of the expansion of power resulted from the passage of two key pieces of legislation—the Judiciary and Removal Act of 1875 and the Evarts Act of 1891—that were part of the Republican Party's efforts to restructure national institutions in order to better facilitate national economic development (see Bensel 2000). The more familiar parts of this political agenda involved currency policy, tariff policy and (eventually) national bureaucratic expansion (Skowronek 1982). However, the expansion of federal administrative capacity only became necessary after economic nationalists were successful at promoting large-scale enterprise by extending more reliable legal institutions to investors and producers who operated within a national market.[2] Federal judges became the principal agents of this agenda after Republicans in the national government retooled the federal judiciary by changing its jurisdiction, reforming its structure, and staffing courts with judges who were reliable caretakers of this new mission.

This account is consistent with the view that judges take on those powers, responsibilities and agendas that are assigned to them by other power-holders in the political system (Peretti 1999, 133). Moreover, given that the two key legislative initiatives leading to federal judicial empowerment were passed by lame-duck Republican Congresses immediately prior to losing control of all or part of the Congress, this argument echoes Ran Hirschl's (2000) "hegemonic preservation thesis," which assumes that elected politicians have a motivation to empower courts when their control over policy outcomes is challenged in majoritarian decision-making arenas. This account is also broadly consistent with what John M. De Figueiredo and Emerson H. Tiller (1996, 438) call a "political efficiency" argument for judicial expansion, which holds that the House of Representatives and Senate have an interest in enacting legislation "expanding" federal courts when they "expect the nominating president and the confirming Senate to appoint judges who will have political preferences consistent with those of the enacting Congress."[3] However, rather than view late nineteenth-century developments as merely an effort by Republicans to achieve short-term political advantages in the staffing of an existing institution, the account developed herein emphasizes the goal of establishing more long-term adjustments in the role or mission of the federal judiciary in American politics.[4]

Within the more familiar judicial politics literature, the approach I am advocating is most closely related to research that links national court behavior to the interests of dominant coalitions and to broader changes in the political system (e.g., Dahl 1957; Graber 1993, 1998a; Klarman 1996). However, rather than focus on the *constraints* imposed on judicial decision making, I want to highlight how the decisions of non-judicial actors reconstructed and *empowered* the institution of the federal judiciary.

The Federal Judicial System Before Reconstruction

To understand the significance of postbellum developments some reminders about antebellum understandings are useful, since during this period the limited nature of federal judicial power also reflected the influence of conventional political considerations.

Early nationalists understood the relationship between strong central authority and a strong federal judiciary that was resistant to local influence— but so did opponents of strong national power, and one of their principal accomplishments in 1789 was preventing the creation of a truly nationalist judiciary (Marcus 1992). Federal judicial districts and circuits were tied to state boundaries. In almost all states only one federal trial judge was assigned (Virginia and Massachusetts received two), and these district court judges had to be residents of their districts. Federal district courts had remarkably limited jurisdiction. They were essentially authorized to hear only admiralty cases plus penalties and forfeitures under the laws of the United States. Circuit courts also acted primarily as trial courts and heard mostly cases involving diversity of citizenship. Importantly, federal district courts had no authority to hear trials on "federal question" suits, which meant that most conflicts over national policy would have to be litigated in state courts.[5] The Supreme Court was given the authority under the infamous Section 25 of the Judiciary Act to review decisions by a state's highest court in which a claim based on federal rights was denied, but it took more than a quarter century before that power was asserted in *Martin v. Hunter's Lessee*,[6] and immediately that authority was subjected to a prolonged siege by resistant states (Warren 1913).

To further mitigate the centralizing potential of the Supreme Court the six justices were required to spend most of their time traveling in the states over which they had circuit responsibilities, where they would serve primarily as trial judges with very limited jurisdiction.[7] When they heard appeals while riding circuit, they were required to participate with the local federal judge who made the original decision. Their circuit responsibilities ensured that these national officeholders would feel deep connections to their assigned states, and antebellum appointment norms solidified these connections by encouraging presidents to choose justices from the region of the country over which they would have circuit responsibilities (O'Brien 2000, 32–103). This tendency to view Supreme Court justices as representing regional interests was reinforced by the Judiciary Act of 1837, which increased the size of the Court from 7 to 9 while also expanding and realigning the circuits to account for western expansion. To reinforce sectional influences no circuit contained both a free and slave state; to ensure the protection of southern regional interests (a goal of the second party system) the slave states were divided into five circuits, meaning that they would enjoy a majority on the Supreme Court (Hall 1973, 18, 19, 448, 451; see generally Frankfurter and Landis 1928, 6–55; and Wheeler 1992).

There were minor adjustments in the structure before the Civil War, but they did not affect the central point: The organization of federal courts was related to larger political considerations about the limited role of the national government in American politics (see Skowronek 1982, 29). More specifically, one of the principal ways in which national power was kept in check was by ensuring that the principal agents of national law would be appointed with local or regional considerations in mind and (for good measure) would be overworked, poorly paid, and authorized to enforce only a subset of federal law (the rest of which would be filtered through state proceedings). Given that this was the goal, it is not surprising that when federal courts experienced serious caseload pressures in the decades before the Civil War, Congress felt no obligation to offer relief.[8]

These courts did do some work for the union (mostly in diversity and admiralty suits) and after *Swift v. Tyson*,[9] they managed a small break from state influence when federal judges were freed from having to follow state law in diversity cases, thus creating a more national forum for interstate economic policy. They were also able (with some difficulty) to enforce some federal policies, most significantly those relating to rights under the federal fugitive slave acts, which were enforced against antislavery forces in the North (Cover 1975). In the Compromise of 1850 Congress also vested the federal judiciary (through the action of federal commissioners) with the responsibility of deciding the status of runaway slaves; when we combine this decision with later partisan urgings to have the Supreme Court address the disintegrating slavery problem in the *Dred Scott* case it is safe to say that there was a consensus among some party leaders that it was politically expedient to channel some aspects of national slavery policy into the federal courts (Graber 1993; Kutler 1968, 32–33). Still, the perceived utility of federal judicial power was very issue-specific, and all antebellum efforts to expand the general significance and power of federal courts in the political system were ignored or rebuffed.[10]

When the slavery interests separated from the national government at the beginning of the Civil War, Republicans had their first opportunity to break southern domination of federal judicial power. They also had their first opportunity to create a strong and effective national court system that could be the agent of Republican interests. But during this period reformers thought more in terms of reworking the traditional model to their partisan advantage rather in terms of serious institutional reconfiguration. Some influential historians of this period argue that Republican efforts in the 1860s represented a strong commitment to the expansion of judicial power to serve the ends of Reconstruction (Kutler 1968, Wiecek 1969), but it is probably more accurate to view these early steps as constrained attempts to marginally change the bias inherent in existing structures.[11] While there were some calls from judges, prominent lawyers and newspapers to increase the number of district courts, create an intermediate court of appeals, and eliminate circuit riding by justices, the Congress was still controlled by representatives committed to localism and regional representation on the Supreme Court (Hall 1975, 180–81). The Judiciary Act of 1862 succeeded in rearranging the circuits so that there were only three wholly southern districts (a number that was reduced to one in 1866) and also gave Ohio and Illinois a prominent role in newly formed northern circuits; Lincoln quickly cemented this traditional model by appointing Samuel Miller of Iowa, David Davis of Illinois, and Noah Haynes Swayne of Ohio to the Supreme Court. A year later regionalism was reinforced again when California and Oregon were brought into the system as a 10th circuit, with Stephen J. Field of California receiving an appointment. The new system ensured that the South could not dominate the federal courts, and thus brought an end to "the judicial embodiment of Calhoun's 'concurrent majority,'" but it did nothing about circuit riding and it made no effort to assist with overburdened dockets at all levels of the federal court system (Hall 1975, 181; Kutler 1968, 16–21).

By 1865 Northern commercial and financial interests were pressuring Republicans to do something about docket overload. The bill that Lyman

Trumbull introduced in late 1868 addressed the problem primarily by creating nine new circuit court judges who would have the same powers and jurisdictions as the assigned Supreme Court justice (who would still be required to attend at least one term of the circuit court during each two-year period). The decision to make these new positions circuit court, rather than district court, appointments was considered a modest way of mitigating traditional local (state-based) biases in the lower federal courts. Still, as Hall (1975, 182–85) summarized these developments, the federal judicial system "ended the decade of the 1860s in much the same condition they had begun, characterized by administrative decentralization and individuality....At least in their institutional structure the federal courts proved resistant to the impact of the Civil War and the first years of Reconstruction. For their part, the Republicans emerged as at best reluctant nationalizers" (see also Fairman 1987; Kutler 1968, 50–63).

From Reconstruction to Economic Nationalism

Initial and tentative efforts to expand the role of federal courts began during the War with the passage of the 1863 Habeas Corpus statute, which for the first time since the "nullification crisis" of the 1830s authorized the "removal" of judicial proceedings from a state court into a federal court if the state proceeding appeared to a defendant's counsel to be prejudiced by reason of the defendant's status as a national officer.[12] The precedent was quickly built upon: Over the next few years Congress passed twelve removal measures extending federal court alternatives to state court defendants (especially blacks) who were not federal officials but who claimed that the protection of federal rights was being jeopardized by local prejudice. Removal also became an option in suits against all corporations (except banking) organized under a law of the United States, suits against common carriers for loss or damage to goods through the hostilities of the Civil War, and diversity suits exceeding $500 where the nonresident party could show local influence or prejudice (Frankfurter and Landis 1928, 61–63; Hyman and Wiecek 1982, 261–63; Kutler 1968, 143–60).[13]

Reconstruction politics also led Congress to engage in piecemeal expansions of the role of federal courts in promoting or protecting national policies. The Federal Enforcement Act of 1870 (a.k.a., the Force Bill) reenacted the 1866 Civil Rights law through the enforcement authority of the Fourteenth and Fifteenth Amendments and also prohibited state election officials from enforcing discriminatory state laws or interfering with voting on the basis of race. While enforcement was assigned to the brand-new Department of Justice, the jurisdiction of federal courts was expanded to hear prosecutions brought under the statute, and removal authority was granted to protect federal officials and rights-holders from prejudicial state court proceedings. Federal judges were also authorized to call for troops to maintain peace at elections, having become now the first line of defense—or offense—for the federal government when confronting challenges to national authority (Hyman and Wiecek 1982, 467). The following year another enforcement act was passed that was aimed primarily at Klan violence.

However, despite a spate of activity culminating in the passage of the Civil Rights Act of 1875, by the mid-1870s the national enthusiasm for the vigorous protection of civil rights was diminishing (Keller 1977, 146; Stampp 1967). President Ulysses S. Grant had effectively halted civil rights enforcement by 1873. Freedmen's Aid Societies in the north disbanded, racism became overt again in the north, and the language of reconciliation became more prominent. Federal patronage flowed from Grant to "respectable" Southern Democrats and convicted Klansmen were pardoned. Many Republicans attempted to kill the Civil Rights Bill, but the advocacy of a dying Charles Sumner led congressional leaders to simply put it off until after the 1874 elections. After stripping the bill of its most controversial feature (the clause requiring integrated schools) an unenthusiastic Republican party passed the bill (Foner 1988, 524–55).

In sharp contrast to their disintegrating commitment to civil rights was the party's increasingly clear focus on nationalism, and especially economic nationalism (Keller 1977, 181).[14] If Morton Keller (1977, 285) is correct that, beyond patronage impulses, "public life in the years immediately after the Civil War was dominated by the conflict between the impulse to foster an active state and a broader national citizenship on the one hand, and deeply rooted countervalues of localism, racism, and suspicion of government on the other," then as a general rule it is fair to say that the former impulse frequently found its center of gravity in the national Republican Party leadership of the period while the latter impulse often found expression in the resurgent Democratic Party (but see Bensel 2000, 101–02). The Republican Party's special focus on economic nationalism intensified after the violence of the Paris Commune in 1871, the rise of the Granger movement, and the Panic of 1873; according to one leading historian of the period it "marked a major turning point in the North's ideological development" as "older notions of equal rights and the dignity of labor gave way before a...preoccupation with the defense of property" and "economic respectability" for large-scale enterprise (Foner 1988, 517, 522). Ultimately, the goal of Republican Party leaders was the creation of "a political economy in which central state power could sweep aside regional and local barriers to the development of a national capitalist market and directly assist in the construction of the physical and financial infrastructure necessary for that market" (Bensel 1990, 4, 11; see also Woodward 1966, 35; Bensel 2000, xix).

This infrastructure was made up of a variety of elements, including tariffs, monetary policy and railroad subsidies. Republican national party platforms during this period were distinguished by their consistent support for tariff protection and the gold standard, while Democrats consistently opposed "all three legs of the Republican developmental tripod, substituting free trade for protection, silver for gold, and government regulation for market-led economic integration" (Bensel 2000, 193). However, the new business practices and social structures generated by postwar economic forces also resulted in new legal issues and disputes, for example, between partners operating across state lines, interstate corporations (large-scale enterprise) and local governments, railroads and farmers, and innovators of new corporate and financial structures. Given that these various issues arose piecemeal in the context of litigation, it was clear that the only way to ensure that this activity remained within the province of national control and direction would be to rethink long-standing convictions about mission and authority of federal courts in the political system.

Federal courts were thus functionally well suited to play an important role in promoting a policy of economic nationalism. The construction of this market required sympathetic supervision of individual transactions rather than general regulative or administrative capacity; federal courts were institutionally positioned to "span the divided between state and national authority" and "constitutional principles provided an effective framework for monitoring federal and state attempts to regulate corporate consolidation and interstate commercial transactions" (Bensel 2000, 9–10). There was also a political advantage to the development of a more active role for federal courts. Federal judges were politically insulated from "hostile popular sentiment," and to the extent that they would act as agents of national economic development, it would be unnecessary for state Republican Party leaders to incorporate into political platforms explicit policy positions on the construction of a national market that might put a strain on regionally specific political coalitions (Bensel 2000, 190–93).

Consequently, in the wake of the midterm elections of 1874, where Democrats regained control of the House of Representatives, Republican leaders in 1875 quickly brought up for consideration in one lame-duck legislative session a subsidy for the Texas and Pacific Railroad, a repeal of the 10 percent tariff reduction of 1872, a mandate that specie payment be resumed within four years, and a bill to expand the jurisdiction of federal courts.

In contrast to earlier removal legislation, which focused on beefing up enforcement of a limited set of civil rights, the main purpose of the Judiciary and Removal Act of 1875 was to redirect civil litigation involving national commercial interests out of state courts and into the federal judiciary. Technically this meant granting the federal judiciary general "federal questions" jurisdiction—that is, the authority to have original jurisdiction in all civil and criminal cases "arising under" the laws of the United States—and removal jurisdiction in state civil cases that raised issues of federal law or that involved parties from different states.[15] The Act attempted to prevent obstruction of removal by authorizing federal judges to hold plaintiffs in default if a state court blocked removal; it also provided that a state court clerk who refused to effectuate a removal was guilty of a misdemeanor punishable by a year of imprisonment and a $1,000 fine (Purcell 1992, 15).

This reconfiguration of federal judicial power was finalized just as Republican Party domination of national politics was coming to an end. The recapture of the House by a more localist-oriented Democratic Party in 1875 (Keller 1977, 252–53), in combination with growing Midwestern and Western hostility to eastern financial interests and national corporations, led to various proposals to repeal or curtail newly expanded federal judicial power. However, given the partisan make-up of Congress and the presidency during this period of intensified two-party competition, these efforts at rollback were unsuccessful. For more than ten years the pattern was for the House Judiciary Committee to favorably report a reform bill and for the Senate Judiciary Committee—now firmly in the hands of the Republican Party—to kill the proposal.[16] As long as Republicans controlled the House, Senate, or presidency, the new role for federal courts would remain entrenched; and given the power of "eastern capital" in the Senate this veto-point remained strong throughout the period (Frankfurter and Landis 1928, 91). The most that was accomplished at the federal level by opponents of federal judicial power was an elimination of provisions that allowed plaintiffs to remove cases, a shortening of the time for filing removal petitions, and an increase in the jurisdictional threshold from $500 to $2,000 (Collins 1986, 738–56; Frankfurter and Landis 1928, 56–102; Purcell 1992, 15). More effective resistance took place at the state level, with some legislatures passing incorporation acts that required corporations to maintain offices in the state (thus ensuring that litigation would not be removable into federal courts under their diversity jurisdiction) or that required nonstate corporations to waive their rights to resort to federal courts (Bensel 2000, 324).

Consolidating Entrenchment Through Reliable Staffing and Institutional Restructuring

If federal courts were going to facilitate the Republican agenda of economic nationalism it was necessary not only to expand their jurisdiction but also to staff them with judges who were ideologically sympathetic to this new mission. Fortuitously, the appointment of federal judges did not require the cooperation of the House of Representatives, which was controlled by the Democratic Party for ten years during the span from 1875–1891.[17] Throughout this period, until Grover Cleveland's inauguration in 1885, the Republican Party controlled the presidency, and combined with their hold on the Senate this meant that Republicans controlled the power to appoint federal judges. Even when Republicans (temporarily) lost the White House, they found that Cleveland's agenda for the Democratic Party was perfectly consistent with their goal of economic conservatism and nationalism.

It was because of this combination of congressionally driven structural changes and executive-driven appointment politics that a system of federal courts which had recently been considered bastions of localism within the federal government were transformed into "forums of order" for national commercial interests seeking a hearing free from the interests and perspectives that dominated state proceedings (Freyer 1978, 1979). Grant alone made a total of forty-one appointments to the federal bench, which by the end of his term resulted in a lower federal judiciary where 64 percent of judges were Grant appointees (posted to twenty-one of the thirty-seven states) and 85 percent were nominally Republican. After President Rutherford B. Hayes, the bench was 91 percent Republican, with 28 percent being Hayes appointees (Barrow, Zuk and Gryski 1996, 29–30).

Of special importance in fortifying this agenda was the decision-making of the United States Supreme Court. The justices would not have the day-to-day responsibilities of administering this policy in individual cases, but their decisions would establish the legal and ideological framework within which these other judges would be operating. A review of the fifteen justices who were appointed between 1870 and 1893 confirms that they "were selected by presidents and confirmed by senators who carefully noted both their devotion to party principles and 'soundness' on the major economic questions of the day," especially their "attitude toward regulation of interstate commerce by the individual states" (Bensel 2000, 7).[18]

1. President Grant started the trend of focusing on conservative economic nationalists by appointing two railroad attorneys and directors, William Strong and Joseph P. Bradley. Two years later he appointed Ward Hunt, who was also identified with railroad interests. Grant's replacement for Chief Justice Chase, Morrison I. Waite, had no prior judicial experience and never held national office, but he had a record as a successful railroad lawyer and director, and also enjoyed the support of the Vanderbilts.

2. After appointing John Marshall Harlan and William Woods, President Hayes attempted to nominate Thomas Stanley Matthews while he was serving as Midwestern chief counsel to financier Jay Gould. The Senate took no action, but Matthews was re-nominated by President Garfield and finally confirmed in 1881 by a vote of 24–23, with opposition arising mostly because of he was considered too openly associated with railroad and corporate interests.

3. President Chester A. Arthur had two appointments: Horace Gray, an experienced state jurist and economic conservative from Massachusetts, and Samuel Blatchford, an experienced circuit judge with connections to New York's business and political elite.

4. The conservative Democrat President Grover Cleveland appointed two: Lucius Lamar, another railroad director and a former professor of political economy who, as a Senator, chaired the Standing Committee on the Pacific railroads, opposed free silver, and vigorously defended Matthews during his controversial nomination (he met strong Senate opposition as the first nominee who had been active in the Confederacy and was finally confirmed by a vote of 32–28 with sixteen senators not voting); and Chief Justice Melville Fuller, a corporate lawyer and sound money advocate who left the Democratic Party after Bryan was nominated on a free silver platform.

5. President Benjamin Harrison had four appointments: David Brewer, a conservative judge with experience in the lower federal courts and

the nephew of iconic conservative Justice Stephen J. Field; Henry Brown, with almost identical credentials as an economic conservative; George Shiras, Jr., a Pittsburgh lawyer with an influential clientele of railroad, banking, oil, coal, iron, and steel interests (and who was specifically supported by Carnegie); and Howell Jackson, a Democrat who was a former colleague of Harrison's in the Senate and a family friend.

6.   Finally, Cleveland had two more nominations: Chief Justice Edward White, a senator and an economic conservative, and Rufus Peckham, a former judge, corporate counsel for New York, and "confidant of tycoons" including Morgan, Rockefeller, and Vanderbilt.

7.   These nominees were not always of one mind on all issues relating to economic nationalism. Still, it is worth emphasizing that all of these nominees fit within a fairly narrow ideological space that supported the assigned mission of federal courts during this period.[19]

Not surprisingly, these justices did not resist Congress' invitation to have federal courts more involved in supervising litigation involving large-scale enterprise. Just a few years after passage of the 1875 statute the Court held that Congress could authorize the removal into federal courts of any case that raised an issue of federal law or that otherwise fell within the federal judiciary's Article III jurisdiction (such as diversity jurisdiction).[20] A year later, Justice Bradley wrote a concurring opinion in which he expressed the view that "No cases are more appropriate to this jurisdiction or more urgently call for its exercise than those which relate to the foreclosure and sale of railroads extending two or more states, and winding up the affairs of the companies that own them."[21] By 1880, in another railroad case, the Court declared that in cases of removal the "only inquiry" was whether the suit was one "arising under the Constitution or laws of the United States."[22] Two years after the Court voided part of the Ku Klux Klan Act of 1871 on the grounds that the protection of individuals from private conspiracies was a state function rather than a national function,[23] a 7–2 majority on the Court ruled in the *Pacific Railroad Removal Cases*,[24] that a suit against federally chartered corporations could be removed into a federal court even if the legal issues implicated ordinary state law claims and defenses. In other cases the Court did impose some minor jurisdictional limits, but the overall record demonstrates that conservative Supreme Court justices were quite willing to support Congress' efforts to expand the control of federal courts over commercial litigation (Collins 1986, 730; Kutler 1968, 157).

Predictably, businesses flocked to these courts seeking more favorable case outcomes and legal doctrines. By January 1, 1878, the federal circuit court in Chicago had 3,045 suits pending, ten times the antebellum average. According to a House of Representatives Report in 1876, diversity cases were "the largest and most rapidly-increasing class of Federal cases," arising from rapid economic development and "the formation of numerous great corporations whose business connections extend into many States" (Purcell 1992, 20). In part, this flood of litigation was motivated by reasons made explicit in the removal language of the 1875 statute, such as a desire to avoid local prejudice. But other advantages should not be overlooked, such as the control that federal judges had over juries (generally regarded as dangerously pro-plaintiff), which included the right to "comment" on the quality or weight of the evidence and direct or set aside verdicts. Verdicts in federal court also required unanimity among twelve jurors, and this was preferable for defendants in comparison to state rules that often allowed smaller or non-unanimous verdicts. Removal also allowed for more "forum shopping" by litigants looking for more sympathetic courthouses. This was particularly important given that the social and professional background of most Republican-appointed federal judges disposed them toward the viewpoints advocated by corporations (Fritz 1991; Hall 1976; Presser 1982, 69–127; Purcell 1992, 24–25). In a nutshell, they were "a remarkably similar, if not insular, social group" that was closely tied to "powerful political and economic actors,...trained and experienced at the bar, steeped in the revered common law, and coming largely from the ranks of the corporate elite" (Purcell 2000, 320).

In a relatively short period of time, with the assistance of an increasingly professionalized bar that viewed itself as obligated to "supervise, direct, and promote the great business interests of the country" (Keller 1977, 350; Twiss 1942), the federal judiciary articulated legal principles that were consistent with the promotion of a more unfettered national market. Federal judges presided over corporate reorganization and addressed problems of railroad finance through the practice of equity receiverships, all with an eye toward promoting more nationalist solutions over regional approaches (Berk 1994; Gordon 1983, 108; Purcell 1999, 732–33). At the top of the hierarchy the Supreme Court increased its supervisory authority over local economic regulation by invoking the commerce clause with unprecedented frequency and interpreting it to require courts to eliminate barriers to the free flow of interstate goods and services (Bensel 2000, 325–49; Freyer 1979; McCurdy

1978). The justices interpreted the Fourteenth Amendment to make it a constitutional violation for a state to regulate a person or a corporation in a way that prevented either from earning a reasonable return on invested capital, thus expanding the supervisory responsibilities of the entire federal judiciary over state regulations of business (Bensel 2000, 334). More generally, the Supreme Court insisted that all levels of government stifle tendencies toward favoritism or prejudice and instead adopt neutral and impartial regulations that were consistent with national standards of due process and equal protection for all (Gillman 1993).[25] In all these cases, doctrines proved extremely beneficial to large-scale enterprise; in fact, by 1890, the *Commercial and Financial Chronicle* commented that "the findings of our highest court are such as to put to rest" the dangers of "Socialistic legislation" and thus mark "an epoch in the industrial and constitutional history of the country" (Bensel 2000, 335).

However, the new mission of the federal judiciary was in such great demand that rising rates of litigation threatened a general collapse. Before institutional reconfiguration the Supreme Court's October Term of 1870 opened with 636 cases on the appellate docket. By comparison, the October Term of 1884 opened with 1,315 cases on the appellate docket; a year later it was 1,340; a year later, 1,396; in 1887, it was up to 1,427; in 1888 it was 1,563; in 1889 the docket was 1,635; and by 1890 the number was an astonishing 1,800 cases—an almost 300 percent increase in twenty years. The story in the lower courts was the same: In 1873 there were 29,013 cases pending in the circuit and district courts; by 1890 the number had risen to 54,194. One result of this caseload overload was that the traditional duty of the justices to attend circuit was practically a dead letter, since a Supreme Court term that went from October to May left only a few months to perform circuit duties that, in the belief of one contemporary, could not be performed in thrice that time (leaving that writer, Walter B. Hill, to lament that "It may well be doubted whether it is a wholesome example for Congress to pass laws relative to the highest judicial tribunal in the land which can only be intended in a Pickwickian sense") (Frankfurter and Landis 1928, 60, 86–87). Nine circuit judges (ten after 1887) were expected to hold circuit courts in sixty-five districts.

Under these circumstances reform legislation might be considered an uncontroversial response to an obvious workload problem. However, during the antebellum period, a Congress that had little interest in promoting federal judicial power was often happy to keep federal judges overworked. Moreover, the caseload pressures of the 1880s resulted from institutional reforms that were still controversial. In fact, the preferred Democratic response to these pressures was not an improvement in the ability of federal courts to manage this workload; it was "complete elimination of all jurisdiction based on diverse citizenship" (Frankfurter and Landis 1928, 98).

Given the opposing views of the two parties on the virtues of broad jurisdiction for federal courts the caseload problem would remain uncorrected as long as divided government prevailed. It was not until 1889, with the start of the 51st Congress, that Republicans once again controlled the House, Senate and presidency and were thus in a position to respond as they saw fit to the pressures on federal courts. By late in 1890 Chief Justice Waite and Justices Harlan and Field each spoke out to urge Congressional action. The American Bar Association influenced President Harrison—who won the presidency with fewer popular votes than President Grover Cleveland—to add a plea for an intermediate court of appeals in his annual message in December 1889.

In April 1890, a reform bill introduced by Congressman John H. Rogers came out of the House Judiciary Committee (Frankfurter and Landis 1928, 97–98). Of the 118 members voting to schedule debate on the bill, 115 were Republicans, two were Democrats (including Congressman Rogers, who in 1896 would later be appointed as a District Court judge by President Cleveland, confirmed by a Republican Senate), and one was a member of the Labor Party; every one of the 101 votes against debating the bill came from Democrats.[26]

The bill's chief sponsor in the Senate, and the eventual namesake of the legislation, exemplifies the political and social forces that were behind judicial empowerment. William M. Evarts was a prominent New York lawyer before the Civil War with a sufficiently impressive reputation that he was retained by the national government to help argue *The Prize Cases*. In 1864, President Abraham Lincoln was urged by many luminaries (including the Massachusetts governor and some Supreme Court justices) to appoint Evarts to replace Chief Justice Taney. He argued a number of cases before the Chase Court, defended Andrew Johnson in the Senate impeachment trial, and then became Johnson's attorney general. When he went back to New York he was a leader of the bar association and helped smash the Boss Tweed ring. He continued a very prosperous law practice, representing mostly railroads and other large commercial interests. He was the lead counsel for Republicans before the electoral commission looking into the disputed Hayes-Tilden election, and not long thereafter he was appointed by Hayes to be Secretary of State, where he advised the president on (among other things) the use of federal troops to put down the Baltimore and Ohio Railroad strike of 1877. When he returned to New York he was instrumental in pushing the state's highest court to adopt due process interpretations that would prove emblematic of the so-called "Lochner era," such as the decision in *In re Jacobs*,[27] striking down the state's Tenement House Cigar Law on the grounds that it amounted to a class-based deprivation of the freedom to labor without any reasonable public health benefit (with Evarts adding that tobacco was a useful method of fumigation). He was elected to the Senate the following year, just in time to lend his reputation, connections, and worldview to the cause of judicial reform (Barrows 1941).

The resulting legislation was patchwork reform rather than reinvention, but it solidified the developments of the previous decades.[28] The original bill introduced by Rogers would have fused district and circuit courts, created nine intermediate circuit courts with final decisions in cases arising solely through diversity of citizenship, and added two additional circuit judges for each circuit. Evarts' alternative, which he had first circulated for comments to the justices of the Supreme Court and selected circuit court judges (Barrows 1941, 481), formally kept both the district and circuit courts but abolished the appellate jurisdiction of the circuit courts, thus leaving them to operate as trial courts alongside the district courts. It also identified defined classes of cases that could be appealed directly from federal trial courts to the Supreme Court, and then channeled all other appeals through nine newly created circuit courts of appeal, which would have the final say in virtually all diversity suits unless the appellate judges certified that the case should be decided by the United States Supreme Court. The three-judge panels on these courts of appeal would be made up of one new court of appeals judge for each circuit plus available circuit or district court judges. Evarts' alternative satisfied some traditionalists who wanted to be able to say that elements of the old structure had been maintained (including circuit riding, which under this proposal would in effect be circuit visiting, since the work would be done by the new intermediate courts).

At conference, the House yielded to the Senate's version and the Evarts Act was finally passed in March of 1891 by the lame-duck 51st Congress (Frankfurter and Landis 1928, 97–102). As with the 1875 legislation this reform came just in time for Republicans. The 52nd Congress that would start later that year had a House of Representatives that was dominated by 235 Democrats and contained only 88 members of the GOP.

The legislation was effective in reducing the Supreme Court's caseload. The number of cases before the justices fell from 623 in 1890 to 379 in 1891 and 275 in 1892. More importantly, the act—the first significant restructuring of the federal judiciary since the Judiciary Act of 1789—made it possible for the 1875 jurisdictional changes to persist. It also helped remove some of the traditional localizing pressures on Supreme Court justices caused by circuit-riding. As a consequence, the Supreme Court could continue its development as a truly national institution, pursuing national political agendas by exercising those expanded powers and responsibilities that had been assigned to it as a result of the postwar political construction of federal judicial authority (Purcell 2000, 40).

Conclusion

The idea of political entrenchment in the judiciary, if not yet adequately incorporated into contemporary political science treatments of partisan politics or judicial empowerment, is nevertheless familiar to students of American constitutional history. When the Federalist Party lost control of the national government in 1800, their lame-duck Congress responded by passing the Judiciary Act of 1801, which expanded the size and jurisdiction of the federal judiciary and gave outgoing President John Adams the opportunity to appoint loyal Federalists to the life-tenured federal bench. Incoming president Thomas Jefferson reacted by uttering his infamous lament: "The Federalists have retired into the judiciary as a stronghold and from that battery all the works of republicanism are to be beaten down and erased." As it turned out, though, Thomas Jefferson's fears never materialized. The Judiciary Act of 1801 was quickly repealed, with the subsequent approval of a besieged U.S. Supreme Court in *Stuart v. Laird*.[29] When Congress began targeting judges for impeachment the remaining Federalists on the bench quickly learned that in order to survive their political climate they had to give up on the hope of using their office as a partisan forum (Whittington 1999). Over the years, John Marshall's Supreme Court was very careful about tailoring its decisions to the evolving preferences of the dominant partisan coalitions in the national government (see Graber 1998b, Klarman 2001).

In the preceding case study, I have tried to show why the sense behind Jefferson's lament is more appropriately directed at the actions of the postbellum Republican Party. These partisans were much more successful than the Federalists at transforming the judiciary into a programmatic stronghold. Why? The principal reasons have to do with some fortuitous political circumstances and a more advantageous institutional environment. Entrenchment was made possible because the Republican Party's post-Reconstruction commitment to an agenda of conservative economic nationalism congealed just as the Party was forced to hand over the House of

Representatives to a resurgent Democratic Party, which means that the federal judiciary was one lame-duck session of Congress away from remaining as relatively weak and marginal as it had been before the Civil War. Republicans were able to control the staffing of these newly empowered courts only because a resurgent Democratic Party was able to win the House but not the Senate, and because two Republican presidents (Hayes in 1876 and Harrison in 1888) were able to win the White House with fewer popular votes than their Democratic opponents. Repeal was avoided throughout this formative period because Republicans maintained a political veto over such efforts by holding onto at least one institution of the national government. The consolidation of this agenda was made possible only because of the Republicans' short-term control of the entire federal government during the 51st Congress.

The fragile and contested nature of the Republican Party's agenda for economic nationalism provides a new perspective on the controversies surrounding the federal judiciary's more active commitment to conservative constitutionalism during the so-called "Lochner era"—a perspective on both why these judges adopted this agenda and why their place in American politics became increasingly controversial as they encountered emergent progressive politics in the twentieth century (Friedman 2001, Gillman 1993, Ross 1994). While the story of the overall development of federal judicial power in the United States does not end with the passage of the Evarts Act in 1891, the lessons of this account may help frame inquiries of later stages. The Evarts Act raised new issues that needed to be cleared up, such as unexpected increases in criminal appeals (addressed in subsequent criminal appeals acts) and the increasingly discordant position of the old (now non-appellate) circuit courts within this new system (leading to their elimination in 1911). The increasingly conspicuous role of the Supreme Court in the political system would be further advanced by the Judges' Bill of 1925 (which gave the justices more control over their decision making agenda) and the subsequent construction of the Court's own building, the so-called the "Marble Temple," in the 1930s.

At around the same time, two prominent law professors wrote an influential account of the political construction of federal judicial power as a way of advancing a different conception of the role of the federal courts in American politics, an agenda that focused on "constraining the reach of the conservative Supreme Court" (Purcell 1999, 684). As one of these writers, Professor Felix Frankfurter, confessed in a letter to his friend Herbert Wechsler, "My central concern and the driving motive of my interest in the field [was the fact that] under the guise of seemingly dry jurisdictional and procedural problems, majestic and subtle issues of great moment to the political life of the country are concealed" (Purcell 1999, 685–86). If we make Frankfurter's concerns our own, we might encourage students of party politics or delegation of powers to focus more attention on the ways in which executives and legislators use judges as extensions of conventional political or policy agendas. Conversely, students of law and courts might be encouraged to locate the scope and direction of judicial decision making into a broader analysis of party systems and partisan control of those institutions that are responsible for the jurisdiction and staffing of courts.

Notes

[1]   This may be due to a number of questionable assumptions: that the nature and scope of judicial power is a pre-constitutional decision rather than a by-product of ongoing political construction; that courts are often policymaking competitors to legislators and thus less likely to be candidates for political empowerment by those legislators; and that courts are not best conceptualized as conventional policymaking institutions, at least not in the same way as bureaucratic agencies or regulatory commissions.

[2]   Skowronek (1982) provides an exemplary account of the development of national administrative capacity, but because the judiciary was not a focus of that analysis he relies too much on accounts that simply stress the conservative orientation of legal elites. No effort was made to analyze the actual steps taken by Congress and the presidency to facilitate judicial power. Still, he is fundamentally correct that "With nationalism, the Court recognized the continental scale of the new economic order and facilitated a concentration of governing authority....[The Court sought] to sharpen the boundaries between the public and private spheres, to provide clear and predictable standards for gauging the scope of acceptable state action, and to affirm with the certainty of fundamental law the prerogatives of property owners in the marketplace" (Skowronek 1982, 41). I would add that this agenda did not originate with the Court, and would not have emerged unless it flowed out of the regime politics of the period.

[3]   During the period discussed in this essay Congress expanded the size of the U.S. Circuit Courts of Appeal seven times (adding nine judges in 1869, one in 1887, nine in 1891, three in 1893, one in 1894, and one each in two separate acts in 1895), and in all but two cases (1887 and 1893) the House, Senate and President were of the same party.

[4]   See also Barrow, Zuk and Gryski (1996) for a discussion of judicial expansion and appointment politics. For my purposes, though, their definition of "institutional change" is overly narrow. They define institutional change as "a function of three components— bench expansion, replacements created by voluntary and involuntary departures, and elevations" of lower court judges to higher courts. This makes quantitative data collection more manageable, but it does not allow for an investigation of the ways in which judicial power may expand as a result of jurisdictional changes and evolving conceptions of the role of federal courts in the political system. While they acknowledge that institutional development may be "either quantitative (increase in 'business') or qualitative (enlargement or upgrading of mission), often connoting alterations of status within the political system as well," they do not provide an assessment of qualitative "mission upgrades" that alter an institution's status in the political system (Barrow, Zuk and Gryski 1996, 7).

[5]   As Casto (1997, 67–73) points out, there was relatively little substantive federal law in the early republic, and so this limit on the authority of federal courts may not as remarkable as it might first appear (see also Purcell 1999, 691–93). At the same time, the decision to channel cases arising out of federal law into state courts demonstrates the level of distrust of national authority, and the prevailing understanding of the relationship between federal court jurisdiction and national power.

[6]   14 U.S. 304 (1816).

[7]   In 1816, Justice Story wrote a "Judge's Bill" that would have conferred on circuit courts the full sweep of judicial power conferred in the Constitution, but Congress never acted (Frankfurter and Landis 1928, 36).

[8]   Hall (1973, 36) reports that in 1841 the Supreme Court had 106 cases pending but disposed of just forty-two; in 1842, 107 pending with fifty-two disposed of; in 1843, 118 and 36; in 1844, 168 and 46; in 1845, 173 and 64. Congress debated reform in 1847 and 1848, but did not act. The situation was even worse in the lower federal courts. In 1849, the Court took matters into its own hand by limiting the amount of time litigants had to make their arguments (two hours per side).

[9]   41 U.S. 1 (1842).

[10]   By the early 1850s southern Democrats attempted to consolidate the protection of slavery by making the first real efforts since the short-lived Judiciary Act of 1801 to nationalize the federal courts and expand their staffing and jurisdiction, but these efforts were successfully resisted by the forces that became the Republican Party, led mostly by Salmon P. Chase (Hall 1973, 107–08, 118, 263, 452).

[11]   "[T]he revisionists' view [which correctly emphasizes that the Republican party was not hostile to judicial power] fails to emphasize sufficiently the local and regional pressures operating on a Republican party squeezed between a traditional commitment to the idea of judicial representation [of regional interests] and the need for more and better administered courts" (Hall 1975, 179).

[12]   Even though a case might be removed into federal court, the judge was obligated to follow the procedures of the state, except Negroes were allowed to testify even against whites and court officers (including lawyers and jurors) had to swear to their past and future loyalty to the Union (Hyman and Wiecek 1982, 261).

[13]   The Supreme Court upheld such removal jurisdiction in *Mayor v. Cooper*, 73 U.S. 247 (1867).

[14]   As Frankfurter and Landis (1928, 57–58) put it, "National authority had to liquidate the institution of slavery, hitherto recognized by all the leading parties as the local concern of the states. By an easy transition other interests previously left to state action were absorbed by federal authority. The central government exerted power in fields which, in the past, would have aroused bitter opposition as encroachments upon the states. Transportation [mostly in the form of land grant aids to railroad and telegraph lines], education [mostly land grant colleges, a form of aid that had been vetoed by Buchanan in 1859 on the grounds that it was unconstitutional], commerce [homestead acts, postal expansions, harbor and canal construction, the encouragement of mining and timber exploitation], were actively promoted by the Federal Government."

[15]   The short-lived Judicial Act of 1801 also bestowed general federal questions jurisdiction, but this last-minute Federalist measure was quickly repealed by the Jeffersonians.

[16]   For fifteen years before the Civil War, the chairman of the Senate Judiciary Committee was a Democrat. By contrast, between 1861 and 1892, a Republican chaired the committee for every Congress except the 46th (1879–1881). See Federal Judicial Center, at http://air.fjc.gov/history/topics/topics_congress_bdy.html (last visited May 15, 2002).

[17]   Democrats controlled the House during the 44th Congress (1875–1877), the 45th (1877–1879), the 46th (1879–1881), the 48th (1883–1885), the 49th (1885–1887), and the 50th (1887–1889). They regained the House during the 52nd and 53rd Congresses.

[18]   The information on these 15 appointments reviewed in the following paragraphs is compiled from Abraham (1999), Bensel (2000), and Myers (1918).

[19]   The failed nominees during this period: Grant's consideration of Senator George H. Williams and Caleb Cushing (another railroad lawyer) to replace Chief Justice Chase (both names were withdrawn because of opposition to their qualifications or character); Hayes' nomination of Mathews (which was successfully resubmitted by Garfield); Arthur's nomination of New York Senator Roscoe Conkling (who was confirmed by the Senate after a bitter fight but who then declined the position); and Cleveland's 1893 nominations of conservative corporate lawyers William B. Hornblower and Wheeler H. Peckham (brother of the person who was successfully nominated two years later), each of whom was unacceptable to the leader of New York's Democratic machine, Senator David Hill (Abraham 1999).

[20]   *Gold-Washing & Water Co. v. Keyes*, 96 U.S. 199 (1878).

[21]   *Removal Cases*, 100 U.S. 457, 480, 482 (1879).

[22]   *Railroad Company v. Mississippi*, 102 U.S. 135, 136 (1880).

[23]   *United States v. Harris*, 106 U.S. 629 (1883).

[24]   115 U.S. 1 (1885).

[25]   Many of these doctrines were also being developed in state courts (Gillman 1993). The argument herein is not that federal judges were alone in elaborating business-friendly doctrines, or that they were consistently more conservative than all state courts. Instead, the point is to explain the innovative inclination of federal courts to federalize certain kinds of precedents that promoted economic nationalism.

[26]   Congressional Record—House, vol. 21, April 15, 1890, 3400.

[27]   98 N.Y. 98 (1885).

[28]   The vote in the Senate to consider the House bill was 36–12, with all opposition coming from Democrats and twenty-nine favorable votes coming from Republicans (Congressional Record—Senate, Vol. 22, September 18, 1891, 10194).

[29]   5 U.S. 299 (1803).

3.

Deregulating the States: The Political Jurisprudence of the Rehnquist Court

R. Shep Melnick

In providing for a stronger central government, therefore, the Framers explicitly chose a constitution that confers upon Congress the power to regulate *individuals*, not *states*. . . . We have always understood that even when Congress has the authority under the Constitution to pass laws regulating or prohibiting certain actions, it lacks the power directly to command the States to require or prohibit that action.

Justice O'Connor, *New York v. United States*[1]

For over a decade now, five members of the United States Supreme Court have been engaged in an effort to restrict the power of the national government and to increase the autonomy of the states. Since 1991, when the appointment of Clarence Thomas gave the "Federalist Five" a majority on the Court, it has struck down in whole or in part a dozen federal statutes on the grounds that they violate constitutional principles of federalism (Keck 2002). In the preceding fifty years, the Supreme Court had struck down only one congressional enactment on federalism grounds, and that controversial decision, *National League of Cities v. Usery* was itself reversed within a few years.[2] For the first time since the constitutional revolution of 1937, the Court has limited Congress's power under the Commerce Clause. It has significantly curtailed the federal judiciary's supervision of criminal proceedings in state court and the treatment of those confined to state prisons. It has limited the federal government's authority to "commandeer" states' administrative apparatus. In a series of decisions announced between 1996 and 2002 the Court has brought state sovereign immunity under the Eleventh Amendment back from the dead. And in a variety of contexts it has refused to impose federal mandates on state governments unless Congress has provided a "clear statement" of its intent. [3]

Yet as anyone who reads the newspaper knows, the Supreme Court has been far from consistent on federalism issues. The same Court that reinvigorated the Tenth and Eleventh Amendments has also upheld *Roe v. Wade*[4] and *Miranda v. Arizona*,[5] invalidated state anti-sodomy laws, limited the states' authority to use affirmative action, imposed restrictions on state and local zoning practices, prohibited states from boycotting the products of foreign countries, and limited punitive damage awards by state courts.[6] To some extent these shifting patterns reflect the influence of the Court's key swing votes, Justices O'Connor and Kennedy. Sometimes they side with Chief Justice Rehnquist and Justices Thomas and Scalia to form the Federalist Five. Sometimes one or both of them will join Justices Ginsburg, Breyer, Souter, and Stevens to place restrictions on state and local governments. It often seems that understanding the Supreme Court's federalism jurisprudence requires psychoanalysis of Sandra Day O'Connor and Anthony Kennedy.

Some federalism cases display a more fundamental shift in voting patterns. For example, in *Lorillard Tobacco v. Reilly*,[7] the Federalist Five ruled that federal law preempts a variety of tobacco advertising regulations established by Massachusetts. Justices Souter, Stevens, Ginsburg, and Breyer dissented. In a variety of affirmative action and takings cases the Court's liberals have supported the states while the conservatives have argued that the constitution limits their authority. This role reversal was particularly apparent in *Bush v. Gore.*[8] The justices, it would seem, endorse federalism when it serves their purposes and abandon it when it does not. Conservatives defer to state legislatures, city councils, and state courts when these bodies institute school vouchers, ignore antidiscrimination rules, and execute minors, but they quickly switch gears—jettisoning both judicial restraint and their dedication to federalism—when states take aggressive steps to protect the environment, regulate HMOs, boycott repressive foreign regimes, or restrict advertising by tobacco companies. The liberals are equally hypocritical, only in the opposite direction. No mystery here! The Court follows the election returns, which on occasion follow the commands of the Court.

Certainly the political ideologies of the justices matter; no one who studies the Supreme Court could deny that, but this does not mean that the conservatism of Justices Rehnquist, Scalia, and Thomas is identical to that of George W. Bush, Tom Delay, or Jerry Falwell, or that Justice Breyer always agrees with his former boss, Senator Edward Kennedy. Consider the following three instances in which the Court's conservatives found themselves at odds both with liberals on the Court and with conservatives in Congress and the punditry.

1. In *City of Boerne v. Flores*,[9] Justices Kennedy, Rehnquist, Scalia, and Thomas joined with Justices Stevens and Ginsburg to strike down the Religious Freedom Restoration Act (RFRA), an act of Congress dear to the heart of many religious conservatives. RFRA was itself an effort to overturn a 1990 opinion written by Justice Scalia that curtailed judicial exemptions from otherwise valid state and federal laws. The religious right was outraged by both opinions. Senator Orrin Hatch spearheaded efforts to pass somewhat narrower legislation that would survive judicial review. By then, though, groups such as the American Civil Liberties Union and the People for the American Way had changed their minds and withdrawn their support for legislation to overturn the Court's decisions (Dinan 2002, 2003).

2. In two 1997 Eleventh Amendment cases, the Court ruled that private businesses could not recover damages from a state agency that had violated federal patent and trademark laws—despite the fact that the Florida state government was running a business that directly competed with the businesses that held the patents and trademarks.[10] Ironically, Justice Scalia argued that the due process clause of the Fourteenth Amendment did not give Congress power to protect the property rights of corporations; Justice Steven's dissent claimed that property should be considered one of the fundamental rights protected by the Fourteenth Amendment. Allowing state agencies blatantly unfair advantages in competing with private companies is hardly a policy favored by most free-market Republicans. Charles Fried, Ronald Reagan's Solicitor General, described the decisions as "truly bizarre" (quoted in Noonan 2002, 94). Republican committee leaders in the House held hearings to consider methods for overturning the Court's decision (Dinan 2002).

3. In 1996, the Court handed down what one might call "the other Gore case," *BMW v. Gore*.[11] An Alabama doctor who had purchased a new BMW discovered that the dealer had repainted part of the car. He sued for damages, and a local jury awarded him $4 million. The State Supreme Court found this a bit excessive for a defective paint job, and reduced the award to a mere $2 million. For the first time the U.S. Supreme Court found a state court award excessive under the Due Process clause of the Fourteenth Amendment. This was one small step in the direction of tort reform as defined by Republicans

in Congress and their business allies. In recent years, few issues have been as partisan as tort reform. Plaintiff attorneys have become a key source of funding for Democrats, especially in the South. Republican efforts to place federal limits on state tort law have routinely been defeated by the Democrats. Yet in the Supreme Court the votes for tort reform came from Justices Stevens, Breyer, Souter, O'Connor and Kennedy. The three most stalwart supporters of federalism, Scalia, Thomas, and Rehnquist joined with Justice Ginsburg in dissent. Tort law, they insisted, was a concern of the states, not the federal government—and certainly not the federal courts acting unilaterally.[12]

As Neal Devins has pointed out, almost all the statutes overturned by the Court on federalism grounds have been the product of broad, bipartisan support (Devins 2002). Conventional understandings of left and right do not adequately capture the nature of the debate within the Court.

The Central Issues

To get a better handle on the federalism debate within the federal judiciary, it is useful to start with what is *not* at the heart of the controversy. First, very few of the cases before the Supreme Court involve the constitutional authority of the federal government to regulate the activity of private citizens. To be sure, in two well-known cases, *United States v. Lopez*[13] and *United States v. Morrison*,[14] the Court limited congressional power under the commerce clause for the first time since 1937. In both instances, the federal legislation regulated matters traditionally under state control. So far no other acts of Congress have been invalidated on these grounds. Lower courts have been reluctant to adopt a broad reading of *Lopez* and *Morrison* (Reynolds and Denning 2000). Moreover, Congress responded to *Lopez* by passing a slightly narrower version of the Gun-Free School Zones Act that would seem to pass constitutional muster (Dinan 2002). Since this legislation is primarily symbolic—a particularly transparent effort to demonstrate that members of Congress support education and oppose gun violence—one could argue that the Court has done little more than provide additional opportunities for position-taking by legislators. The bottom line is that the Court has placed very few constitutional restrictions on Congress's power to regulate private conduct, tax private citizens, spend for the "public welfare," or impose conditions on states' use of federal funds. The New Deal and most of the Great Society are perfectly safe.

Second, the Supreme Court does not seem much concerned with the issue so important in the early Republic and the contemporary European Union (EU): state-erected barriers to trade. Dormant commerce clause cases have been relatively rare; in fact, the Court has decided only one such case in the last five years.[15] The Rehnquist Court has continued to follow the meandering path laid out by the New Deal court in the 1940s. Justices Scalia, Rehnquist, and Thomas, who, one might think, would be free-trade enthusiasts, have argued (unsuccessfully) that the Court should simply abandon its dormant commerce clause jurisprudence.[16] At times the Court's conservatives have been somewhat less inclined than its liberals to allow the states to supplement federal regulatory programs. But it is difficult to detect any clear patterns either in voting patterns or in the Court's overall direction in preemption cases (Greve 2004).

What, then, is at the heart of the federalism "revival" or "revolution"? One key feature of the Court's controversial federalism decisions is that they almost always involve federal regulation of state and local governments and officials. For example, in *Printz v. United States*[17] the Court ruled that state and local law enforcement officials could not be forced to help the federal government enforce the Brady Handgun Violence Protection Act. The federal government could do the job by itself or it could offer the states incentives for participating. But it could not "commandeer" state and local officials. In *Seminole Tribe v. Florida*[18] the Court held that the governor of Florida could not be compelled to enter into "good faith negotiations" with Indian tribes over casino gambling licenses. In *Alden v. Maine*[19] the Federalist Five ruled that state courts could not be required to hear federal Fair Labor Standards Act suits brought under the state government. As different as these cases are, in each instance the issue is whether the federal government can regulate subnational governments, not private citizens.

Second, for reasons that are by no means readily apparent, many of the Court's recent federalism decisions involve questions about the jurisdiction of the federal courts. The Eleventh Amendment, the constitutional provision at the heart of the most controversial of those rulings, is nothing more than a limitation on the types of cases federal courts can hear: "The Judicial power of the United States shall not be construed to extend to any suit in law or equity, commenced or prosecuted against one of the United States by Citizens of another state, or by Citizens or Subject of any Foreign State." Other important decisions have restricted the right of private citizens to bring suit against state and local officials under 42 U.S.C. §1983, part of a

Reconstruction era statute that was given new life by the Supreme Court in the 1960s. The Court has also become reluctant to recognize private rights of action against state and local officials. Paradoxically, the Court has engaged in considerable judicial activism—striking down federal statutes and overturning precedents—in order to reduce the jurisdiction of the federal courts.

These two issues—federal regulation of subnational governments and the jurisdiction of federal courts—are closely linked. That is because *private lawsuits currently constitute the most important method for interpreting and enforcing federal regulation of state and local governments.* To the extent the Court reduces the jurisdiction of the federal courts it reduces federal control over subnational governments.[20]

In some instances the Court has limited private parties' opportunities to file suits alleging violations of constitutional rights. For example, both in its own *habeas corpus* jurisprudence and in its interpretation of federal legislation passed in 1996, the Court has restricted prisoner suits involving claims of defective criminal procedures or cruel and unusual punishment. The Court has also limited so-called *Bivens* actions for damages against federal law enforcement officials and expanded various forms of official immunity.[21] Far more important, though, is the way the Court has restricted *statutory* claims against subnational governments, for example those alleging violation of Title VI of the Civil Rights Act of 1964, Title IX of the Education Amendments of 1972, the Americans with Disabilities Act, the Social Security Act, the Individuals with Disabilities Education Act, and the Age Discrimination in Employment Act.

Neither political scientists nor legal scholars have paid nearly enough attention to the importance of private suits for enforcing these federal statutory mandates or the extent to which judicial enforcement of statutory requirements lies at the heart of the Supreme Court's new federalism. The political science literature contains extensive discussion of the new forms of federal regulation of subnational governments that emerged in the 1960s and 1970s, but has ignored the legal complexities of enforcing these rules. Conversely, legal scholars familiar with the nuts and bolts of federal court litigation (this usually means those who teach courses on Federal Courts, not Constitutional Law) have paid little systematic attention to the transformation of federal rules governing state and local officials. Moreover, so much attention has been lavished on the most controversial constitutional rulings (such as *Lopez* and *Morrison*) that the significance of seemingly mundane statutory cases has been overlooked. As Justice Breyer wrote in a 2001 opinion, "[I]n today's world, filled with legal complexity, the true test of federalism principles may lie not in the occasional constitutional effort to trim Congress's commerce power at its edges, or to protect a State's treasury from a private damage action, but rather in the many statutory cases where courts interpret the mass of traditional doctrine that is the ordinary diet of the law."[22] The remainder of this paper attempts to describe the various streams—political and legal, constitutional and statutory—that flow into the broad river of the Supreme Court's new (and still evolving) doctrines on federal regulation of subnational governments.

Federal Rules and Judicial Enforcement

Before 1964, Congress and the executive branch rarely issued rules regulating the behavior of state and local officials. About the only exception was the conditions attached to the grants-in-aid programs that proliferated during the New Deal. Yet even these were relatively few in number and weakly enforced. Congress was reluctant to impose many restrictions on the states. Federal administrators' ability to enforce legislative conditions was hampered by the fact that the sanction for non-compliance—the funding cut-off—was both politically dangerous and administratively cumbersome. Few federal administrators wanted to kill state programs in order to improve them.

This changed dramatically in the mid-1960s. New federal regulation of the states started with civil rights, but spread rapidly to a wide variety of other areas. According to the Advisory Commission on Intergovernmental Relations (ACIR), prior to 1960, Congress had passed only two statutes significantly regulating the behavior of state and local officials. It passed thirteen "regulatory federalism" statutes in the 1960s, twenty-two in the 1970s, and twenty-seven in the 1980s (ACIR 1993, 46).

One form this new intergovernmental regulation has taken is the so-called "cross-cutting requirement." "Cross-cutting requirements" are rules that apply to all subnational governments accepting certain categories of federal financial assistance. The earliest and still most important cross-cutting requirement is Title VI of the Civil Rights Act of 1964, which prohibits racial discrimination in any program receiving federal aid. Title IX of the Education Amendments of 1972 prohibits gender discrimination in all education programs receiving federal funding. Section 504 and the Americans with Disabilities Act (ADA) bar discrimination on the basis of disability in all federally financed programs.

Another set of federal laws establish binding rules for state and local governments in their capacities as employers and polluters. In 1972 Title VII's ban on racial and gender discrimination in employment was applied to subnational governments. In 1974 the Fair Labor Standards Act was extended to all state and local employees. During the 1970s and 1980s, a variety of environmental laws set uniform national standards for municipal sewage, waste disposal and drinking water systems.

A third set of intergovernmental regulations establishes uniform national rules backed by the threat of draconian fiscal sanctions. For example, Congress has at various times decreed that states will lose highway and mass transit funding if they do not establish a 55 mph speed limit, raise the legal drinking age to twenty-one, endorse nationally uniform size and weight requirements for trucks, establish minimum standards for licensing commercial drivers, and meet air pollution reduction targets. These are often referred to as "crossover sanctions" since they involve fiscal penalties for activities that do not themselves directly receive federal financial assistance (ACIR 1984, 1–24).

Just as important as the growth of these new forms of "regulatory federalism" is the multiplication of "strings" that apply to individual grant-in-aid programs. I am not aware of any quantitative measures of this change, but anyone familiar with federal education, welfare, transportation, health care, or environmental programs will readily attest to the increasing number, specificity, and enforceability of the strings produced by Congress and federal administrators. James Q. Wilson has noted that the legislation governing one major joint federal-state program, highway construction, grew from twenty-eight pages in 1956 to 293 pages in 1991. The 1956 Federal Aid Highway Act imposed few restrictions on either state governments or federal administrators. The Intermodal Surface Transportation Efficiency Act of 1991, in contrast, not only provided money for highway construction and mass transit, but

> mandated that the secretary of transportation relieve congestion, improve air quality, preserve historic sites, encourage the use of auto seatbelts and motorcycle helmets, control erosion and storm water runoff, monitor traffic and collect data on speeding, reduce drunk driving, require environmental impact studies, control outdoor advertising, develop standards for high-occupancy vehicles, require metropolitan area and statewide planning, use recycled rubber in making asphalt, set aside 10 percent of construction moneys for small business owned by disadvantaged individuals, defines women as disadvantaged individuals, buy iron and steel from U.S. suppliers, establishes new rules or renting equipment, give preferential employment to native Americans if a highway is to be built near a reservation, and

control the use of calcium magnesium acetate in performing seismic retrofits on bridges. (Wilson 1994, 43)

Almost all of these commands to federal administrators must be translated into federal regulations of those state and local officials who do most of the work designing, building and patrolling highways and running mass transit systems. The well known and often lamented tendency of the post-1970 Congress to "micromanage" federal programs usually also means federal "micromanagement" of state and local programs. Not surprisingly, the cost of complying with these various forms of federal regulation have gone up significantly. During the high-deficit 1980s, federal financial assistance to the states shrank as federal mandates grew (ACIR 1993, chap. 5; Conlan 1998, chaps. 10–11; Nivola 2002, 3–9 and 102–08; Walker 2000, 151–56).

The rapid expansion of federal regulation of subnational governments helps explain a feature of contemporary government that might otherwise seem paradoxical: While the reach of the federal government has grown enormously since the mid-1960s, federal civilian employment has fallen. The workforce of state and local governments, in contrast, has grown by leaps and bounds, reaching 14 million by 1987—almost five times the size of the federal workforce (Fesler and Kettl 1996, 138). State and local governments provide almost all the "street-level bureaucrats" who carry out programs established—and partially funded—by the national government. Public school teachers, police, welfare administrators, highway and environmental engineers, health and safety inspectors, public health officials—all are employed by subnational governments but subject to a wide variety of federal rules.

It is one thing to establish legal mandates and conditions, quite another to enforce them. How do federal officials ensure that their state and local counterparts follow these rules and spend federal funds properly? An important feature of American government is that federal officials cannot issue direct commands to state and local administrators. They cannot hire, fire or reassign the thousands of "street-level bureaucrats" on whom they rely so heavily. Of course, the federal government can use money to encourage programs it likes and to starve those it would like to scale back. Federal administrators can try to develop close ties with like-thinking professionals in state and local governments. As useful as all these tools can be for establishing the general direction of policy, they are not designed to ensure that each and every federal rule is followed or, more importantly, that each potential beneficiary receives the treatment promised by federal law.

In many instances federal officials have the authority to cut off funding to state and local programs that fail to comply with federal law. This sanction lies behind "cross-cutting" and "crossover" rules as well as the ordinary conditions on grants-in-aid. But from long experience we know that federal administrators are reluctant to impose such sanctions. In the early years of a program, federal administrators might be able to use the threat of fiscal sanctions to achieve major policy change; but over time the effectiveness of such threats fades. Moreover, most conditional spending laws require "substantial" non-compliance before funds can be terminated. Similar problems frequently plague federal regulatory programs administered by the states: The penalty for failure to follow federal rules is usually a federal take-over of enforcement; but the federal government seldom has the resources, expertise, or political will to displace state regulators (Melnick 1983). Cross-cutting regulations present an additional problem: The federal officials charged with enforcing the cross-cutting rules are not the ones charged with supervising the programs in question. Administrators in, say, the Department of Transportation will be reluctant to reduce transportation funding to enforce rules announced by the Department of Justice (Katzmann 1986).

Another potential enforcement tool—one that is both more focused and more credible—is a lawsuit brought by the United States against state and local governments. Federal *administrators* may not be able to issue direct orders to state and local officials, but federal *judges* most definitely can, and frequently do. As city councilors in Yonkers, New York learned a few years ago, public officials who ignore federal court injunctions can be held in contempt of court, fined, and even imprisoned. Hamilton's famous claim that the judiciary "has no influence over the sword or the purse" ignores a key feature of American federalism: Federal judges can use their injunctive sword—backed by an army of federal administrators and, ultimately, the guns of U.S. Marshals—to control the purse strings of state and local governments. As state and local officials know (but political science professors are for some reason loathe to admit), federal judges routinely issue such orders, and state and local officials routinely obey them.

The federal courts have long recognized the authority of the United States to file suit against either private parties or subnational governments to enforce the terms of federal laws. Private parties may need statutory authority to file federal court suits, but the national government does not. Nor does the Eleventh Amendment's limitation on suits against state governments apply to the U.S. Federal judges have power to issue commands to state officials; federal administrators have both the authority to initiate litigation and the capacity to monitor compliance: The combination would thus appear to constitute a highly effective compliance mechanism.

Yet outside school desegregation and voting rights the United States government does not often go to court to insist that subnational governments comply with federal mandates. Perhaps this is because such litigation normally must go through the Department of Justice, which is both risk-averse and perpetually short-handed. Perhaps federal administrators worry about disrupting relations with their state counterparts. Perhaps political executives worry about the political fallout of such a visible and adversarial stance. Or perhaps it is simply easier to let private parties take the initiative—and the political heat. In a 1999 case Justice Kennedy complained about the Justice Department's enthusiasm for handing these sensitive intergovernmental matters over to private litigants:

> The Solicitor General of the United States has appeared before this Court...and asserted that the federal interest in compensating the States' employees for alleged violations of federal law is so compelling that the sovereign State of Maine must be stripped of its immunity and subjected to suits in its own courts by its own employees. Yet, despite specific statutory authorization . . . the United States apparently found the same interests insufficient to justify sending even a single attorney to Maine to prosecute this litigation.[23]

One of the messages the Supreme Court has been sending to federal administrators in recent years is that if they want to assert federal authority, they need to accept political responsibility.

Thus, we arrive at the enforcement mechanism that has become ubiquitous since the 1960s: Private suits against subnational governments for failure to comply with federal laws and administrative rules. Private rights of action have the advantage of offering those with the greatest stake in government decisions and the most knowledge of the circumstances—for example, welfare recipients denied benefits, students subjected to sexual harassment, or employees who were the victims of racial discrimination—the opportunity to lodge a complaint, demand compliance, and receive financial compensation. But they are not without their drawbacks. Since complete enforcement is seldom either possible or desirable, private rights of action give private parties the power to set public priorities. In criminal law we rely entirely on public prosecutors to decide which cases are worth pursuing. We do not want the enforcement of criminal to depend on the litigiousness or vindictiveness of private parties. Public prosecutors are politically accountable in the way that private parties are not. Private rights of action also make enforcement of federal requirements highly decentralized and unpredictable. The extent of compliance will vary from state to state and even from city to city, depending on the inclination of judges and the resources and litigiousness of interest groups. Such variation can at times become extreme, creating serious problems for federal officials charged with administering federal law in a uniform manner.

In thinking about judicial enforcement of federal mandates, it is also important to keep in mind that *enforcing* a law or regulation is inextricably linked with *interpreting* that law or regulation. This means that private rights of action give federal judges the opportunity to determine the content of federal mandates. Many federal requirements are inherently ambiguous: What does it mean to "discriminate" on the basis of race, gender or disability? What constitutes "available" income, "reasonable and adequate" reimbursement, or an "appropriate" education? Some judges will defer to federal administrators' interpretation of these terms. Some will defer to the interpretation offered by state officials. Some will do neither. Some judges will look only at the text of the federal statute, others at its legislative history or general purpose. Some will favor broad interpretations of statutory entitlements; others will be hesitant to increase financial burdens on subnational governments. Most of the time this discretion will be exercised, not by the Supreme Court, but by district and circuit court judges. Over the past 40 years, the federal courts have used private rights of action to build up what is in effect a vast common law—based partly on federal statutes, partly on administrative rules, and partly on case law—regulating state and local officials.

Jurisdiction Expanding …

Before 1960 private suits to force state and local officials to comply with federal statutes and federal administrative rules were extremely rare. Only a handful of cases involving federal grants ever reached court, and in most instances plaintiffs went away empty-handed. Federal courts are not courts of general jurisdiction. That means that they cannot hear cases that have not "been entrusted to them by a jurisdictional grant by Congress" (Wright 1994, 2). Legislation establishing grant programs seldom explicitly authorized private suits against state or local governments. A few cases—less than 300 in total—had been brought against state officials under 42 U.S.C. § 1983, which authorizes damage suits against those acting "under color of state law." Almost all of these involved alleged denial of constitutional rights. Judges generally refused to find "implied" private rights of action in federal statutes. In other words, no explicit authorization, no jurisdiction for statutory claims (Coppalli 1979, 1–11; Chemerinsky 1999, 453–66).

All this changed very suddenly between 1961 and 1964. The Supreme Court's 1961 decision in *Monroe v. Pape*[24] expanded the federal courts' jurisdiction under § 1983. *J.I. Case v. Borak*[25] allowed judges to read "implied" private rights of action into federal statutes so long as such litigation seemed to serve the general purpose of the legislation. Another 1964 decision made it easier for courts to skirt the Eleventh Amendment by claiming that a state had consented to be sued.[26] More important than the precise holdings of these cases was the general attitude of the Warren Court about jurisdictional issues: To be blunt, they did not really care about them. For example, in the pivotal AFDC case *King v. Smith*[27] the Court imposed unprecedented requirements on state AFDC programs without ever explaining why it had jurisdiction. The Court ignored the issue for over a decade—until it decided that in fact it did *not* have jurisdiction over most AFDC cases.[28] Judge Henry Friendly, one of the federal judiciary's leading expert on jurisdictional matters, later described the Court's position as "inexplicable."[29] Eventually (to make a very long story mercifully short), the Supreme Court expanded its interpretation of § 1983 to cover almost all statutory claims against state and local officials.[30] These later rulings provided post-hoc justification for what most federal courts had been doing for a decade and a half.

The Supreme Court and almost all lower courts also assumed—again without explanation—that the proper remedy for violation of a condition attached to a federal grant was an injunction requiring the state to amend its policy, rather than termination of federal funding. This meant that these conditions became binding rules, unless, of course, the state took the initiative to refuse the federal money. Freed from the onus of having to enforce their rules, federal administrators wrote increasingly elaborate rules governing the use of federal funds.

The new judicial rules on enforcement of federal regulations emerged just as Congress was multiplying the number of federal rules. The first wave of legislation came before anyone had any idea what the courts were doing. By the early 1970s, though, it was clear to state and local officials, federal administrators, advocacy groups, and attentive members of Congress that most of the new laws and concomitant administrative rules would now be enforceable in court. The transformation was hard to ignore. Excluding cases filed by prisoners, the number of § 1983 cases rose to 13,000 per year in 1977 and almost 25,000 per year in 1992 (Wright 1994, 132; Eisenberg 1981, 74)

Despite years of Republican appointments to the Supreme Court, by 1990 there remained few barriers to judicial enforcement of federal rules or conditions. The Court had announced that it would no longer attempt to protect the integrity or traditional authority of state governments—this was up to the "political process." State sovereign immunity was virtually a dead letter. A combination of Supreme Court decisions and congressional action made § 1983 available to almost anyone claiming that state or local officials had violated federal laws or regulations.[31] Federal judges regularly used their injunctive power to enforce very broad interpretations of federal statutes. Occasionally Justices Rehnquist, O'Connor, Powell, and Burger (as well as Scalia, who replaced the Chief Justice in 1986) would pick up a fifth vote to limit enforcement of such federal mandates. But usually they were outvoted.[32]

...and Contracting

Placed against this backdrop, the pattern of recent Supreme Court decisions becomes easier to understand. The Federalist Five want to reduce federal control of subnational governments. One way to do this is to define those "core state functions," "indisputable attributes of state sovereignty," and "historic powers" that are so central to federalism and republican government that they cannot be invaded by the federal government. For example, the Court has refused to allow Congress to dictate how state legislatures must write laws on disposal of nuclear waste. The federal government can offer incentives, or it can take on the job of regulating this waste itself. But it cannot tell states what legislation they must pass.[33] The Court has implied (but not explicitly held) that Congress cannot override state laws establishing the tenure of state judges.[34] But the Court has had great difficulty defining these constitutionally protected core activities, and has been understandably reluctant to establish clear constitutional limits on the power of the national government.

Instead the Court has discovered a variety of ways to keep private suits against subnational governments out of court altogether. Sometimes the Court has employed constitutional arguments, usually the Eleventh Amendment. Sometimes it has used statutory interpretation, especially to narrow the scope of § 1983. Sometimes it has simply announced new judicial rules, for example, on limited immunity for public officials. Behind all these rulings lies a strategy that Michael Greve has described as one of "noncooperation": "The expansion of sovereign immunity partakes of a larger trend toward an increased judicial reluctance to cooperate with Congress in dismantling state and local autonomy" (Greve 1999, 76).

Seldom does the Court totally preclude judicial enforcement of federal mandates. If Congress expresses its intent unambiguously, then the Court will look more favorably on judicial enforcement. If the Department of Justice, the Equal Employment Opportunity Commission (EEOC), or another federal agency has the time or the guts to file suit, then the federal courts will not invoke sovereign immunity. But when Congress has whispered rather than shouted its intent to direct the states and when the executive branch has sat on its hands, the courts (to use yet another metaphor) will remain on the sidelines. To put the matter another way, the Court has significantly raised the political cost of imposing federal requirements on state and local governments.

A quick look at two cases will illustrate the Court's strategy. The first, *Kimel v. Florida Board of Regents*,[35] is one of the Court's controversial recent Eleventh Amendment cases. The second, *Blessing v. Freestone*,[36] is a little known § 1983 case decided in 1997. In both cases, the Court refused to force state officials to comply with federal rules.

Like many important Supreme Court decisions on federalism, *Kimel* involved state employment practices. A college professor at a state college sought damages under the Age Discrimination in Employment Act (ADEA), which had been extended to state employees in 1974. By a 5–4 vote the Court held that despite explicit authorization from Congress, state sovereign immunity recognized by the Eleventh Amendment barred the federal judiciary from hearing private ADEA damage suits. Congress could not abrogate the states' immunity because the ADEA and the 1974 amendments had been passed under the Commerce Clause, not § 5 of the Fourteenth Amendment. The Fourteenth Amendment amends the Eleventh Amendment. Thus, legislation within the scope of § 5 is not constrained by state sovereign immunity. But, the Court held, Congress's authority to regulate state action under § 5 does not encompass the ADEA because age discrimination is not a violation of the Fourteenth Amendment's Equal Protection or Due Process clauses. In short, since the Court has never found age discrimination unconstitutional, Congress does not have authority to authorize private damage suits for age discrimination in state employment.

If this seems rather convoluted, consider the consequences of the decision. First, the Court substantially undercut enforcement of most federal regulation of state employment practices. This represents a substantial blow to the position the Court took in *Garcia v. San Antonio Municipal Transit Authority*.[37] In a 1999 decision, the Court had held that the Eleventh

Amendment also prevents state employees from pursuing such federal claims in state court.[38] Rather than explicitly overturn *Garcia*, the Rehnquist Court has whittled away at it.

Second, the Court left in place all existing mechanisms for enforcing most federal rules against two other forms of discrimination, those based on race and gender. That is because the Court has held that racial and gender discrimination also violate the Equal Protection clause. Two years after *Kimel* the Court ruled that most discrimination on the basis of disability, like discrimination on the basis of age, is not a violation of the Fourteenth Amendment. Chief Justice Rehnquist explained that "Congress is the final authority as to desirable public policy, but in order to authorize private individuals to recover money damages against the States, there must be a *pattern of discrimination by the States which violates the Fourteenth Amendment*, and the remedy imposed by Congress must be *congruent and proportional to the targeted violation*."[39] In 2003, in contrast, the Chief Justice and five other members of the Court announced that the Eleventh Amendment does not bar private suits to enforce the Family and Medical Leave Act (FMLA) since that law was a valid exercise of Congress's authority under § 5.[40] Because the FMLA, unlike the ADEA and the ADA, was designed to attack state gender discrimination, "it was easier for Congress to show a pattern of state constitutional violations." The states' history of "unconstitutional participation in, and fostering of, gender-based discrimination in the administration of leave benefits is weighty enough to justify the enactment of prophylactic § 5 legislation."[41]

Needless to say, this leaves the Court with a great deal of discretion to decide what is enforceable through private damage suits and what is not. For example, in 2004 the Court allowed private damage suits against states that failed to make courthouses accessible to the handicapped. Since the section of the ADA at stake in *Tennesseee v. Lane* was designed "to enforce a variety of other basic constitutional guarantees" secured by the Due Process clause of the Fourteenth Amendment, the five-member majority (Stevens, Breyer, Souter, Ginsburg, and O'Connor) gave Congress broad power under § 5. The dissenters argued that the legislative record "contains only a few anecdotal handwritten reports of physically inaccessible courthouses, again with no mention of whether States provided alternative means of access." This dispute over the application of the "congruent and proportional" standard led Justice Scalia to disown it entirely, describing it as yet another "flabby test" that provides "a standing invitation to judicial arbitrariness and policy-driven decision[]making."[42] At this point the reach of § 5 of the Fourteenth Amendment—and consequently of state sovereign immunity under the

Eleventh—depends largely on what Justice O'Connor finds to be a reasonable method for protecting constitutional rights.

If the Court had made it easier for states to escape punishment for engaging in racial or gender discrimination, it would quickly have been accused of undermining the seminal case of modern constitutional law, *Brown v. Board of Education.*[43] This, no doubt, would have mobilized civil rights groups and women's groups against the Court—as was the case when the Court raised the barriers to similar suits against private employers (Melnick 1994, 4–6). The ability to distinguish claims of racial and gender discrimination from other forms of regulation of the states is crucial to the political success of the Court's project.

Third, the Court did not leave those subject to discrimination on the basis of age or disability without legal remedies. Justice O'Connor noted that "State employees are protected by *state* age discrimination statutes, and may recover money damages from their state employers, in almost every State in the Union" (Opinion at 91). Her opinion also implied that if Congress had established a clear pattern of unreasonable and systematic discrimination, the Court might view things differently. Taking an unusually nasty swipe at Congress, O'Connor wrote, "Our examination of the ADEA's legislative record confirms that Congress's 1974 extension of the Act to the States was an unwarranted response to a perhaps inconsequential problem" (89). In addition, the EEOC remained free to file suit against the states, as it had at times done in the past. In *Garrett,* Justices Kennedy and O'Connor note that "what is involved is only the question whether the States can be subjected to liability in suits brought not by the Federal Government...but by private persons." Congress has in fact taken some small steps to circumvent these decisions. In 1998, it passed legislation authorizing the United States to file suit on behalf of veterans seeking redress for state violations of the Uniformed Services Employment and Reemployment Rights Act. In 2002, the Senate Committee on Health, Education, Labor and Pensions reported out legislation to make waiver of sovereign immunity under the ADEA a condition for receiving federal assistance. But this bill never made it to the Senate floor (Dinan 2002; 2003).

The second case, *Blessing v. Freestone,*[44] involved enforcement of conditions attached to Title IV-D of the Social Security Act, which provides federal funding for state child support programs. Title IV-D specifies the services that all participating states must provide, and establishes deadlines for passing through to needy families the child support payments collected by the state from absent parents. It allows federal administrators to reduce funding to states that fail to meet federal standards, but does not explicitly authorize private suits against the states.

In *Blessing* several families claimed that the state of Arizona had denied them services and child support payments mandated by Title IV-D. Everyone (including the federal Department of Health and Human Services) agreed that Arizona had done a miserable job complying with federal requirements. The Ninth Circuit ruled that beneficiaries could sue the state under § 1983 in order to bring the state into "substantial compliance" with federal law. But the Supreme Court disagreed. Writing for a unanimous court in 1997, Justice O'Connor explained that "in order to seek redress through § 1983" a plaintiff "must assert the violation of a federal *right*, not merely the violation of a federal *law*."[45] The plaintiff not only must identify the "particular statutory provision" that "gives rise to a federal right," but must also convince the court that Congress had intended to single out for assistance particular beneficiaries rather than to provide collective benefits to a broad sector of the population. Moreover, the plaintiff must demonstrate that the statutory right "is not so 'vague and amorphous' that its enforcement would strain judicial competence." The statute "must *unambiguously* impose a *binding* obligation on the States" by couching the right "in mandatory, rather than precatory, terms." Meeting these tests only produces "only a rebuttable presumption that the right is enforceable under § 1983." A judicial remedy is foreclosed if Congress had expressly forbidden recourse to § 1983 or, more importantly, if Congress had created "a comprehensive enforcement scheme that is incompatible with individual entitlements under § 1983." The plaintiffs in *Blessing* could not surmount these numerous hurdles. According to the Court,

> [T]he requirement that a state operate its child support program in 'substantial compliance' with Title IV-D was not intended to benefit individual children and custodial parents, and therefore it does not constitute a federal right. Far from crafting an *individual* entitlement to services, the standard is simply a yardstick for the Secretary to measure the *systemwide* performance of a State's Title IV-D program. Thus, the Secretary must look to the aggregate services provided the State, not to whether the needs of any particular persons have been satisfied.[46]

The Court did not foreclose the possibility that some parts of Title IV-D might create rights enforceable through § 1983—which probably explains why this was a unanimous opinion. But *Blessing* shows how reluctant the Court has become to discover individual entitlements in grant-in-aid programs.

Blessing was just one of several post-1991 cases to narrow the scope of statutory rights protected by § 1983. For example, in a 1992 case, *Suter v. Artist M,*[47] the Court refused to enforce a provision of the Adoption Assistance Act that required participating states to make "reasonable efforts…to prevent or eliminate the need for removal of the child from his home and to make it possible for the child to return to his home." This language, Chief Justice Rehnquist claimed,

> does not unambiguously confer an enforceable right upon the Act's beneficiaries. The term 'reasonable efforts' in this context is at least as plausibly read to impose only a rather generalized duty on the State, to be enforced not by private individuals, but by the Secretary in the manner previously discussed.[48]

Justice Blackmun objected that the Court had in effect "inverted its established presumption that a private remedy is available under § 1983 unless Congress has affirmatively withdrawn [it]." According to Blackmun, the Court had "contravened twenty-two years of precedent," "changing the rules of the game without offering even minimal justification."[49] In a similar decision handed down in 2002, Chief Justice Rehnquist stated that "if Congress wishes to create new rights enforceable under §1983, it must do so in clear and unambiguous terms."[50] Justice Stevens' dissenting opinion correctly noted that by placing the "burden of showing an intent to create a private remedy on §1983 plaintiffs," the Court had "eroded—if not eviscerated—the long-established principle of presumptive enforceability of rights under § 1983."[51] One might question whether precedents announced abruptly in the 1970s are "long-established," but Justice Stevens is clearly right in his description of the change.

The Politics of the Supreme Court's New Federalism

Earlier in this chapter, I argued that the agenda of the Federalist Five was not political in the simplistic sense that it corresponded to the platform of the Republican Party or the voting patterns of members of the Republican caucus. Yet the doctrines of the Court's emerging new federalism are "political" in at least three respects.

First, taken together, these doctrines represent a significantly modified version of the "political safeguards of federalism" argument originally formulated by Herbert Wechsler and endorsed by the Court in 1985. According to Justice Blackmun's majority opinion in *Garcia*, "The principal means chosen by the Framers to ensure the role of the states in the federal system lies in the structure of the Federal Government itself."[52] Since the states are so well represented in the legislative process, the federal courts need show no special solicitude for them; the judiciary can simply stand aside and let the political process work. One could make a strong argument that the Court embraced the "political safeguards of federalism" soon after these safeguards had disappeared (Derthick 2001). Whether or not one accepts the claim that the states are adequately represented in the contemporary congressional process, it remains indisputable that Justice Blackmun's "political safeguards of federalism" position does not really call for judicial passivity. Rather, it calls for extensive judicial participation on behalf of those seeking to impose federal rules on subnational governments. The *Garcia* case, after all, was a suit by employees of a public transit authority seeking money damages from their employer.

When judges hear these enforcement cases, difficult federalism issues once again rear their ugly head. Seldom is the meaning of key statutes and regulations crystal clear. How broad a reading of the federal statute should the court adopt? How much deference should judges accord to federal administrators? How broadly should they interpret the remedies available to federal judges? The answers courts give to these questions significantly influences the balance of power not only between the levels of government, but among the branches of government as well.

In the period stretching roughly from 1965 to 1985 the federal courts adopted an expansive interpretation of federal statutes, of the authority of federal administrators, and of the powers of federal judges. In some instances they went far beyond any plausible interpretation of the words of federal statutes and the expectations of members of Congress (Melnick 1994, 83–102). As the Deputy General Counsel of the Department of Health Education and Welfare (HEW) explained in 1970, intervention by the courts "permitted a sort of four-sided game of leapfrog," in which each set of federal actors could impose new restrictions on the states. "If for some reason the federal administrators were inhibited in the development of new rules—perhaps because of the disapproving views of members of an appropriations committee—the courts could assume the lead in developing new legal requirements." At the same time, federal administrators could embed a judicially developed policy in their rule book "perhaps even embellishing it a bit." Reform "could thus proceed in an ever-ascending spiral with no single participant in the process having the capacity to block progressive development" (Barrett 1970; see also Halpern 1995; Davies 2002; Melnick 1994). To put it bluntly, behind the deferential rhetoric of the "political safeguards of federalism" lay a concerted subconstitutional attack on subnational governments.

In the 1990s, the Court began to establish a new set of presumptions about federal regulation of state and local governments: Ambiguity would be resolved in favor of state autonomy; the closer federal regulation came to traditional state functions and prerogatives, the clearer the statute must be. These new presumptions can easily be justified in terms of the "political safeguards of federalism:" in order for these safeguards to work, state and local governments must be given adequate notice of the consequences of proposed legislation. Judges and administrators should not discover expensive or restrictive mandates in vague legislation and then tell state and local official, "Don't complain, you had your chance in the legislative process." In short, because federal judges play such a key role in the enforcement of federal mandates, they inevitably lay down many of the rules of the game that establish the contours of the "political safeguards of federalism." In the 1960s and 1970s, the courts established new rules that increased federal control. In recent years, they have revised these rules to raise the political cost of imposing federal mandates.

The Court decisions discussed in this paper are political in a second sense as well: They prudently seek to strengthen the states without attacking either the New Deal or the civil rights revolution. Despite all the hoopla about the possible implications of *Lopez* and *Morrison*, the court has placed virtually no limits on Congress's ability to regulate economic activity or to use its spending power to encourage certain types of state activities and discourage others. The regulatory practices the Court has attacked did not arise until nearly thirty years after President Franklin Delano Roosevelt launched the New Deal. Similarly, the Court has explicitly (and cleverly) excluded from its sovereign immunity restrictions almost all disputes involving racial and gender discrimination and some involving the rights of the disabled. The back-pedaling exhibited in *Nevada v. Hibbs* and *Tennessee v. Lane* helps explain why these jurisdictional decisions have generated little political opposition despite the anguish they have provoked among law professors.

Moreover, the Court has allowed aggrieved constituencies several means of redress. For example, state employees unions can work to convince state legislatures to waive sovereign immunity in cases under the Fair Labor Standards Act and Age Discrimination in Employment Act. Or they could ask the federal government to file suit on their behalf. Or Congress can make waiver of immunity a condition for receiving federal financial assistance. In several instances, Congress has already taken action to undo court decisions

(Dinan 2002, 2003). Strong political coalitions will get around the barriers erected by the Court. This gives them little reason to attack the Court directly.

Finally, the Court has frequently justified its federalism rulings by arguing that it is increasing the political accountability of government at all levels. "When the Federal Government asserts authority over a State's most fundamental political processes," Justice Kennedy claimed in *Alden v. Maine*, "it strikes at the heart of the political accountability so essential to our liberty and republican form of government." In particular,

> A general federal power to authorize private suits for money damages would place unwarranted strain on the States' ability to govern in accordance with the will of their citizens. Today, as at the time of the founding, the allocation of scarce resources among competing needs and interests lies at the heart of the political process.[53]

In a 1982 dissent, Justice O'Connor argued that the federal government should not be allowed to tell state public utilities commissions which issues they must consider:

> Local citizens hold their utility commissions accountable for the choices they make. Citizens, moreover, understand that legislative authority usually includes the power to decide which ideas to debate, as well as which policies to adopt. Congressional compulsion of state agencies, unlike pre-emption [i.e., a full federal take over of the policy arena] blurs the lines of political accountability and leaves citizens feeling that their representatives are no longer responsive to local needs...[Citizens] cannot learn the lessons of self-government if their local efforts are devoted to reviewing proposals formulated by a faraway national legislature. If we want to preserve the ability of citizens to learn democratic processes through participation in local government, citizens must retain the power to govern, not merely administer, their local problems.[54]

Sounding themes familiar to political scientists, the Federalist Five have also pointed out ways in which federal commands can disguise the costs of government programs. For example, in *Printz* Justice Scalia wrote,

> By forcing state governments to absorb the financial burden of implementing a federal regulatory program, Members of Congress can take credit for "solving" problems without having to ask their constituents to pay for the solutions with higher federal taxes. And even when the States are not forced to absorb the costs of implementing a federal program, they are still put in the position of taking the blame for its burdensomeness and for its defects.[55]

If the feds should not be able to pass the buck to the states, Justice O'Connor argued in another case, neither should state officials be able to pass the buck to the feds:

> [T]he facts of this case raise the possibility that powerful incentives might lead both federal and state officials to view departures from the federal structure to be in their personal interests. Most citizens recognize the need for radioactive waste disposal sites, but few want sites near their homes. As a result, while it would be well within the authority of either federal or state officials to choose where the disposal sites will be, it is likely to be in the political interest of each individual official to avoid being held accountable to the voters for the choice of location. If a federal official is faced with the alternatives of choosing a location or directing the States to do it, the official may well prefer the latter, as a means of shifting responsibility for the eventual decision. If a state official is faced with the same set of alternatives—choosing a location or having Congress direct the choice of a location—the state official may also prefer the latter, as it may permit the avoidance of personal responsibility. The interests of public officials thus may not coincide with the Constitution's intergovernmental allocation of authority.[56]

Justices O'Connor and Scalia clearly understand what Kent Weaver has termed "blame avoidance" (Weaver 1986, 371). They are against it.

Justices Stevens and Breyer have noted that the Court's solicitude for the states might end up enlarging the federal bureaucracy. As Justice Stevens wrote in his *Printz* dissent,

> By limiting the ability of the Federal Government to enlist state officials in the implementation of its programs, the Court creates incentives for the National Government to aggrandize itself. In the name of State's rights, the majority would have the Federal Government create vast national bureaucracies to implement its policies. This is exactly the sort of thing that the early Federalists promised would not occur, in part as a result of the National Government's ability to rely on the magistracy of the states.[57]

In *College Savings Bank* Justice Breyer complained that the Court had "made it more difficult for Congress to decentralize governmental decisionmaking and to provide individual citizens, or local communities, with a variety of enforcement powers."[58]

The Federalist Five have responded that a somewhat larger federal bureaucracy is the price we must pay for accountability. When the federal government is forced to act on its own, Justice O'Connor has argued, it

> makes the decision in full view of the public, and it will be federal officials that suffer the consequences if the decision turns out to be detrimental or unpopular. But when the Federal Government directs the States to regulate, it may be state officials

who will bear the brunt of public disapproval, while the federal officials who devised the regulatory program may remain insulated from the electoral ramifications of their decisions.[59]

According to Justice Kennedy,

> A suit which is commenced and prosecuted against a State in the name of the United States by those who are entrusted with the constitutional duty to "take Care that the Laws be faithfully executed," differs in kind from the suit of an individual...Suits brought by the United States require the exercise of political responsibility for each suite prosecuted against a State, a control which is absent from a broad delegation to private persons to sue nonconsenting States.[60]

Given the amount of influence plaintiffs' attorneys wield in negotiating consent decrees and the provisions of structural injunctions, increasing the role of government lawyers and reducing the role of private lawyers could have broad and important ramifications.[61] Just as the Warren Court believed that the political process would not work properly if "discrete and insular minorities" were excluded from participation, the Federalist Five seems to believe that the political process cannot work properly if politicians can engage in extensive blame- and cost-shifting. It is not my intent here to examine the validity of the Court's arguments about participation and accountability or to evaluate the extent to which the Court has succeeded in promoting republican government. At this point, I would simply point out that the Court's new federalism is based on political arguments, and that there is nothing wrong with this. The real question is, How *good* are these political arguments? How will the new rules of the game change political incentives, the shape of government programs, and the nature of political participation? These, I would suggest, are more interesting questions than why members of Congress objected to the *Chisholm* decision in 1793 or the inherent meaning of "under color of state law." Rather than condemning judges for engaging in political analysis, we should help them do it well.

Notes

1   488 U.S. 1041 (1992).
2   *Garcia v. San Antonio Metropolitan Transit Authority* 469 U.S. 529 (1985), *overruling National League of Cities v. Usery* 426 U.S. 833 (1976).
3   *Raygor v. Regents*, 534 U.S 533 (2002) (clear statement); *Owasso Independent School v. Falvo*, 534 U.S. 426 (2002) (clear statement); *Gregory v. Ashcroft*, 501 U.S. 452 (1991) (clear statement); *Dellmuth v. Muth*, 491 U.S. 223 (1989) (clear statement); *Printz v. United States*, 521 U.S. 898 (1997) (commandeering); *New York v. United States*, 488 U.S. 1041 (1992) (commandeering); *Miller v. French*, 530 U.S. 327 (2000) (criminal procedure and prison conditions); *Felker v. Turpin*, 518 U.S. 651 (1996) (criminal procedure and prison conditions); *Coleman v. Thompson*, 501 U.S. 72 (1991) (criminal procedure and prison conditions); *McKleskey v. Zant*, 499 U.S. 467 (1991) (criminal procedure and prison conditions); *Teague v. Lane*, 489 U.S. 288 (1989) (criminal procedure and prison conditions); *Federal Maritime Commission v. South Carolina State Ports Authority*, 535 U.S. 743 (2002) (Eleventh Amendment); *Board of Regents v. Garrett*, 531 U.S. 356 (2001) (Eleventh Amendment); *Kimel v. Florida Board of Regents*, 528 U.S. 62 (2000) (Eleventh Amendment); *Alden v. Maine*, 527 U.S. 706 (1999) (Eleventh Amendment); *College Savings Bank v. Florida Prepaid*, 527 U.S. 666 (1999) (Eleventh Amendment); *Florida Prepaid Postsecondary Education Expenses Board v. College Savings Bank*, 527 U.S. 627 (1999) (Eleventh Amendment); *Idaho v. Coeur d'Alene Tribe*, 512 U.S. 261 (1997) (Eleventh Amendment); *Seminole Tribe of Florida v. Florida*, 517 U.S. 44 (1996) (Eleventh Amendment); *United States v. Morrison*, 529 U.S. 598 (2002) (limiting congressional power under commerce clause); *United States v. Lopez*, 514 U.S. 549 (1995) (limiting congressional power under commerce clause).
4   410 U.S.113 (1973).
5   384 U.S. 436 (1966).
6   *Planned Parenthood v. Casey*, 505 U.S. 833 (1992) (abortion); *Lawrence v. Texas*, 539 U.S. 558 (2003) (affirmative action); *Shaw v. Hunt*, 519 U.S. 899 (1996) (affirmative action); *Richmond v. J.A. Croson Co.*, 488 U.S. 69 (1989) (affirmative action); *Crosby v. National Foreign Trade Council*, 530 U.S. 363 (2000) (foreign policy); *Dickerson v. United States*, 530 U.S. 428 (2000) (Miranda rights); *State Farm v. Campbell*, 538 U.S. 408 (2003) (punitive damages); *BMW v. Gore*, 517 U.S. 559 (1996) (punitive damages); *Palazzolo v. Rhode Island*, 533 U.S. 606 (2001) (takings); *Monterey v. Del Monte Dunes*, 526 U.S. 687 (1999) (takings); *Lucas v. South Carolina Coastal Commission*, 505 U.S. 1003 (1992) (takings).
7   533 U.S. 525 (2001).
8   531 U.S. 98 (2000).
9   521 U.S. 507 (1997).
10 *Florida Prepaid Postsecondary Education Expenses Board v. College Savings Bank*, 527 U.S. 627 (1999); *College Savings Bank v. Florida Prepaid*, 527 US 666 (1999).
11 517 U.S. 559 (1996).
12 *State Farm v. Campbell*, 538 U.S. 408 (2003).
13 514 U.S. 549 (1995).
14 529 U.S. 598 (2002).

[15] *Hillside Dairy v. Lyons*, 539 U.S. 59 (2003). The most recent previous case was *Camp Newfound/Owatanna v. Harrison*, 520 U.S. 565 (1997).

[16] E.g., *Camp Newfound/Owatanna v. Harrison*, 520 U.S. 565 (1997); *West Lynn Creamery v. Healy*, 512 U.S. 186 (1994); *Tyler Pipe Industries v. Washington State Dept. of Revenue*, 438 U.S. 232 (1987). See generally *Redish and Nugent* (1987); Eule (1982).

[17] 521 U.S. 898 (1997).

[18] 517 U.S. 44 (1996).

[19] 527 U.S. 706 (1999).

[20] In order to emphasize the Court's broad purposes and strategy, in this chapter I gloss over an important legal issue: the distinction between prospective, injunctive relief and retrospective monetary damages. For decades the Supreme Court allowed injunctions against state and local officials, but not damage awards against unconsenting states. This was the uneasy and often troublesome compromise struck by the Court in *Ex Parte Young*, 209 U.S. 123 (1908) and confirmed in *Edelman v. Jordon*, 415 U.S. 651 (1974). This meant, for example, that federal judges could order states to increase future welfare benefits, but not to repay past benefits improperly withheld. Some of the Supreme Court's recent decisions have narrowed Congress's ability to abrogate sovereign immunity and thus to authorize money damages against the states. Others, though, have ignored the prospective-retrospective distinction. In *Seminole Tribe v. Florida Chief*, Justice Rehnquist wrote,

> [W]e have often made it clear that the relief sought by a plaintiff suing a State is irrelevant to the question whether the suit is barred by the Eleventh Amendment. . . . The Eleventh Amendment does not exist solely in order to 'prevent federal court judgments that must be paid out of a State's treasury' . . . ; it also serves to avoid 'the indignity of subjecting a State to the coercive process of judicial tribunals at the instance of private parties.'

116 U.S. at 1124. Statements such as this lead some legal scholars to believe that the majority is rethinking Ex Parte Young, the foundation of a great deal of federalism jurisprudence. In *Verizon Maryland v. Public Service Commission of Maryland*, 535 U.S. 635 (2002), the Court reaffirmed its commitment to *Ex Parte Young*.

[21] For example, *Correctional Services Corp v. Malesko*, 534 U.S. 61 (2001), and the cases cited in Chemerinsky (1999), 578–83 and 536–38.

[22] *Engelhoff v. Engelhoff*, 532 U.S. 141, 160–61 (2001).

[23] *Alden v. Maine*, 527 U.S. 706, 759 (1999).

[24] 365 U.S. 167 (1961).

[25] 377 U.S. 426 (1964).

[26] *Parden v. Terminal Railway*, 377 U.S. 184 (1964).

[27] 392 U.S. 309 (1968).

[28] *Chapman v. Houston Welfare Rights Organization*, 441 U.S. 600 (1979); see Melnick 1994, 48–51 and 83–88.

[29] *Almenares v. Wyman*, 453 F.2d 1075, 1082 (2d. Cir. 1971).

[30] *Maine v. Thiboutot*, 448 U.S. 1 (1980); *Monnell v. New York City Department of Social Services*, 436 U.S. 658 (1978).

31 *Pennsylvania v. Union Gas*, 491 U.S. 1 (1989); *Garcia*, 469 U.S. 528, 551–55 (1985); *Maine v. Thiboutot*, 448 U.S. 1 (1980); *Owen v. City of Independence,* 445 U.S 622 (1980); *Monnell v. New York City Department of Social Services*, 436 U.S. 658 (1978).

32 Compare *Pennhurst State School and Hospital v. Halderman*, 465 U.S. 89 (1984); *Middlesex Co. Sewage Authority v. National Seaclammers Association*, 453 U.S. 1 (1981); and *Atascadero State Hospital v. Scanlon*, 473 U.S. 234 (1985) with *Hodel v. Virginia Surface and Mining Reclamation Association*, 452 U.S. 264 (1981); *FERC v. Mississippi*, 456 U.S. 742 (1982), *Wilder v. Virginia Hospital Association*, 496 US 498 (1990); and the cases discussed in the preceding paragraphs.

33 *New York v. United States*, 505 U.S. 144 (1992).

34 *Gregory v. Ashcroft*, 501 U.S. 451 (1991).

35 528 U.S. 62 (2000).

36 520 U.S. 329 (1997).

37 469 U.S. 528 (1985).

38 *Alden v. Maine*, 527 U.S. 706 (1999).

39 *Board of Trustees v. Garrett*, 531 U.S. 356, 375 (2001).

40 *Nevada Department of Human Resources v. Hibbs*, 538 U.S. 721 (2003).

41 538 U.S. at 735.

42 See Stevens, Rehnquist and Scalia's opinion in *Tennessee v. Lane*, 124 S.Ct. 1978, 11, 9, 4 (2004).

43 347 U.S. 483 (1954).

44 520 U.S. 329 (1997).

45 520 U.S. at 340 (emphasis in original).

46 520 U.S. at 343.

47 503 U.S. 347 (1992).

48 503 U.S. at 363.

49 503 U.S. at 376–77.

50 *Gonzaga University v. Doe*, 536 U.S. 273, 290 (2002).

51 536 U.S. at 302.

52 469 U.S. 528 (1985).

53 527 U.S. at 750–51.

54 *FERC v. Mississippi*, 456 U.S. 742, 787, 790 (1982).

55 521 U.S. at 930.

56 *New York v. U.S.*, 505 U.S. at 182–83.

57 521 U.S. at 959.

58 527 U.S. at 705.

59 505 U.S. at 168–69.

60 527 U.S. at 756.

61 For a graphic example, see Sandler and Schoenbrod (2003, chap. 3).

II. The European Context

• • •

4.

Judicial Authority and Market Integration in Europe

Alec Stone Sweet

Martin Shapiro is unquestionably the dominant figure in the study of law and courts in American political science over the past half-century. His impact registers across theoretical divides, modes of analysis, legal domains and court systems, and several generations of scholars. My own intellectual debts to Shapiro began accumulating as a graduate student, with my dissertation (Stone Sweet 1992); they have mounted through subsequent collaboration (Shapiro and Stone Sweet 1994, 2002).

In this chapter, I show that a framework for analyzing European legal integration can be built from materials found in Shapiro's work, which I then use to help explain the construction of judicial authority over market integration in the European Union (EU). The paper is organized as follows. I begin (part I) with a relatively abstract discussion of the theory that guides the empirical analysis. I then turn (part II) to the relationship between the European legal system and integration, before tracing (part III) the impact of the European courts on the evolution on the EU's trading institutions.

Judicialization, Commitment and Lawmaking

I began research on European integration in 1997, in order to test a theoretical model (published as Stone Sweet 1999) of how a particular type of social system—a rule of law polity—emerges and evolves, with what political consequences. I developed the theory of "judicialization," which is expressed as an abstract deduction, without reference to the European Community (EC). After compiling comprehensive data on the various processes associated with European integration, my collaborators and I began testing hypotheses derived from judicialization, blending quantitative and qualitative methods. Our main findings are summarized in part II.

I consciously made use of three strains of ideas developed by Shapiro. His reductive move to conceptualizing the relationship between dyads and triads made it possible to develop a dynamic model of what I called the judicialization of politics; his arguments about federalism–as–cartel focus attention on dilemmas of cooperation, and the use of law and courts as commitment devices; and his ideas about judicial lawmaking (through interpretation, balancing and precedent) link the techniques of legal reasoning to those of policymaking more generally. I now take up each of these strains of thinking, and discuss how they were combined.

Dyads and Triads

In *Courts* and *Courts: A Comparative Political Analysis* (1975, 1981a), Shapiro elaborated a simple, reductive, but general theory of courts capable of organizing comparative research across time and space. At its core is an insight first made by anthropologists, namely, that the social demand for third-party dispute resolution (TDR) is so intensive and universal that we can find no human community that has failed to supply it in some form or another. Shapiro focused on what he recognized as deeply *political* aspects of moving from dyadic conflict to triadic dispute resolution. When two parties in a dispute ask a third party to help them, they build, through a consensual act of delegation, a mode of social authority or mode of governance. This mode of governance, the triad, contains a fundamental tension that threatens to destroy it. The dispute resolver knows that her social legitimacy rests in part on the consent of the parties, and thus on the perception that she is neutral vis-à-vis the dispute. Yet, if she declares a winner and a loser, she creates a two-against-one situation, which will erode that perception. Consequently, mediators and arbitrators have developed a host of techniques to settle conflicts without neatly declaring a loser. Old-fashioned legal anthropology (Collier 1973) and newfangled law and economics (Ellickson 1991) have both shown that consensual TDR in closeknit societies functions more to reassert preexisting norms than to evolve new ones (see also Hart 1994, chap. 2; Stone Sweet 1999, 159–63).

Adjudication, of course, is institutionalized, compulsory triadic *government*. The triad is permanently constituted by jurisdiction, and coercion and office that substitute for consent. Courts still avoid or mitigate the effects of declaring a loser through the development of settlement regimes, splitting the costs of a decision among the parties, processing appeals and so on. Just as important for politics, they generate a rhetoric of normative justification for their decisions. Judges are agents of the state, or of the law; and when they invoke legal norms they authoritatively bring a governmental interest to bear on the parties. Once activated by litigation, they normally must make a ruling. All of this means that in moving from consent to compulsion, "the problem of perceived two-against-one is aggravated" (Shapiro and Stone Sweet 2002, 212). As a result, Shapiro brilliantly argued (1981, chap. 1), a powerful myth about judicial authority that emerged and formalized as "the prototype of courts." The prototype works to provide legitimacy to judges, given the quasi-permanent "crisis" in which they find themselves.

In *Courts*, Shapiro showed that judicial institutions are part and parcel of their greater political environments, and that judges respond to similar inputs in similar ways when compared to other organs of government. Famous for emphasizing judicial decision making-as-policymaking elsewhere (Shapiro 1964b, 1969), Shapiro had nearly nothing to say about judicial lawmaking in *Courts*. In my elaboration of the judicialization model, I focused heavily on the question of why judges give normatively grounded justifications for their decisions, and the conditions under which such justifications, once understood as a style of rulemaking, will shape the decision making of other actors. Shapiro sought to explain why courts are so often "like" other political institutions; I tried to show that courts were a microcosm of governance itself, and how non-judicial actors and institutions could be governed by rules developed by judges in their decisions. I further argued that in social settings characterized by rising levels of interdependence (i.e., increased social differentiation and division of labor), in which transaction costs are relatively high, the functional demand for TDR overlaps a rising demand for rule adaptation. In such situations, consensual TDR, with its emphasis on settling conflict and the (re)enactment of existing social norms, is often insufficient to sustain increasing levels of social exchange. Commitment devices—law and adjudication—are needed. If litigation is sustained, adjudication necessarily becomes governance, which I defined as the process through which rule structures (including law) are adapted to the purposes of those who live under them. As important, "judicial" and "legislative" authority become increasingly interdependent, even interchangeable.

Judicialization and the Construction of Governance (Stone Sweet 1999), elaborates on a deductive theory of governance, focusing on the development of specific causal relationships between three factors: dyadic contracting or social exchange, third-party dispute resolution or judging, and institutions or law. The model shows how two sets of processes can become linked to one another to produce an expansive, self-sustaining system of governance. These processes can be expressed as testable propositions, which I adapted to the study of European integration. The first set of claims concerns the relationship between dyadic contracting, or social exchange, and TDR. As social exchange grows and becomes more complex and differentiated, so will the demand for TDR; given certain conditions, TDR will be increasingly activated and thereby implicated in governance. The second set of claims concerns the underlying dynamics of judicial rulemaking: the clarification, modification or creation of rules through triadic decision making. Critical to the theory is the enormous social pressure put on the judge to announce reasons to justify her decisions. The more the judge does so, the more likely she will be to insist that those with whom she interacts also defend their behavior with reasons, a point to which I will return shortly. The paper sets out the conditions under which argumentation, deliberation and justification not only become basic to how all actors in the system pursue their underlying interests, but also to how the rule system evolves. Judicialization is a feedback effect, observable as the impact of triadic rulemaking on how individuals take decisions and interact with one another (see also Stone Sweet 2000, chaps. 3, 7).

Delegation and Commitment

The logic of pre-commitment, or self-binding, has always lurked behind arguments for constitutional review within federal arrangements. As Shapiro (1998, 1999a, 1999b) emphasized in both the American and European contexts, federations are cartels and, as such, they are unstable. One classic rationale for federalism has been to build larger and more open markets (Mattli 1999). Let us assume that the members of the cartel have decided to pursue their collective interests to liberalize trade across borders, and that they have done so by adopting rules to govern such trade. The resulting situation is typically modeled as a prisoner's dilemma. Each member can gain advantage vis-à-vis other members if it chooses to ignore the obligation to open markets while others obey it. We have good reason to expect that the outcome will be that no cartel member complies fully with the agreement. One means of stabilizing incentives to cooperate is to build a system capable of effectively monitoring and enforcing the rules governing federalism. Courts provide such a mechanism.

Shapiro argued further that federal systems sustained through effective constitutional review can be expected to evolve in ways that centralize power. The result hinges in part on the extent to which the court performs its assigned role, and in part on dynamics within the federation itself. If the joint gains of cooperation are important enough, each constituent member of the cartel has an interest in ensuring that every other member obeys the rules of the federation; and thus, the cartel has an interest in supporting the court, even if some decisions go against it. The logic of long-range reciprocity comes to govern the arrangement, reducing debilitating concerns about short-term relative gains and losses, and legitimizing judicial authority.

More generally, contracting generates a functional demand for judicial discretion, and certain forms of constitutional contracting—the establishment of federalism and rights—imply the need for an effective mechanism of constitutional judicial review. The link between (a) the problems of imperfect commitment and incomplete contracting and (b) the extent of political power, or discretion, delegated to the constitutional judge should be obvious (see also Stone Sweet 2000, chap. 2). Further, constitutional obligations are typically expressed in quite general, even vague, language, not least because vagueness can facilitate the reaching of agreement in the first place. As Shapiro noted, "the more general the text, the more discretion to the interpreter" (Shapiro 1999a, 323). And constitutions are often more difficult to amend than other forms of public law, reflecting the fact that the underlying commitment problem is often more acute. Obviously, the harder it is for non-judicial authority to nullify the effects of the court's decision making, "the greater the political power" of the court (Shapiro 1999a, 323–24).

The argument can be formalized. The strategic "zone of discretion" enjoyed by any court (Stone Sweet 2002) is determined by (a) the sum of powers delegated to the court, or possessed by the court as a result of its own accreted rulemaking, minus (b) the sum of control instruments available for use by non-judicial authority to shape (constrain) or annul (reverse) outcomes that emerge as the result of the court's performance of its delegated tasks. Constitutional courts, including the European Court of Justice, operate in an unusually permissive strategic environment: Their zones of discretion are close to unlimited. A third determinant of discretion is endogenous to a court's own decision making. Relative levels of discretion will vary as a function of the court's case law (at any given time, in any given substantive area of the law), but only if some minimally robust idea of precedent governs its decision making. In elaborating constraints that bind all governmental authority in the constitutional system, the court also constrains itself.

Functional logics can help to explain why delegation to courts occurs. Yet, when it comes to how systems of constitutional review actually operate, purely functional perspectives (seeing courts as general institutional solutions to the general problem of credible commitments) are woefully inadequate as explanatory theory. The dynamics of constitutional interpretation and lawmaking always subvert efforts to predict what will happen from the preferences of those who delegated to judges in the first place, or from the details of institutional design. Constitutional review helps to define the paths along which the polity develops through clarifying, supplementing or amending outright the constitutional law on an ongoing basis. Where there is a steady case load, where judges justify their decisions with constitutional reasons, and where the constitutional text can be amended only with great difficulty or, in practice, hardly at all, we expect to find that the court—through its case law—dominates the overall process of constitutional development. Simply put, those who construct such systems are unlikely to control how they will evolve.

For these and other reasons, the "principal-agent" (P-A) literature of the so-called "positive theorist" typically miss what is most important when it comes to constitutional judicial review. In the language of Majone (2001), the agency metaphor that animates standard P-A models of the politics of delegation, with its emphasis on the goals and resources of the principal(s), is not well-chosen. Far more appropriate is the notion of *trusteeship*. When those who have delegated review powers have transferred, for all practical purposes, the relevant "political property rights" to the court, the judicial duty is a fiduciary one (Moe 1990; Stone Sweet 2002). The court possesses fiduciary responsibilities, usually in the name of some fictional entity (e.g., the Sovereign People). The extent to which those who delegate are in fact able to rein in (or otherwise shape the use of) such authority should not be presumed, but rather constitutes a crucial empirical question of the social scientist (Moe 1987; Pierson 1998; Thatcher and Stone Sweet 2002).

Normative Indeterminacy and Judicial Lawmaking

Pervading Shapiro's various approaches to law and courts is the claim that the law is fundamentally indeterminate, at least from the perspective of adjudication. Indeterminacy constitutes a rationale for delegating to courts— it motivates litigation—and it serves to justify discretion and incremental lawmaking. Given that "the prototype of courts," normative indeterminacy also pushes judges to behave as professional "liars" (Shapiro 1994). Abetted by the academy, judges must routinely deny that they make law, except insofar as lawmaking can be dressed up as a marginal adjustment to precedent, and thus redeemed by the doctrine of *stare decisis* (Shapiro and Stone Sweet 2002, chap. 2). Here I will discuss only two aspects of Shapiro's ideas on the relationship between indeterminacy and lawmaking: precedent and balancing.

Precedent. Following from Shapiro's analysis of the move from dyad to triad, practices associated with precedent can be understood as a response to the basic existential crisis that judges continuously face. The judge is expected to resolve legal disputes with reference to the law. However, the law, being a social abstraction, cannot be applied to any concrete dispute, situation or set of facts without adaptation. Normative indeterminacy thus generates a second-order social demand, this time for judicial discretion and governance. The crisis blooms when judges actually do their jobs, in that they reveal that judicial lawmaking inheres in dispute resolution; judicial lawmaking, in turn, reveals that the disputants could not have known the precise content, nature or scope of the applicable norms at the time their conflict erupted.

Judges typically respond to this crisis by propagating an overarching principle of governance which, for simplicity's sake, I will simply call precedent. Judges, supported by legal positivists (Hart 1994; MacCormick 1978), portray precedent as an inherently legal constraint on discretion and lawmaking. In its idealized form, governance through precedent proceeds incrementally, through formal exercises in normative deliberation and analogic reasoning. A court that does not actually or always proceed in this way, nonetheless, typically pretends to the rest of us that it has. Judges package decisions in ways that make their rulings appear to be self-evident, redundant, deductive extensions of pre-existing law (Shapiro 1972). In this way, precedent camouflages lawmaking, while enabling it. More broadly, the crisis engendered by judicial lawmaking generates mountains of legal materials—judicial decisions, commentaries and treatises—whose purpose it is to re-assert the underlying stability and permanence of the law, and therefore, the legitimacy of courts with reference to precedent and settled canons of interpretation and reasoning.

Shapiro (1970, 1972) argued that precedent-based judicial lawmaking also serves a related, defensive purpose. Because adjudication constitutes a relatively non-hierarchical, decentralized mode of governance, courts seek to structure their environments in ways that will both reduce "noise" from below and enhance systemic coherence through guidance from above. Practices associated with precedent allow judges to do both. Lawyers counsel clients and develop litigation strategies from cues given in existing case law, and these cues would have little meaning without some conception of precedent and coordination (both horizontal and vertical) between courts.

I wrote the paper, *Path Dependence, Precedent, and Judicial Power* (Shapiro and Stone Sweet 2002, chap. 2), partly with these points in mind. The paper seeks to explain why the judicial mode of governance tends to be incremental and path-dependent (see also Shapiro 1968). Legal institutions can be said to be path-dependent to the extent that litigation and judicial rulemaking, in any given area of the law at any given point in time, are fundamentally conditioned by how earlier disputes have been sequenced and resolved. The paper develops a model of adjudication in which legal norms and reasoning are brought to bear on strategic action and decision making through the propagation of discursive choice-settings—doctrine—what I prefer to call "argumentation frameworks" (following Sartor 1994). Such frameworks are formalized analogies, assembled from materials found in past decisions, on related cases. Judges self-consciously curate precedents in order to organize their environments in ways that make judicial governance possible. Argumentation frameworks give some measure of determinacy to legal norms and thus help to legitimize judicial lawmaking. They also help lawyers and judges build "litigation markets," enabling legal actors to achieve effective communication and coordination with one another (Shapiro and Stone Sweet 2002, 96, 294), even when they are widely dispersed in space and time.

Balancing. Shapiro focused on the politics of balancing in his dissertation (ultimately published as Shapiro 1966) and returned to these politics regularly (e.g., 1971, 1986). In balancing situations, judges are most clearly exposed as policymakers. In pure constitutional balancing situations (that is, when a court is faced with resolving a dispute in which each of the parties, pleads a legitimate constitutional right, interest or value), it is the judges reading of the situation—not of the law per se—that determines the outcome. In developing balancing and proportionality tests, judges exploit the social logic of long-term reciprocity among potential litigants (society), and construct the law as a flexible instrument of dispute resolution (Stone Sweet 2000, 97–99, 142). These tests make it clear that each litigant's legal interest is a legitimate one; the court, nonetheless, must make a decision by weighing each side's interest against the other; and future cases pitting the same two legal interests against one another may well be decided differently, depending on the facts. Balancing and proportionality tests (1) hold sway precisely where the law is most indeterminate, and (2) are most in danger of being constructed in a partisan way. Balancing tests constitute normative tools for managing this indeterminacy over time; they also enable the judges to maintain their own room to maneuver in cases likely to come before them in the future.

When it comes to balancing rights claims against a constitutionally-derived public interest pursued by government, Shapiro (e.g., 1992a, 130–31) predicts that a steady stream of such cases will lead judges to develop a highly intrusive form of review: proportionality or least-means testing. The microfoundations of this prediction, in my view, are laid out by Shapiro (1992b, 2001) in an analysis (applied to another context) of the dynamics of "giving reasons." In these papers, Shapiro showed how sustained litigation could drive courts to perfect a very particular technique of judicial control over the discretion of public authorities: requiring government officials to defend their actions with reasons. Under certain conditions, the following sequence ensues: (a) the rule that those being controlled must provide a reason to justify an action gives way to (b) the rule that only a good or sensible reason can be justified, which in turn develops into (c) the rule that the best possible reason will be strictly scrutinized, and even then may not be enough to prevail in court. Proportionality, or a strict least-means balancing standard, requires the judge to ask if government could not have proceeded in ways that would have caused less harm, say, to the rights of individuals. If the answer is yes, then the government's interest must be outweighed by an individual's. If, in balancing, courts necessarily become legislators and administrators, the reverse is also true: In enforcing least-means tests, courts push lawmakers and administrators into a judicial mode, requiring them to reason as the judge will, that is, to consider the proportionality of their own activities (Shapiro and Stone Sweet 2002, chap. 6).

Summary

It should be obvious how these ideas can be connected. We have good *a priori* reasons to expect that the pace and scope of judicialization will be partly determined by the size of the zone of discretion enjoyed by the court. A court that operates in a relatively large zone of discretion—e.g., a trustee court that exercises fiduciary duties with respect to a constitution—is far more likely to gain decisive influence over the institutional evolution of a polity than one that operates in a relatively restrictive environment. Trusteeship, however, will never be enough in and of itself. For steady judicialization to proceed, there needs to be a steady case load to which judges respond by building a precedent-based case law. It will not proceed if judges produce capricious decisions, with no concern for the coherence of their own jurisprudence. Yet again, the greater the zone of discretion, of course, the more likely it is that the specific modes of reasoning and decision making developed by judges—e.g., those associated with balancing—will consolidate and diffuse as general modes of governance within the system.

The Constitutionalization of the Legal System

European legal integration, provoked by the European Court of Justice (ECJ) and sustained by private litigants and national judges, has gradually but inexorably "transformed" (Weiler 1991) the EU. The so-called *constitutionalization* of the treaty system not only displaced the traditional, state-centered "international organization" of the diplomat and the "regime" of the international relations scholar (Burley and Mattli 1993; Stein 1981; Stone 1994; Weiler 1981, 1999). It progressively enhanced the supranational elements of the EU and undermined its intergovernmental character (Stone Sweet and Caporaso 1998), federalizing the polity in all but name (Cappelletti, Seccombe, and Weiler, 1986; Lenaerts 1990; Mancini 1991). Today, the ECJ has no rival as the most effective supranational judicial body in the history of the world; on any dimension, it compares favorably with the most powerful constitutional courts anywhere.[1]

Here, I focus on the impact of the ECJ on the overall course of integration, setting aside many other important and relevant issues.[2] For brevity's sake, I assume basic familiarity with the Court's "constitutional" case law and the scholarly discourse on "constitutionalization."[3] In this section, I will discuss the major consequences of constitutionalization for integration, in light of the theoretical materials laid out in part I. I begin by briefly summarizing the results of a project to develop and test a dynamic and macro-institutional theory of integration. I then provide an overview of the ECJ's case load and decision making. Both provide strong support for the dominant integration narrative propagated by the best legal scholarship, while seriously undermining social science theories of integration that ignore the steady expansion of judicial power within the EC.

Integration and the Legal System

My collaborators and I (Stone Sweet and Brunell 1998a, 1998b; Stone Sweet and Caporaso 1998; Fligstein and Stone Sweet 2002; Stone Sweet 2004) have sought to test a dynamic and macro-institutional theory of integration, the results of which can be briefly summarized. We built the theory from materials developed in North (1990), recent economic sociology (Fligstein 2001), and my own model of judicialized governance (Stone Sweet 1999). We explicitly incorporated the basic constitutionalization narrative into the theory and tied that story to other key narratives of integration studies (see Fligstein and Stone Sweet 2002, 1213–26). After deriving hypotheses and considering alternative propositions, we gathered comprehensive data on the various processes most closely associated with European integration. We then tested the theory, using econometric and other statistical techniques, as well as doctrinal analysis and process tracing. We showed, through varied measures and methods, that the activities of market actors, lobbyists, legislators, and litigators and judges had become connected to one another in various ways. These linkages, in turn, produced a self-reinforcing, causal system that has largely determined the pace and scope of integration, and given the EU its fundamentally expansionary character.

These outcomes depend on certain *necessary* conditions, the most important being the constitutionalization of the Treaty of Rome: The diffusion of the Court's rulings on supremacy, direct effect, and related doctrines within national legal orders (Slaughter, Stone Sweet and Weiler 1998). In our analysis of period effects, we also found that two parameter shifts—whereby important qualitative events generate quantitatively significant transformations in the relationships among variables—had occurred in the evolution of the EU. The first shift began roughly around 1970, the second in the mid 1980s. The EU's developing legal system was implicated in both transitions, first through constitutionalization, and then as the legal system developed robust means of controlling compliance with EU law, especially with regard to rules governing the common market.

The research also explored the impact of adjudicating EU law on legislating and treaty-revision in detail. We identified two basic motivations for litigating EU law in national courts. First, actors engaged in transnational economic exchange would ask national judges to remove national laws and administrative practices that obstruct their activities in order to expand their markets, and to fix market rules in their favor. As transnational activity increases, the pool of potential litigants expands, as does the diversity of situations likely to give rise to conflicts between private economic actors and states. Second, individuals and groups *not* directly engaged in cross-border economic activity—such as those seeking to enhance women's rights or the protection of the environment—would use the courts to destabilize or reform national rules and practices they found disadvantageous. As the corpus of EU law (including both secondary legislation and the Court's case law) becomes more dense and articulated, so do the grounds for pursuing these "diffuse interests" at national bar. We found that both dynamics have tended to be self-sustaining.

We also attended to the impact of adjudicating EU law on treaty-revision and legislating. To do so necessarily requires a focus on governments. We now make a brief detour into the arcane world of integration theory, but not for the last time. "Intergovernmental" is an adjective that helps to describe certain modes of governance in place in the EU (and in many other federal polities). All extant theories of integration attend, if in diverse ways, to governments and the intergovernmental aspects of the EU. But such a focus does not entail adopting "intergovernmentalism" as theory, which is at once a body of particular concepts, a strategy for doing research, and a set of claims about the nature of integration and how it proceeds. We found that the adjudication of article 234 references not only pushed the integration project further than Member States' governments would have been prepared to go on their own, it also worked to structure intergovernmental bargaining and legislating at both the national and supranational levels.

These results bear on certain long-standing concerns of EU studies, three of which deserve emphasis. First, they provide broad empirical support for the core claims of "neofunctionalist," regional integration theory, developed by Ernst B. Haas (1958, 1961; see also Burley and Mattli 1993) some forty years ago, as we have modified it. Haas and his followers argued, among other things, that economic interdependence and the growth of transnational society would push the European Community's organizations, like the Commission and the Court of Justice, to work creatively to facilitate further integration, while raising the costs of intergovernmental inaction. In drawing connections between Haas' neofunctionalism and our research, I meant to emphasize commonalities that become apparent at a relatively abstract theoretical level. Haas (1961) focused on relationships between (a) European rules, (b) supranational organizations (especially organizational capacity to resolve disputes), and (c) the behavior and dispositions of those political and economic actors relevant to integration. In Europe, he theorized these three elements could evolve symbiotically through positive feedback loops that would, under certain conditions, push steadily for deeper integration. What I find important in this formulation are notions of how integration could develop an "expansive logic," as the activities of an increasing number of actors, operating in otherwise separate arenas of action, became linked.

These are quite similar to logics theorized in the model of judicialization discussed in part I.

Second, our results conflict sharply with propositions derivable from the strong intergovernmentalism of Andrew Moravcsik (1991, 1993) and Geoffrey Garrett (1992). Moravcsik (1991, 75) argued that "the primary source of integration lies in the interests of states themselves and the relative power each brings to Brussels," whereas private actors and the EU's organizations never play more than a secondary role. Among other things, he proposed that intergovernmental modes of governance typically produce outcomes that reflect the "minimum common denominator of large state [France, Germany and the United Kingdom (UK)] interests," given the "relative power positions" of states and unanimity decision rules. Although Moravcsik ignored the legal system entirely, Garrett (1992, 556–59) bluntly declared, "Decisions of the European Court are consistent with the preferences of France and Germany." If it were otherwise, the Member States would have punished the Court, and moved to reconstruct the legal system.

Beyond the founding of the communities themselves, the single most important institutional innovation in the history of European integration has been the constitutionalization of the Rome Treaty. The ECJ, in complicity with national judges and private actors, authoritatively revised the normative foundations of the treaty without the consent of Member State governments. Strong intergovernmentalism utterly fails to account for legal integration and its effect. Further, we found—in legal domains as different as free movement of goods, sex equality and environmental protection—that adjudicating EU law systematically subverted lowest common denominator policy outcomes that had been reached under unanimity, ratcheting them upwards. We also collected and analyzed comprehensive data on the Court's decision making, in these and other legal domains. The data firmly refute the view that the Court's rulings follow from state preferences, at least when states clearly and formally signal their policy preferences in their observations (briefs) to the Court (Cichowski 1998, 2001; Stone Sweet and Brunell 1998a; Stone Sweet and Caporaso 1998; and confirming Kilroy 1996).

Not surprisingly, strong intergovernmentalism has been abandoned. The theory could not explain the steady expansion of supranational governance within the interstices of treaty-making, or the impact of the Commission and the Court on policy. Moravcsik (1998) retreated into a far weaker brand of intergovernmentalism, grafting a simple P-A account of delegation onto his basic framework in order to link the major episodes of state-to-state bargaining with the ongoing, day-to-day processes of supranational governance. He now stresses that states design (and re-design) European institutions and organizations to help them resolve certain commitment problems. States confer on EU organizations the power to act against the short-term preferences of some governments in order to help achieve their more basic, long-range and collective objectives. In this way, "state purposes" infuse the system, animating supranational governance and encapsulating its evolution.

This strategy raises critical theoretical issues. Most important, the use of delegation theory cannot distinguish weak intergovernmentalism from other theories of EU institutions, including my own (see also Pollack 1998; Tallberg 2002). Quite the contrary, the heirs of Haas and others explicitly invoked P-A logics in their critique of intergovernmentalist theory (e.g., Pierson 1998; Sandholtz and Stone Sweet 1998). What remains distinctive about Moravcsik's improved approach, apart from the narrow empirical focus on state-to-state bargains, are two claims. Although it is increasing economic interdependence that is the key exogenous, independent variable in the theory, just as it is in neofunctionalism, Moravcsik denies that transnational society or interests exist; instead, private interests can only be domestic. He also insists (e.g., Moravcsik 1998, chap. 7) that the EU's organizations have done nothing to "influence the distribution of gains," or the configuration of economic interests, in ways that could help to determine the preferences of governments.

Third, it is sometimes asserted that "negative integration," the process through which barriers to cross-border economic activity within Europe are removed, and "positive integration," the process through which common, supranational public policies are made and enforced, are governed by separate social logics. Although I will not dwell on this issue here, we found that negative and positive integration, far from being distinct processes, are in fact connected in important ways (they are meaningfully endogenous to one another).

How has the legal system been able to have such an impact on the course of integration? One way of responding is to focus on judicial discretion: the authority of judges to interpret and apply legal rules to situations in order to resolve disputes. In part I, I emphasized three factors. The first concerns the nature and scope of the powers delegated to judges by the contracting parties. The Rome Treaty charges the Court with enforcing treaty rules, most importantly, against the contracting parties themselves, and it establishes further details of jurisdiction. Discretion is also built into the treaty: In addition to direct grants of authority to the Court by the Member States, the contracting parties have also delegated in a tacit or implicit manner. The Rome Treaty, like all modern constitutions, is an incomplete contract generated by what Milgrom and Roberts (1992, 127–33) have called "relational contracting." The parties to it do not seek to fully specify their reciprocal rights and duties; instead, they broadly frame their relationship through establishing basic "goals and objectives," outer limits on acceptable behavior, and procedures for completing the contract over time. Adjudication functions to clarify, over time, the meaning of the contract, and to monitor compliance.

The second factor is the mix of control mechanisms available to the contracting parties, vis-à-vis the judge. Direct controls are formal (they are established by explicit rules) and negative (they annul or authoritatively revise the court's decisions, or curb the court's powers). The following point can hardly be overemphasized: The decision rule that governs reversal of the Court's interpretations of the Treaty—unanimity of the Member States plus ratification—constitutes a weak system of control. Put differently, the ECJ operates in an unusually permissive environment when it interprets the Rome Treaty. When it interprets secondary legislation, permissiveness shrinks in those domains governed by majority or qualified majority voting, other things equal.[5]

Indirect controls operate only insofar as the judges internalize the interests of the contracting parties, or takes cues from the revealed preferences of the latter, and act accordingly. The extent to which any court does so is commensurate to the credibility of the threat that direct controls will be activated. Given that the system of direct controls favors the ongoing dominance of the ECJ over the constitutional evolution of the system, we have no good reason to think that the ECJ, when it interprets the treaties, will be systematically constrained in its use of its discretionary powers for fear of being punished. A fatal flaw in strong intergovernmentalism was its under-theorized assumption that the EU's organizations behaved as relatively perfect agents, under the control of their principals, the Member States.

Taken together, we see that, compared with most courts in the world, the ECJ operates in a zone of discretion that is unusually large. When the Court interprets the Rome Treaty, its discretionary powers are close to unlimited.

Conceptualizing discretion in this way cannot tell us what the ECJ will actually do with its powers. The question—what values are judges maximizing when they exercise discretion—is a central one if we are to make sense of European legal integration and the impact of the construction of the legal system on non-legal actors. I proceed on the assumption—implicitly shared by nearly all legal scholars who have sought to understand the dynamics of legal integration—that the Court seeks to enhance the effectiveness of EC law in national legal orders, to expand the scope of supranational governance, and to achieve the general purposes of the treaty broadly conceived. The Court cares about compliance with its decisions because compliance serves these values. I see no compelling or *a priori* institutional reason to model the Court (or the European judiciary) as servants of national governments. Where governments work to promote the same values, they work in tandem with judges; where they do not, they court judicial sanction.

The third determinant of the Court's discretion is endogenous to the Court's own decision making, that is, relative levels of discretion will vary as a function of the Court's case law, but only if some minimally robust idea of precedent governs the Court's decision making. The capacity of the Court to organize integration prospectively depends on its success in generating a relatively coherent jurisprudence on the Treaty. Of course, in elaborating constraints that bind all actors in the EU system, the Court also constrains itself.

Agency and Trusteeship

At first glance, the discussion in the preceding section appears to fit easily with the so-called "positive theory" of delegation noted in part I. The analyst typically begins with an exposition of the underlying functional logics for delegation, in order to "explain" why "principals" delegate to "agents" (new governmental organizations). The standard line is that delegation is functional for principals insofar as delegation reduces the costs associated with governing: bargaining and commitment, monitoring and enforcing agreements, and developing rational policies in the face of technical complexity, incomplete information, and powerful incentives for rent-seeking. The analyst then turns to how the P-A relationship is constructed, focusing on the mix of *ex ante* and *ex post* incentives and control mechanisms that principals use to (a) preprogram the agent's performance with respect to their policy preferences, and (b) monitor and punish the agent for non-performance.

There are good reasons to be dissatisfied with this approach to delegated governance, the first of which I repeat again: the P-A framework loses much of its relevance in a trusteeship situation.[6] The second problem relates to testing. The "positive theory of delegation," like Moravcsik's notions of delegation, offers appropriate, but pre-packaged, logics that can be applied to virtually any governance situation at the EU level. As causal theory, it remains woefully inadequate, unless the analyst clearly specifies variables or causal mechanisms that would make the formulation of testable hypotheses or comparative research on governance-through-delegation possible (Huber and Shipan 2000). Most important, because the framework fetishizes the *ex ante* functional needs of principals, it is poorly equipped to deal with the evolutionary dynamics of agency, let alone trusteeship.

Any theory of integration must attend to the motivations of the Member States in choosing to establish or enhance the powers of supranational organizations. Functional logics can help us to do so. They can also help to generate some very general expectations about how the system of governance constituted by delegation is likely to evolve. A trustee, for example, will likely to exert more independent impact on the evolution of EU institutions than will an agent. The Court operates in an expansive zone of discretion, and its activities—such as its interactions with national judges and private parties—cannot be directly controlled by the Member States. Ultimately, trusteeship constitutes a necessary condition for the kind of feedback that is at the heart of judicialization to emerge and become entrenched.

I, an intergovernmentalist or a neofunctionalist can always "explain" some of the scope of supranational governance, at any given moment, through reading outcomes produced by the EU's organs back to some previous act of delegation. The Member States chose to constitute the Court and the Commission as trustees on a host of matters, for rational purposes. They did so, obviously enough, because a trustee would be more likely to succeed in helping them build the common market than an agent would be, or the states would be, given the prisoner's dilemma characteristics of political cartels. But questions of how supranational governance actually proceeds—through what processes, generating what kinds of outcomes, with what effects?—cannot be answered in this way, except in the most mundane, *post hoc* and circular way.

Unfortunately, weak intergovernmentalism fails to offer testable propositions concerning how the law or supranational governance evolves. By definition, the greater the Court's or the Commission's zone of discretion, the less able the analyst is to predict the outcomes of supranational governance from the preferences of the Member States at *any* selected moment in time. Moravcsik's strategy is to stipulate some underlying functional need of the Member States for supranational governance, and then to interpret outcomes produced by the EU's organizations in light of a prior act of delegation, thereby "explaining" them. Outcomes of interest *always* fall within the parameters fixed by state purposes. The move, however, does little to help us understand how the EU's organizations actually operate, or what kinds of outcomes they will produce. Instead, the empirical domain is eviscerated: Integration proceeds, supranational governance spreads and deepens; but the intergovernmentalist's model of the EU, and of state control of the system, never changes. Indeed, intergovernmentalists like Garrett and Moravcsik assert that the system has never produced important "unintended consequences."

The ECJ: Case Law and Decision Making

The constitutionalization of the Treaty of Rome constitutes an "unintended consequence" of monumental proportions. The Member States had designed an enforcement system that I would characterize as "international law plus," the "plus" being (a) the compulsory nature of the Court's jurisdiction, and (b) the obligatory participation of the Commission in various proceedings. Under article 227, a Member State may bring a complaint against another Member State if the Commission determines that the complaint is founded, and if the defendant state refuses to settle, the case may go to the Court. Article 227 is virtually a dead letter, used (I believe) in only two instances to date. Under article 226, the Commission may initiate infringement proceedings against a Member State; rounds of negotiation with a recalcitrant government then ensue and, if these fail, the Court might hear the case. For various reasons, the Commission was reticent to use article 226 aggressively until the late-1970s, a posture abandoned as constitutionalization through article 234 proceeded. Article 234 establishes a preliminary reference procedure in order to avoid conflicts of interpretation; it was not meant to be an enforcement mechanism at all, at least not in any direct sense. As everyone now knows, article 234 is the linchpin of constitutionalization, and thus, of legal integration (Appendix 1).

Figure 1 tracks article 234 activities since the first reference in 1961. Levels of references were very low during the 1960s, and then began to pick up in 1970, as common market rules entered into force, and as national judges began to make use of the doctrines of supremacy and direct effect. references doubled by 1980, and shot up again after the Single European Act.

Figure 1
Annual Number of Article 234 References to the ECJ

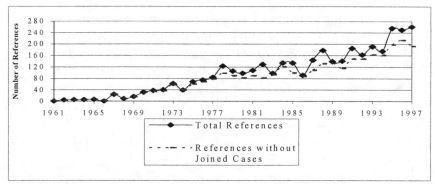

Note: The line plots the annual number of article 234 references to the ECJ. The broken line plots the annual number of references minus those that have been joined to another case. The ECJ typically joins together references that involving similar disputes (although each involves a separate litigating party).
Source: Alec Stone Sweet and Thomas L. Brunell Data Set on Preliminary References in EC Law, 1958–98, Robert Schuman Centre for Advanced Studies, European University Institute (San Domenico di Fiesole, Italy, 1999). Available online at http://www.nuff.ox.ac.uk/Users/Sweet/index.html. See Stone Sweet and Brunell (2000).

Table 1 records the extent to which reference activity has expanded in scope and intensity across an increasing number of legal domains. During the 1970–74 period, over 50 percent of the total number of areas invoked fell within just two domains: agriculture and the free movement of goods, while these areas today are the source of barely 20 percent of total activity. In the meantime, we see an important rise of reference activity in other domains, such as environmental protection, taxation, commercial policy and competition, and the free movement of workers. Strikingly, in the 1990s, nearly one-in-twelve references concerned "social provisions," which mostly invoke sex discrimination law. Thus, today, the legal system operates as much as a vehicle for more diffuse, "public" interests, as it does for traders and producers.[7]

Table 1
Distribution of Preliminary References by Legal Domain and Period
(Article 234)

Subject	Total 1958– 98*	1958– 69	1970– 74	1975– 79	1980– 84	1980– 89	1990– 94	1995– 98*
Agriculture (%)		13	41.5	35.8	26.9	21.4	15.3	9.5
(number)	1,008	13	129	232	202	170	163	99
Free Movement		18	18.7	19.4	21.6	21.3	16.2	12.3
of Goods	832	17	58	126	162	169	172	128
Social		27	10.3	12.2	7.9	8.9	10.2	6.5
Security	444	26	32	79	59	71	109	68
Taxation		14	3.2	4.2	6.1	7.4	8.1	9.8
	344	14	10	27	46	59	86	102
Competition		12	7.1	4.3	4.9	5.5	10.5	6.1
	318	12	22	28	37	44	112	63
Approximation		1.0	1.0	1.5	4.9	4.2	3.9	8.9
of Law	217	1.0	3	10	37	33	41	92
Transportation		0	1.6	1.5	1.2	1.1	3.6	1.5
	77	0	5	10	9	9	28	16
Establishment		1.0	1.9	3.7	2.1	6.4	8.4	9.8
	289	1.0	6	24	16	51	89	102
Social		0	0.3	1.2	2.8	3.9	8.5	8.2
Provisions	236	0	1.0	8	21	31	90	85
External		1.0	2.6	2.3	3.1	1.8	1.6	3
	109	1.0	8	15	23	14	17	31

(Table continued on next page)

Free Movement		1.0	2.9	2.9	2.9	5.2	3.7	6.8
of Persons	202	1.0	9	19	22	41	39	71
Environment		0	0	0.2	1.7	1.0	1.0	4.1
	75	0	0	1.0	13	8	10	43
Commercial		0	1.3	1.2	1.3	1.4	2.4	1.4
Policy	72	0	4	8	10	11	25	14
Other		11	7.7	9.6	12.5	10.5	7.9	12.3
	483	11	24	62	94	83	84	12.5
Total Claims	**4,706**	**97**	**311**	**649**	**751**	**794**	**1065**	**1039**
Percent of Total Claims by Period	100**	2.1	6.6	13.8	16	16.9	22.6	22.1

* The data for 1998 is incomplete, ending, for most countries in May or June 1998.
** 'Joined references' (see figure 1) are excluded from these calculations. Due to rounding, percentages of total claims by period add to 100.1percent.
Source: Alec Stone Sweet and Thomas L. Brunell Data Set on Preliminary References in EC Law, 1958–98, Robert Schuman Centre for Advanced Studies, European University Institute (San Domenico di Fiesole, Italy: 1999).

Underlying judicial authority is prospective, precedent-based lawmaking. The EC was founded as an international legal order by Member States sharing civil law traditions. Although neither international nor civil law formally recognize the doctrine of *stare decisis*, the Court has worked to develop what are now robust, taken-for-granted practices associated with precedent. It has propagated increasingly nuanced doctrinal frameworks, and these have helped to structure the evolution of the legal system (Stone Sweet and McCown 2003). These frameworks typically render the law more coherent (more determinate) for those who are networked by and participate in the system (see Bengoetxea 2003). They are also primary mechanisms of Europeanization, powerfully conditioning, among other things, how actors develop litigation strategies. Not only do the number of decisions using precedent-based arguments increase over time, but so do the number of precedent-based rules used to construct each argument. Figures 2 and 3 provide some indication of these developments.

Figure 2
Annual Percentage of ECJ Preliminary Rulings
Citing Prior ECJ Judgments

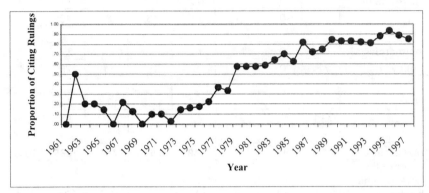

Source: Margaret McCown and Alec Stone Sweet. 2002. *Dataset on European Court of Justice Citation Practices in Preliminary Reference Rulings, 1961–1998.* Nuffield College, Oxford. For analysis, see Stone Sweet and McCown (2003).

Figure 3
Average Annual Number of Citations in ECJ Preliminary Rulings

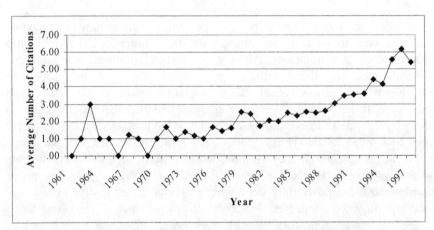

Source: Margaret McCown and Alec Stone Sweet. 2002. *Dataset on European Court of Justice Citation Practices in Preliminary Reference Rulings, 1961–1998.* Nuffield College, Oxford. For analysis, see Stone Sweet and McCown (2003).

The Court of Justice and Market Integration

If the legal system operated only to enforce existing European law, an exclusive focus on the functional needs of the Member States and the EU's legislators might be defensible. But, in interpreting the Rome Treaty, the Court regularly recasts the strategic settings in which governments and legislators find themselves. Treaty-revision in the EU has always been partly about governments responding to market integration with more political integration, and partly about judicialization, that is, governments playing catch-up with the Court and the Commission.

In this section, I focus on the constitutional politics of one story: the impact of the evolution of the Treaty of Rome's trading institutions on the EU system as a whole. The free movement of goods domain comprises the classic core of the market integration project, and the Court's jurisprudence on article 28 has rightly been the subject of sustained theory-driven doctrinal research (e.g., Poiares Maduro 1998; Weiler 1998). In political science, the revival of integration studies (Sandholtz and Zysman 1989) and rise of intergovernmentalist theory (Moravcsik 1991, Garrett 1992) began with a focus on the relationship between market-building, the legislative process and treaty-revision. I summarize this episode primarily to test theory against data (for the full account, see Stone Sweet 2004, chap. 3). Although I report results for the free movement of goods domain as a whole, my primary concern is on the knottiest problem of all: non-tariff barriers.

Given my theoretical priorities (part 1), I expected the adjudication of trading disputes in the EU to be patterned in predictable ways.[8] One set of expectations concerned logics of litigating. Traders would use article 28 instrumentally, to remove national barriers to intra-EU trade, targeting—disproportionately—measures that hinder access to larger markets relative to smaller ones. As negative integration proceeds (that is, to the extent that the legal system sides with traders against national authorities), further litigation will be stimulated. A second set of expectations concerned the kinds of outcomes the legal system would be likely to generate. Given a steady supply of preliminary references, it will be the Court's case law, and not the preferences or decision making of Member State governments, that determines how the domain evolves. On the basis of assumptions about litigants' and judges' interests, the Court can be expected to produce rulings that (a) facilitate expansion of intra-EU trade, (b) undermine national control over such activity, and (c) press the EU's legislative bodies to extend the scope of the polity's regulatory capacities. These expectations are conditioned by the Court's zone of discretion in this area: The Court is a trustee of the Treaty, not an agent of national governments.

Alternative propositions have been put forward. Recall that Garrett (1992) argued that the Court's decisions would serve to codify, in case law, the policy interests of the dominant states. In a follow-up piece, Garrett (1995, 178–79) argued that the Court seeks to enhance its own legitimacy by pursuing two, sometimes contradictory, goals: (a) to curry the favor of powerful states and (b) to ensure Member State compliance with its decisions. The ECJ, he argued, will sometimes censure 'powerful governments,' but only in 'unimportant sectors' of the economy, while 'accepting protectionist behavior' in more important sectors, since strong governments are unlikely to comply with adverse decisions. Apparently, no stable predictions are derivable when it comes to 'less powerful governments.' As in all his work, Garrett resolutely ignores the litigants and national judges, a choice left undefended.

Unfortunately, it is all but impossible to derive relevant testable propositions from Moravcsik's weak intergovernmentalism. Since the Member States established the authority of the Commission and the Court in the free movement domain through purposive acts of delegation, their activities serve the fulfillment of the Member States' grand designs. Nonetheless, Moravcsik makes at least one straightforward causal claim, in the guise of the assertion that delegate governance has never produced "unintended consequences." He insists (1998, 482–90), that while governments set the agenda for the EU's organizations, the latter never "alter the terms under which governments negotiate new bargains." The argument is repeated (1998, ch. 5) in his analysis of the Single European Act (SEA).

Article 28 of the Treaty of Rome

The Rome Treaty required the Member States to eliminate national barriers to intra-EC trade by the end of 1969, including non-tariff barriers. Article 28 states that "Quantitative restrictions on imports and all measures having equivalent effect [MEEs] shall be prohibited between Member States." Article 30 permits a Member State to derogate from article 28, on grounds of public morality, public policy, public security, health, and cultural heritage, though derogations may "not…constitute a means of arbitrary discrimination or a disguised restriction on trade between Member States." In ex-article 33, the Member States charged the Commission with producing directives to fix a "procedure and timetable" for states to abolish MEEs. Compared with import quotas or border inspection fees, non-tariff barriers—MEEs—negatively affect intra-EU trade in less visible, more indirect ways; further, being part of national regulatory regimes, they can always be justified as serving legitimate state purposes. In the system designed by the Member States, MEEs were to be removed through two mutually reinforcing processes: States would abolish such measures on their own, or be pushed to do so by infringement proceedings, while the EC legislation would gradually replace national regulations with "harmonized" ones.

On the eve of the entry into force of free movement of goods provisions, this system was in deep trouble. Member States had made little effort to abolish MEEs on their own, and the Luxembourg Compromise (important EC legislation was to be adopted by unanimity voting in the Council of Ministers, rather than through qualified majority, applicable from 1966) threatened to paralyze the Commission's harmonization efforts. To jumpstart matters, the Commission issued Directive 70/50 (December 1969) pursuant to ex-article 33 (reproduced in Oliver 1996, 424–28). The Directive gave article 28 an expansive reading. First, it listed nineteen types of rules or practices that Member States were to rescind, including discriminatory policies on pricing, access to markets, advertising, packaging and names of origin. Pushing further, it announced what we will refer to as a "discrimination test": measures that treated domestic goods differently than imported goods—say, by limiting the availability or the marketing of imports, or by giving "to domestic products a preference" in the domestic market—were prohibited under article 28. Second, the Commission raised the sensitive question of the legality of measures that states applied to domestic and imported goods equally, but were nonetheless protectionist. The Directive proposed that such "indistinctly applicable measures" [IAMs] ought to be captured by article 28, if they failed a test of proportionality. Where the "restrictive effects of such measures…are out of proportion to their [public policy] purpose," and where "the same objective can be attained by other means which are less of a hindrance to trade," the IAM constitutes an illegal MEE. With Directive 70/50, the Commission had gone far beyond its remit. The Member States had not delegated to the Commission the power to define the legal concept of MEEs, nor had they ever meant for article 28 to apply to IAMs. Note, however, that the Commission, while being an agent of the Council of Ministers in the harmonization process, is a trustee of the Treaty under ex-article 33.

In a series of rulings responding to references from national judges, the Court superseded the Commission on the first point, and absorbed the second, elaborating a highly intrusive form of judicial review of national regulatory regimes in the process. In *Dassonville* (ECJ 8/ 1974), the Court announced that "all trading rules [later replaced by "all measures"]...capable of hindering directly or indirectly, actually or potentially" intra-EC trade constitute MEEs. Traders bear no burden to show that a national measure actually reduces levels of exchange, or is *de facto* equivalent to a quota (the position defended by most if not all Member States at the time). In subsequent cases, the Court not only formally required national judges to apply a least-means/proportionality test to claimed exceptions under article 30, but sometimes did the balancing for the judge of reference, thereby determining the outcome (the classic case is *De Peijper*, ECJ 104/1975). In *Cassis de Dijon* (ECJ 120/1978), the Court extended the *Dassonville* framework and least-means balancing to IAMs, that is to the whole of national regulatory regimes, a move tempered somewhat by making available a new set of justifiable derogations from article 28. Claimed article 28 derogations are available to states only in areas of regulation that have not been harmonized, and are subject to strict proportionality review. Last, in now famous *dicta*, *Cassis* suggested that the treaty implied, and perhaps required, what came to be known as the "mutual recognition" of national production and marketing standards.

The Emergence and Consolidation of the "Dassonville Framework"

The basic doctrinal structure governing free movement of goods developed quickly, in a series of cases decided in the 1970s. The crucial elements of the framework are the following: First, trader's rights are conceived broadly and expansively, while the prerogatives of national governments are conceived restrictively. Second, there exist no clear limits to the reach of judicial authority into national regulatory regimes. Third, through the enforcement of a least-means, proportionality test, the framework makes judges the ultimate masters of trade law. Thus, the doctrinal structure encourages traders to use the courts as a means of negative integration, while denying that national authorities possess secure political property rights when it comes to the regulation of market activities. Perhaps most important, since the framework authoritatively organized the relationship between articles 28 and 30, it also *per force* organizes a discursive politics on the nature of European constitutionalism and the limits of national sovereignty (see Poiares Maduro 1998).

Dassonville: Hindrance to Trade, Direct or Indirect. The *Dassonville* case
(ECJ 8/74, 1974) provided the Court with its first important opportunity to
consider the meaning of free movement of goods provisions.

In 1970, Mr. Dassonville imported a dozen bottles of Johnnie Walker
Scotch Whiskey into Belgium, after having purchased it from a French
supplier. When Dassonville put the scotch on the market, he was prosecuted
by Belgian authorities for having violated customs rules. The rules prohibited
the importation from an EU country, in this case France, of spirits that
originated in a third country, in this case Britain, unless French customs rules
were substantially similar to those in place in Belgium. Dassonville was also
sued by a Belgian importer who possessed, under Belgian law, an exclusive
right to market Johnnie Walker. Dassonville argued that, under article 28 of
the Treaty, goods that had entered France legally must be allowed to enter
Belgium freely, and that exclusive rights to import and market goods were
not valid. The Belgian court appeared to agree and requested guidance from
the ECJ.

Dismissing the objections of the UK and Belgium, both of which argued
that such rules were not prohibited by article 28, the Court found for
Dassonville. Much more important, the Court declared the following:

> All trading rules enacted by the Member States, which are capable of hindering,
> directly or indirectly, actually or potentially, intra-Community trade are to be
> considered as measures having an effect equivalent to quantitative restrictions.

With no supporting argument, the Court had repudiated the two rival
understandings of article 28 then current. In its official brief to the Court, the
UK had argued that only measures that actually resulted in a "quantitative
reduction in the movement of goods" might be captured by article 28. The
UK's position, which would have placed the burden on the trader-plaintiff to
show that a given national measure had caused direct, deleterious effects on
trade, had wide support among the Member States and legal scholars at the
time (see Oliver 1996, 90–92). With Directive 70/50, the Commission had
sought to destroy this interpretation. The Court replaced the Commission's
discrimination model with its own, even more rigorous, "hindrance to trade
test" (Gormley 1985, 22). If put to a vote, the ECJ's interpretation of article
28—more expansively integrationist than any in circulation at the time—
would certainly not have been accepted by the Member State governments.

The Court had, after all, placed no limits to the reach of article 28: All
national laws or administrative practices that negatively impact the activities
of traders, including those that do so only "indirectly or potentially," are
presumptively prohibited. This Court had thus raised a delicate political

issue, which proved inseparable from how the law would come to develop. The wholesale removal of national regulations would strip bare legal regimes serving otherwise legitimate public interests, such as the protection of public health, the environment and the consumer. Further, where the Council was unable to produce harmonized legislation in a timely fashion, this lack of protection might not only endure, but could weaken public and political support for integration down the road. In response, the ECJ announced, in *Dassonville* and subsequent decisions, that the Member States could, within reason, continue to regulate the production and sale of goods in the public's interest, pending harmonization by the EU's legislator. The Court stressed that: (a) the condition of "reasonableness"[9] would be controlled strictly, (b) such regulations—as with national measures justified under article 30 grounds—could not "constitute a disguised restriction on trade between member states," and (c) the European judiciary would review the legality of these exceptions to article 30 on a case-by-case basis.

Thus, not only did the *Dassonville* decision define article 28 as broadly as possible, it laid the foundations for balancing, and therefore, for judicial dominance over trade policy within the EU.

De Peijper: Least-Means Proportionality. The ECJ's ruling in *Dassonville* showed traders that litigation of article 28 in the national courts could be an effective means of subverting national laws that hurt them, and of shaping the evolution of EU institutions in their favor. At the time, the legal establishment (in Brussels, Luxembourg and the academy) still clung to the idea that the appropriate way to review breaches of Treaty law by the Member States was through infringement proceedings organized by the Commission (article 226 EC). The Court, however, had made it clear that the rights of traders must be defended by national judges, and that national judges must do so in particular ways. Most important, *Dassonville* requires national judges to assess the reasonableness of national measures that might affect trade. In *De Peijper*, the Court (ECJ 104/75, 1976) demonstrated that such a requirement entails the judicial review of the decision making of national lawmakers, in micro-detail if necessary.

The case concerned criminal charges brought by Dutch prosecutors against an importer of the pharmaceutical, Valium. Mr. De Peijper had distributed the Valium to a hospital and pharmacy, after having purchased it from an English wholesaler and repackaged it under his own company's name. He was accused of violating a law that prohibited the marketing of medicinal products without the prior consent of the Public Health Inspector, in the absence of certain documents, to be verified by the Inspector, certifying the origin and composition of imported medicines. In his defense, Mr. De Peijper pleaded article 28. He could do so since the files and reports required by the Public Health Inspector could be completed only by designated "experts" who, in practice, were pharmacists employed by a company that was also the official importer of Valium into the Netherlands. Since Mr. De Peijper's company sold Valium at a lower cost than the official importer, he believed he would not be able obtain the latter's help in completing the required documents. The national court of referral asked the ECJ if the measures in question, as applied to parallel imports, constituted a "measure having an equivalent effect" under article 28 and, if so, whether the measure could be justified on article 30 grounds, namely, under the heading of "public health." Once the oral proceedings before the ECJ had been completed, the Commission instituted infringement proceedings against the Netherlands, under article 226.

The Advocate General sided with the importer, noting that Valium circulated lawfully in other Member States under various licenses and other public controls, which could, in principle, be used by national authorities to trace the origin. The Dutch and British governments defended the measures in question, first as non-discriminatory, then on article 30 grounds. But they also argued, joined by the Danish government, that the measures simply implemented existing EU directives, and thus, were presumptively valid under EU law. These directives prohibited the marketing of "medicinal products" in the absence of "a prior authorization issued by the competent authority in the Member State"; and they obliged distributors of imported medicines to show to this authority documents, to be completed with the aid of designated "experts," certifying the product's "composition and the method of preparation." In response, the Advocate General argued that the case implicated only the relationship between articles 28 and 30, and that EU secondary legislation could not expand the scope of "the residuary powers left to the Member States by article 30."

A final issue concerned the judicial function of the preliminary reference procedure, relative to infringement proceedings. In his report, the Advocate General (642–43, 649) noted:

> Although it is not within the scope of the Court's jurisdiction under [a]rticle 234 to give a ruling on the compatibility of the provisions of a specific national law with the Treaty, it acknowledges...that it has jurisdiction to provide the national court with all the factors of interpretation under Community law which may enable it to adjudicate upon this compatibility.

"There is no doubt," the Advocate General continued, "that the normal way of testing the compatibility of national laws [with EU law] is by means of...article 226," rather than through a reference from a national court. Yet, he argued, "if the Court wishes to give a helpful answer to the national court," it would be "impossible for it...to avoid examining this problem of compatibility." Further, given his expressed view on how the case ought to be decided, "the question then arises how Netherlands law should be adjusted in order to encourage free trade to the greatest possible extent while complying with the well-known requirements of public health." The Advocate General suggested that the Court could avoid the question for now, leaving it to be resolved through the Commission's infringement proceedings.

The Court ruled that the Dutch measures fell within the purview of article 28, taking care to restate the *Dassonville* formula. It then proceeded to balancing, generating an explicit least-means test:

> National rules or practices do not fall within the exception specified in [a]rticle 30 if the health and life of humans can be as effectively protected by measures which do not restrict intra-Community trade so much.

The ECJ then insisted that the national court apply such a least-means formula to resolve the case.

The Court could have ended the matter there. Instead, it chose to evaluate the proportionality of the Dutch measures on its own, showing how a Member State might secure the public's interest in ways that would hinder trade less than the Dutch rules at hand. Among other solutions, the Court suggested that national authorities "adopt a more active policy" of helping traders acquire necessary information, rather than "waiting passively for the desired evidence to be produced for them," or making importers dependent upon a competitor. More broadly, a Member State could hardly claim to be acting to protect public health, the Court declared, if its policies discouraged the distribution of lower cost medicines. Finally, the Court ruled that the various EU directives harmonizing regulation of pharmaceuticals had no effect on the scope of articles 28 and 30.

De Peijper illustrates some crucial aspects of the dynamics of judicial balancing under least-means proportionality tests. Courts do not enforce such tests without reenacting the decision-making processes of those whom they are being asked to control. That is, "they...put themselves in the latter's shoes, and walk through these processes step-by-step" (Stone Sweet 2000, 204). Inevitably, judges speak to how governmental officials should have behaved, if the latter had wished to exercise their authority lawfully. In doing so, judges lay down prospective rules meant to guide future decision making. Lawfulness, balancing courts are telling policymakers, entails reasoning through the legal norms as judges do, as balancers of rights against the public interest. Not surprisingly, ongoing enforcement of least-means tests tends to generalize judicial techniques of governance, inducing other public officials, if they hope to defend their interests adequately, to engage in the style of argumentation developed in the pertinent case law (Stone Sweet 2000, ch. 6).

The *De Peijper* ruling supplemented *Dassonville* in ways that quickly locked in these dynamics with respect to European market integration. The Court served notice to the Member States that national regulations bearing on trade could only be justified under the most restrictive of conditions. It demonstrated to litigators and the Commission that the preliminary reference procedure comprised an effective means of reviewing the conformity of national with EU law, parallel to, but not restricted by, the infringement procedure. And the ECJ ordered national judges to engage in least-means testing, while promising to instruct them exactly how to do so, where necessary.

Cassis: Mutual Recognition and Strict Scrutiny of Mandatory Requirements. A third seminal ECJ decision, *Cassis de Dijon* (ECJ 120/78, 1979), completed the construction of a comprehensive framework for adjudicating trade disputes under article 28. With Directive 70/50, the Commission had sought to bring within the ambit of article 28 IAMs: those national measures that did not, on their face, discriminate between domestic and imported goods, but which nonetheless restricted market access to imports, or otherwise disadvantaged them relative to domestic goods. In *Cassis*, the Court extended the *Dassonville* principles to this class of national regulation. Put very differently, the Court had decided that traders should not be asked to bear the costs of the Member States' failure to produce harmonized EU market rules.

In 1976, the German federal agency that regulates the marketing of spirits denied a request to import the French liqueur, *Cassis de Dijon de Dijon*, a black currant syrup typically mixed with wine as an aperitif, because its alcohol content fell below a minimum that would, under German law, allow it to be sold on the German market. Restated in general terms, the national judge asked the ECJ if article 28 could cover national laws that fixed different mandatory requirements for the marketing of products relative to those in place in other Member States. In its defense, the German agency claimed that IAMs were not presumptively captured by article 30, referencing Commission Directive 70/50 in support. In the absence of harmonization through EU directives, counsel for the German agency argued, "each Member State retains full legislative jurisdiction" over the technical characteristics upon which the marketing of beverages and foodstuffs is made conditional." As a second line of defense, the agency dutifully trotted out arguments to the effect that its rules on alcohol content served various public interests, covered under various headings of article 36. The Advocate General rebutted each of these arguments in his report, stating, that the Court had rejected the more "limited interpretation" of Directive 70/50 being relied on by the defendant.

The Court agreed with the German agency that where harmonized rules were not in place, "it is for the Member States to regulate all matters relating to the production and marketing of...alcoholic beverages...on their own territory." However, it also ruled that "disparities between the national laws" that hinder trade in such products would be "accepted only in so far as [such laws] may be recognized as necessary...to satisfy mandatory requirements relating in particular to the effectiveness of fiscal supervision, the protection of public health, the fairness of commercial transactions, and the defense of the consumer." After rehearsing and dismissing each of the justifications given by the German agency, the Court then declared that it could not divine

> [any] valid reason why, provided that they have been lawfully produced or marketed
> in one of the member states, alcoholic beverages should not be introduced into any
> other member states.

Through *dictum*, the Court had floated a new principle: that of the mutual recognition, on the part of each Member State, of the national production and marketing standards in place in the other Member States.

The Court's judgment extended the logic of *Dassonville*, while innovating in several important ways. With *Cassis*, no aspect of national regulatory policy touching on the market for goods could be considered *a priori* exempt from judicial scrutiny. The ruling required national judges to attend to the effects on traders of "disparities" between national legal regimes, thus, making them supervisors of the politics of harmonization. At the same time, the Court made available to the Member States a new set of justifications for derogating from article 28, although these are valid only in the absence of harmonization.[10] In subsequent cases, the Court imposed a least-means proportionality test to scrutinize such claims, which it taught to national courts by way of example.

Precedent. This trio of founding cases produced a set of general doctrinal principles that governed the domain until its partial mutation in the 1990s (discussed briefly below). In our analysis (Stone Sweet and McCown 2003) of the structure of the system of argumentation in the domain, we found that over one-third of all of the Court's article 234 decisions on MEEs under article 28 cite at least one of these three rulings. Of those rulings that combine multiple arguments from more than one decision, more than one-half do so. As adjudication in the area proceeded, litigators and judges developed increasingly refined structures—derivations of the basic principles—for dealing with particular problems. Litigators learned to build arguments from rulings on trading situations that most resembled those in which they found themselves; and the Court typically treats these arguments, and its own precedents, at relatively sectorally based. For example, intellectual property rights decisions tend to draw on previous cases dealing with trademark and copyrights questions, rather than advertising or labeling requirements, even when the legal question at issue deals with rather general balancing rules that are applied in the same way in all free movement of goods disputes. At the same time, a precedent-based discourse on the various justified exceptions to article 28 also developed, which varies subtly across the article 30 headings and the mandatory requirements under article 28.

The development of a minimally coherent, precedent-based discourse on article 28 is a necessary condition for the range of outcomes—feedback effects of the Court's case law—to which we now turn.

Outcomes

The Court's case law on article 28 combined with the doctrines of supremacy and direct effect to give traders rights that were enforceable in national courts. After *Cassis*, no part of the regulatory state was *a priori* insulated from the reach of judicial review. Although important, the production of favorable doctrines does not conclude the story. The more the EU's legal system actually removes barriers to markets, for example, the more intra-EU trade and subsequent litigation will be stimulated. Positive outcomes for traders will attract more litigation, negative outcomes will deter it. Further, the more effective the legal system is at enforcing article 28, the more pressure adjudication puts on the EC's legislative organs to harmonize market rules. I now turn to the dynamic effects of this doctrinal structure on the greater integration process, culminating in the Single Act.

Figure 1 depicts the annual number of article 234 references for the domain as a whole, and for article 28, through mid-1998. References have steadily increased since *Dassonville*, and spike upward after *Cassis*. Breaking down the data crossnationally shows that only two of the original EU-6, France and Germany, have generated a disproportionate number of references in this legal domain.[11] Of the original EU-12, French, German, Italian, and UK judges have produced 73 percent (591/805) of all references in the domain. Trader-litigators, in fact, do target large markets, relative to smaller ones. The finding seems unsurprising: Traders have a far greater interest in opening larger markets relative to smaller ones; and higher levels of cross-border trade, strongly correlated with larger markets, will generate relatively more trading disputes than would smaller markets (see Stone Sweet and Brunell 1998a). In contrast, Garrett (1992, 1995) claimed that the ECJ and the legal system only work effectively against smaller states.

Analysis of the dispositive outcomes produced by the Court provides a more direct test of such claims. We examined all of the ECJ rulings pursuant to article 234 references that expressly invoked article 28 (n=254). For each ruling, we coded for whether the Court declared the type of national rule or practice at issue to be a violation of article 28, or not. The ECJ ruled in favor of the trader-plaintiff in exactly half of all decisions in which such a determination was clearly made (108/216). Traders have a higher success rate in France, Germany and Italy—well over 50 percent—than they do in Belgium, the Netherlands and the UK; and they enjoy the best success rate (60 percent) in Germany. Member State briefs to the Court—revealed state preferences on how the Court should decide cases—failed to presage or influence the Court's rulings. German interventions were found to be particularly ineffectual in generating outcomes (see also Kilroy 1996). In contrast, the Commission's observations "predicted" the Court's decision about 85 percent of the time. Thus, there is no evidence to support the view that governments constrain the Court in any important, let alone systematic, way. Similarly designed studies of adjudicating EU social provisions and environmental protection confirm these results (Cichowski 1998, 2001; Stone Sweet 2004, chaps. 4, 5).

We also examined the types of national rules and practices that have come under attack in references, and the data shows legal integration to be an inherently expansionary process. In the 1970s, the vast majority of references attacked national measures that required special certification and licensing requirements, border inspections and customs valuations for imports. After *Cassis*, a host of IAMs, such as those that impose purity or content requirements, came onto the Court's agenda. By the early-1980s, traders began attacking an increasingly broad range of national rules, such as those related more to the marketing (rather than the production) of goods: minimum pricing, labeling and packaging requirements, Sunday trading prohibitions, and advertising. The absence of any clear limit to the reach of *Dassonville-Cassis* made these dynamics—which progressively extended the reach of article 28 to more and more indirect hindrances to trade—possible.

Given the nature of least-means balancing, the ECJ and national judges inevitably came to play a powerful lawmaking role, not least in providing templates of lawful market regulation. In its article 28 case law, the Court routinely generated such templates, which could then become harmonized law in one of two ways. National regimes could adapt themselves to the Court's case law, in order to remain competitive and to insulate themselves from litigation. Or, more efficiently, the Commission could propose legislation of the kind that had passed review by the Court, thus, providing the Member States with legal shelter.

Both routes were facilitated by how the Court actually decided cases. In a very important piece of research, Poiares Maduro (1998) examined how the ECJ balances trading rights against derogations from article 28 claimed by Member State governments, in that part of the domain governed by *Cassis* (i.e., the review of the conformity, with article 28 of IAMs). The data show that the judges engage, systematically, in what Poiares Maduro calls (1998, 72–78) "majoritarian activism." When the national measure in question is more unlike than like those equivalent measures in place in a majority of Member States, the ECJ strikes it down as a violation of article 28. (We found that the Court began, in the early-1980s, to ask the Commission to provide such information on a regular basis.) Poiares Maduro found no exceptions to this rule. On the other hand, he found that the Court tends to uphold national measures in situations in which no dominant type of regulation exists, although there are important exceptions. In this way, the Court generates a "judicial harmonization" process. Majoritarian activism undermines the logic of minimum common denominator outcomes asserted by intergovernmentalists. At the same time, the Court would have little to fear in the way of reprisals, since a majority of Member States would likely be on its side on any given case.

No systematic research on the relationship between the Court's article 28 case law and legislative harmonisation in the EU has been undertaken. It is, however, routinely noted that the Court replaced the Council of Ministers as a force for positive integration prior to the Single European Act (Craig and De Burca 1998, chap. 14; Oliver 1996, chap. 6), and a smaller piece of literature (Empel 1992; Berlin 1992) focuses on how the Court's caselaw required or provoked governments to act legislatively. In any case, dozens of EU directives adopted prior to the Single European Act codified, as secondary legislation, specific rulings of the Court. Much more attention has been paid to the impact of *Cassis de Dijon*, from which the Commission developed a new strategy for achieving market integration.

Following the Court's ruling in that case, the Commission took the unusual step of issuing a "Communication," in the form of a letter sent to the Member States, the Council and the Parliament (reproduced in Oliver 1996, 429–31). The letter asserted that the Court had effectively established mutual recognition as a constitutional principle, which the Commission went on to interpret in the broadest possible manner. The Court had shown how states might retain their own national rules, capable of being applied to within the domestic market, while prohibiting states from applying these same rules to goods originating elsewhere. Reliance on mutual recognition could obviate the need for extensive harmonization. Indeed, the Commission announced, it would henceforth focus its harmonization efforts on IAMs, particularly those "barriers to trade...which are admissible under the criteria set by the Court." Almost immediately, the large producer groups and associations of European business proclaimed their support of the initiative, and the new strategy— mutual recognition, minimal harmonization—came to be dominant in the discourse on how best to achieve market integration.

Concurrently, the Commission began to use article 226 more aggressively for the first time, in order to increase the pressure on governments. Markus Gehring and Stone Sweet have collected the data on infringement proceedings brought, withdrawn and decided by the Court. Prior to *Cassis*, the Court produced only two article 226 rulings on article 28. From the date that *Cassis de Dijon* was rendered to the date the Single Act was signed, the Commission filed forty-six cases on article 28 leading to final judgments by the Court. Member States lost 85 percent of these cases. During this same period, the Commission formally filed thirty-six more article 28 suits against Member States that were subsequently withdrawn by defendant Member States that decided to settle before going to court. In the crucial 1980–84 period, free movement of goods cases comprised more than one-in-three of all article 226 rulings; and nearly 30 percent of all rulings concerned MEEs under article 28.

The literature on the sources of the Single European Act, of which mutual recognition was an important part, has sufficiently demonstrated the extent to which the EU's supranational organizations and transnational business were ahead of governments in the process of "relaunching" Europe (Alter and Meunier-Aitsahalia 1994; Dehousse 1994; Fligstein and Mara

Drita, 1996; Sandholtz and Zysman 1989; Stone Sweet and Caporaso 1998; Weiler 1991; but see Moravscik 1991, 1995). Governments acted, of course, in the form of a Treaty that codified integrative solutions to their own collective action problems, including the renunciation of the Luxembourg compromise. But these solutions had emerged from the activities of the EU's organizations and transnational actors, against the backdrop of pent-up demand for more, not less, supranational governance. Of course, the process was not only to do with transnational activity, law, courts, and trusteeship. It was propelled forward by a growing sense of crisis (brought on by globalization), the failure of go-it-alone policies to sustain economic growth, and an accumulation of legal precedents that empowered traders and the Commission in legal disputes with national administrations.

In his most recent account of the SEA, Moravcsik (1998, ch. 2) denies all of this, declaring that the EU's organizations "generally failed to influence the distribution of gains" that could have had an effect on the preferences of governments to negotiate. With respect to the impact of the Court and the legal system, what evidence does Moravcsik (1998, especially 353–55) marshal to support this view? In my view, none. First, he does not discuss the sources and consequences of litigating article 28 and related provisions, and thus, is not in the position to address if or how adjudication "influence[d] the distribution of gains." During the crucial 1979–84 period, levels of article 226 and article 234 litigation under article 28 rose sharply, rulings of non-compliance proliferated, and national regulatory frameworks were placed in a creeping "shadow of the law." Second, Moravcsik (based on the error made by Alter and Meunier-Aitshalia 1994)[12] wrongly claims that *Cassis* was actually a "retreat from previous ECJ jurisprudence," but he does not defend the view. In fact, *Cassis* extends *Dassonville* to IAMs, a deeply controversial area that governments had not contemplated being covered by the treaty until the Commission's 1970 directive. Third, he argues that mutual recognition "was not a new innovation," but had been floated as early as the late-1960s. Yet, if by Moravcsik's own admission, the governments knew of this proposal, they did not adopt it. Instead, they pursued an intergovernmental politics that continued to fail miserably. In the end, they adapted to *Cassis*, for obvious, "rational" reasons, including the fact that the Court had constructed article 28 in ways that redistributed resources toward those actors pushing for more supranationalism.

Last, Moravcsik argues that (a) governments fulfilled their own "demand" for mutual recognition and majority voting, and (b) "*Cassis*, at most, accelerated the single market program," but "was not a necessary condition." Since he nowhere specifies the conditions necessary for the SEA, it is not obvious how one might assess or respond to this claim. The Member States' "demand" for mutual recognition and harmonized market regulations was heavily conditioned by outcomes produced by the legal system, and Moravcsik fails to show otherwise. The Court's steady and expansively integrationist interpretation of article 28 undermined national regulatory sovereignty, enhanced the role of transnational actors and national judges to participate in market integration, and empowered the Commission, in both legislative and judicial processes. Clearly, the "distribution of gains," however conceived, had been altered, raising the cost of intergovernmental inaction considerably.

A broader point deserves emphasis. To take imperfect commitment and delegation in the EU seriously requires us to abandon an exclusive focus on governments, and to examine the dynamics of agency and trusteeship. In this story, the Member States did *not* design the EU's trading institutions, nor did they design the mode of governance that best served to enforce them. The Court did. When *Cassis* was rendered, the Legal Service of the Council of Ministers actually produced a finding that rejected the ruling's main principles, asserting the viability of the Commission's (pre-*Dassonville*, Directive 70/50) discrimination test![13] A simple counterfactual might provide the best test: In a world without direct effect and supremacy, in a world in which the Member States actually controlled the evolution of the EU's trading institutions, how far would market integration have gone after the Luxembourg compromise?

Mutation of the Dassonville Framework

The *Dassonville* framework remained remarkably stable until 1993, when, in *Keck* (ECJ 167/1991) the Court removed national regulation of certain "selling arrangements" from the corpus of IAMs covered by article 28 (see also Weiler 1998). I view this decision as an adjustment dictated largely by the evolution of adjudication in the domain, that is, more to do with factors that are endogenous to the legal system's own activities rather than with exogenous factors. The aggressively interventionist approach taken by the Court in *Cassis* had led to three sets of interrelated problems. First, as noted above, in the 1980s market actors who were *not* primarily involved in intra-EC trade began to use article 28 to attack national regulations they did not like. This led to a great deal of doctrinal soul-searching about the absence of limits to the reach of *Cassis*, worries that we can assume were shared by the Court (Advocate General Van Gerven in *Torfaen* [145/1988], Mortelmans

1991, Rawlings 1993, Steiner 1992). In the end, the Court adopted the solution proposed in a beautifully argued article (White 1989) produced by a lawyer in the legal affairs department of the Commission. In *Keck*, the Court announced, the legal system would continue to monitor and enforce article 28 rules against one class of IAMs—mandatory requirements related to the characteristics of products—but would greatly reduce or abandon altogether the review of restrictions placed on the circumstances (i.e., the time, place and manner) of selling goods. In essence, *Keck* tells a large class of potential litigants—merchants not directly engaged in importing or exporting goods—that "enough is enough." Second, the Court was responding to signals from their most important interlocutors: the national courts. Many national judges had all but refused to subject IAMs to least-means proportionality testing. I examined, for the *Cassis* through *Keck* period, every national decision on IAMs reported by courts in three EC Member States (France, Netherlands and the UK). Most judges, at least implicitly, used a discrimination test, not the "actual or potential, direct or indirect" hindrance to trade test announced by *Dassonville*. In all three countries, national judges were often unwilling to enforce article 28 rules against the state when the litigant was not directly involved in moving goods across borders (see also Jarvis 1998). Third, the marginal returns to market integration of an aggressive approach to IAMs had, by the time Keck was decided, fallen virtually to zero (see also Shapiro 1999a, Weiler 1998). In my view, the approach was a victim of the Court's more general successes. After the Single Act, the legislative process opened up (data reported in Fligstein and Stone Sweet 2002) and harmonization proceeded steadily, thereby withdrawing, prospectively, whole classes of cases from the Court's docket. The Court's role in market regulation has become less high-profile since, and necessarily so (as predicted by Weiler 1991).

Summary

The Court of Justice provides a dramatic case of judicialization; as Shapiro (1992a, 123) puts it, "in a very real and concrete sense, the Court of Justice constituted the European Community." It did so, in part, through drawing other actors and organizations into processes the Court managed and controlled; and it did so, in part, because the Member States had largely failed to make progress on market integration on their own. It seems to me that the members of the Court proved to be far better political economists— with a better and more subtle understanding of the varied purposes of delegation and self-binding, and of the logics of incrementalism—than have the social scientists who have studied integration.

Conclusion

I conclude with a few words about theory-testing. In part I, I surveyed three sets of Martin Shapiro's ideas about judicial power which, in combination, provide the core of a general approach to the evolution of judicial authority in any political system. My project on European integration mixed deductive theorizing, econometric and other quantitative methods, and relatively traditional "process tracing" of the evolution of doctrine. The aim was to test causal theory against relatively comprehensive data. I do not claim that my approach to judicialization, or to the evolution of the European legal system, is the "right" or "best" one. But a start has been made toward a particular end: hypothesis testing. The point leads to another of Shapiro's admonitions that the viability of a social science of courts depends on the development of theories that can be tested, across time and legal systems (Shapiro 1980; Shapiro and Stone Sweet 2002, chap. 4). In his own work, Shapiro has provided masterly examples of two kinds of testing: the "crucial case" method of falsification (see Eckstein 1975), which organizes the presentation in *Courts* (Shapiro 1981a); and the "structured-focused comparison" (see George 1979) of two cases, using time-staging techniques, as in his analysis of the evolution of the "giving reasons" requirement, first in the U.S. and then in the EU (Shapiro 1992b, 2001a). I would guess that Shapiro would not want this part of his agenda—the building and testing of a causal theory of judicial politics—to be obscured by the various conceptual debates about the nature of law and courts with which he is otherwise associated.

Notes

1   In the past decade, political scientists have published more articles on the ECJ than they have on any other court, with the exception of the U.S. Supreme Court. As important, social scientists, who otherwise do not study law and courts, today trace the Court's impact on discrete policymaking episodes.

2   Thus, I pay more attention to theories of integration than to, say, the growing literature on the "Europeanization" of national law and politics, despite the fact that the latter is a hugely important phenomenon (Stone Sweet 2002).

3   The "constitutionalization of the treaty system" refers to the process by which the Treaty of Rome has evolved from a set of legal arrangements binding upon sovereign states, into a vertically integrated legal regime conferring judicially enforceable rights and obligations on all legal persons and entities, public and private, within EC territory. In its decisions, the ECJ implicitly treated its terms of reference as a constitutional text since the early 1960s; by the 1990s, it was openly calling the Treaty a "constitutional charter," and "the constitution of the Community." More formally, "constitutionalization" refers to the (multidimensional) impact of the consolidation of the doctrines of direct effect and supremacy on litigating, judging and lawmaking in the EC. Among other things, the doctrine of direct effect enables private actors to plead rights found in EC law against public authorities in national courts, and the doctrine of supremacy requires national judges to resolve conflicts between EC and national law with reference—and deference—to the former. Two basic dynamics were quickly established (Stone Sweet and Caporaso 1998). First, transnational economic actors litigated to remove national hindrances to their activities; and second, individuals and groups not directly engaged in cross-border exchange—such as those who seek to enhance women's rights—sought to use the EC legal system to destabilize or reform national rules and practices. In many legal domains, including those governing the free movement of goods and of workers, social policy, and environmental protection, the operation of the legal system has pushed the integration project a great deal further than the Member State governments, operating under existing decision rules, would have been prepared to go on their own (see Stone Sweet 2004, chaps. 3–5).

4   See Haas (2001) on Moravcsik.

5   Other things, however, are not equal, since in legislative processes the Court's principal is a complex and hybrid one, including the Commission, the Council of Ministers and the Parliament.

6   A situation in which the judge's task is to govern the principals, and when the agent's rulemaking is effectively insulated from *ex post* controls.

7   For an analysis of parallel information on infringement proceedings (article 226 activity), see Stone Sweet (2004, chap. 2).

8   Hypotheses are derived and tested more formally in Stone Sweet and Brunell (1998a), Stone Sweet and Caporaso (1998), and Fligstein and Stone Sweet (2002).

9   Reasonableness as a criterion for legality is common in European administrative and constitutional law. The rule normally implies proportionality: a law or administrative act is unreasonable if it produces effects that are out of proportion to its purpose.

10 In *Cassis*, the Court generated four possible derogations (for "mandatory requirements" related to fiscal supervision, the protection of public health, the fairness of commercial

transactions, and the defense of the consumer), which were later supplemented by two other headings: the improvement of working conditions (ECJ 155/80, 1981), and the protection of the environment (especially ECJ 302/86, 1988). Although the Court treats the source of these derogation to be article 28, each is, nonetheless, subject to exactly same judicial standards of scrutiny as are justifications claimed by the Member States under article 30 (see Oliver 1996, 181).

[11] See Stone Sweet and Brunell (2000) for a discussion of how expected proportions are calculated.

[12] Alter and Meunier-Aitshalia (1994) emphatically claim that, beyond its *dicta* on mutual recognition, the Court's ruling does not innovate on the basic *Dassonville* framework. The error is critical, and it undermines their analysis of the ruling's impact.

[13] Which some, and perhaps all, governments opposed at that time.

5.

Deconstructing Government?

Carol Harlow

Government and Governance

In a recent paper deploring a slippage in the vocabulary of public administration from "government" to "governance," Martin Shapiro (2001b) wrote:

> Administrative law as it has historically been understood presupposes that there is something called administration. The administrator and/or the administrative agency or organization exist as a bounded reality. Administrative law prescribes behavior within administrative organizations; more importantly, it delineates the relationships between those inside an administration and those outside it. Outside an administration lie both the statutemaker whose laws and regulations administrators owe a legal duty to faithfully implement and the citizens to whom administrators owe legally correct procedural and substantive action.
>
> More generally, the political and organization theory that inform our administrative law have traditionally viewed public administration as a set of bounded organizations within which decisions are made collectively. On this view, these "organs of public administration" are coordinated with one another, subordinated to political authority, and obligated to respect the outside individuals and interests whom they regulate and serve.
>
> In today's public administration and political science literature, however, the word "governance" has largely replaced the word "government." This change in vocabulary announces a significant erosion of the boundaries separating what lies inside a government and its administration and what lies outside them. To be sure, governments and their administrative organizations still make collective decisions, but now everyone, or at least potentially everyone, is also seen as a participant in the collective decision-making process.
>
> Today, elected and nonelected government officers, nongovernmental organizations, political parties, interest groups, policy entrepreneurs, "epistemic communities," and "networks" are all relevant actors in the decision-making processes that produce government action. The decision-making process is no longer seen as one in which private activity occurs around government decision-making, or seeks to influence government decision-making. Rather, the very distinction between governmental and non-governmental has been blurred, since the real decision-making process now continually involves, and combines, public and private actors.

As a succinct description of the pattern of government as it has evolved in democratic western states during the twentieth century, this can hardly be bettered. There is perhaps less emphasis on a constitution and on formal, triadic separation of powers than one might expect from an American constitutional lawyer (compare Lindseth 1999), but it is nonetheless, a classical portrait of limited government, containing a number of shared understandings about the boundaries inside which public administration and its shadow, administrative law, are expected to operate. Implicitly, for example, "government" is seen to function within the framework of a constitution that is at one and the same time constitutive of the institutions of government and of the administrative law system by which the organisms of government are further structured and confined. (Whether the constitutional framework assumed here most closely follows the liberal, liberal-democratic or republican pattern is not important. It is enough to realize that the author assumes a post-Enlightenment constitutional history, according to which "the growing power of the nation state and its expanding capacity to determine and control the life of its subjects created the need for extra protection from the power of government and administration" (Castiglione 1996).

Shapiro does not press the distinction between government and administration nor does the portmanteau term "executive" appear; the emphasis lies on a largely operational "administration." There is no attempt to examine the structural arrangements of government nor to explicate the complex symbiosis between government, administration and other public authorities and agencies. This reflects a gap in classical constitutional theory that will prove to be of some importance in the European context and may be taken by the public administrator as partial justification for the transition from "government" to "governance." Essentially, we have here a reductionist view of the executive function of government, which downplays and understates the policymaking dimension assumed to be essential within the framework of "big government"; a twentieth-century legacy on one side of the Atlantic Ocean of Franklin Delano Roosevelt's New Deal and on the other of the social welfare states which followed the European earthquake of World War II. In Shapiro's picture, administration exists to "implement" laws and policies generated by a "statutemaker"—an unfamiliar substitution for the classical term "legislature" which may or may not intentionally denote realization of the important role played by the executive in modern statute-making. But as with the majority of administrative law texts aimed at lawyers, the emphasis here is on control functions and not on the division of labor within government.

It is well to pause at this point to reflect on the slippery term "governance," an innocent word used originally to denote "the act of governing" (Rhodes 1996).[1] Of the six usages identified by Robert Rhodes as prevalent in the last decade, the reference to "corporate governance" can here be left to one side. Again, there is little quarrel over the phrase "good governance," denoting a set of public service standards and "an efficient, open, accountable and audited public service which has the bureaucratic competence to help design and implement appropriate policies and manage whatever public sector there is" (a description borrowed by Rhodes from Leftwhich 1993). The link with the ideology and terminology of "New Public Management" (Aucoin 1990) is more relevant, in that Rhodes explains the introduction of the term as specifically designed to denote a break with traditional accounts of government, including both the "Westminster" model of cabinet government and the American separation of powers model that form the background to Shapiro's article. These traditional accounts are institutional in character and cover both the activity or process of governing and the people charged with the duties of governing and administration. They are also based on methodological assumptions concerning the study of government, seen as involving the use of legal and historical skills to explain government in terms of rules, procedures and institutions (as exemplified in Oakeshott 1951 and Oakeshott 1962). For Rhodes, the switch to the terminology of governance introduces "a new process of governing; or a changed condition of ordered rule; or the new method by which society is governed" (Rhodes 1997).

In contrast, Rhodes draws on the allegedly more scientific disciplines of systems analysis and managerial public administration to provide a study of what he calls "differentiated polity," focused on "interdependence, a segmented executive, policy networks, governance and hollowing out" (Rhodes 1997). In this conception of "governance without government," the public/private border is deliberately collapsed, governance (or the act of governing) being described as a "socio-cybernetic system" composed of "self-organizing networks." This interpretation which, we shall find, figures conspicuously in debates concerning the governing of the European Union, is emphatically not part of the familiar liberal-democratic world in which decisions and decision-makers are clearly identifiable and fixed; in fashionable terminology, "nested" or "billeted." We have moved instead into an inchoate postmodern world where there is "no longer a single sovereign authority" and in which regulatory mechanisms do not need to be endowed with formal authority to function effectively. The consequence is a "centerless society" or polycentric state characterized by multiple centers, in which the amorphous task of government is described in unaccustomed fashion as being "to enable socio-political interactions; to encourage many and various arrangements for coping with problems and to distribute services among the several actors" (Rhodes 1997). Government, to put this differently, is not to govern but to mediate.

So these accounts of the postmodern transition from government to governance do not merely demolish the public/private boundary. They overturn liberal constitutionalism, exposing its notions of "bounded government" as complacent. They brush to one side traditional ideas of democratic accountability and the values of representative democracy on which it is based. They replace hierarchical and centered structures of government with a de-centered state where, as Walter Kickert bluntly puts it, "Government does not have enough power to exert its will on other actors" (Kickert 1993). The demolition of the traditional control system leaves a vacuum in which policy networks are left largely to control themselves. In Kickert's euphemistic narration, "autonomy not only implies freedom, it also implies self-responsibility" (Kickert 1993). According to Rhodes, the state has been "hollowed out" (Rhodes 1994), its powers not only sloughed off sideways to private actors—Shapiro's main reason for disquiet—but also lost to international actors on a stage where public and private meet on equal terms, where the role of governments, absent a clear mandate at this level to legislate or regulate, becomes uncertain and it is questionable too whether administrators possess sufficient legitimacy to act as "guardian of the public interest" or "to claim a privileged position" in the networks they have established (Rhodes, 1997). This is a world of "gouvernance sans frontières" in which both constitutionalism and national governments are being bypassed.

Governance and the European Union

Government Without Executive

Whether the European Union (EU) is or should become a limited system of "bounded government" or merely a set of structures and networks to which the term "governance" is applicable, has always been contestable (Bankowski and Christodoulidis 1998). An institutional account might at first sight suggest that the EU is becoming, or perhaps aspires to become, a classical system of bounded government, federal or quasi-federal in character and the Draft Constitutional Treaty, which simplifies but in many cases makes significant changes to the present institutional provisions of the European Community (EC) Treaties, in some ways confirms this direction.

Closer acquaintance with the way in which the European Commission actually operates, however, taken together with the Commission's own recent proposals in a White Paper on Governance (European Commission 2001) discussed below, points to a system so "heavily dependent for its operation on co-operative action through policy networks as to epitomize "governance" in the sense in which Rhodes uses the term (Rhodes 1997). Although Simon Hix has talked of it in terms of "cabinet government" based on collective responsibility (Hix 1999), it is hard to accept the European Commission as a "government," even less so one which is "subordinated to political authority." The Commission is in a different position than national governments, since it is not elected, but appointed by the Council of Ministers, the primary EU law- and policy-maker, following approval nowadays by the European Parliament (article 214). Commissioners are charged by article 213 to be "completely independent in the performance of their duties," neither seeking nor taking instructions "from any government or from any other body," this despite the fact that they are nominated by and to this extent represent the individual Member States. The effect is that the Commission is not—and never has been—subordinate or directly responsible to the Council which appoints it. The initial perception of the Commission was of an élite rather than a technocracy, with obligations to the abstract notion of Community and Community interest. A measure of independence was deliberately bestowed on it to counteract the pursuit of national self-interest thought likely to ensue from the governments of the Member States acting in Council (see Moravscik 1993). From a political standpoint, therefore, the Commission stands in a different position to that occupied by a national government, conforming neither to the American or German models of federalism, in which the federal executive is responsible to a directly elected political officer, nor to the Westminster model of cabinet government, in which the political head of the executive is an elected member of the Parliament. As neither the President nor the College of Commissioners is subject to the normal democratic discipline of suffrage, the Commission remains essentially free-floating.

Although its primary function is to regulate and to promote regulation, the Commission does not present policies to a European electorate. It has been described as a "policy entrepreneur" (Laffan 1997), collecting views and recommending policies for action, and then acting as watchdog over the Community interest to see those policies implemented at national level. In this respect, the Commission has been said to operate more like an American agency than as a national administration (Shapiro 1997). Yet, in areas where the EU has competence, the Commission, unlike an agency,[2] possesses its own power of decision, and participates in the shaping of measures taken by the Council and by the European Parliament in the manner provided for in the Treaty (article 211). Again, it resembles an agency in being less directly accountable than most executives. It could not at first be democratically accountable to a parliament, as none yet existed. A directly elected European Parliament first came into being in 1979 and almost immediately set about the process of bringing Commission activity under control, a process in which it has had some success, through clever use of its budgetary powers and use of committees.[3] It has to be remembered, however, that neither the Commission nor Parliament directly control supply, since funds are raised through a levy on Member States negotiated and agreed by their representatives in Council. These peculiarities confirm the view of democracy deficit in the EU: Representative democracy as generally experienced by western nations remains in a nascent state. Article I-25.5 of the Draft Constitution proposes that the Commission would take on a collegiate responsibility to the European Parliament, with the president assuming individual responsibility for the activities of his commissioners. This, if agreed, would represent a move towards a model of political accountability.

Descending from the political to the bureaucratic level, the Commission differs markedly from a national civil service. It has some "bounded physical reality," as its unfriendly nickname of "Brussels" indicates. In contrast to the U.S. federal government, however, it does not duplicate national civil services or operate through local offices situated on the territory of Member States. In this way it more closely resembles the German model of federal government, which normally operates through the administrations of the Länder. Even here we find a crucial difference in the fact that "the federal authorities in Germany have considerable powers to intervene in the local execution of federal legislation, to the point where they can place the administration of the Länder under the control of the federal government" (Diez-Picazo 2002). The Commission powers of implementation are less direct. They involve a lengthy process of negotiation and service of a formal "reasoned opinion" before a defaulting government can be brought before the Court of Justice and, ultimately, fined (article 226). This process can take several years.[4] In the case of a breach of EU law by regional administration, the procedure is less direct still, as the Commission's implementation powers extend only to Member States; action against the defaulting unit is governed by the national constitution, which may render coercion very difficult both for the Commission and for the national government of a Member State.[5]

Network Management

For the most part, however, the Commission is a body which, to paraphrase the famous aphorism of David Osborne and Ted Gaebler (1992), steers but does not do much rowing. The Commission's areas of direct administration are strictly limited, lying mainly in the field of competition law. It possesses no service delivery functions, unless one counts the administration of EU grants and even this function is limited, as payments under programs such as the Common Agricultural Program are actually distributed to individuals by national administrations or agencies. Consequently, it has remained small in size, too small in fact for the tasks unthinkingly loaded on it in recent years by a Council notoriously unwilling to provide further resources (Nugent 2001). The Commission largely operates through national administrations. In the regional policy and structural funding programs, however, where the Commission is responsible for the distribution of large sums of money in development grants to underresourced regions, the Commission has introduced the "partnership principle" (Council Regulation 1988). This not only enables the Commission to work directly with regional and local government rather than through the Member State government, but also with the institutions of civil society, business and voluntary organizations, meeting together at policy round tables. Semi-autonomous agencies less directly subject to the control of Member State governments may also be involved. Finally, under-staffing has meant that the Commission has had perforce to "contract out" to numerous private companies that cluster around it in Brussels; to technical assistance offices established by the Commission or, more particularly in the case of overseas aid programs, to the voluntary sector. These agents have proved notably difficult to control, if only because it is not always clear which legal system governs their operation. These are classical "new public management" techniques, placing the Commission in its preferred role of "facilitator," or "regulator" of a public/private network, its role being to create, foster and maintain relationships. This role, according to Rhodes, who actually uses the structural funding procedures as a case study, typifies "governance" (Rhodes 1994). In such a process, the public/private divide is blurred in just the way to which Shapiro takes exception.

A dazzling searchlight on the way in which the Commission actually operates came in 1999 from a "Committee of Independent Experts" working for the European Parliament (Committee of Independent Experts 1999). This Report, which was to result ultimately in the fall of the Commission headed by President Jacques Santer, provides apt illustrations of the networking characteristics of EU projects. The MED program, for example, was a program of aid to states bordering the Mediterranean and badly affected by the Gulf War. Set in place by the Commission with funding provided by the Council, MED in fact consisted of five linked programs. Each involved regional authorities, local universities, private enterprises based in, and often set up under the laws of, MED countries, research centers, and the media. At the apex stood the Commission, working with the executives of autonomous private bodies registered under the law of three different European countries, responsible for administrative and financial management. At the grass roots level, there were 496 individual and differing projects. The whole was held together by a ramshackle construct of committees, some with Commission participation, others without. The administrative networks over which the Commission presided in MED were typical of other EU projects: long chains of responsibility, operating across national boundaries, moving through different political, legal, administrative and—most important of all—audit systems (Harlow 2002a). This rambling configuration clearly presents problems of linguistic and cultural co-ordination with which national administrations do not usually have to grapple and with which the Commission naturally finds it hard to deal. The Commission is cast in the role of supervisor or "network organizer," a difficult role resembling the task of a regulatory agency, for which the Commission's staff, recruited through competitions designed for national civil servants or co-opted from national civil services, may not be particularly well fitted (Metcalfe 1996).

The steps recommended by the Independent Experts to introduce appropriate systems for management and accountability in the Commission contrast rather sharply with this fluid picture of governance. Far from accepting like Kickert (1993) that participants in a network should be left to control themselves through a process of self-responsibility and equilibrium, the Experts returned to first principles of democratic government, stressing the principle of hierarchy both inside the Commission and in its dealings with external bodies. Hierarchical, bureaucratic controls by the Commission were to be stiffened by enhanced accountability to the EU's representative assembly, the European Parliament. "Governance" was, in short, to be transformed into "Government" by the application of classical principles of responsibility and representative democracy. Subsequently, some steps towards reform have been taken, but unsurprisingly, the total package has never materialized.[6]

Adding Agencies

Just as national systems of government are breaking down and their institutions being transformed, so are experiments with governance by network are undercutting the institutional balance of the EU. At one level, the concept permits the Commission to operate in fields in which the EU has no competence, or only doubtful competence, in which its intervention may be contested. In this context, the gradual accretion to the EU administration of a set of agencies could crucially undermine efforts to install a system of responsible government. In the area of Justice and Home Affairs, indeed, there is some evidence that this is precisely how the Member States intend agencies to be used. Both Europol, an agency designed to promote active co-operation between national police forces and Eurojust, which exists to work on judicial co-operation, have been used to open up areas that, in the early stages, fell outside the competence of the EU. Describing the development of transnational policing, Loader is in no doubt that we are seeing "the transference of governmental functions to barely accountable agencies who are increasingly adopting responsibility for both the 'rowing' and 'steering' of policing systems" (Loader 2000; Walker 2002). Progressive transfer of functions from national governments to supra-statal bodies has marked every stage of the transformation of intergovernmental co-operation on matters of immigration and asylum and latterly, terrorism, through the so-called "Third Pillar" machinery introduced by the Treaty of Amsterdam, into the present "Area of Freedom, Justice and Security" (Title VI) (Harlow 2002a; and see Guild 1998). Like Shapiro, Loader is concerned for accountability and demands "a renewed role for institutions of government...as active regulators whose task it is to ensure that "public interest" considerations pertaining to such matters as equity and democratic liberalism are sustained in the face of multi-organizational, fragmented policing systems" (Loader 2000, 336).

The majority of EU agencies depart from the U.S. paradigm in that their function has so far been to gather information and not to regulate or implement (Shapiro 1997).[7] This limited function has been encouraged both by the Commission's determination, in the name of institutional balance, to keep its hands on the levers of power and by the Court of Justice. In *Meroni*,[8] the Court built the classical administrative law rule of non-delegation into the Treaties, ruling that, for reasons of "institutional balance," the Commission could not delegate anything more than purely operational functions. The decision provides justification for the typical structure of EU agencies, on which the Commission is always represented, as also for their limited, advisory and informative functions. Some agencies, such as the advisory European Environmental Agency (EEA), certainly possess the potential to act as the focal point of a network composed of national and international agencies, trans-national, commercial enterprises and non-governmental organizations as representative of civil society (Ladeur 1997); although the EEA still lacks the regulatory and executive powers of its U.S. counterpart, the Environmental Protection Agency (EPA). Other agencies are beginning to emerge, notably the recently established European Food Safety Authority, empowered to set in place a network of national agencies and possessing some crisis avoidance powers.[9] This is a matter of concern to those who favor a federal outcome for the EU, since it could mean displacing the Commission from its role at the center of EU government with a monopoly power of initiating EU law, in favor of a model of resembling that of Sweden, where agencies, local authorities and other governmental entities, possessing a considerable degree of autonomy from central government, are loosely linked together for purposes of accountability to the national parliament (Ziller 2001). This decentered version of EU administration would presage a move away from both the "institutional balance," which the Court of Justice sees as incorporated into the Treaties, and the classical "Community method" of operating, which envisages a shared responsibility of the main EU institutions (for these purposes mainly Council, Commission and European Parliament).

Rulemaking by Comitology

A similar analysis can be applied to the "comitology" a network of "management" or "regulatory" committees, with a membership of experts and national civil servants, set in place by the Council as a means of inserting an intergovernmental perspective into, hence Council control over, the procedure for making "implementing regulations."[10] For Shapiro, whose view is hostile, the comitology blurs the public/private border in rulemaking, replacing it by the negotiatory or "reg-neg" model of rulemaking so popular with administrators, proponents of participatory democracy and devotees of regulatory and governance models of administrative law (Shapiro 2001a; see also Ziamou 2001). Shapiro quite simply condemns the comitology as a secretive, unrepresentative and undemocratic vehicle for special pleading by interest groups in the making of rules (Shapiro 2001a). Leaving aside the issue of secrecy, perhaps improved by recent reforms, the other main criticisms of comitology remain valid. The comitology is unrepresentative, with a largely official composition only occasionally leavened by selected representatives of civil society—a useful limitation some may think on rulemaking by interest groups. It is also in a double sense undemocratic. First, comitology procedure has the effect of cutting the European Parliament (EP) out of the lawmaking process; indeed, the EP sees the comitology as lending to Commission implementing measures the full authority of the Council, while concealing the fact that the Council has often never been consulted (Bradley 1999). Second, from a national perspective, the procedure has the effect of transferring rulemaking power to national bureaucrats freed from the constraints of national control systems.

While it is possible to explain the comitology as participatory in terms of a "transformed" administrative law—further discussed in a later section of the paper—it has to be said that it sits more comfortably with the paternalist structures of corporatist government that characterized many of the early EU institutions: the Economic and Social Committee and "social partnership" of management and labor for example. Harm Schepel, like Shapiro, blames globalization for installing scientific expertise and experts at the center of denationalized decision making processes, with the effect that traditional lawmakers are rendered impotent. Schepel demands "public institutionalization and designs for legal process which would ensure accountability" (Schepel 1998), but so far, reform proposals have usually taken the form of an American-style Administrative Procedures Act (Dehousse 1999; Joerges and Dehousse 2001), opening them to criticism of lawmaking by interest groups; at the same time, cumbersome, formal, legal protections inevitably give rise to demands from infuriated administrators for the introduction of informal, streamlined, "reg-neg" procedures such as those described in the next paragraph. The Convention has been persuaded to take a more radical approach to comitology: The procedure would be replaced by a more classical form of delegated legislation, allowing the Commission the open-ended power to enact "delegated regulations to supplement or amend certain non-essential elements" of law or framework law, which would be enacted jointly by the Council and EP. The only limitations imposed are that, where this is specifically provided for in the legislation, the Council or EP may revoke the delegation or prevent the regulations entering into force.[11] These provisions lend a positively benign aspect to the contested comitology!

Soft Law, Soft Governance

The "soft" techniques of "governance" are highly advantageous to interest groups in areas where, unable to gain political support for their policies, their position in international policy networks allows them to push for the circumvention of a stalled political process. Environmental activists or Greens—who, be it noted, although they have held governmental office, have never come to power in any EU Member State—find this technique particularly useful in lending legitimacy to their infiltration of the policymaking process. To exemplify, the 1993 Commission White Paper "Towards Sustainability"[12] introduced the concept of "shared responsibility," said to require "a much more broadly based and active involvement of all actors, including government, enterprise and the public." Under the Aarhus Convention (1996), a "soft law" document to which Member States subscribed (see Lee and Abbot 2003), states acquired rights to participate in cross-border environmental policymaking on the condition that, if they decided to do so, information had to be passed to the "public concerned in the territory of the Member State likely to be significantly affected." By 2001, this had been fleshed out into a cross-border right for the public to express their opinions, with a corresponding obligation for the way in which and extent to which these opinions have been considered to be expressed by the decision makers in a reasoned decision.[13] The Commission is now expressing concern that "the public" may not be able adequately to avail themselves of this new opportunity, creating space for the publication of policy papers on legal aid,[14] enabling a further foray on to the terrain of national governments.

    More generally, the Commission wishes to develop the "open method of coordination," modeled on experiments carried out in the context of employment rights and European Monetary Union (Hodson and Maher 2001). According to the Commission in its White Paper on European Governance (European Commission 2001), the Open Method of Coordination (OMC) "is a way of encouraging co-operation, the exchange of best practice, and agreeing common targets and guidelines for Member States....It relies on regular monitoring of progress to meet those targets, allowing Member States to compare their efforts and learn from the experience of others." In certain areas, an action plan may be arrived at: The European Employment Strategy, for example, consists of a list of guidelines which set benchmarks towards which Member States are supposed to work. The extent of Union action consists of "report back" mechanisms including "peer review," the only "sanction" being recommendations for improvement issued by the Commission and Council. Whether this softest of soft law as yet amounts to a system of "governance" is perhaps questionable; clearly, however, it may have the effect of diffusing responsibility for policy and blurring accountability lines. It divests the Commission of its supervisory functions and responsibilities as network regulator, leaving it with its preferred "soft" function of policy entrepreneur. As Oliver Gerstenberg forcefully observes of OMC

> It unfolds in a space devoid of formal legal constraints apart from the Treaty provisions themselves. There is no attempt legally to control the outcome, and it is difficult to conceive how the OMC process could conceivably be monitored (and its democratic legitimacy reinforced) through law... The OMC is expressis verbis designed as a non-law-based approach, precisely in order to allow governments to collaborate closely even in areas where it would be impossible to move forward through a common legal framework. (Gerstenberg 2002)

Similar fears were expressed by Convention working groups, several of which proposed that OMC should be anchored firmly inside the framework of a Constitution.

Government and Administrative Law

While constitutional law "strives to billet mighty decision makers in conspicuous sites where they can be carefully monitored" (Holmes 1995, 6), administrative law "structures and confines" administrative action and discretion. The negative constitutionalism that marks Shapiro's paper provides the context for a largely negative and (see Davis 1976). It is depicted by Shapiro as largely mechanistic administrative law, its functions being internal to regulate relationships between administrative entities and external to govern relationships with citizens, to whom is owed a formalist obligation of "legally correct procedural and substantive action." The mention of citizens serves to draw a crucial "them-and-us" bright line between the public servants and the civil society they serve, but also presupposes the existence of a state or nation in the framework of which administrative law functions. This bright line is a matter of importance to Shapiro, whose main purpose in the passage cited is to deplore the erosion of the public/private boundary, an attrition which, he suggests (Shapiro 2001b, 372),[15] facilitates an "amorphous method of policy-making," reflected in the governance concept. This view has its challengers.

It must always be borne in mind that until the time of the Treaty of European Union signed at Maastricht in 1992, the EU possessed neither citizens nor any concept of citizenship; even the Draft Constitution accepts a national basis for citizenship. In fact the "citizens" to whom the EU administration owed duties of "legally correct procedural and substantive action" largely were—and remain—multi-national corporations, for whose convenience, it may be thought, the concept of "governance" has been introduced. One consequence of the public/private bright-line is, however, that individual and corporate interests are, for the purposes of administrative law, largely conflated, an important element in the call for a "reformation" of administrative law to make space in the decision making process for under-represented citizens and the civil society organizations which purport to represent them.

But the classical or "rule of law" model of judicial review is generally agreed to be about control: The executive, the subject of review, is subjected on the one hand to control by the legislature, on the other to the law courts, which see themselves in the guise of protectors of citizens' rights or private interests. It is courts that in liberal democracies police and often designate the boundaries of administrative action and take upon themselves the duty to enforce standards of administrative behavior, frequently defining what those standards shall be. Codes of administrative conduct are, at least in the first instance, usually judge-made and in this respect the EU is no exception (Schwarze 1993). Without stepping too far or too often outside the accepted boundaries of adjudication, courts can wage a war of attrition against audacious agencies and administrators with whose social judgments and decisions they disagree. They tend to move steadily—though a pattern of ebb and flow is evident—from "light touch" to "hard look" review. Shapiro describes a process of "synoptic dialogue," which commits agencies to

> respond adequately not only to all issues actually raised by interested parties, but also to all issues. In short, the demand is that the agency do a perfect job of decision-making with the strong implication that the agency must arrive at the perfect, or at least the best, decision. (Shapiro 1992c)

At its best, this process can be seen as strengthening deliberative decision making, though it has not yet succeeded in emerging as a form of participatory democracy, as we shall see later. At its worst, courts have been able to impose time-consuming and often wasteful procedures on administrators, virtually bringing agency action to a halt. This is a criticism often made of the American Administrative Procedures Act.

Although courts have usually assumed responsibility for defining their own jurisdiction,[16] their scope in this respect is not unlimited; within a framework of bounded government, courts have typically set limits to their own competence. The bright-lines, dictated by classical separation of powers doctrines, traditionally fall on the border between, on the one side, principle and procedure, accepted by positivists as the proper field of judicial activity; and on the other, policy, substance and merits, all three of which lie within governmental terrain. Thus, in classical administrative law systems courts, see substitution of their own decision for that of politicians and administrators as unwarrantable trespass on executive and administrative terrain. This does not mean that we can assume that judicial intervention will necessarily be negative or restrictive in character. Not every administrative judge necessarily subscribes to classical theories of judicial review, and amongst the administrative law systems of the Member States are to be found important administrative law systems markedly more administration-friendly than Shapiro's classical, republican model (see Debbasch 1976; and Bell 1998). And the European Court of Justice (ECJ) has arguably far exceeded its remit in article 220 "to ensure that in the interpretation and application of this Treaty the law is observed," developing a permissive, pro-Commission ethos commensurate either with a facilitative view of administrative law or with the Court's consciousness of the Commission's position as regulator (below). In so doing, it has justly been charged with an integrationist stance.[17]

In constructing an administrative law system for the EU, the ECJ had slight foundations on which to build. The Treaties endow it with jurisdiction to "review the legality of acts...on grounds of lack of competence, infringement of an essential procedural requirement, infringement of this Treaty or of any rule of law relating to its application, or misuse of powers" (article 230). A provision, later to become central to the judicial enterprise, instructed the Court when awarding compensation against the EC institutions (article 235), to employ "the general principles common to the laws of the Member States" (article 288). To Anglo-American observers, the remedies at its disposal were limited; in review proceedings, the ECJ at first possessed only the power to declare acts void (article 231); subsequently, and following on a judicial revolution, which introduced the doctrine of Member State liability in damages,[18] a further paragraph allowing for fines was added to article 228 by the Maastricht Treaty.

The way in which these laconic provisions were used to construct an administrative law for the European institutions is in some ways surprising, in others predictable. They seemed on their face to authorize construction by the judiciary of an administrative law directed at the Community institutions and more particularly the Commission, charged with the function of implementation. This would in time combine with national systems of administrative law, which would retain control over the EU administrative process when conducted by national entities. What was not predictable was the extent to which these separable systems would become entangled and entwined.[19]

As predicted contemporaneously by Shapiro (1992, 180), the ECJ progressed rapidly down the path of procedural review, using as its pattern-book the procedural law of the Member States, while at the same time exploiting to its full potential article 253 (ex-article 190), which obliges the institutions to "state the reasons on which [their decisions] are based." This requirement Shapiro sees as the basis of all judicial review. The control function of judicial review is articulated clearly in a passage which constantly recurs in the Court's jurisprudence[20] to the effect that

> In imposing upon the Commission the obligation to state reasons for its decisions, Article 190 is not taking mere formal considerations into account but seeks to give an opportunity to the parties of defending their rights, to the Court of exercising its supervisory functions and to Member-states and to all interested nationals of ascertaining the circumstances in which the Commission has applied the Treaty.

This standard formula justifying reasoned decisions has been used to extend an embryonic principle of access to documents towards a wider constitutional doctrine of transparency. In this progression, the advent of the Court of First Instance (CFI) has been significant: It is the CFI which has tightened the ratchet, subjecting the EU institutions in recent cases concerning access to information held by official bodies to the balancing test of proportionality.[21] Like American courts in the heyday of hard look review, the CFI is prepared carefully to check the Commission's fact-finding process and show "enhanced responsiveness" to the factual points and evidence put forward by the parties to the litigation. According to Hanns-Peter Nehl, its stance is more intrusive than that of the ECJ, and it has shown an inclination to develop new "process standards," such as an incipient duty of good administration or vestigial duty of care in administering a file (Nehl 1998; see also Lenaerts and Vanhamme 1997).

The ECJ has also promulgated a number of "general principles" which go beyond the procedural, of which the celebrated proportionality principle is probably the most significant.[22] Procedural in its origins, the proportionality principle allows the judge to examine the evidence and weigh the "means against the ends," making possible an unusually intensive degree of judicial review (Tridimas 1999, 66; see also de Burca 1993). Taking citizens' rights as its starting-point, the proportionality principle admits only such administrative measures as are necessary, appropriate for the proper achievement of government goals and objectives, and in themselves reasonable—all highly subjective tests (Sullivan 1992). Like rights of property, capable of weighting the balance heavily towards existing interests, proportionality can easily become a recipe for static administration. Once general principles achieve constitutional status, the principle transcends procedure, allowing goals and objectives to be subjected to a test of proportionality that weighs them against protected constitutional values or human rights charters. Perhaps still more significantly, the nostrum can be extended to the legislator.[23] Much of the same is true of the parallel principle of "legitimate expectation," according to which a rule or policy may be annulled if those subject to the policy have acted with the expectation that it will not for the foreseeable future be changed. The ECJ subscribes less frequently to this doctrine, highly restrictive of political action and capable when used aggressively of holding regulators and administration to outdated policies, better revised (Kadelbach 2002, 182). These developments are suggestive that judge-made administrative law has settled into a strong version of the classical or rule of law mould.

It can, however, be argued that once judicial review has reached this degree of penetration the classical model has been transformed or perhaps even been superseded. The scope and ambit of judicial input into rulemaking and policymaking procedures within the administration has changed in character, limiting the policymaker's scope for action too severely. The rigidity induced by too strict a judicial supervision is a prime reason why administrators turn to informal rulemaking techniques, and "soft law" replaces hard law as an element in "governance." As indicated when discussing OMC, soft law is often used by the Commission as a "tin-opener," to open up areas of policy-making blocked by the Member States in Council (Snyder 1994) or where the EU has no or only limited competence. Again, in the context of structural funding, discussed briefly above, a spokesman for one German Land has described the progression from "soft" policies and memoranda through "hardened" guidance to hard law in the shape of directives: "First there are 'proposals;' and the next time the proposals are seen they are evaluation 'guidelines'; guidelines which the Commission is going to apply ex cathedra throughout the Member States and which it uses skillfully to circumvent the regulation texts" (Bauer 2002). Thus, soft law is very much a technology of governance, the use of which may in several ways rebound on the system of government. It needs to be constrained by a judiciary confident in its mandate to fill the gap left at Union level by the absence of a controlling legislature (the so-called "democratic deficit"). This, the Court of Justice, integrationist by instinct, has not always done.[24]

Where courts have obtained—or more usually invested themselves with—powers to review and invalidate legislation, representative democracy is curtailed; the judicial tendency to "confine and structure" the policy-making and rule-making powers of representative democratic institutions has indeed been termed by Daniel Wincott a "perversion of democracy" (Wincott 1984). This is the process started by the seminal case of *van Gend en Loos*[25] where, in Shapiro's telling metaphor (Shapiro 1999a), "the cat was let loose" on the Member States and, at the point when the Court of Justice imposed liability in damages on Member States in some cases where national law was out of line with EU law,[26] the cat had grown into a leopard. The system of EU law now constrains Member State legislatures, often reducing them to the point of a principal/agent relationship and in some Member States, notably the United Kingdom, a power of constitutional review of legislation had been handed to judges who had not previously possessed it.[27] In short, the Court of Justice has facilitated a transfer of power from governments accountable to national parliaments to transnational institutions, including national governments, which are notably less accountable, whether to courts or democratic bodies. We are seeing a "hollowing out" of the national legislative power through a horizontal transfer of power to the executive, coupled with a vertical transfer to a transnational judiciary. To revert to metaphor, it is time for the cat to sharpen its claws on the EU institutions, more especially the Council and Commission. The vehicle might have been the concept of "subsidiarity" first introduced by the Treaty of Maastricht, according to which "the Union shall act only if and insofar as the objectives of the intended action cannot be sufficiently achieved by the Member States."

The steady leaching of power upward is perhaps the most powerful argument for an EU Constitution to provide a framework in which judicial review would be more firmly anchored and perhaps more impartial,[28] but although the Draft Constitution contains frequent references to subsidiarity, the proviso that the Union is able to act where centralized action is likely to be more effective "by reason of the scale or effects of the proposed action" is a let-out of a type all too familiar in the history of federalism. In the case of the EU, this easy escape route is shored up by the principle of "loyal cooperation" built into the Treaties and strenuously enforced by the ECJ (see Harlow 2002a). Thus, the steady drift to centralization we have been experiencing is unlikely to be stemmed. Moreover, despite prolonged debate during the course of the Convention, and a general feeling that national parliaments should possess a general competence in the matter, no specific provisions have been included as to who shall police questions of subsidiarity. No doubt the Convention hopes that the Court will settle the thorny issue for them with a new van Gend en Loos.

Administrative Law and Participatory Democracy: An Unlikely Partnership?

Shapiro argues that the "reformation" of American administrative law famously advocated by Richard Stewart and others and designed to make policy-making process more permeable, to provide a platform for groups disadvantaged in the political process, and to open decision making to a wider group of participants (Stewart 1975), in fact, contributed substantially to blurring the public/private boundary, to the point that "everyone involved in the decision-making can fairly be viewed as a partner" (Shapiro 2001b, 372). Once the insider/outsider definition has lost its meaning, the agency or administration "almost ceases to be the decision-maker" and takes on the role of mediator or facilitator. Thus, Richard Stewart's "reformation" of administrative law is at least a contributory factor in the "transformation" of the surrounding governmental system. Although I have some sympathy with this argument, it is, I think, too large a claim. The reformation of administrative law undoubtedly operated to change its focus quite dramatically. The judicial process became more fluid, internal boundaries were broken down, standing was—at least temporarily—widened[29] and intervention rights granted to third parties. A hybrid style of judicial review procedure was produced, which mimics, while affording a pale shadow of, political debate and discussion (Harlow 2002b). In a few cases, though only in the United States, judicial remedies changed their nature to take in the so-called "structural injunction." But though these shifts may breach the classical, separation of powers framework of the model of government, it is not accurate to talk of slippage from government to governance in the sense that Shapiro objects to, since the judicial decision maker remains a responsible public official.

The primary thrust of the movement for reformation of administrative law was in any event directed towards control of what came to be portrayed by public choice theorists as a self-interested government/legislative alliance, affording privileged access to both the political and legal process to particular groups which dominated them (Buchanan et al. 1998). It should be made that this alliance was not composed only of public actors, but was, in fact, highly permeable to influence by corporate interests. This was the situation of privilege in which under-privileged groups and interests sought the help of courts to make their voices heard: very much the contention of the modern "governance" movement. The intention was not to destabilize the institutions of representative democracy, but to open them up and provide lawmakers and policymakers with information about public opinion on which acceptable decisions could be based. Deliberative and participatory democracy came together and, as they often do, covered the same ground. In terms of administrative law, the movement asked for group access to policymaking and rulemaking processes, with a view to substituting prospective for retrospective control of government through judicial review of administrative action in individual cases. Shapiro is right also to note the focus on transparency, an essential tool of participatory and deliberative democracy.

The participatory model of administrative law did nevertheless contain the seeds of a largely unanticipated threat to representative democracy. This was to materialize in several ways. When administrative law began to dominate rulemaking procedure, it encouraged the growth of soft law and "reg-neg" as effective alternatives to formal rulemaking procedures, in time creating a threat to democratic lawmaking through a partial substitution of participatory for representative democracy. And once their claims could be based on a fully fledged human rights mandate, emerging at global level during the 1980s, courts became bolder, promoting a constitutional right of access to judicial process. Taken together with the encouragement given to courts to set themselves up as "an alternative political forum," accessible to social action and public interest groups as a platform for the articulation of alternative policy options, the scene was set for a serious erosion of the traditional barrier between law and politics. But even if administrative law connived at slippage from representative to participatory democracy, this is not the same thing as slippage from government to governance.

It is in any case fair to say that the ECJ has not shown itself particularly favorable to the model of participatory democracy. Nor has it yet identified the "governance" phenomenon as presenting any special challenge to the rule of law. True, one could read the shift in European administrative law from a right of access to personal files and information, resembling the right to reasons and justified on similar grounds, towards a general democratic right of access to information as signifying a shift towards the participatory model. On the other hand, the ECJ has clung to its non-delegation rule. In *Rothmans*,[30] two strands came together when the CFI, faced with a request for access to documents, ruled against the autonomous identity of a comitology committee, holding the Commission, which services its meetings, responsible for purposes of access to committee documentation. In the later case of *Alphapharm*,[31] the Council was declared responsible for a legislative act based allegedly on insufficient consultation with scientific advisers by the Commission. These cases point to a judicial tendency to place accountability squarely on public actors and require from them reasoned decisions, proof against moderately hard-look review.

Again, the Courts' standing provisions are relatively restricted in comparison to many national jurisdictions, which have tended to move in the direction advocated by Stewart (above). The basic provisions are not particularly protective of individual interests, as article 230 has a double requirement of "direct and individual concern" in respect of individuals. The ECJ has clung tenaciously to this rule[32] and both courts have resisted the blandishments of public interest groups to permit public interest actions. The leading case is *Stichting Greenpeace*.[33] The Spanish Government sought to use EU funding allocated by the Commission to erect power stations in the Canary Islands, a development hotly contested by the local population. Greenpeace International funded litigation in the CFI, appearing in its own name with individuals affected. Both were met by the classic argument against that environmental interests are "common and shared," hence, standing must be denied as nobody was "individually" affected. The negative decision makes it virtually impossible for any representative action to be mounted under the courts' existing interpretation of the rules. Taken with *Unión* and *Jégo Quéré*, the consequence for individuals and campaigning groups, which may find it hard to participate and express their views in the early stages of decision making, is that they cannot easily challenge decisions taken jointly by national and EU authorities.[34] A gap has opened up that protects decisions made under jointly administered programs—a serious deficiency of "billeted" government that attracts cries for greater flexibility. But opinion remains sharply divided as to whether the EC Justice should open up the standing rules as the CFI would prefer, or whether the present limited rules of access should be maintained.[35]

In the *UEAPME* case[36] the CFI was asked to protect rights of participation in rulemaking procedures. A classic "reg-neg" procedure was involved, in which representatives of the "social partners" are allowed to negotiate the rules and standards under which they will operate, and it falls to the Commission to promote "consultation of management and labor at Community level." A double consultation was required: first, before the Commission submitted any regulatory proposals, second if the Commission, after consultation, considered regulation desirable. The outcome of the second "dialogue," if not left to contract or informal action, could be implemented at national level or formalized into a Council decision on a proposal by the Commission. The Commission established a list of potential consultees on which UEAPME figured as representing the views of small business concerns. It was consulted and responded by a letter in the first, but not the second, round of consultations.

The reasoning, claimed as an instance of "serious engagement" by the CFI with the concept of "new governance" (Scott and Trubek 2002), it merits a closer look. The Council argued that UEAPME had no locus standi: It had never participated in negotiation and, in any case, the Commission "is not in charge of the negotiatory stage of the second procedure and the document which emerges is an agreement between private parties." In this way, the negotiated rulemaking process circumvented public law controls. How, then, did the CFI react? Admittedly, it listened to the argument that, without UEAPME participation, the representation was unbalanced—a classic interest-representation argument consonant with pluralist democratic theory—but ultimately the plea fell on deaf ears. The Court said that it was "proper to stress the obligation incumbent on the Commission and the Council to verify the representativity [of the consultees]."[37] This could be read as a move to engage with the participatory governance processes since the CFI went on to say that "the participation of the two institutions in question has the effect...of endowing an agreement between management and labor with a Community foundation of a legislative character, without recourse to the classic procedures..." (Scott and Trubek 2002). Because these rulemaking procedures excluded the EP, the need arose for "the participation of the people [to] be otherwise assured."[38] So the judgment is ambiguous, recognizing participatory rights but firmly based on classical principles of representative democracy with a possible leaning towards corporatist tradition in management/labor relations. Accepting that the mandatory consultation procedures had been followed, the CFI went so far as to scrutinize the list maintained by the Commission and to consider whether the participants in the second round were in fact broadly representative. It was, however, easily satisfied and UEAPME, which had to a limited extent participated at the first stage of the proceedings, was denied standing to sue. To sum up, the CFI used classical administrative law reasoning to interpret a statutory framework for consultation so as to place responsibility for procedural correctness squarely on the public actors, while leaving them substantial discretion as to whom they wished to consult. A weak outcome but one, it has to be admitted, in line with classical control systems of administrative law.

Governance, Regulation and Accountability

At the root of Shapiro's antagonism to the governance concept lies the suspicion that it is anti-democratic. The institutions used for policymaking, the agencies around which networks cluster and networks of public and private actors, are used to legitimate and disguise a substantial transfer of power from institutions of representative democracy to unaccountable bureaucratic elites and interest groups. While on the surface devoted to a deepening of democracy, transparency and public accountability, the methodology of governance in fact dilutes all three. The seemingly widely accessible information can in practice be digested, used and acted on only by the experts, bureaucrats and interest groups who stack the committees, assuming the policymaking powers. Thus, while professing allegiance to participatory democracy, practices and institutions of governance (such as the comitology) shut the people out of government and maximize the influence of experts. Democratic accountability is destroyed, as voters have no idea whom "to blame or reward for results they like or dislike." Indeed, they have largely lost the capacity to hand out the prizes and punishments, as their powers have been irreversibly "delegated" to the experts. All in all, this adds up to "more government and less democracy," encouraging—as if encouragement were needed—"pervasive micro-management" by the bureaucracy (Shapiro 2001b, 374).

To apply the term "good governance" to new developments sited within established systems of government and public administration is not an abuse of language. Inside the framework of the state, solutions to problems of governance are possible and are developing. Regulation, a subset of administrative law nicely poised to straddle the public/private border, was introduced precisely because it was thought capable of devising appropriate systems of accountability to deal with public/private networks (see, e.g., Freeman 1997; Freeman 2000). Some years after regulation had crossed the private border, the concept was modified to introduce the idea of "decentred regulation," (Black 2000) in order to cover the position where regulatory agencies charged with the duty of controlling and overseeing the corporate sector use their semi-autonomy to set in place a network in which the actors come together to harmonize goals and objectives and synchronize the work of national regulatory bodies. While this may at first largely involve public actors, in time interest and campaigning groups start to cluster around the regulator, creating networks which assume a regulatory function. Notice how this account of regulation mirrors the portrayal of the evolution of networks in the process of "new governance."[39]

The first models of regulation, established in a framework of government, were state-centered: The state possessed not only the capacity to command and control, but was assumed to be the only legitimate commander and controller. Once this assumption was supposedly discredited by the "hollowing out" phenomenon, a search for defensive strategies naturally followed. The role of the EU (then Community) was at first equivocal. On one view, the Treaties were a liberalizing force, unbinding international capitalism and unleashing its potential; on the other, the danger to democratic government came primarily from global capitalism and the EU stood as a moderately forceful state-substitute or regulator (Jachtenfuchs 2001; Majone 1994; Majone 1996; see also Everson 1998), affording capacity for the regulation of global capitalist forces. The fact that its regulatory functions were directed at areas of highly specialized technical knowledge inside the boundaries of a common market—as for example, food and products safety, pharmaceuticals or biotechnology—made the EU a prime candidate for elite, corporatist governance in which democracy had arguably no part to play. This was a structure in which administrative law operated largely in the interests of transnational commerce, which soon learned to use its machinery skillfully to stifle regulatory control (Harding 1992; Stone Sweet and Brunell 1998b).

Joanne Scott and David Trubek criticize "traditional conceptions of law" as too hierarchical; by setting in place the false god of sovereignty, these establish the judiciary at the apex of a hierarchical accountability system (Scott and Trubek 2002, 8). They see the machinery of "new governance" as enabling a wider and less hierarchical system of accountability, based on a fragmentation and dispersal of authority and on "fluid systems of power sharing." This analysis—which Shapiro would surely deplore—is guilty of blurring two arguments which ought to be distinguished: On the one hand, the authors apparently ask for a less negative and more facilitative form of administrative law, especially in courts; on the other, they seem willing to accept the outright transfer of law's traditional control functions to governance through participatory democracy in the limited sense of popular participation in decision making. In this reasoning, the terminology of governance can be seen to cover much the same ground and to serve the same purpose as that of decentered regulation. It also embodies the same paradox: In both cases, postmodern terminology is used to blur a crucial distinction between the machinery of control and what is being—or not being—controlled.

Regulatory theory is in any event notably weak on accountability, showing a marked preference for discretion and for negotiated methods of problem solving (Ayres and Braithwaite 1992). In the interdependence model of regulatory accountability developed by Colin Scott (Scott 2000), participants in a network are portrayed as "dependent on each other in their actions because of the dispersal of key resources of authority (formal and informal), information, expertise and capacity to bestow legitimacy such that each of the principal actors has *constantly to account for at least some of its actions* to others within the space, as a precondition for acting" (Scott 2000, 50) (emphasis added). This is no more than a portrait of decentered regulation and tells us little about what will happen when actors in the network join together in concert or act arbitrarily. In Scott's redundancy model, hierarchical responsibility is replaced by the horizontal responsibility of markets, through contract, competition and public procurement law, to the point that "overlapping (and ostensibly superfluous) accountability mechanisms reduce the centrality of any one of them" (Scott 2000, 52). This account does little more than describe a policy network, while replicating the political argument for privatization. Both models need strengthening to incorporate a necessary element of control, supplied in the model of government and administrative law. Unfortunately, there is a dearth of attempts to define the role of administrative law in the global context and efforts so far are largely descriptive. Aman, for example, nicely captures the phenomenon of governance in his description of the new blends of public and private power which are emerging, necessitating a redefinition of the boundaries (Aman 1997, 2002). Like Shapiro, Aman fears diminution in public participation "through the institutions of democracy" and the emergence of bargaining and negotiatory models of decision-making. But is Aman (2002) describing a new administrative law or, as his title hints, merely pleading for a new administrative law in terms of a description of the terrain on which it must operate?

In this unsettled context, the Commission's flirtation with the governance concept must be construed. In addition to experiments with the "open method of co-ordination" and "reg-neg" methods of rulemaking by interested parties, to which Scott's interdependence model of accountability are perhaps applicable, we find in the White Paper on European Governance issued by the Commission a leaning, perhaps unintentional, towards participatory democracy (European Commission 2001; for a critique, see Follesdal 2003; Armstrong 2002). The White Paper promises "wide participation through the policy chain—from conception to implementation" (European Commission 2001, 10). It promises to "reach out to citizens and "involve civil society" (European Commission 2001, 14), construct and consult better networks and, less ambitious, establish procedures and time-tables for consultation. All this sounds positive, like moves in accordance with principles of good administration and the fashionable values of transparent, accountable governance. There is, however, a sting in the tail for campaigning groups that wish to take up the Commission's offer. Reasoning that "with better involvement comes greater responsibility," the White Paper admonishes civil society organizations that, before they can find a place on the list of potential consultees or receive Commission funding, they must bring themselves into line with the Commission's standards of democratic representativity and accountability (European Commission 2001, 15, 17 and 18). Teubner has argued that the inevitable consequence of taking over tasks perceived as public in character is that private actors must swallow the "poisoned pill" of intrusive regulation of their own affairs (Teubner 2000). Here we see this beginning to happen. Under recently introduced Commission procedures,[40] groups are being sorted into "hierarchically ordered and functionally differentiated categories, recognized and licensed (if not created) by the state and granted a deliberate representative monopoly within their respective categories in exchange for observing certain controls on their selection of leaders and articulation of demands and supports" (Schmitter 1979). A form of globalized corporatism is developing and civil society is being co-opted by bureaucracy.

In any event, the Commission's simple faith in participatory democracy as a solution for problems of democratic deficit in the EU is likely to be disappointed. In the first place, it is doubtful that the Commission possesses the administrative resources and expertise to implement its ideas. It seems unaware too of the extent to which it will be operating in a cold climate, where public participation, even through the simple act of voting, is declining as an activity. There is too a little empirical evidence to the effect that interest group representation does not promote trust amongst the general public, but only among the members of participating organisations (Öberg 2002). The Commission's version of participatory democracy is unlikely, therefore, to contribute greatly to institutional legitimacy. The more probable outcome is that bureaucratic hallmarking will have the effect of detaching campaigning groups from the civil society which they purport to represent and tugging them across the private/public border, demoted in the eyes of the public to clients of the bureaucracy on which they have become dependent. Perhaps, then, it is fortunate that opposition from Europe's numerous representative institutions, scenting a threat to orthodox representative democracy, has prompted a retreat from the terrain of participatory democracy back to the more orthodox ground of administrative consultation.[41]

Conclusions: Bottling the Genie?

Behind the switch to the terminology of governance as a panacea for the ills of EU government lies unease over the health of representative democracy: a set of arguments centering on the so-called "democratic deficit." In this condition of deficit, some believe that participatory democracy is capable of legitimating transnational governance. Others believe that gaps in present governmental systems of representative democracy should, in any event, be filled by resort to techniques of participatory and associative democracy in the interests of making society more inclusive (see Gerstenberg 2002). The danger is that the governance ideology will rebound on functioning national systems of government to produce a perversion of representative democracy, which can only hasten the "hollowing out" of the state and its institutions. This outcome may be positively welcomed, not only to proponents of participatory democracy, but also to the transnational bureaucracies and epistemic communities of experts to whom policymaking has been handed over by governments anxious to free themselves from the familiar political controls of national governmental systems. This is the first lesson of the European experiment in transnational government. The second is that when courts, which seem to function more effectively in the supranational stratosphere, move in to fill the gap—as they have been praised for doing in the European Union—they may, as argued earlier, add to the democratic deficit and widen the accountability gap. In the EU context, this process can only be reversed if the Court of Justice can learn to function less as a constitutional and more as an administrative court; metaphorically speaking, to show a greater willingness to "unloose the cat" against the EU and its power-hungry institutions.[42]

A more profound difficulty lies in the fact that the European Union is trying to work with two incompatible models of administration. Arguably, neither the Constitutional Convention nor the EU institutions, by no means all pulling in the same direction, can hope to produce a convincing blueprint for European governance without a decision on the fundamental issue of integration. Is the EU progressing, as the European élite has always hoped, to a centralized federal state or is it, as the present enlargement process suggests, drifting inevitably back to a bottom-weighted confederation of sovereign states? The first outcome dictates a classical governmental structure, incorporating the machinery for control and accountability assumed by Shapiro in the passage that heads this paper. The second points to further experiments with "soft" techniques of governance, such as the OMC, soft law and "reg-neg" mentioned earlier in this Chapter, essential to hold the disparate networks and units of the confederation together in a fluid and plural system. This is the model to which the European Commission in its White Paper on European Governance seemingly aspires, though whether in formulating its various proposals the Commission has paid sufficient respect to presently functioning systems of representative democracy or to the control systems sited inside them, is a very moot point.

There are, however, hints reported in this paper that the choice may not be so stark as the last paragraph suggests. Perhaps the classical model of "bounded government" favored by Shapiro and the "governance" model of organized and monitored "networks" are really symbiotic? Each comes into play as a notional cure for the other's imperfections. If so the traditional institutions of government will in time move in to control the new governance procedures by shaping them into a controlled but relatively static "model of government." It will then fall to the various actors concerned in the business of government to open up new space, again bypassing the restrictive machinery of government via a fluid and dynamic process of governance. What the role of administrative law will be at the various stages is hard to predict. It is the negative or control model of administrative law depicted by Shapiro which sits most comfortably inside the model of government. The EU has, however, experienced law as highly creative and dynamic. Whether this dynamism can effect a transformation of its judge-made administrative law into the less negative and more facilitative system demanded by Scott and Trubek seems rather doubtful.

Notes

[1] The six categories, which self-evidently overlap, are: the minimal state, corporate governance, new public management, good governance, a socio-cybernetic system and self-organizing networks.

[2] France is unusual in allowing an independent executive lawmaking power: see Article 37 of the French Constitution.

[3] For a helpful overview of the budgetary process, see Lenaerts and Verhoeven (2002).

[4] For detailed exposition, see Snyder (1993).

[5] See the case of Greece, discussed by Theodossiou (2002).

[6] Steps taken include a new financial regulatory framework, the establishment of an anti-fraud unit, which has had some successes, see Pujas (2003); and a general program of reform outlined in European Commission (2000).

[7] There are, however, exceptions; for an early attempt at classification see Everson (1995).

[8] Case 9/56 *Meroni v High Authority* [1957-8] ECR 133. The doctrine of institutional balance, a softer version of separation of powers, is helpfully described by Lenaerts and Verhoeven (2002).

[9] Regulation 178/2002, OJ L31/1, of the European Parliament and Council laying down the general principles of food law, establishing the European Food Safety Authority and laying down procedures in matters of food safety. See more generally Chiti (2000).

[10] Set up by Council Decision 99/468 of June 28, 1999 laying down procedures for the exercise of implementing powers conferred on the Commission, OJ L184/23. Implementing regulations were designed to be used to complete the Single Market after the Single European Act of 1986.

[11] Draft Constitution, Article I-35 1 and 2.

[12] OJ 1993 C138/5

[13] Directive, 2001. See Macrory and Turner (2002). For radically different perspectives, see Rose-Ackerman (1995), reviewed by Lindseth (1996).

[14] See papers *at* http://europa.eu.int-comm-environment-aarhuis-complaintsappeals/ and europa.eu.int-comm-environment-impel-access_to_justice/

[15] See, however, Horwitz (1982) arguing that the public/private distinction, functional in restricting monarchical power and carving out an area of freedom from state interference, lost its potency in the late nineteenth century, when "large-scale corporate concentration became the norm."

[16] Compare *Marbury v Madison*, 1 Cranch 137 (1803) with Case 26/62 *Van Gend en Loos v Nederlandse Administratie der Belastingen* [1963] ECR 1.

[17] Justified in Mancini and Keeling (1994, 1995). First as Advocate-General, later as a judge, Federico Mancini was an important influence at the ECJ.

[18] Cases C-6, 9/90 *Francovich and Bonafacio v Italy* [1991] ECR I-5357.

[19] Kadelbach (2002, 167–79), adds a third category of "overspill" into national systems in cases with no EU connection.

[20] From Case 24/62 *Germany v Commission* [1963] ECR 69.

[21] Case T-14/98 *Hautala v Council* [1999] ECR II-2489. Arguably, the CFI nudged the ECJ forward, always pushing against the limiting ECJ decision of Case C-5894 *Netherlands v Council* [1996] ECR I-2169. See for the intervention of the legislator Regulation 1049/2001 of the European Parliament and Council of May 30, 2001 regarding public access to EP, Council and Commission Documents [2001] OJ L145/43.

[22] For the early development, see Lorenz (1964); Akehurst (1981). See also Ellis (1999).

[23] Case 280/93 *Germany v Council* [1994] ECR I-4973.9

24 See Lindseth (1999, 701) on the Court's "preference for Europe." See also Weiler (1993); Ward (2000).

25 Case 26/62 *Van Gend en Loos v Nederlandse Administratie der Belastingen* [1963] ECR 1.

26 This occurred in *Francovich, supra* note 21. The case set some limitations on liability.

27 C-213/89 *R. v Transport Secretary ex p. Factortame* [1990] ECR I-2433.

28 Thus, Weiler (1997) has argued for an autonomous tribunal composed in part of national judges to decide issues of subsidiarity. The Constitutional Convention considered the use of national parliaments for the purpose but this approach is generally considered too cumbersome to be practical.

29 See *Friends of the Earth, Inc. v. Laidlaw Environmental Services*, 528 U.S. 167 (2000); *Lujan v. Defenders of Wildlife*, 504 U.S. 555 (1992); Sunstein (1992); Lanza (2000); Miller (2000).

30 Case T-188/97 *Rothmans v Commission* [1999] ECR II-2463. Note also that the European Commission (2001) in its White Paper on Governance, argues that committees should become advisory.

31 Case T70/99 *Alphapharm v Council* (Judgement of 11 September 2002). After "hard look" scrutiny of the scientific evidence, the CFI ruled against Alphapharm.

32 Case C-50/00 P *Unión de Peqeños Agricoltores v Council* [2000] ECR I-6677 and Case C- 263/02P *Jégo Quéré* (1 April 2004) overruling the Court of First Instance in Case T-177/01 *Jégo-Quéré et cie v Commission* [2001] ECR II-2365.

33 Case T-585/93 *Stichting Greenpeace Council (Greenpeace International) v Commission* [1995] ECR II-2205 and, on appeal to the ECJ, [1998] ECR I-1651. And see Harlow (1992).

34 The cumbersome answer lies in an action in domestic courts coupled with a preliminary reference under article 234 on a point of EU law to the Court of Justice, see Case C-74/99 *R v Health Secretary ex p Imperial Tobacco* [2000] ELR I-8599.

35 Compare the judgement of the European Court of Justice in Case C-50/00 P *Unión de Peqeños Agricoltores v Council* [2002] ECR I-6677 with the Opinion of Advocate-General Jacobs in the same case and with Case T-177/01 *Jégo-Quéré et cie v Commission* [2002] ECR II-2365 in the CFI.

36 Case T-135/96 *UEAPME v Council* [1998] ECR II-2335.

37 Case T-135/96 *UEAPME* at para. 88.

38 At para. 89.

39 As in the sketch of European environmental policymaking at pages 153-54. See also Picciotto (2002).

40 Commission Communication, "The Commission and Non-governmental Organisations: building a stronger partnership" COM(2000) 11 final and "general principles and minimum standards for consulting non-institutional interested parties" COM(2002) 277. The list of consultees together with the bodies with which they interact is published by the Commission and can be viewed at the CONNECS site, *at* http://europa.European Union.int/comm/civil_society/connecs/index.htm.

41 For progress so far, see European Commission (2003, 11–18).

42 How this could be done is discussed and evaluated by Lindseth (1999).

6.

The Constitutionalization
of Community Administration

Paul Craig

This chapter has three related objectives. The first is to point to the increasing constitutionalization of Community administration. The term constitutionalization has a plethora of meanings. Its use here signifies, in formal terms, that the principles governing Community administration have now been enshrined in a norm, the new Financial Regulation, that is of constitutional importance. The term constitutionalization signifies, in substantive terms, the emergence of overarching principles that frame the entirety of Community administration.

The second is to convey an understanding of Community administration. Much has been written on topics such as Comitology. There is, however, a paucity of material on the different ways in which the Community administers its policies. The divide between shared and direct administration is imperfectly understood.

The third objective is to examine the role of law in Community administration. Judicial review is but part of this story. It will be seen that law, both hard and soft, plays a plethora of roles in this area. Law, in the form of general Community legislation, establishes the overarching principles to govern Community administration, as exemplified by the new Financial Regulation. Law, in the form of specific Community legislation, encapsulates choices that can markedly affect success or failure, as exemplified by the Common Agricultural Policy. Law will be used to legitimize new institutions for policy delivery, such as executive agencies. Law, in the form of judicial review, has a Janus-like focus. The Community courts will control abuse of administrative power. They can also use judicial review to read Community legislation in the manner that best conforms to the Community's interest. We must also be mindful of the limits of the law. The bypassing of formal legal norms by key players, and the legal response, is a fascinating part of the story.

The Emergence of a Constitutional Framework for Administration

The recognition that Community policies are administered in different ways is not new. The work of the Committee of Independent Experts, nonetheless, constituted a major step forward. The Committee was established to investigate claims of mismanagement and fraud in Community administration. Its First Report[1] precipitated the downfall of the Santer Commission. In its Second Report, the Committee distinguished between shared and direct management. Shared management is concerned with "those Community programs where the Commission and the Member States have distinct administrative tasks which are inter-dependent and set down in legislation and where both the Commission and national administrations need to discharge their respective tasks for the Community policy to be implemented successfully."[2] The Common Agricultural Policy (CAP) and the Structural Funds are the principal instances of shared management. Direct management covers those Community programs administered by the Commission itself, either "in house," or by contracting-out. The Committee's Report had a marked impact on the Commission's thinking. The White Paper on Reforming the Commission[3] drew heavily on the Committee's analysis of direct and shared administration.

This distinction has been embodied in the new Financial Regulation. The previous Financial Regulation was enacted in 1977, and amended on many occasions.[4] The new Financial Regulation[5] now provides a legal framework for the structure of Community administration.

The detailed provisions of the new Regulation concerning direct and shared management will be considered below. The present discussion will focus on the structural aspects of the Regulation. These are dealt with in Title IV, Implementation of the Budget, Chapter two of which is concerned with Methods of Implementation. Article 53(1) of the Financial Regulation provides that the Commission shall implement the budget either on a centralized basis, by shared or decentralized management, or by joint management with international organizations. These methods of implementation must be considered separately.

Centralized management covers those instances where the Commission implements the budget directly through its departments, or indirectly.[6] The principles concerning indirect centralized implementation are set out in Article 54. The Commission is not allowed to entrust its executive powers to third parties where they involve a large measure of discretion implying political choices. The implementing tasks delegated must be clearly defined and fully supervised.[7] There will clearly be problems in deciding whether the task allocated to third parties is ultra vires, in the sense that it involves "a large measure of discretion implying political choices," within the meaning of Article 54(1). Within these limits the Commission can entrust tasks to the new breed of executive agencies, or Community bodies that can receive grants.[8] It can also, within the limits of Article 54(1), entrust tasks to national public-sector bodies, or bodies governed by private law with a public service mission guaranteed by the State.[9] These national bodies can only be entrusted with budget implementation if the basic act concerning the program provides for the possibility of delegation, and lays down the criteria for the selection of such bodies. It is also a condition that the delegation to national bodies is a response to the requirements of sound financial management, and is non-discriminatory. The delegation of executive tasks to these bodies must be transparent, and the procurement procedure must be non-discriminatory and prevent any conflict of interest. There must be an effective internal control system for management operations, proper accounting arrangements, and an external audit.[10] The Commission is not allowed to entrust implementation of funds from the budget, in particular payment and recovery, to external private-sector bodies, other than those which have a public service mission guaranteed by the State.[11] The Commission is, however, empowered to entrust such private-sector entities with tasks involving technical expertise, and administrative, preparatory or ancillary tasks involving neither the exercise of public authority, nor the use of discretionary judgment.[12]

Where aspects of the budget are implemented by shared management, tasks are entrusted to the Member States in accordance with specific provisions of the new Financial Regulation concerning the European Agricultural Guidance and Guarantee Fund (EAGGF), Guarantee Section, and the Structural Funds.[13]

Cases of decentralized management cover those instances where funds are intended for third country beneficiaries. These funds can be disbursed directly by the Commission, or by the authorities of the beneficiary state.[14]

The following discussion will consider direct management. There will then be an analysis of shared management within the Common Agricultural Policy.

Direct/Centralized Management

The Rationale for Direct/Centralized Management

The traditional pattern of Community administration has been shared: The Commission works directly with national bureaucracies to implement the CAP and the Structural Funds. The Commission has, however, increasingly undertaken administration directly. This was in part because the enabling provisions did not establish any general pattern of shared management. It was in part because the subject matter did not necessarily lend itself to shared management. It was in part also because the Commission felt that certain policies were best implemented through non-governmental organs. The appropriations for directly managed operations are approximately one-sixth of the Community budget, in the order of 14 billion Euros per year.

Delivery of Direct/Centralized Management and Contracting Out

Direct management captures the idea that the Commission will implement a program without formal, systematic co-operation with national bureaucracies. It does not mean that the Commission carries out the entirety of the activity itself, "in house." It is common in relation to direct management for the Commission to contract out part of the work. The motivations for contracting out were eclectic. In some areas, such as nuclear safety, expertise was the key factor. In others, there was a desire to involve civil society in service delivery. The rationale for contracting-out in the context of humanitarian assistance was that specialist aid organizations would be better placed to deliver the aid than the Commission. Shortage of staff within the Commission was another reason for contracting out.

Direct/Centralized Management, the Fall of the
Santer Commission and Internal Reform

There had been concern in the EC for some considerable time about fraud and mismanagement. This culminated in the setting up of a Committee of Independent Experts, convened by the European Parliament and the Commission, with a mandate to detect and deal with fraud, mismanagement and nepotism. The Committee produced its first report in March 1999.[15] The Report spoke of the mismatch between the objectives assigned to the

Commission, and the way in which it fulfilled them.[16] It led to the resignation of the Santer Commission.

It is, however, only by reading the Report in its entirety that one can understand what went wrong (Craig 2000). It is readily apparent that the difficulties encountered were those inherent in contracting-out by a public arm of government. The line between policy formation and policy implementation became blurred. It was difficult to ensure that the private contractor did not breach its contract with or defraud the Commission. The Commission's mismanagement resided principally in its failure to detect these problems and to address them.

Romano Prodi, the new Commission President, sought to restore faith in the institution. He introduced a new Code of Conduct for Commissioners.[17] This was followed by the creation, in September 1999, of the Task Force for Administrative Reform (TFRA), for which Neil Kinnock was given responsibility. The TFRA produced a White Paper,[18] which was heavily influenced by the Second Report of the Committee of Independent Experts.[19]

This Second Report dealt, inter alia, with the different ways in which Community services are delivered. In relation to direct management, the Committee accepted that the Commission would have to contract out tasks.[20] It was equally firm in its belief that the existing arrangements were imperfect. The Committee proposed a new type of executive agency.[21]

The Commission's White Paper acknowledged the contributions made by the Reports of the Committee of Independent Experts,[22] and the DECODE exercise.[23] The general theme of the White Paper was the need for the Commission to concentrate on core functions such as policy conception. Delegation to other bodies would enable the Commission to concentrate on its core activities.[24] "Externalisation" was only to be used where it was the most efficient option, and would not be pursued at the expense of accountability. "Externalisation" should not, therefore, be used where real discretionary power was involved.[25] There was to be a new type of implementing body.[26] Important recommendations were also made about staffing and financial control.

Direct/Centralized Management and Law

Direct/Centralized Management and Externalization: Four Choices

The new Financial Regulation provides a framework for those activities directly managed by the Commission. Such programs can be directly managed within the Commission; management tasks can be undertaken by executive agencies, some tasks can be delegated to networks of national agencies, and certain activities can be contracted-out.

These modes of direct management inter-relate. Thus, even where it is decided to use an executive agency, there will still be important aspects of the program overseen by the Commission, since the management tasks that can be delegated to such agencies are limited. Moreover, the contracting-out of certain tasks can be used in conjunction with any of the other modes of direct management. Thus, as will be seen, it is possible for an executive agency to contract-out certain of its assigned tasks.

Management by the Commission: Recasting Responsibility for Projects

Public lawyers will be aware of the importance of proper control systems when dealing with contracting out and the like. The Committee of Independent Experts revealed that many of the problems with direct management were integrally linked to deficiencies in relation to financial controls. The basic provision was the Financial Regulation of 1977,[27] but two fundamental tenets remained largely unchanged.

First, the authorization of expenditure and the collection of revenue were both in the hands of the Financial Controller of each Community institution. It was the Financial Controller that would give the "visa" authorizing the expenditure, and it was the Financial Controller that would collect the revenue.[28] Second, there was a separation of function between the authorizing officer and the accounting officer. The former entered into the financial commitments, subject to the grant of a "visa" by the Financial Controller, and the latter actually carried out the relevant operation.

The Committee of Independent Experts was critical of this regime.[29] The Financial Controller's responsibility for ex ante control and ex post audit could lead to a conflict of interest. The centralization of ex ante control in the Financial Controller through the visa system was ineffective. Control of expenditure should be decentralized to the Directorates-General. The responsibility for authorization of expenditure should be linked to responsibility for the carrying out of the operation.[30]

These ideas were taken up directly into the White Paper on Reforming the Commission. The aim was to create "an administrative culture that encourages officials to take responsibility for activities over which they have control—and gives them control over the activities for which they are responsible."[31]

The new Financial Regulation gives legal force to these ideas.[32] The duties of the authorizing officer and the accounting officer are separated.[33] The latter is responsible for payments, collection of revenue, keeping the accounts, and the like.[34] It is, however, the authorizing officer that is central to the whole scheme. Each institution "performs" the duties of authorising officer.[35] It lays down rules for the delegation of these duties to staff of an appropriate level, and specifies the scope of the powers delegated and the possibility for subdelegation.[36] The authorizing officer to whom power has been delegated makes the budget and legal commitments, and validates expenditure and authorizes payments.[37] Before an operation is authorized, staff members other than the person who initiated the operation must verify the operational and financial aspects.[38]

The provisions on expenditure reinforce the centrality of the authorizing officer. Every item of expenditure must be committed, validated, authorized and paid.[39] The budget commitment consists of making the appropriation necessary to cover a legal commitment. The legal commitment is the act whereby the authorizing officer enters an obligation to third parties, which results in expenditure being charged to the budget. The same authorizing officer undertakes the budget and legal commitment,[40] and the former must precede the latter.[41] It is for the authorizing officer, when adopting a budget commitment, to ensure, inter alia, that the appropriations are available, that the expenditure conforms to the relevant legal provisions, and that the principles of sound financial management are complied with.[42] It is the authorizing officer that is responsible for validation of expenditure.[43]

The internal auditor is also central to the reform package. The idea was strongly advocated by the Committee of Independent Experts,[44] and endorsed by the Commission White Paper.[45] The central idea was to establish an Internal Audit Service, the auditors of which would advise the institutions about proper budgetary procedures, and the quality of their management and control systems. The new Financial Regulation made provision for internal auditors,[46] and the Internal Audit Service has published a Charter to describe its role.[47]

Management by Executive Agencies: Policy and Implementation, Power and Responsibility

The origins of executive agencies are to be found in the Committee of Independent Experts' Second Report. The Committee noted that technical assistance offices were nothing more than contractors, who undertook work for the Commission.[48] It was the weak controls over such firms that led to the problems highlighted in the Committee's First Report. The creation of implementing agencies was seen as a way of alleviating these problems.[49] The new Financial Regulation makes provision for such executive agencies.[50]

There is now a framework Regulation dealing specifically with these agencies.[51] The objective is to foster flexible, accountable and efficient management of tasks assigned to the Commission. Policy decisions remain with the Commission, implementation is assigned to the agency.[52] The conjunction of power and responsibility, a principal theme of the new Financial Regulation, is carried over to this new regime.

It is fitting to begin with the rules relating to the establishment and winding-up of executive agencies. Executive agency covers a legal entity created in accordance with the Regulation, to manage a Community program.[53] The Commission may decide after a cost-benefit analysis to set up such an agency.[54] The cost-benefit analysis shall take into account factors such as the justification for outsourcing, the costs of co-ordination and checks, the impact on human resources, efficiency and flexibility in the implementation of outsourced tasks, possible financial savings, simplification of the procedures used, proximity of the outsourced activities to final beneficiaries, the need to maintain an adequate level of know-how in the Commission, and the visibility of the Community as promoter of the Community program. The Commission will determine the lifetime of the agency, which can, within limits, be extended.[55] When the services of the agency are not required, it will be wound up.[56] The creation of a particular agency requires approval under the Comitology regulatory procedure,[57] and a new Comitology Committee is established.[58]

In terms of legal status, executive agencies are Community bodies, with a public service role. They are legal entities with the capacity, inter alia, to hold property and be a party to legal proceeding.[59]

The staffing arrangements are a blend of the old and the new. The operational head of the agency is the director, who must be a Community official within the staff regulations. The Commission makes the appointment, which is for four years renewable.[60] The director is responsible for the agency's tasks, and draws up an annual work program.[61] The director is assisted by a Steering Committee of five members, who do not have to be Community officials. They are appointed by the Commission for at least two years renewable.[62] The Committee is to meet at least four times a year. Its main tasks are to adopt the agency's annual work program presented by the director, to adopt the agency's budget, and to report annually to the

Commission on the agency's activities.[63] The agency staff are comprised of Community officials, seconded to the agency, and non-Community officials recruited on renewable contracts.[64]

There are important provisions specifying the agency's tasks. The Commission can entrust the agency with any tasks required to implement a Community program, with the exception of "tasks requiring discretionary powers in translating political choices into action."[65] Policy choices remain for the Commission, implementation is for the agency. This is confirmed by the examples of tasks that can be assigned to executive agencies.[66] The tasks include management of projects within a program, by adopting relevant decisions using powers delegated to the agency by the Commission, adopting the instruments of budget implementation for revenue expenditure and the award of contracts on the basis of powers delegated by the Commission, and gathering and analyzing data for the implementation of the program.

While the intent is clear, the actual wording in article 6 to delimit the agency's power may be problematic. This wording is similar to that found in Article 54(1) of the new Financial Regulation, which precludes delegation of executive powers to executive agencies involving a "large measure of discretion implying political choices."[67] There are, however, crucial differences between the two formulations. Article 54(1) of the Financial Regulation prevents delegation of discretionary political choices. Article 6(1) of the Regulation on executive agencies precludes delegation of tasks requiring discretionary power in translating political choices into action. In this formulation, the executive agency is not only prevented from making the initial political choices, but also from exercising discretionary power when translating those choices into action. This will, if taken literally, severely limit the tasks that can be given to agencies. This conclusion might be avoided by reading the phrase "discretionary powers" more narrowly. In this view, the mere existence of choices as to how to, for example, manage a project would not be regarded as the exercise of "discretionary powers."

The financial arrangements for the new agencies are important. The principles of the new Financial Regulation concerning financial transparency, internal and external audit and the like, are carried over into the scheme for executive agencies.[68] This is especially so in relation to the fusion of financial power and responsibility. The director is the authorizing officer for budgetary matters within the agency.[69]

The new Regulation specifies rules on agency liability in damages. The law applicable to the contract governs contractual liability.[70] Article 288(2) concerning non-contractual liability has been extended to the executive agency.[71] This follows the legal technique used in relation to "older" agencies, such as the European Environment Agency.[72]

The provisions on review of legality have been more controversial. The initial draft Regulation stipulated that the legality of the acts of an executive agency could be reviewed under article 230 on the same conditions as the acts of the Commission itself.[73] It is questionable whether article 230 could have been used to challenge the legality of actions of executive agencies, since these actions are not included in the list of reviewable acts under article 230(1). The better view is nonetheless that such agency decisions could, as a matter of principle, be reviewed under article 230. The Court of Justice has read Article 230 broadly so as to facilitate review of the European Parliament (EP)[74] and Court of Auditors.[75] Moreover, Community legislation has provided for challenge to the legality of decisions made by bodies such as the Office for Harmonization in the Internal Market.[76] The EP, nonetheless, argued that the executive agency was the Commission's responsibility, and the Commission should be legally responsible under article 230.[77] The Commission counter-argued that the executive agency had its own legal personality, and therefore, the Commission should not be liable for the legality of its actions.

The final version of the Regulation is a compromise between these two views: the initial legal responsibility lies with the agency, and the legality of its acts can be reviewed by the Commission, with a further review of the Commission by the Court of Justice under article 230 if the Commission rejects the appeal.

Article 22(1) of the Regulation provides for a novel form of internal review of agency decisions by the Commission. An act of an executive agency that injures a third party can be referred to the Commission, by any person directly and individually concerned or by a Member State, for a review of its legality. Such actions must be brought within one month of the day on which the applicant learned of the challenged act. The Commission, after hearing arguments, must make a decision within two months. If it does not do so, it means that the action has been implicitly rejected. The Commission is also able, of its own volition, to review an act of the executive agency.[78] The Commission can suspend implementation of the measure or prescribe interim measures; it can also, in its final decision, uphold the measure, or decide that the agency must modify it in whole or in part.

This regime for internal monitoring by the Commission is complemented by recourse to article 230. Thus, article 22(5) states that an action for annulment of the Commission's explicit or implicit decision to reject an administrative appeal may be brought before the Court of Justice in accordance with article 230.

The rules on the legality of agency acts raise a number of technical legal issues. The grounds for review are not spelled out, although the assumption is that they will be those used under article 230. It seems, moreover, that any act of the executive agency that injures a third party can be reviewed, irrespective of whether it is binding; although the requirement that the act should cause injury may impose an indirect qualification in this respect. There also seems to be an asymmetry as to recourse in the Court of Justice. Article 22(5) is framed in terms of an annulment action where the Commission rejects the administrative appeal. It seems, therefore, that the executive agency itself has no such recourse where the Commission upholds the appeal.

The rules on the legality of agency acts also raise important issues of principle. Article 22 has introduced a novel form of internal review of the legality of executive agency action by the Commission. The procedure will require careful thought. Executive agencies are only accorded limited implementing powers. Policy formation remains the prerogative of the Commission. This raises two important points of principle. It is, on the one hand, important who hears such cases within the Commission. It is not clear whether they will be heard by the Directorate General (DG) to which the executive agency is attached. If the cases come to the same DG that established the agency, there is a danger of a conflict of interest. It is not easy to keep policy formation and implementation distinct. If an action challenging implementation implicates policy, there could be real objections to the Commission sitting as a "judge." There is, on the other hand, an issue of principle arising from the fact that the executive agency seems to have no recourse to the Court of Justice where the Commission upholds the appeal. The executive agency may feel that the Commission is using its internal power of review to impose a view concerning detailed matters of implementation that is legitimately within the agency's sphere.

The rules on the legality of executive agency acts also prompt thought about broader issues of "legal design." These rules require us to reflect on the optimal structuring of legal liability. The mere fact that a body has a separate legal personality, so that it can hold property, bring actions in its own name, etc., does not a priori preclude making another body liable for its actions. The principled argument for holding the Commission responsible for the executive agency is that the program has been assigned to the Commission itself. The Commission may choose to deliver this program in-house or through an executive agency. That choice should not affect legal liability, which should remain with the Commission. The argument to the contrary is as follows: Executive agencies are lawful. They are Community bodies and have a legal personality. Placing liability directly on the executive agencies best serves the broader objectives of the administrative reforms considered above. It reinforces the conjunction of power and responsibility that is central to the new Financial Regulation.

Networks of National Agencies

It is clear from the Commission's White Paper that externalization could be pursued through devolution of tasks to certain national public bodies.[79] This was confirmed by the new Financial Regulation.[80] Centralized management of Community activities can be undertaken by, inter alia, national public sector bodies or bodies with a public service mission guaranteed by the state.[81] The conditions described above apply to these bodies, just as much as when externalization is pursued through executive agencies.

The Commission's thinking about the use of such bodies is clearer from a Communication devoted to the topic.[83] The idea is to devolve executive responsibilities to national bodies, which are either public or have a public service mission guaranteed by the state. These bodies are collectively referred to as "national agencies," and this status can be conferred on existing or new entities. The agencies then act as partners in the implementation of Community policies, but the Commission retains overall responsibility for service delivery.[84] The intention is to devolve detailed implementation to national agencies, so that they have no margin of discretion on Community policy.[85]

The Commission perceives a number of advantages of using national agencies.[86] It facilitates proximity to the beneficiaries of the policy, as in the case of education and training. It fosters complementarity, since there will often be national agencies with experience of a particular policy. National agencies can offer greater flexibility than executive agencies, since it is easier to adapt to local circumstance. The Commission has established criteria for when networks of national agencies will be appropriate.[87]

The Commission is against a general framework regulation for management by networks of national agencies.[88] The preferred approach is to provide for management by national agencies within the specific regulation governing a particular program. There will then be a Commission decision laying down the responsibilities of the Commission and the Member States in relation to the national agencies.

Contract Award, Contract Specification and the Allocation of Contractual Risk

Contracts are used to secure the delivery of many of the programs directly administered by the Commission. Problems surrounding such contracts played a large part in the fall of the Santer Commission, and the Court of Auditors has revealed difficulties in other areas.[89] It is, therefore, unsurprising that subsequent reforms have been directed towards these contractual relationships.

The new Financial Regulation contains rules as to the type of activities that can be entrusted to another body. The implementing tasks must be clearly defined and supervised, and the Commission is not allowed to entrust its executive powers to third parties where "they involve a large measure of discretion implying political choices."[90] Much will depend on how intensively the Community courts decide to review such matters.

The new Financial Regulation contains rules as to the type of bodies to whom such tasks can be assigned. Within the limits specified in the previous paragraph, the Commission can entrust tasks of public authority, and budget implementation, to the new breed of executive agencies, Community bodies that can receive grants, and national public-sector bodies, or bodies with a public service mission guaranteed by the State.[91] The Commission is not allowed to entrust implementation of funds from the budget to external private-sector bodies, other than those which have a public service mission guaranteed by the State.[92] The Commission is, however, empowered to entrust private-sector entities with tasks involving technical expertise, and administrative, preparatory or ancillary tasks involving neither the exercise of public authority, nor the use of discretionary judgment.[93] The dividing line between technical expertise or administrative tasks, and the exercise of public authority or discretionary judgment, will be difficult to maintain.

In relation to the award of contracts, the basic strategy of the new Financial Regulation is to apply the directives on public procurement to contracts awarded by the Community institutions.[94] There is an obligation to put such contracts out to tender, using the open, restricted or negotiated procedure, or for there to be a contest.[95] There are safeguards against fraud by contractors. Thus, firms are excluded from the tendering process if they are bankrupt, guilty of grave professional misconduct and the like.[96] A contract cannot be awarded to a firm that has a conflict of interest, or that has been guilty of misrepresentation.[97] The specification of the terms of the contract is equally important if the mistakes of the past are to be avoided. Fraud and financial irregularities perpetrated by contractors will be prevented in part by the provisions concerning the exclusion of certain firms from the tendering process. This can, however, only be part of the overall strategy. It is also important to ensure the effective discharge of Community policies by those to whom tasks have been contracted out. The specification of the contract terms is all-important. Contracts are bargains, which allocate risks. The Committee of Independent Experts was critical of Commission practice in this respect.[98] There is an integral connection between the specification of the contract terms and the contractual objective. If the objective is set at too high a level of generality, it will be difficult to devise concrete contractual terms that can operate as a meaningful constraint on the other contracting party.

Reflections on Direct Management and Law

The shock waves from the fall of the Santer Commission generated a radical re-thinking by the Commission of the delivery of programs for which it has direct management responsibility. The Commission might well have retreated into a defensive shell after the Report of the Committee of Independent Experts. It did not do so. It embraced the majority of the Committee's suggestions. Three more general observations on the new administrative order are warranted.

First, the Commission's overall strategy is based on the conjunction of power and responsibility, with the authorizing officer being the key figure in this regard. The divide between policy and implementation is equally central[99]: policy remains the preserve of the Commission, with implementation devolved to executive agencies, networks of national agencies, or managed through contracting-out subject to Commission oversight. It can be accepted that the divide between policy and implementation is difficult to preserve. This does not mean that the overall strategy is misguided. It is inevitable, for the reasons considered above and below, that the Commission will have to externalize the administration of some programs. Given that this is so, it is right that the central policy choices should be made by the Commission. It is right for this to be enshrined in the new administrative order, even if in some instances an executive agency might "cross the line" and make some limited discretionary policy choices.

Second, the effective delivery of policy is an endemic problem within national polities, so too when programs are administered at the Community level. The Commission cannot administer all policies in-house. Therefore, the Commission has to "externalize" the administration of some programs.

Nor will one technique of externalization serve for the plethora of differing programs that the Community manages. In some cases the best technique will be to maintain control within the Commission, but to contract-out detailed implementation. In other cases executive agencies will be the most appropriate institutional form. In yet other instances, existing national agencies will be the most fitting medium.

Third, there are several layers to the legal realization of these administrative reforms. This is not excessive legalism. The new Financial Regulation is at the apex. It is of constitutional significance. It contains the budgetary principles, orders the different forms of Community administration, establishes principles governing the allocation and exercise of administrative power, and allocates financial power and responsibility. The next level down are the Regulation on Executive Agencies. No such general regulation is contemplated for networks of national agencies. The use of such networks will, nonetheless, be legitimized through Community legislation in the specific areas where they are used. There is a further legal level concerned with the detailed operation of an executive agency, or network of national agencies. Specific Community legislation, combined with operating agreements, defines the tasks of such bodies in particular areas.

Shared Management

We have already seen that the new Financial Regulation contains provisions dealing with shared management, as well as direct/centralized management.[100] It is, nonetheless, important to press further in order to understand the difficulties posed by this mode of administration, and the role of law within this area. This is more so given that a number of these problems are not addressed by the new Financial Regulation. These problems will be explored in the context of the Common Agricultural Policy.

The Common Agricultural Policy: Treaty Foundations

The Treaty foundations for the CAP have not altered in substance since the inception of the Community, articles 32–38 (ex-articles 38–46). The objectives of the CAP are laid down in Article 33(1). They are:

1. to increase agricultural productivity by promoting technical progress and by ensuring the rational development of agricultural production and the optimum utilization of the factors of production, in particular labour;
2. thus to ensure a fair standard of living for the agricultural community, in particular by increasing the individual earnings of persons engaged in agriculture;
3. to stabilise markets;
4. to assure the availability of supplies;
5. to ensure that supplies reach consumers at reasonable prices.

The Treaty provides further guidance as to the attainment of the objectives listed in article 33(1). In positive terms, article 34(2) stipulates that the common organization of agricultural markets may, inter alia, be directed towards price regulation, production and marketing aids, and storage arrangements to stabilize imports and exports. In negative terms, article 34(2) provides that there shall be no discrimination between producers or consumers within the Community.

Implementation: From Price Support towards Income Support

The detailed story of the CAP has been told elsewhere (Usher 1988; Snyder 1990, chap. 4–5; Grant 1997; Nugent 1999, chap. 15; McMahon 2000; Rieger 2000; George and Bache 2001, chap. 24). It is, however, necessary to understand the outline of this story, in order to comprehend the regime of shared management.

The principal focus of CAP policy has been on price support. A rationale for the EC has always been that goods should be able to move unhindered by trade barriers, subsidies and the like. This regime has not applied to agricultural produce. The Council established common prices for most agricultural goods. There is a target price, this being the price that it is hoped farmers will be able to obtain on the open market. There is an intervention price, which is the price at which the Commission will buy up produce from the market. There is also a threshold price, this being the price to which imports are raised when world prices are less than those prevailing in the EC.

The price support system has proven very costly for the EC, consuming the largest share of the Community's budget. Community prices have, on the whole, been higher than those obtainable on the open markets. This has encouraged production, and generated surplus goods. These then have to be stored, a further significant cost.

The EC adopted a variety of measures to ameliorate the consequences of the CAP price support regime. Quotas and the like were introduced to reduce the impact of the system. The degree of price support for particular agricultural goods was reduced. Farmers were encouraged to set aside certain farmland, and hence, reduce production. There was a realization that the existing regime could not continue in the light of enlargement. Incentives for CAP reform also came from external sources. The EC was under pressure from the United States and other countries to reform its protectionist agricultural policies. These pressures became particularly forceful during the Uruguay round of the General Agreement on Tariffs and Trade (GATT) negotiations in the early 1990s. The Agriculture Commissioner, MacSharry, put together a package of reforms that that were accepted after much hard bargaining within the EC, and with the United States. The CAP reforms in 1991–1993 were of more long-term significance, since it was acknowledged that support for farmers could be disaggregated from production.

This was the beginning of the shift from price support to income support. Fischler, the Agriculture Commissioner in the Santer Commission, continued this trend. Support for farmers began to be seen separately from support for production.[101] This theme was developed in the Commission's Agenda 2000 document.[102] The Commission proposed large reductions in support prices, coupled with direct compensation to farmers. These proposals were, however, watered down in the Council meeting of the Agriculture Ministers in March 1999, as a result of French opposition. Further opposition from President Jacques Chirac in the Berlin European Council[103] led to a greater dilution of the original proposals. The Commission, nonetheless, sought to make the "best" of the outcome of the Berlin European Council, emphasizing those aspects that fitted with its Agenda 2000 initiative. More detailed plans have also been forthcoming to deal with enlargement. The decoupling of support from production is central to this strategy.[104] It has not been easy to secure agreement on such changes. However the pressures of enlargement, and the EU's negotiating position with the World Trade Organization (WTO), were the principal factors leading to an agreement in June 2003, the foundation of which is the disaggregation of financial support from production.

It is clear that the CAP has been "not only a tool for the technical arrangement for the management of agricultural markets, but also a tool of commercial and humanitarian policy" (Rieger 2000, 186). It has as a consequence been directly concerned with the distribution of income.

The Framework of Shared Management

The administration of the CAP is "shared," in the sense that the various forms of price support payments are administered jointly by the Commission and the Member States.[105] This is done through the European Agricultural Guidance and Guarantee Fund (EAGGF). The Guidance section deals with EC expenditure relating to agricultural structures; the Guarantee section covers payments relating directly to the regulation of agricultural markets, refunds on exports and intervention payments. It is the latter that is of principal concern here.

The main enabling provision for many years was Regulation 729/70.[106] The Member States designated the bodies within their countries that would make the payments covered by the Guarantee section,[107] and the Commission would make the funds available to the Member States for disbursement by those bodies.[108] The Member States were under an obligation to take the necessary measures to satisfy themselves that the transactions financed by the Fund were actually carried out correctly, to prevent and deal with irregularities, and to recover sums lost as a result of irregularities or negligence.[109] However, in the absence of total recovery, the financial consequences of irregularities or negligence were borne by the Community, with the exception of the consequences of irregularities or negligence attributable to administrative bodies of the Member States.[110] The Member States and the Commission had the power to carry out inspections to ensure the probity of the transactions financed by the Fund.[111]

In addition to the provisions of Regulation 729/70 protection of the Community Budget was to be secured, inter alia, through the system of clearance of accounts. This was particularly important since the Commission made payments to national bodies on a monthly basis, and sought to recover, thereafter, sums that should not have been paid. Prior to 1995 the Commission was required to clear the EAGGF Guarantee accounts by the December 31st of the year following the financial year concerned, that is, by December 31st of the year n + 1. The Member States were meant to submit the accounts of their paying agencies by March 31st of the year n + 1. The Commission then examined the accounts. The accounts were, however, rarely closed on time. The Commission could order a correction in relation to a particular irregularity. It could also order flat rate corrections when it discovered a systemic weakness in the procedures of a paying agency.

Three major changes to Regulation 729/70 were made in 1995. First, it was stipulated that paying agencies had to be accredited by the Member States. Only such agencies could make payments.[112] Second, the accounts of the paying agencies had to be certified by a body that was operationally independent of the paying agency.[113] Third, the timetables and procedures for accounting and compliance were separated within the system for clearance of accounts.[114] These changes were incorporated in Regulation 1258/99.[115]

Shared Management, the CAP and Law

The Role of Law within Shared Management

It is interesting to reflect on the role of law within the pattern of shared management that characterises the CAP. There are, unsurprisingly, a number of dimensions to this inquiry.

It is fitting to begin by considering legislative objectives. It is clear that there is tension between the collective interests of the Member States in the Council, and the interests of individual Member States as recipients of CAP funds. The Member States in their collective capacity have an interest in the allocation of the Community budget, and in the proper use of funds within that allocation. There is, however, a tension between this objective, and the accountability of individual Member States for the correct disbursement of CAP funds. Individual states have sought to minimize their liability for incorrect CAP allocations. This leads naturally to the design and content of legislation. Legislation will contain procedural and substantive conditions for eligibility to funds. It will specify rules as to liability if things go wrong. Law creates incentives or disincentives to certain types of action. This can be seen from three examples, the first of which concerns the complex system of export refunds. This is intended to bridge the gap between Community prices and those on the world market. The provisions differentiate payments according to product type and export destination. It has been highly susceptible to fraud and difficult to police.[116] A second example relates to the 1995 legislative reforms that introduced the ideas of accreditation and certification of accounts. The Commission argued that it should be responsible for the accreditation of paying agencies, and for the approval of the national certifying bodies, but these suggestions were rejected by the Council. The Member States are empowered to accredit agencies[117] and specify the certifying bodies.[118] This has been problematic, with bodies being accredited that did not fulfil the relevant criteria. The third example of the importance of legislative design is provided by article 8 of Regulation 729/70.[119] Member States have an obligation to prevent irregularities, and to recover sums lost as a result of irregularities or negligence. However, in the absence of total recovery, the financial consequences of irregularities or negligence are borne by the Community, with the exception of losses attributable to irregularities or negligence by administrative bodies of the Member States. This creates, as the Committee of Independent Experts noted, a particular pattern of incentives:

> It is difficult to believe that the administrative authorities…in the Member States are always inclined to highlight for the Commission instances of irregularity or negligence on their part which would result in them bearing the resulting financial consequences. It is also difficult to believe that they are never negligent. In other words the arrangements which this basic Regulation established and which still pertain do not provide the immediate disbursers of 48% (at one time as high as 70%) of the Community's budget, the EAGGF paying agencies in the Member States, with any immediate incentive for rigour and tight control of what is in effect someone else's, that is the Community's, money.[121]

Formal law, howsoever framed, can only do so much. The history of shared management in this area provides ample testimony to the way in which formal legal norms were undermined in the operation of the CAP. We have already noted the differing incentives of the Member States collectively, and those of individual Member States as recipients of CAP funds. Member States have bypassed formal law when it suited their interests. This can be exemplified by the accreditation of paying agencies. Article 4 of Regulation 729/70[122] was clear: Member States were obliged to submit to the Commission details of the paying agencies, and the accounting conditions for payment. However, prior to 1996 there were "hundreds of unnotified small de facto agencies making EAGGF Guarantee payments in the Member States without any structured procedures for checking on their activities or accounts."[123] This illegality was practised by the Member States and tolerated by the Commission.[124] This point can also be exemplified by the system for clearance of accounts. The time scale for this procedure was rarely adhered to, in part because the Member States were late in submitting the accounts of paying agencies.

The interplay between formal legal norms, and practical reality, is evident in the response to the preceding problems. The law attempted to "catch up" and address the problems caused by shared management. There have been many changes in the CAP regulations. The major changes have been motivated by the need to address shortcomings of the previous legal structure, as exemplified by the 1995 Regulations. The accreditation requirements, the stipulation that there must be a co-ordinating body where there was more than one paying agency, the certification of accounts, and the divide between accounting and compliance were all directed towards this end.

We must, however, also consider the effectiveness of law reform. The provision of revised legal norms may be a necessary condition for the improvement of the CAP regime. It is not, however, sufficient. The effectiveness of these new norms must be evaluated. The Court of Auditors looked at these issues twice. Its conclusions were that the revised regime was certainly better than before, but that the new system still had deficiencies. Both reports revealed weaknesses in the accreditation system. The 1995 reforms gave power of accreditation to the Member States. The Court of Auditors found that there were major shortcomings in many paying agencies, which ought to have led the Member States to withdraw accreditation.[126] Its later Report found that there had been improvements, but that there were still causes for concern. There were still too many paying agencies, some of which failed to meet the criteria for accreditation, but the Member States had not generally withdrawn their accreditation.[127] The independence of certifying bodies had been resolved, but there were shortcomings in the conduct of audits.[128] The Committee of Independent Experts expressed itself more forcefully. It concluded that the "leeway which the Commission has allowed the Member States on accreditation and certification amounts to a lax implementation of the Regulation."[129]

The legal regime for the CAP has also been markedly affected by the Conciliation Procedure. There will inevitably be differences of opinion between the Member States, and Commission that arise in the clearance procedure. The Commission can exclude expenditure by paying agencies where it is not in compliance with Community rules.[130] Before such a decision is finalised, the Member State can invoke the Conciliation Procedure, which was introduced in 1994.[131] The Conciliation Body[132] is instructed to try to reconcile the divergent positions of the Commission and the Member States.[133] This is not however binding on the Commission, nor does it preclude a Member State from using article 230.[134] The effect of the Conciliation Body has, however, been mixed. The number of cases in which it secures agreement is relatively low,[135] and there has not been a marked drop in the cases submitted to the Court of Justice.[136] In more general terms, the Committee of Independent Experts described conciliation as a "win-win" procedure for the Member States, enabling them to delay recovery of undue payments, while reserving the right to challenge the Commission's final decision before the Court.[137]

The discussion of law in CAP shared management would be incomplete if it did not take account of the role of the Court of Justice. There has been a steady stream of cases in which Member States have challenged Commission decisions concerning recovery of payments unduly made by national paying agencies. These have been brought under article 230. The ECJ has interpreted the legislation in a teleological manner, largely in support of the Commission.

The Court of Justice has allocated the risk of incorrect interpretation of the Community rules to the Member States. The Member States argued that the implication of article 8(2) of Regulation 729/70[138] was that losses flowing from an incorrect, but bona fide, application of a Community rule by a national authority should be borne by the Community, except where there was negligence at the national level. The Court disagreed. It held that the text of article 8(2), viewed in the light of the preparatory documents and the language versions, contained "too many contradictory and ambiguous elements to provide an answer to the question at issue."[139] The Court decided the case on the basis of articles 2 and 3 of the same Regulation, from which it concluded that only sums paid in accordance with the relevant rules, correctly interpreted, could be charged to the EAGGF. It was for the Member States to bear the burden of other sums paid.[140] The Court of Justice reasoned that otherwise states might give a broad interpretation to the relevant rules, thereby benefiting their traders as compared to those in other states.

The Court also made it easier for the Commission to impose financial corrections on the Member States in the clearance procedure. Most actions for judicial review involve a challenge to the legality of flat rate corrections. These are made by the Commission when it discovers a systemic weakness in the procedures of a paying agency, and concludes that a series of irregular payments have been made. Flat rate corrections can be 2, 5 or 10 percent of the value of the moneys disbursed, depending upon the seriousness of the deficiency, and the degree of probable loss to Community funds.

The Court enunciated the following principles when dealing with these cases. It is for the Member State, in accordance with article 8(1),[141] to ensure the correct implementation of the CAP, prevent irregularities and recover sums lost due to irregularity or fraud.[142] It is for the Commission to prove an infringement of the CAP rules, and to give reasons explaining the defect in the national procedures.[143] However, the Commission is not required to demonstrate exhaustively that the checks carried out by national authorities are inadequate, or that there are irregularities in the figures submitted by them, but to adduce evidence of "serious and reasonable doubt on its part regarding those checks or figures."[144] The rationale for this "mitigation of the burden of proof" is that it is the Member State that is best placed to verify the data required for the clearance of the EAGGF accounts. Therefore, it is for the State to adduce evidence to show that it has carried out the necessary checks, or that its figures are accurate, and that the Commission's assertions are inaccurate.[145]

This judicial reasoning legitimized the system of flat rate corrections, without which the compliance aspect of clearance would be unworkable. It limited the damaging force of article 8(2), under which the financial consequences of irregularities or negligence are borne by the Community, unless attributable to irregularities or negligence by the national agencies. The Commission will carry out inspections of national procedures, and conclude that there is a serious and reasonable doubt as to the soundness of the national procedures, or the correctness of the national figures. The "mitigation" of the burden of proof means that it is for the Member State to adduce evidence to dispel those doubts. It is, in this sense, much easier to attribute the irregularities to the Member States, denying them the safe haven of article 8(2).

The Role of Law within Shared Management: Conclusions

Two related conclusions can be drawn concerning the role of law in the administration of the CAP.

First, sharing the administration of a complex activity is difficult. This is a trite statement, but an important one nonetheless. It was both natural and inevitable that the administration of the CAP should be shared between the Commission and national bureaucracies. The interplay between Member States and the Community in the design of the CAP, and the rules for its administration, was never going to be straightforward. The complexity of the legislative norms, combined with the divide between the collective and individual interests of Member States, produced a regime the administration of which is inherently difficult. Moves towards the simplification of the CAP legislation are to be welcomed in this respect.[146]

Second, we should be careful about the ascription of blame when things go wrong. The tendency has been to lay the fault at the door of the Community, and more especially the Commission. This suits the Member States, and anti-European commentators. The Commission has of course been at fault through, for example, tolerating departures from existing rules, and by allocating insufficient personnel to the EAGGF section. To suggest that the entire malaise of the CAP can be laid at its door, or that of the Community, is a gross oversimplification. The Community is not some reified entity that desired the CAP in its present format. The existing regime is largely the result of Member State preferences expressed in the Treaty provisions and in the CAP legislation (Rieger 2000, 180).

Conclusion

The reforms to Community administration undertaken since the fall of the Santer Commission are to be welcomed. The new Financial Regulation contains a framework of principles for the management of Community policies of a kind that have not existed hitherto. These principles are important for both direct and shared management. The creation of the new breed of executive agencies should also foster accountability in the area of direct management. It should, nonetheless, be recognized that law, in the form of specific Community legislation, encapsulates choices that will affect the success or failure of the particular regime, and this remains so notwithstanding the reforms discussed above. The difficulties encountered over the years with the Common Agricultural Policy provide a fitting example. For Community administration to be accountable, efficient and legitimate, we must pay attention to both the overarching principles contained in the new Financial Regulation, and also to the rules that govern particular areas of Community policy.

Notes

[1] Committee of Independent Experts. 1999. *First Report on Allegations Regarding Fraud, Mismanagement and Nepotism in the European Commission* [hereafter First CIE].

[2] Committee of Independent Experts. 1999. *Second Report on Reform of the Commission: Analysis of Current Practice and Proposals for Tackling Mismanagement, Irregularities and Fraud*, vol. I, par. 3.2.2 [hereafter Second CIE].

[3] *Reforming the Commission*, COM (2000) 200.

[4] *Financial Regulation of 21 December 1977 Applicable to the General Budget of the European Communities* [1977] OJ L356/1.

[5] Council Regulation 1605/2002, *on the Financial Regulation Applicable to the General Budget of the European Communities* [2002] OJ L248/1. For background, see, *Proposal for a Council Regulation on the Financial Regulation Applicable to the General Budget of the EC* COM(2000)461 final; *Amended Proposal for a Council Regulation on the Financial Regulation Applicable to the General Budget of the EC* COM (2001)691.

[6] Council Regulation 1605/2002, supra n. 5, Art. 53(2).

[7] Ibid., Art. 54(1).

[8] Ibid., Art. 54(2)(a) and (b).

[9] Ibid., Art. 54(2)(c).

[10] Ibid., Art. 56(1).

[11] Ibid., Art. 57(1).

[12] Ibid., Art. 57(2).

[13] Council Regulation 1605/2002, supra n. 5, Arts. 149–60.

[14] Ibid., Arts. 163–71.

[15] First CIE, *supra* note 1.

[16] Ibid, para. 9.4.5.

[17] *The Formation of the Commission*, 12 July 1999. See also, *Operation of the Commission*, 12 July 1999.

[18] Supra n. 3.

[19] Second CIE, *supra* note 2.

[20] Ibid., vol. I, par. 2.3.1. See also, pars. 2.0.1, and 2.3.8.

[21] Ibid., vol. I, par. 2.3.27–2.3.31.

[22] *Reforming the Commission*, supra n. 3, Part I, p. 2.

[23] *Designing Tomorrow's Commission, A Review of the Commission's Organisation and Operation*, 7 July 1999.

[24] *Reforming the Commission*, supra n. 3, Part I, p. 6.

[25] Ibid, Part I, p. 7.

[26] Ibid., Part I, p. 7.

[27] Supra n. 4.

[28] Ibid., Art. 24.

[29] Second CIE, *supra* note 2, pars. 4.6–4.7.2.

[30] Ibid., par. 4.7.

[31] *Reforming the Commission*, supra n. 3, Part I, p. 19.

[32] Council Regulation 1605/2002, supra n. 5.

[33] Ibid., Art. 58.

[34] Ibid., Art. 61.

[35] Ibid., Art. 59(1).

[36] Ibid., Art. 59(2).

[37] Ibid., Art. 60(2).

[38] Ibid., Art. 60(4).

[39] Ibid., Art. 75.

[40] Ibid., Art. 76(1), subject to limited exceptions.

[41] Ibid., Art. 77(1).

[42] Ibid., Art. 78.

[43] Ibid., Art. 79.

[44] Second CIE, *supra* note 2, par. 4.13.

[45] *Reforming the Commission*, supra n. 3, Part I, p. 22.

[46] Council Regulation 1605/2002, supra n. 5, Arts. 85–86.

[47] *Charter of the Internal Audit Service of the European Commission* SEC(2000)1801/2.

[48] Second CIE, *supra* note 2, par. 2.3.4.

[49] Ibid., par. 2.3.27.

[50] Council Regulation 1605/2002, supra n. 5, Arts. 54(2)(a), 55.

[51] Council Regulation 58/2003, *Laying Down the Statute for Executive Agencies to be Entrusted with Certain Tasks in the Management of Community Programs* [2003] OJ L11/1, (hereafter *Executive Agencies*). For background, see *Amended Proposal for a Council Regulation laying down the Statute for Executive Agencies to be Entrusted with Certain Tasks in the Management of Community Programs* COM(2001)808 final, replacing the earlier version COM (2000)788 final.

[52] Council Regulation 58/2003, supra n. 51, recitals 5–6.

[53] Ibid., Art. 2. Community program covers any activity, set of activities or other initiative which the relevant basic instrument or budgetary authorization requires the Commission to implement for the benefit of one or more categories of specific beneficiaries, by committing expenditure, Art. 2(b).

[54] Ibid., Art. 3(1).

[55] Ibid., Arts. 3(1)–(2).

[56] Ibid., Art. 3(2).

[57] Ibid., Arts. 3(3), 24(2).

[58] Ibid., Art. 24(1).

[59] Ibid., Art. 4.

[60] Ibid., Art. 10.

[61] Ibid., Art. 11.

[62] Ibid., Art. 8.

[63] Ibid., Art. 9.

[64] Ibid., Art. 18.

[65] Ibid., Art. 6(1).

[66] Ibid., Art. 6(2)(a)–(c).

[67] *Council Regulation 1605/2002*, supra n. 5, Art. 54(1).

[68] *Executive Agencies*, supra n. 51, Arts. 12–16, 20; *Council Regulation 1605/2002*, supra n. 5, Arts. 55–6.

69   *Executive Agencies*, supra n. 51, Arts. 11(3), 16(2).
70   Ibid., Art. 21(1).
71   Ibid., Art. 21(2).
72   *Council Reg. 1210/90 on the Establishment of the European Environment Agency* [1990]
     OJ L120/1, Art. 18.
73   COM (2000)788 final, Art. 21.
74   Case 249/83 *Parti Ecologiste – "Les Verts" v. European Parliament* [1986] ECR 1339.
75   Cases 193–4/87 *Maurissen v. Commission* [1989] ECR 1045.
76   *Council Reg. 40/94 on the Community Trade Mark* [1994] OJ L11/1, Art. 63.
77   *Report of the European Parliament on the Proposal for a Council Regulation laying
     down the Statute for Executive Agencies* A5–0216/2001, Amendment 12.
78   *Executive Agencies*, supra n. 51, Art. 22(2).
79   *Reforming the Commission*, supra n. 3, Vol. I, p. 10.
80   *Proposal for a Council Regulation*, supra n. 5, Explanatory Memorandum, p. 19.
81   *Council Regulation 1605/2002*, supra n. 5, Art. 54(2)(c).
82   See supra, pp.
83   *Communication from the Commission, Management of Community Programs by
     Networks of National Agencies* COM(2001)648 final.
84   Ibid., para. 3.1.
85   Ibid., para. 5.2.
86   Ibid., para. 4.1.
87   Ibid., para. 5.1.
88   Ibid., para. 5.3.
89   Court of Auditors, Special Report 16/2000, *On Tendering Procedures for Service
     Contracts under the Phare and Tacis Programs* [2000] OJ C350/1; Court of Auditors,
     Special Report 12/2000, *On the Management by the Commission of European Union
     Support for the Development of Human Rights and Democracy in Third Countries* [2000]
     OJ C230/1.
90   *Council Regulation 1605/2002*, supra n. 5, Art. 54(1).
91   Ibid., Art. 54(2).
92   Ibid., Art. 57(1).
93   Ibid., Art. 57(2).
94   *Council Regulation 1605/2002*, supra n. 5, Arts. 104–6.
95   Ibid., Arts. 90–91.
96   Ibid., Art. 93.
97   Ibid., Art. 94.
98   Second CIE, *supra* note 2, pars. 2.2.4–2.2.14.
99   There are clear analogies to reforms of the administrative landscape within national
     polities, such as the United Kingdom, with the shift to core departments, and Next Steps
     Agencies. *Improving Management in Government: The Next Steps* (1988); D.
     Goldsworthy, *Setting Up Next Steps: A Short Account of the Origins, Launch, and
     Implementation of the Next Steps Project in the British Civil Service* (HMSO, 1991).
100 Council Regulation 1605/2002, supra n. 5, Arts. 149–60.
101 Commission, *The Agricultural Situation in the European Union* (1995).
102 Commission, *Agenda 2000: For a Stronger and Wider Union* (1997).

[103] 25 March 1999.
[104] Commission, *Enlargement and Agriculture: An Integration Strategy for the EU's Member States* (2002).
[105] Second CIE, *supra* note 2, par. 3.6.3.
[106] Council Reg. *729/70 on the Financing of the Common Agricultural Policy* [1970] OJ L94/13.
[107] Ibid., Art. 4(1).
[108] Ibid., Art. 4(2). There is evidence of shift to pre-financing by Member States, *Council Regulation 1605/2002*, supra n. 5, Arts. 151–52.
[109] Reg. 729/70, supra n. 106, Art. 8(1).
[110] Ibid., Art. 8(2).
[111] Ibid., Art. 9.
[112] *Comm. Reg. 1663/95 Laying Down Detailed Rules for the Application of Council Regulation 729/70 Regarding the Clearance of Accounts of the EAGGF Guarantee Section* [1995] OJ L158/6, Art. 1.
[113] Reg. 1663/95, supra n. 112, Art. 3.
[114] *Council Reg 1287/95 Amending Regulation 729/70 on the Financing of the Common Agricultural Policy* [1995] OJ L125/1, Art. 1.
[115] *Council Reg. 1258/99 on the Financing of the Common Agricultural Policy* [1999] OJ L160/103. See also, *Proposal for a Council Regulation Amending Regulation 1258/99* COM(2000)494 final.
[116] Second CIE, *supra* note 2, pars. 3.13.2–3.13.5.
[117] Reg. 1258/99, supra n. 115, Art. 4.
[118] Reg. 1663/95, supra n. 112, Art. 3.
[119] Supra n. 106. The provision has remained unchanged in Reg. 1258/99.
[120] Second CIE, *supra* note 2, par. 3.7.5.
[121] Second CIE, *supra* note 2, par. 3.7.5.
[122] Supra n. 106.
[123] Second CIE, *supra* note 2, par. 3.9.6.
[124] Ibid., par. 3.9.6.
[125] Supra n. 112.
[126] Court of Auditors, Special Report 21/98, *Concerning the Accreditation and Certification Procedures as Applied to the 1996 Clearance of Accounts for EAGGF-Guarantee Expenditure* [1998] OJ C389/1, para. 2.11.
[127] Court of Auditors, Special Report 22/2000, *On Evaluation of the Reformed Clearance of Accounts Procedure* [2000] OJ C69/1, paras. 13–23.
[128] Ibid., paras. 31–47.
[129] Second CIE, *supra* note 2, par. 3.9.10.
[130] Reg. 1258/99, supra n. 115, Art. 7(4).
[131] *Comm. Dec. 94/442 Setting Up a Conciliation Procedure in the Context of the Clearance of Accounts of the EAGGF Guarantee Section* [1994] OJ L182/45.
[132] It is composed of five members appointed by the Commission after consulting the EAGGF Committee. The members must be highly qualified in EAGGF Guarantee Section matters or in the practice of financial audit. Comm. Dec. 94/442, supra n. 131, Art. 3, as amended by Comm. Dec. 2000/649 [2000] OJ L272/41.

133 Ibid., Art. 1(1)(b).
134 Ibid., Art. 1(2).
135 Court of Auditors, Special Report 22/2000, supra n. 127, paras. 65-68.
136 Ibid., para. 72.
137 Second CIE, *supra* note 2, par. 3.11.1.
138 Supra n. 106.
139 Case 11/76 *Netherlands v. Commission* [1979] ECR 245, para. 6.
140 Ibid., para. 8.
141 Reg. 1258/99, supra n. 115.
142 Case C-235/97 *France v. Commission* [1998] ECR I-7555, para. 45; Case C-278/98 *Netherlands v. Commission* [2001] ECR I-1501, para. 92.
143 Case C-253/97 *Italy v. Commission* [1999] ECR I-7529, para. 6; Case C-278/98 *Netherlands v. Commission*, supra n. 142, para. 39.
144 Case C-54/95 *Germany v. Commission* [1999] ECR I-35, para. 35; Case C-278/98 *Netherlands v. Commission*, supra n. 142, para. 40.
145 Case C-278/98 *Netherlands v. Commission*, supra n. 142, para. 41.
146 *Commission Report on Simplification of Agricultural Legislation* COM(2001)48 final.

III. Comparative Contexts

...

7.

Judicial Independence in Latin America: The Lessons of History in the Search for an Always Elusive Ideal

Javier A. Couso

Introduction

Ever since his 1964 book *Law and Politics in the Supreme Court*—a primer in the then-nascent field of "political jurisprudence"—Martin Shapiro has managed to make insightful contributions to the understanding of the relationship between law and politics, or, as it is now often said, "the politics" of law and courts. A major example of such a contribution is his groundbreaking work, *Courts: A Comparative and Political Analysis* (1981a), in which Shapiro articulated one of the most powerful analytical accounts of judicial institutions available. In this book, Shapiro emphasized the crucial role played by judicial independence for the legitimacy of courts, while also noting the complexity involved in the achievement of this ideal, particularly with regard to autonomy from the government.

In this chapter, I analyze this subject as it plays out in the context of new and non-consolidated democracies, specifically in Latin America, which includes many states organized on the United States model of separation of powers. As we shall see, Shapiro's insights on judicial independence, and his proverbial capacity to connect the study of the courts to the larger political system, provides an excellent point of departure for the analysis of judicial independence in fragile democracies, such as those of Latin America, in which there is a strong separation of powers regime.

The chapter is organized as follows. First, it briefly introduces the importance of, and obstacles to, the implementation of judicial independence in new democracies. The next two sections address the concept of judicial independence, describing the many dimensions of this phenomenon and then focusing on so-called "external independence" from government. This is followed by a case study of the Latin American country of Chile, where a reasonable degree of external judicial independence has been achieved, and which may provide valuable lessons for other new and non-consolidated democracies organized as a system of separation of powers.

As we shall see in this chapter, the Chilean experience is of interest because it suggests that judicial independence in presidential regimes may be dependent on the prior existence of a strong legislative branch, which manages to become independent from the president, and can then provide the courts with the necessary political backing to assert themselves against the latter, which is the traditional enemy of judicial independence in new democracies.

The Rule of Law, Judicial Independence and Non-Consolidated Democracies

To assert that judicial independence is an essential element of the rule of law is to state a truism.[1] We know that without a judicial branch that adjudicates impartially the law of the land, the rule of law cannot exist. The problem consists in figuring out how to actually facilitate independent judiciaries in regions where the rule of law has traditionally been an elusive ideal, as is the case in Latin America and most non-consolidated democracies.[2]

When it comes to the problem of furthering judicial independence, most of the available literature tends to concentrate on the structure and organization of the judiciary, and typically prescribes the constitutional entrenchment of transparent and a-political mechanisms of appointment and removal of judges, and the introduction of autonomous bodies in charge of the process of judicial recruitment and promotion.[3] This intellectual effort eventually received the backing of multilateral organizations such as the World Bank and the Inter-American Development Bank, which over the last decade have been promoting the implementation of a series of policy innovations in this field, including the introduction of national councils of the judiciary and other mechanisms directed at strengthening judicial independence in developing countries.

Although it is still too soon to evaluate the actual impact of these structural reforms on judicial independence (since they have been in place for less than two decades, which in constitutional history is a rather short period of time), there are already indications that such new procedures are not by themselves enough to guarantee judicial independence. Indeed, there has been rather brutal interference by the executive branch into the judiciary in Latin American countries that have already implemented reforms aimed at furthering judicial independence, such as Venezuela under Hugo Chavez in 1999, Peru under Alberto Fujimori in 1992, and Argentina under Carlos Menem in 1990. This suggests that the mere introduction of changes in the formal structures of appointment and promotion of judges is not enough to guarantee judicial independence in non-consolidated democracies.[4] This rather disappointing experience with constitutionally entrenched judicial independence is not restricted to Latin America, but has also been evident in other transitional regimes, such as Russia in 1993 when President Boris Yeltsin disbanded the first Constitutional Court.

Given this rather frustrating record, it seems that although convenient, constitutional engineering aimed at giving formal autonomy to the courts is not sufficient to actually obtain judicial independence. As Peter Russell has put it:

> In emergent liberal democracies, where there has not been a strong tradition of judicial independence, it may be wise to ensure that judicial independence is included in the new constitution's catalogue of fundamental principles .... But valuable as such constitutional languages may be in these contexts, particularly from a symbolic and educational perspective, it would be foolish to rely on constitutional protections—and their interpretation by the judiciary—for the implementation of judicial independence. (Russell 2001, 22–23)[5]

All this suggests that it is necessary to return to the drawing board and try to understand what other elements impinge on the institutionalization of judicial independence. In order to better understand the nature of the phenomena we are dealing with, it is important to address the question of what exactly it is meant by the concept of judicial independence.

Conceptualizing Judicial Independence

The notion of judicial independence is highly complex and equivocal. To begin with, it is of course related to the idea of courts, which, according to Martin Shapiro's classic definition, entails an independent judge applying preexisting legal norms to reach a dichotomous decision after an adversarial proceeding (Shapiro 1981a, 1).[6]

As Shapiro himself recognizes, of the four "prototypic" elements just mentioned, judicial independence is the one that contributes the most to the social legitimacy of courts.[7] Indeed, the notion that judicial adjudication ought to be made by an independent judge constitutes an important ideal expected from courts everywhere in the world.

Having said so, there are two different levels of judicial independence that play a role in the adjudicative function of courts. The first is the independence of a court from the parties to a lawsuit. This type of judicial independence, also known as "judicial impartiality," is a universal goal of any judicial system. Indeed, without impartiality it is hard to conceive how the rule of law would be possible at all.

There is, however, more to the idea of judicial independence, as Martin Shapiro reminds us. In fact, when political scientists talk about judicial independence, they typically have in mind a different issue, that is, the political autonomy of the judiciary from the other branches of government. At first glance, it would appear that this concern is just an extension of the problem of securing judicial impartiality writ large. That is, the point of ensuring the political autonomy of the judiciary would presumably be to maintain its impartiality even in cases in which the government is a party to a case, thus maintaining a measure of equality among the parties. In effect, there is a sense in which this is precisely what the political independence of the judiciary can offer. But there is more to it. Judicial independence is also critical in a far more relevant situation: when a court is asked to intervene in protection of an individual whose rights are being threatened by the police or other administrative agency acting in violation of the law. This protective function of courts, which can be traced to the habeas corpus writ and the Magna Carta, requires politically independent courts to be able to stand up to the government. This sort of independence, however, is harder to obtain, because the courts themselves have historically been part of the state bureaucracy, and thus, dependent on the government.[8]

As Martin Shapiro has pointed out:

> In the most basic and usually the least important sense, independence would mean that the judge had not been bribed or was not in some other way a dependent on one of the parties. But when we ensure this kind of independence, by creating the office of judge within some governmental structure, in a far more important sense he is not independent, for he is a dependent of those for whom he holds office. Thus explicators of the prototype have come to define independence not so much as independence from the contending parties as independence from those to whom the judge owes his office. (1981a, 19–20)

Notice that here Shapiro argues that the independence of the courts from the government is in a sense more important than judicial impartiality vis-à-vis the parties. The irony is that the judicial impartiality is a function of state support to the courts (i.e., providing them with the help of the coercive power of the state—the police—and material resources to conduct their adjudicative function without feeling the pressure of the parties). Indeed, the very governmental support that makes judicial impartiality possible paradoxically makes the political independence of the courts such a difficult task.

All the above suggests that to develop judicial independence in the less trivial, more political, sense consists of a two-step process: First, a fully formed nation-state ought to exist. In other words, the "Hobbesian" problem of ensuring public order and the monopoly of state coercion, rule-making and adjudication has to be finished (not a self-evident proposition in some areas of Latin America). Second, only when a fully developed state already exists can the courts start to slowly consolidate their functional autonomy from the executive and legislative powers. This is apparent in the history of judicial institutions in Latin America, which follows a similar path as the one experienced by the English courts described by Shapiro (1981a, 65–125), although with a considerable delay in time, as we shall see later in this chapter.

In addition to the autonomy of the judiciary from government, another aspect of judicial independence that is often highlighted if the so-called "internal independence," that is, the autonomy enjoyed by lower judges vis-à-vis their superiors, which can also be a source of undue influence on the rulings of the former.[10] This dimension of judicial independence can be in fact as important as that which concerns the autonomy of the judiciary as a whole (that is, vis-à-vis the other branches of government and other societal forces), which is called "external independence."

The recognition of the many facets of judicial independence is all the more relevant once it is understood that often the strategies designed to further say, external independence, can actually undermine internal independence (and vice versa). This has been the case with what Mirjan Damaska (1986) calls "hierarchical" judicial systems—characteristic of continental European and other civil law countries, in which a highly bureaucratized and disciplined judiciary manages to isolate itself from the "political" branches of government and thereby gain external independence, while at the same time the superior courts use their autonomy to exercise tight control over the lower courts through their power to recruit and promote judges within the hierarchy, thus, sacrificing internal independence.

All the above makes the elaboration of a general theory or model of judicial independence rather complicated. Therefore, it is important for any study of this issue to start specifying with clarity the domain or dimension of judicial independence that it will address. Following this prescription, I want to make clear that the goal of this chapter is to analyze the obstacles that the Latin American judiciaries face when attempting to gain "external independence" from the government (the executive branch), which has been the historical enemy of judicial autonomy in the region—as has also been the case in other non-consolidated democracies elsewhere. The reason for this choice is of course the wide scholarly agreement that the most important threat to judicial independence in Latin America has historically been of an external nature (Rosenn 1987; Verner 1984; Dodson and Jackson 2001).

The Contours of the "External Independence" of the Courts

Although the ideal of judicial independence involves the notion that courts perform their sensitive work independently from all external sources of influence—public or private—the most challenging task in developing nations has been the attainment of reasonable degrees of judicial independence from the government, which has historically been tempted to engage in what was known in the former communist regimes of Eastern Europe as "telephone justice," an expression meant to convey the idea that an authority of the government calls a judge in order to press her to rule in a way that pleases the administration.

As with the other dimensions of judicial independence, the external autonomy of the courts involves the relationship of the courts with other entities. In the case of new democracies, the issue is how the judiciary relates to the other bodies of the political system. Given this, it is rather surprising that most analyses of judicial independence in new democracies fail to specifically address this problem from the perspective of the rest of the players of this drama, that is the legislative and executive branch. This neglect is particularly puzzling in the case of presidential regimes such as those of Latin America, in which there is a clear separation and interaction of powers between congress, the president, and the judiciary. Given the nature of this interaction, it is in fact unfortunate that most analyses and proposals for furthering judicial independence in the region limit themselves to either formalist solutions such as constitutional and legal engineering or, when they dare study the issue from a more politological point of view, focus exclusively on the relationship between courts and the administration, while leaving the role of congress out of the picture.

The lack of any analysis of the role that the legislative branch can play in new democracies in presidential regimes is all the more unsatisfactory, because it does not take into account that in this "game" of three basic actors, the potential alliance between congress and the judiciary represents the best chance for the latter to achieve a minimum of judicial independence that allows it to perform its judicial function in a proper way. Of course, any attempt to approach the issue of judicial independence from this perspective presupposes the existence of a political party system sufficiently organized so that it allows congress to exhibit a minimum of institutional differentiation from the executive branch (something that is not often the case in new democracies), which in turn makes the notion of a three party game meaningful. When this is the case, there are important incentives for congress to actually support the judiciary's independence vis-à-vis the executive branch.

The most evident such incentive is that an independent set of courts that honestly attempts to implement the statutes approved by the legislative branch operates as a de facto agent of congress, since it is the ultimate implementer of the decisions made by the latter. Given this important role as collaborator of the legislature, there are strong functional incentives for congress to actually defend the autonomy and professionalism of the courts.[11]

As we shall see in the following section of this chapter, this sort of institutional partnership between the legislative and the judicial branch was precisely the key factor contributing to the independence of the Chilean judiciary, providing an historical example of the operation of this model.

The Struggle for External Judicial Independence in Chile

Within the context of Latin America, Chile distinguishes itself for having a highly institutionalized state apparatus, capable of delivering governance with efficacy. This feature, which in the developed world is taken for granted, is nonetheless, still tenuously realized in most of Latin America, a region where often the state does not even control all the territory under its formal jurisdiction. The reason for Chile's early and successful process of state-formation is still a matter of inquiry among both historians and social scientists, but it is often said to have roots in events that took place over the nineteenth century.[12]

As a result of this achievement, Chile has a public administration characterized by degrees of transparency and adherence to legality that are rare in the region. This has allowed the country to exhibit levels of corruption comparable to that of Organization for Economic Co-operation and Development (OECD) countries (Hodess 2003). More relevant for this chapter, Chile has a judicial branch that is widely regarded as an independent branch of government (some observers would argue that it is too autonomous from society as a whole).[13]

What makes the study of the process by which the Chilean judiciary obtained independence from the government relevant for the topic of this chapter, is the fact that Chile shares with the rest of Latin America many common social and cultural characteristics, as well as a similar constitutional structure. We now turn to the account of the relationship between law and politics in Chile, particularly as it pertains to judicial independence. The analysis relies heavily on the legal and constitutional history of Chile, particularly that of the period in which judicial independence became institutionalized, towards the end of the nineteenth century.[14]

The Judicial Function in Colonial Chile

Legal and judicial mechanisms played a crucial role in the bureaucratic structure of the Spanish Empire. Indeed, a large part of the royal bureaucracy in America consisted of legally trained officials familiar with the complex set of laws and regulations decreed by the King since the beginning of the conquest. This abundant legislation regulated everything from economic and commercial matters to religious and criminal matters. The monarchy exercised tight control of its overseas territories with the help of a sophisticated administrative apparatus which enabled it to rule over vast areas located thousands of miles away, in an era in which transportation and communication technologies were still very primitive (Perry 1990; Góngora 1975; Gibson 1964; Morse 1954, 71–93). In this governmental scheme, the judiciary was considered to be part and parcel of the large royal administrative apparatus designed to rule over the American dominions by the Spanish Empire. The intimate connection between governing and adjudicating then prevalent was considered natural, as it was in most monarchical regimes before the emergence of constitutional monarchies.[15]

The administrative regime implemented by the Crown included delegation of royal powers to the *viceroys, oidores*, and *corregidores*, which were considered to be direct representatives of the Crown in Spanish America. The viceroys were the top executive officers in charge of the administration, taxation and defense of the territories under their care. Below the viceroys, but not their subordinates, was a secondary tier of officials, the *oidores*, who made up the *real audiencias,* followed by the *corregidores*, in charge of the government over more peripheral areas.

The vast powers delegated by the King to the viceroys and the other colonial authorities were counter-balanced with the royal obsession of having a vigilant eye over all his representatives in America, in order to minimize the loss of the great wealth produced by the American territories, as well as the abuses of power by the Crown's representatives. Monitoring the authorities was not an easy task due to the precarious means of communication and transportation then available, but was accomplished through a variety of cleverly designed mechanisms. Prominent among these were first, a bureaucratic structure characterized by redundancy and overlapping among the top colonial authorities, each of them keeping an eye on one another and reporting any illegality or irregularity directly to the King, and second, a set of quasi-judicial procedures designed to evaluate the performance of those authorities.

The most salient example of overlapping authority enjoyed by different royal offices, was that between the powers of the *viceroys* and the *audiencias*. Indeed, although the viceroys had mostly executive functions, they were also in charge of some judicial matters. Conversely, the *audiencias*, the top judicial bodies in the seaborne territories, also had important executive functions. This overlap of governmental functions worked as a system of checks and balances, since the shared jurisdiction was a constant source of distrust and often hostility among these royal agencies, which, in turn, contributed to the King's control of each of them.

Strictly speaking, the "judiciary" had a pyramidal structure with the King at its pinnacle, followed by the rest of the courts. In fact, the Spanish crown exercised tight control over the judicial function, both because the King was the supreme "court" of appeals, and through the practice of delegating jurisdictional functions to agencies enjoying both executive and judicial functions. As a result of this legacy, although the new independent states of Latin America formally adopted the republican separation of powers doctrine in their constitution, in practice, the judiciary was long understood to be part and parcel of the administrative apparatus of the government, and therefore, heavily dependent on the executive power. Consistent with the generally centralizing and absolutist spirit of the whole structure of government, the King was the supreme judicial authority. In practice, however, the immense distance separating Spain from America made appeals to the King exceedingly expensive and slow. This made the *real audiencia* the effective court of last resort in the American territories.

In addition to the regular system of courts just described, the Crown authorized special courts for the protection of the natives against abuses by the white population,[16] as well as special commercial courts (*cabildos*) to deal with commercial disputes. Moreover, the traditional military and ecclesiastical courts existing in Spain at the time of conquest also had jurisdiction over cases involving military men, regular priests, and the members of the religious orders in Spanish America. All these parallel justice systems were linked at the top to the King's justice.

The nature of the colonial organization of the judiciary—in particular the fact that the administration of justice was often exercised by the executive authorities—may be at the root of the traditional difficulty experienced by Latin America's courts in achieving independence from government intervention. Indeed, this factor seems to have been at work in the failure of the courts to become truly autonomous from the government even though the republican constitutions that followed the imperial regime solemnly recognized a constitutional separation of powers and guarantee judicial independence.[17]

State, Law and Politics in Chile's State-Formation Period (1810–1890)

After its independence from Spain, Chilean leaders had to re-invent the architecture of government. The war of independence against the Spanish Crown (1810–1818), made the adoption of monarchical regimes politically unpalatable to most patriots.[18] Moreover, the *creole* elite, which took hold of power, was heavily influenced by the French and American revolutions and the republican ideals represented by them. Therefore, the only viable system of government for the new independent nation appeared to be some kind of republican regime.

Following a brief period of political instability (1818–1830), in which a number of constitutional experiments were tried, including a short-lived attempt to introduce federalism,[19] Chile finally achieved political stability when the conservatives defeated the liberals in the civil war of 1829–1830. In the aftermath of this conflagration, the former acquired a tight grip on power and set themselves to institutionalizing a new 'conservative order.' This found institutional expression in a new Constitution, promulgated in 1833.

The constitutional design introduced by the 1833 charter represented a response by the conservatives to what they regarded as the unrealistic attempt to introduce a liberal-democratic regime in a nation they thought was not ready for such a form of government. Indeed, beneath republican forms, the Constitution of 1833 established a highly centralized and autocratic regime centered on the president. This reliance on a quasi-monarchical president has led some commentators to contend that republican Chile did not fundamentally change the political ethos prevalent in the colonial era, characterized by respect for traditional authority, acceptance of social hierarchies, and authoritarian government. According to this approach, in spite of the change in Chile's political regime from the bureaucratic patrimonial state of the colonial era to the republican state of the nineteenth century, a quasi-imperial regime remained intact.

The authority of the president was supreme. The constitution gave him not just vast administrative powers, but also legislative functions, which he shared with a bicameral congress, and even some judicial tasks. In addition to these, the Constitution of 1833 gave the president the power to declare "states of emergency," allowing the government to suspend civil and political rights during times of social unrest. Although the president needed congressional approval for declaring a state of emergency, this requirement could be waived when congress was in recess, in which case the president could decree an emergency on his own and obtain approval later. This was precisely what often happened, because congress was in recess most of the year (in one year, 1838, it did not function at all), thus, giving the executive the opportunity to restrict and suspend individual liberties at will, and then to obtain retroactive congressional confirmation of the states of emergency.

Unfortunately, the use of "emergency powers" proved to be a key political tool for the executive power during the formative years of the Chilean state. Indeed, as Loveman (1993) documents, during the thirty years of the "authoritarian republic" (1833–1861), the president ruled with the aid of emergency powers nearly one-third of the time, thus rendering moot the individual rights solemnly declared by the charter (see also Collier 1995, 55).

The new constitutional structure centralized political power both at the level of the central government, with the president being the overriding political power over a subordinated Congress and Judiciary, and territorially, with the capital controlling provincial governments through presidential delegates known as *intendentes*.

The president was elected by a very small minority of the population, since the franchise was restricted to approximately five percent of the adult male population under an 1833 electoral law which explicitly denied voting rights to peasants and artisans (*jornaleros y peones gañanes*), the clergy, and the lower ranks of the armed forces.[20] In addition to these explicit prohibitions, the 1833 Electoral Law added stringent literacy and property requirements, further limiting the franchise.[21]

The Judicial Branch and Its Gradual Path Toward Independence from Government

It is difficult to assess the character and role of the Chilean courts in the nineteenth century because there are almost no studies addressing this issue (compare Fruhling 1984). The traditional legal history dominating the field among Chilean scholars, which gives priority to the study of the development of legal doctrine over the actual performance of the legal system, is in part to blame.[22] Although in recent years there have been a few studies attempting to remedy the dearth of scholarship on this matter (de Ramón 1989), the fact is that we still know very little about the actual behavior of the courts during the nineteenth century, a critical time in which Chile introduced sweeping changes in its legal system in an attempt to modernize both its substantive law and the judicial process from its patrimonial bureaucratic background to a regime of codified law. With that in mind, I will summarize the few things we do know about the Chilean judiciary in the nineteenth century, especially concerning its independence.

Soon after independence, the Chilean patriots faced complications deriving from the fact that the imperial bureaucracy, including most judicial offices, had been staffed with Spaniards, not *creoles*, thus, requiring the training of new judicial personnel from the ranks of the Chilean patriots. In addition to the necessary changes in judicial personnel, soon after independence Chile started to introduce modifications to the structure of the judiciary, such as the establishment of new lower courts and courts of appeals (which replaced the *audiencias*), and the even more significant introduction of the first Supreme Court of Chile.[23] This was followed by special legislation introduced in 1824, the *Reglamento de Administración de Justicia*, which was the first systematic piece of legislation regulating the functioning of the judiciary since Chile's independence.[24] According to this framework, the judicial branch was hierarchically organized around the Supreme Court located in Santiago, which was the top court, and three Courts of Appeals (one in Santiago and the other two in the provincial cities of *La Serena* and *Concepcion*). Immediately below in the judicial hierarchy were the numerous courts of general jurisdiction, followed by an even larger group of courts under the wing of the executive power, the *juzgados de subdelegación* and the *juzgados de distrito*. Parallel to the regular judicial structure, these executive-sponsored courts maintained special jurisdiction, inherited from colonial times, over ecclesiastical, military and commercial matters.

The political instability experienced by Chile in its first decade as an independent state contributed to the administrative disarray of the judicial system. This disarray was not, however, solely a function of political anarchy, but the result of a judicial system that, albeit structured on a republican constitutional context, was still working with colonial laws and procedures.[25] Indeed, for a number of decades after independence, the Chilean courts were left with the task of administering justice under a complex mix of legislation enacted by the post-independence authorities and legislation from the colonial period that remained in force. [26]

Even though the Chilean Constitution of 1833 solemnly declared the independence of the judiciary from the government, the judiciary maintained the subordinated status it had had in colonial times, continuing to be regarded as just another set of agencies of the state providing a public good—in this case, justice. The fact that the Constitution gave the president and his "Council of State" the power to nominate judges was, of course, an important source of dependence by the judiciary on the executive.[27] The entanglement of judicial and administrative functions was more apparent in the countryside and in small towns, where over ninety percent of the population lived. Indeed, during most of the nineteenth century, representatives of the executive power in the provinces and towns, the *gobernadores* and *intendentes*, served as judges as well.[28] Equally troubling, most cases arising deep in the countryside were legally within the "jurisdiction" of the landowners where the conflicts had arisen (Fruhling 1984, 59). Such overlapping of executive and judicial powers in the same individuals led a Chilean constitutional observer to note that many judges of the period had an unacceptable "participation in the electoral struggles of the time, unconditionally giving the government their support in its electoral intervention practices" (Guerra 1929, 452–53).

The overwhelming dependency of the judiciary on the executive power (which, as I have stressed before, represented the continuation under republican forms of a centuries-old colonial tradition of treating the judiciary as part of the government bureaucracy), would only start to change toward the last third of the nineteenth century, thanks to the action taken by a legislative branch which had itself managed to become autonomous from the president sometime around the middle of the century. This process unfolded in the following way. First, members of congress opposed to the president managed to have a constitutional reform approved that prohibited the reelection of the president, a measure that contributed to reduce the hitherto formidable status of the latter in Chile's fabric of government. That was followed by a series of reforms aimed at separating the boundaries of the legislative and executive branches, such as the constitutional amendment making incompatible the position of parliamentary deputy and minister of government (as well as any other presidential appointment), and eliminating the president's electoral intervention. Finally, a more empowered legislative branch was able to take away from the president his control over the judiciary, which had been under his power since the 1830s. In Fruhling's words, "The constitutional and legal amendments that were enacted from 1871 to 1874 not only strengthened the role of congress vis a vis the executive, but they also enhanced the autonomy of the judges" (1984, 51–52).

The first important reform concerning the judiciary was a constitutional amendment that, in 1874, restricted presidential oversight of the official conduct of judicial personnel.[29] As important was the approval in 1875 of the landmark *Law of Organization of the Judiciary*, which, for the first time in Chile's republican history, organized in a systematic way the judicial branch, providing that the simultaneous exercise of judicial and executive posts was prohibited and that the judiciary would have jurisdiction over most of the judicial disputes of the country (many of which have been distributed in special jurisdictions of military, administrative and religious nature). This last set of reforms allowed the judicial branch to become functionally separate from the rest of the administration, which in turn provided it with more legitimacy (Fruhling 1984, 58). Furthermore, the laws regulating the organization and functions of the judiciary allowed the Chilean courts to enter an era characterized by an increased professionalization and specialization (Fruhling 1984, 53).

The increased institutional autonomy of the judiciary from the administration did not mean, however, that the courts achieved complete political independence. To the contrary, in the years of the so-called "parliamentary republic" (1891–1920), characterized by the preeminence of congress over the president, the judiciary's subordination to the political branches shifted from its traditional dependency on the executive to an equally strong dependency on the legislative branch. Signaling this change was the role that congress started to play in the nomination of judicial personnel between 1891 and 1924, through its partial control of the 'Council of State,' the body in charge of pre-selecting candidates to fill judicial vacancies.[30] At any rate, given the more fragmented nature of the legislative branch, as well as the modernization processes taking place in the judiciary at the time, the net result was increased political autonomy for the Chilean judiciary.

In 1925, a new Constitution increased the autonomy and powers of the courts by giving the judiciary a role in the nomination process for judicial vacancies, thus, ending the previous government control of judicial nominations. In addition to this, the Constitution of 1925 introduced a limited mechanism for judicial review of the constitutionality of legislation. Indeed, article 86 of the new charter established that the Supreme Court could declare "non-applicable" laws that it deemed in violation of the constitution. Although a ruling on the unconstitutionality of a given statute would only be applied to the case at hand—that is, had merely an inter partes effect—it was a major innovation that raised expectations among constitutional scholars of a new era marked by the enforcement of constitutional supremacy by a more independent judiciary.[31]

Although the autonomy-oriented clauses of the new constitution of 1925 would eventually contribute to a more independent judiciary, the years immediately following the passage of it witnessed a short period of regression into government intervention in the courts, when the first military dictator in a century took power in 1927. This regime, which lasted until 1932, repeated the pattern of government control of the judiciary in the absence of an autonomous legislative branch.[32]

Once constitutional rule was restored and Congress was reinstated in 1932, the judicial branch regained its hard-won autonomy from government, this time enjoying a long period of stability, which lasted for over fifty years, until 1973, when another military dictatorship would threaten the independence of the judiciary. During this long period of institutional stability, the Chilean judicial branch developed a strong corporate identity, consolidating a peculiar understanding of its political independence that led it to isolate itself completely from the political system, in what has been characterized by some scholars as judicial solipsism (Peña 1994). Such reticence to get involved in the political fray, nonetheless, had important consequences, such as the Chilean Supreme Court's highly deferential use of its power, granted in the 1925 charter, to review the constitutionality of legislation. Indeed, there is widespread agreement among Chilean constitutional scholars on the failure of the Supreme Court to actively use these review powers (Brahm 1999; Gomez 1999; Peña 1996). This failure, however, did not extend to the ordinary (that is, non-constitutional) judicial business of the Chilean courts, which was adjudicated with professionalism and independence.

The calm and stability enjoyed by the courts lasted for over half a century, until 1973, when the second military coup of Chile's history occurred. As in the previous military regime, the judicial branch lost its independence from government after the latter's suppression of the legislative branch. The loss of autonomy from the new military regime is summarized by the response given by a top Supreme Court justice to an opposition politician who approached him to complain about the scandalous inaction of the courts vis-à-vis the systematic human rights violations of the time. The justice's brief answer was: "The time of law will come later."[33]

Thus, again deprived of the protection of the legislative branch, the judiciary sunk into dependency toward the government, limiting itself to the adjudication of routine cases. This time, however, the courts' lack of independence would have tragic consequences due to the fact that Pinochet's dictatorship, unlike that of the 1920s, engaged in gross human rights violations. But as happened after the end of military rule in 1932, once General Pinochet's regime ended and constitutional rule was returned to Chile in 1990, the judiciary gradually recovered its independence from the executive branch.

Conclusion

Judicial independence represents one of the most crucial elements of the ideal of the rule of law. At its core, the idea is to let judges perform their dispute resolution tasks impartially and free from pressures from either government or the parties to a lawsuit. Although judicial independence has many dimensions, one of the most elusive aspects to implement in new democracies has been autonomy of the judiciary vis-à-vis the government.

Indeed, this aspect of judicial independence is of critical relevance in cases in which an individual or group asks the courts to protect it from illegitimate governmental action. In such cases, the existence of a politically independent judiciary can make the difference between life and death. At the end of the day, only independent courts can enforce the declarations of rights that most constitutional charters solemnly recognize. For this reason, the question of the best path toward the implementation of this important ideal remains one of the most challenging issues of the day, particularly in polities that have no or a minimal tradition of democracy and rule of law.

The problem with the prescriptions for achieving judicial independence that are typically offered, however, is that they tend to rely on constitutional engineering aimed at changing the structure of recruitment, promotion and retirement of judges, and other proposals of that sort. Such an approach fails to recognize that judicial independence from the government is mostly a political problem that needs to be analyzed by taking into account all the actors involved in the drama of contemporary politics. If this is so, it is crucial to consider the role that the legislative branch can play in helping the courts to become independent from the executive branch. When this exercise is performed, it is surprising how important the former can be in furthering judicial autonomy.

This is precisely what the historical trajectory of the Chilean judiciary reveals. Indeed, it was only when the legislature acquired a minimum of autonomy from the president that the courts started to separate from the administration. By the same token, on the two occasions in which Chile regressed into an authoritarian regime, the fall of congress led to the loss of judicial independence. This suggests that new democracies organized as presidential regimes should consider strengthening their legislatures if they want to obtain judicial autonomy. If the Chilean experience is of any guide, strong legislatures have powerful incentives for supporting judicial autonomy, because independent courts can operate as delegates of congress able to police the government's respect of the compromises between the two big players of the legislative 'game' in presidential regimes, where law is the product of a negotiated process between congress and the administration.

Notes

[1] The link between judicial independence and the rule of law has a long history. For a good analyses of this topic, see Rose-Ackerman (1999), Kriegel (1995), Shapiro (1994), and Elster and Slagstad (1988). It must be noted, however, that in recent years there have been some observers who have voiced the need for a measure of responsiveness of the courts to the rest of the political system, such as Owen Fiss (see below). The justification offered for demanding a minimum of political accountability—or, in other words, a degree of politicization—by the judiciary springs from the growing recognition that courts do not merely apply pre-existing law, but they also create law. In this scenario, the argument goes, a court system which is absolutely autonomous from—and indifferent to—the rest of the political system seems to violate democratic principles. This is the concern voiced by Owen Fiss, who writes (1993, 56–58)

> It is simply not true that the more insularity the better, for a judiciary that is insulated from the popularly controlled institutions of government—the legislative and executive branches—has the power to interfere with the actions or decisions of those institutions, and thus has the power to frustrate the will of the people....We are thereby confronted with a dilemma. Independence is assumed to be one of the cardinal virtues of the judiciary, but it must be acknowledged that too much independence may be a bad thing. We want to insulate the judiciary from the more popularly controlled institutions, but should recognize at the same time that some elements of political control should remain.

Note that Fiss' warning against too much judicial autonomy from the rest of the political system is premised on the power of the courts to interfere with the elected branches of government. His cautionary note on the perils of too much judicial independence is particularly relevant to constitutional adjudication, in which the judiciary or a special constitutional court can directly frustrate the policy preferences of the democratic delegates of the people. For all his point's intuitive appeal, however, Fiss' hypothetical "judicial dictatorships" constitute a rare species, even in countries with the most activist judiciaries (Dahl 1957; Rosenberg 1991).

[2] For a historical account of the difficulty experienced by Latin American countries in achieving a working rule of law, see Adelman (1999b) and Loveman (1993).

[3] For the case of Latin America, good examples of this literature are Larkins (1996, 610), Jarkin and Carrillo (1998), and Dakolias (1995, 168).

[4] In these countries, the government intervened the judicial branch in spite of the formal mechanisms aimed at guaranteeing judicial independence. For a review of the political context surrounding government interventions in these judicial systems, see Pásara (2003), Miller (2000) and (1994), and Schor (1999).

[5] Going even further in his skepticisms concerning the role of constitutionally entrenched judicial independence, Russell argues that, on top of not being a sufficient condition, to include the former in the constitution may not even be a necessary condition for obtaining judicial independence. He writes,

> Though constitutional entrenchment may be a useful devise for safeguarding judicial independence, the comparative record of liberal democracy does not obviously support the generalization that it is a necessary condition. Look around the world of the liberal democracies and at their actual experience and ask yourself whether it is really clear that the judiciary in countries like Israel, New Zealand, the United Kingdom, or Sweden–all countries that have not constitutionally entrenched judicial independence—have enjoyed less independence than their counterparts in countries with constitutional guarantees, for example, the United States amd Australia. (2001, 22)

[6] This simple ideal type (or "prototype," as Shapiro calls it) represents the distillation of what seems most essential to courts everywhere, and represent as close a universal model as it is possible to get of a commonsensical understanding of judging, one that Shapiro claims, gives them the basic political legitimacy or "social logic" of courts' (Shapiro 1981a, 1).

[7] In Shapiro's words

> Only the prototypic element of judicial independence remains relatively pure in the context of conflict resolution. For neither of the conflicting parties is likely to accept anything other than pure mediation from a third who is tied to his oponent. That is, so long as the third exercises any independent influence over the outcome, he must demonstrate his independence of the party who achieves the more favorable outcome if he is to achieve the consent of the less favored... (1981a, 16).

[8] And it is not only history, because even under modern conditions, the judiciary remains dependent on the government when it comes to the enforcements of adjudication. As Shapiro highlights, "Courts, we are repeatedly and rightly told, have neither the purse nor the sword. Perhaps more important, they rarely have the administrative resources to follow up on their resolutions" (1981a, 13).

[9] Ibid.

[10] This dimension of judicial independence is stressed by Peter Russell, who writes, "Judicial independence as a relational term does not refer to a single kind of relationship ——a single lack of dependency between two things. Judicial independence is best understood as a two-dimensional relationship. First, in terms of the sources of dependency, external controls and influences. Second, in terms of the targets of influence or control, the individual judge must be distinguished from the judiciary as a collective whole or institution" (Russell, 2001, 11) .

[11] Of course, it is possible that if the president's political party also gains control of congress, the dynamic just described could not develop, but this is not necessarily so.

[12] For an account of Chile's early state-formation process see Halperin-Donghi (1987, 295–320). Adelman and Centeno (1997) share Halperin-Donghi's conclusion on the highly institutionalized shape of the Chilean state.

[13] This is the position taken by Hilbink (1999a) and Correa (1999, 281–315).

[14] The choice of doing a historical analysis echoes Jeremy Adelman and Miguel Angel Centeno's call for an institutional analysis that is sensitive to history:

We think that the troubles of legality in Latin America beg larger contextual and historically-derived questions; they are not amenable to technocratic solutions (as Salinas once promised) nor remediable by reference to internal rejuggling of legal rules (as some jurists might contend). Legal regimes are not freestanding, but embedded, and part of this embeddedness is made of historical experience. (Adelman and Centeno 1997, 6)

[15] The congruence of judging and administering in imperial settings was also noted by Shapiro (1981a, 22).

[16] In Gibson's account of early colonial Mexico, criminal and civil cases involving Indians were heard and settled before native *alcaldes* (Gibson 1964, 180).

[17] The traditional conceptualization of courts as part and parcel of the government continued to inform Latin Americans attitudes towards the judicial system, even though this conception was contrary to the republican rhetoric and aspirations proclaimed by Latin American states since the time of independence. Thus, the persistence of old conceptions of the role of the judiciary exemplifies the paradigm in which, underneath the formal republican surface, the legacy of colonial patrimonialism retains some of its force.

[18] Nonetheless, the prospect of constitutional monarchy was not ruled out by a few *Creoles*, such as José de San Martín and Andrés Bello, who were originally attracted by the British monarchical model (see Jaksic 2001).

[19] The list of constitution-like charters adopted since the year of Chile's independence in 1810 include: the *Provisional Regulation* of 1811, the *Provisional Constitutional Regulation* of 1812, the *Regulation for the Provisional Government* of 1814, the *Constitution of 1818*, the *Constitution of 1822*, the *Constitution of 1823*, and the *Constitution of 1828*. For an account of Chile's constitutional history, see Harriet (1963).

[20] It is worth noting that these prohibitions were not stipulated by the Constitution of 1833, but only by the Electoral Law of the same year, which was evidently unconstitutional, because it unduly deprived large groups of voters of their franchise (see Huneeus 1880, 470).

[21] The Electoral Law of 1833 gave the municipal authorities, subordinates of the President of the Republic, the power to select the members of the so-called *Juntas Calificadoras*, the bodies in charge of conducting the electoral process, including the crucial decision of who had the franchise. These gave the President of the Republic almost absolute control over the electoral administration. It is interesting to note that the first electoral laws of the period explicitly forbade peasants and artisans from voting (see Huneeus, 1880, 450).

[22] This sort of legal history includes a variety of works, which rarely provide an appropriate historical or intellectual context. Examples include Carrasco Albano (1858), Bravo (1888) and Roldán (1913).

[23] The Supreme Court was then constitutionally recognized by article 156 of the Constitution of 1823. Although this constitutional charter was abrogated two years later, its clauses referring to the Supreme Court survived.

[24] The judicial clauses of the Constitution of 1823 and 1828 continued in existence after the promulgation of the Constitution of 1833, as prescribed by transitional articles 2 and 3 of the latter. To the basic framework set up by these constitutional and legal norms were added some minor reforms in 1843 and 1866 (see Huneeus 1880, 247).

25 Edwin Borchard has listed the following colonial laws as still having legal validity after independence of Chile. They include: (1) The decrees, ordinances, orders, and royal *cédulas* issued for America, and communicated by the Council of the Indies from May 1680 to the period of independence; (2) the *Recopilación of the Laws of Indies*; (3) The *Novísima Recopilación of the Laws of Spain*; (4) The *Leyes de Estilo*; (5) The *Fuero Real*; (6) The *Fuero Juzgo*; and (7) The *Siete Partidas* (see Borchard 1917, 383 and 385).

26 This appears to have been the same dilemma confronting the judiciary in other Spanish American countries. Indeed, as Jeremy Adelman's important work on the early republican era in Argentina shows, the crisis in the justice system after independence in Argentina derived in part from the clash between, on the one hand, a new political regime centered around republican forms and rhetoric and, on the other hand, a judicial sphere still anchored in the ways and forms of a radically different, absolutist regime. In the latter, such cornerstone ideals of republicanism as equality before the law did not exist. In fact, quite to the contrary, the legal and judicial practices under Spanish absolutism were premised on the critical role that status played in judicial procedures (see Adelman 1999b).

27 According to the Constitution of 1833, the Supreme Court prepared a list of candidates that was sent to the "Council of State," which, in turn, chose three candidates from among the names on that list. Finally, the President of the Republic was in charge of selecting the actual judge to the position to be filled from among the three candidates sent to him by his Council of State. The relevant clause of the Constitution, article 73, number 7th reads: "It is within the power of the President to: 7th Designate the Justices of the superior courts, as well as the Judges of First Instance within a list prepared by the Council of State...."

28 Huneeus reports that the *gobernadores* had jurisdiction on over "a hundred types of cases," in addition to what special legislation—such as a 1834 law on contracts between theater owners and artists and a 1842 law on roads—gave them (see Huneeus 1880, 236).

29 This last measure was adopted through a constitutional reform in 1874 (Fruhling 1984, 52). Fruhling explains that although the 1874 constitutional amendment reproduced the president's constitutional prerogative to exercise on oversight of judges established by the Constitution of 1833, it introduced a more formalized system (requiring the president to ask the *Ministerio Público* to enforce disciplinary measures before the proper court) for the performance of such important function. According to Fruhling, this change led to an increase in judicial autonomy.

30 According to Guerra, an important jurist of the first half of the twentieth century critical of the parliamentary regime that ruled over Chile from 1891 to 1924, the Congressional influence in the nominating process of judicial personnel contributed to what he called a "judicial parliamentarism" which, in his view, tended to "politicize the judiciary, lowering the quality of the judges, because most of the new judges were political caudillos, or subordinated to congressional caudillos" (Guerra 1929, 440).

31 Guerra, praising the new power given to the Supreme Court wrote, "This clause is of the highest relevance and would prove very useful, because it imports a corrective against possible abuses of the legislative power, and an important guarantee for the nation's inhabitants" (1929, 458–59).

32 The dictator at the time, Carlos Ibáñez del Campo, first shut down Congress, and then established a non-elected one that he completely dominated.

[33] The justice was Rafael Retamal, who replied in this way to the then leader of the opposition, Patricio Aylwin, who would later become President of the Republic once the dictatorship ended (see Aylwin 1998, 59). As this quotation and the historical record indicates, the judiciary lost its independence vis-à-vis the government under Pinochet's rule despite the formal declaration by the dictatorship tha it would "guarantee the full efficacy of the faculties of the Judicial Power and will respect the constitution and the laws of the republic as far as the circumstances allow it" (Decree Law No. 1 of the The Military Junta).

8.

Beyond Judicial Review: Ancillary Powers of Constitutional Courts

Tom Ginsburg

Introduction

Much of the literature on the global judicialization of politics consists of documenting the spread of constitutional review around the globe, first in Europe and increasingly in Asia, Africa and Latin America. The paradigm power of these courts is constitutional review, in which a court evaluates legislation, administrative action, or an international treaty for compatibility with the written constitution. It is natural that writers on the new constitutional courts have concentrated attention on judicial review, for it is here that the court's lawmaking power is at its apex. Relatively free of the threat of correction from other political actors, courts exercising judicial review are rather obviously policymaking bodies.[1] But in their understandable eagerness to assess new systems of review, scholars have paid little attention to the other functions of constitutional courts.

This chapter is concerned with what I will call the ancillary powers of constitutional courts, those powers that fall outside the prototypical constitutional review function described above.[2] Perhaps because of the very success of constitutional review as an institution, constitution-drafters have given new courts a wide range of other tasks. Just as Martin Shapiro (1991) has argued that scholars of American law and courts have paid too much attention to judicial review, so scholars of the new constitutional courts risk an incomplete understanding of courts as political institutions if they ignore these other powers of constitutional courts, which often place the courts in the midst of politically charged controversies. This chapter is a first attempt to call attention to these powers.

I will argue that many of these functions are in fact closer to the triadic social logic of courts as identified by Shapiro (1981a) than the prototypical function of constitutional review. This is because the essential function of courts in many of these cases is that of dispute resolution, pure and simple.

As we will see, the ancillary powers vary in the extent to which they require the court to refer to a constitutional text, and some of them do not involve the constitution even nominally. By moving away from the core task of constitutional courts, we actually highlight the basic social logic of courtness in their institutional design.

The chapter is organized as follows: I begin with a review of the recent literature on constitutional review as a lawmaking process. I then describe some of the ancillary powers of constitutional courts around the world, both as provided by constitutional text and as exercised in practice. I conclude by speculating on the tension that emerges between lawmaking and dispute resolution in the exercise of these ancillary powers.

Constitutional Review and Judicial Lawmaking

Constitutional review can be divided into two different kinds of tasks with very different political logics: dispute resolution among multiple lawmakers and protection of individual rights. Both of these involve constraint of present day political authorities on the basis of fundamental principles in the constitutional text. First, consider the logic of dispute resolution among multiple lawmakers. Here, we can include the classic federalist rationale for judicial review so apparent in the early history of the United States Supreme Court and in Hans Kelsen's model for the Austrian Constitutional Court. With two levels of lawmaking authority, each with its own area of competence, a neutral third party is needed to ensure that neither lawmaker steps over the boundary into the other jurisdictional domain. The oft-noted affinity between federalism and judicial review reflects this. [3]

We can also include horizontal separation of powers schemes as drawing on the logic of dispute resolution. Where two parallel bodies have different zones of lawmaking authority, a neutral third is needed to police the boundary. The scheme of divided lawmaking between the executive and legislature in the Constitution of Fifth Republic France is the paradigm example here (Stone Sweet 1992). The French system allows the Executive to make law by decree, and established a *Conseil Constitutionnel* in large part to keep parliamentary legislation from impinging on the Executive's zone of authority. In the United States, one can think of constitutional disputes over executive competence, such as the proper scope of the commander-in-chief power, or issues related to judicial control of administration in situations of congressional delegation to agencies. Each of these problems involves defining the boundary between multiple lawmakers, and enforcing the founding bargain that set up the institutions in the first place.

The second major function of judicial review is individual rights protection. The image here is of the judge as hero and policymaker. Rather than triadic dispute resolution among governmental bodies, the judge is siding with the individual against the mighty apparatus of the state to advance particular substantive goals of liberal democracy. The policymaking role of courts is more apparent here because the logic of dispute resolution does not really mask it. When the court substitutes its own judgment for that of the government or legislature, it cannot be doing anything other than policymaking.

Much work, by Shapiro and others, has shown how courts created to play the basic dispute resolving function can transform their role into one that involves much more explicit policymaking. Again, French experience provides a paradigm example. Some years after its creation, the *Conseil* discovered that of the 1789 French Declaration of the Rights of Man formed a part of the French Constitution (Stone Sweet 1992). This gave it a human rights mandate that it had not previously exercised. The similar transformation of the American Supreme Court from its early focus on centralizing federalism into a rights-guardian began before *Lochner*[4] and has expanded with fits and starts since then. Again, a court shifted from dispute resolver to rights protector over time.

Regardless of whether the court is conducting boundary-guarding dispute resolution or rights-enforcing constraint of government, a common thread in both forms of constitutional review is judicial lawmaking. This feature of lawmaking is inherent in the judicial and administrative process (Shapiro 1968, 1981a, 1986). In lieu of the Montesquieuan conception of rule-making as practiced solely by the legislature, we must accept judicial lawmaking if we are to characterize adjudication as applying general principles to particular cases. And if judges simply lie about what they are doing, that is part of the game, for their power is drawn from the image of applying pre-existing rules (Shapiro 1994).

The lawmaking function of constitutional review has been highlighted in two literatures bridging political science and law. The first is comparative work, by Stone Sweet and others, that focused initially on the *Conseil Constitutionnel* (Stone Sweet 1990, 1992, 1995). The French system of pre-promulgation abstract review highlights the lawmaking function, since the *Conseil*'s declarations of unconstitutionality almost always lead to revision and resubmission of the legislation to conform with the constitutional dictates of the *Conseil*. Stone Sweet observed that this type of review turns the *Conseil* into a specialized third chamber of the legislature (Shapiro 1999, 197). Stone Sweet used this insight to develop a broader "legislative" approach to abstract review, in which judicial lawmaking is not the particular and retrospective type identified by Shapiro, but rather shares with the legislative process the elaboration of general norms for prospective application.

The lawmaking function of constitutional courts is emphasized in a second literature that is emerging as the central paradigm in public law studies of law and courts, namely strategic accounts of judicial power. The core insight of the strategic model is that courts can make law, but are constrained by other actors in the political system. This work originated in the context of "dynamic" statutory interpretation in the United States (Eskridge 1994; Ferejohn and Weingast 1992). The court can adopt its preferred interpretation of a particular piece of legislation. Whether this judicial interpretation is stable depends on the preferences of other actors, conceived of in spatial terms as distance from their ideal policy preferences. If both Houses of Congress and the president disagree with the court and can agree on a more preferred interpretation, they will cooperate to pass new legislation overturning the court. The process then starts all over again. Over time, the court and Congress continue to develop the law together; the law is simply the equilibrium outcome of their games of power. Much empirical work has documented the back and forth of Congress and the Court engaging in "constitutional dialogues" in particular policy areas (Fisher 1988; Devins 1996; Epstein and Knight 1998).

This work has positive and normative implications. The positive implication is that judicial "activism" is a continuous variable reflecting the zone of space where other actors cannot agree on overturning judicially enacted policy. This means that the ability of courts to deviate from the desired preferences of politicians will vary as those preferences themselves diverge from each other. For example, judicial lawmaking power should expand in periods of divided government, since politicians will find it more difficult to agree (Whittington 2003). The constitutional structure will also play a key role in determining the extent of judicial power: In the proverbial state of other things being equal, more actors involved in the legislative process should lead to more policy space for the court to work in because of the difficulty of passing new legislation. It is thus, not surprising that courts in the United Kingdom, with its single house of parliament controlled by a legislative majority, are less active than courts in the United States, with weak parties and three separate institutions that must collaborate to make new law (Cooter and Ginsburg 1996). Nor is it surprising that the European

Court of Justice has a great deal of strategic space to operate in, with many diverse states involved in the formal lawmaking process (Stone Sweet, this volume; Cooter and Ginsburg 1998).

The key distinction between statutory and constitutional interpretation in this view is the greater difficulty of overruling the court in the constitutional context. Constitutional amendments are more difficult to obtain than ordinary legislation. A judicial decision to treat a policy area as a constitutional matter will render the court much more powerful, both because of the normative significance attached to the constitution, but also because overruling constitutional interpretation requires constitutional amendment.

This work on judicial lawmaking also has a normative implication. A judicial interpretation that deviates from the statutory or constitutional text may in fact be legitimate if it is within the tolerance zones of other sitting political actors. William Eskridge has argued forcefully for just this kind of "dynamic" approach to statutory interpretation (Eskridge 1994). The court's creativity plays a role in keeping the system up to date and saves the legislature the trouble of having to continually amend legislation. The positive observation of judicial lawmaking now has normative significance.

These two literatures, the comparative constitutional literature and the strategic model focused on the United States, are now coming together in comparative work on constitutional courts, describing how the extent of the "policy space" limits lawmaking in comparative terms (Epstein and Knight 2001). Weiler's work on the role of the European Court in "transforming" Europe implicitly supports this point of view (Weiler 1991). The story goes like this. In the early years of the European Communities, integration proceeded at a modest pace, but with the adoption of the Luxembourg compromise allowing any state to veto new law, the political organs of Europe became paralyzed. As the difficulty of passing legislation increased, the space of judicial discretion increased accordingly, and the Court became the primary vehicle for integration. Shapiro has suggested how this led to a backlash from the Member States who feared a judicially sanctioned "race to the bottom" in regulatory standards, so that the States eventually came together to develop and control a new program of integration (Shapiro 1992a, 51–52; Cooter and Ginsburg 1998). The Court's power was thus constrained, but it had played the key role in jump-starting European integration.

All this work on constitutional review and constitutional courts has developed the basic insight, that courts make law, into a sophisticated framework for understanding judicial power in particular political contexts. But the very success of the research program has obscured other questions.

Judicial power becomes equivalent to the extent of lawmaking discretion in any particular context. As we shall see, however, a complete survey of powers allocated to constitutional courts goes beyond lawmaking.

Ancillary Powers

Besides the core task of constitutional review of legislation and administrative action, constitutional courts have been granted other powers, including such duties as proposing legislation[5]; determining whether political parties are unconstitutional[6]; impeaching senior governmental officials[7]; and adjudicating election violations.[8] United States federal courts have some of these and other powers, including rulemaking,[9] and until recently a role in appointing special prosecutors.[10] Constitutional courts have been given a wide range of other powers that move even more far afield from the paradigm role of judicial review. The Constitutional Court of Belarus has the power to "submit proposals to the Supreme Council on the need for amendments and addenda to the Constitution and on the adoption and amendment of laws."[11] The Azerbaijani draft Constitution gave the constitutional court power to "dissolve parliament if it repeatedly passes laws that violate the Constitution,"[12] though this, thankfully, did not survive into the final draft. The South African constitutional court must certify the constitutions of provinces for conformity with the Constitution.[13] Armenia's constitutional court can supervise decisions on states of emergency.[14]

The Constitutional Court of Thailand, set up as part of an effort to clamp down on corruption, exercises a wide array of ancillary powers. It can confirm findings of and evaluate disclosures submitted to the new National Counter-Corruption Commission (NCCC), review whether any appropriations bill would lead to involvement of an elected official in the expenditure of funds,[15] determine whether an Emergency Decree is made in a real emergency,[16] determine whether Election Commissioners should be disqualified,[17] and decide whether political party regulations violate the Constitution or fundamental principles of Thai governance.[18] Because of the overarching concern with corruption that animated the 1997 Constitution, the Court has the power to demand documents or evidence to carry out its duties. In this sense, it is a kind of inquisitorial Constitutional Court exercising a wide gamut of ancillary powers.

The following table lists some of the functions given to constitutional courts in new democracies, drawn from the post-socialist context as a convenient source of comparative data.

Table 1: Ancillary Powers of Post-Socialist Courts

Country	Supervise elections or referenda	Impeachment	Constitution-ality of political parties	Other
Albania	X	X		enforce provision preventing parliamentary deputies from making money with state property
Armenia	X	X	X	
Belarus		X		
Bosnia				resolve disputes over House of Peoples' vetoes of lower house legislation
Bulgaria	X	X	X	
Croatia	X	X	X	establish if President cannot perform duties
Czech Republic	X	X	X	
Estonia				establish if President cannot perform duties
Hungary		X		Approve dissolution of local government bodies
Lithuania	X			establish if President cannot perform duties
Macedonia	X	X	X	establish if President cannot perform duties
Mongolia	X	X		
Poland				determine if temporary impediment to exercise of presidential power
Rumania	X	X	X	
Russia		X	Not after 1993	propose legislation in areas of competence
Slovakia	X	X		
Slovenia	X	X	X	
Ukraine	X	X		Supervise amendments

We will now consider some of these powers in terms of the basic functions of courts. Recall that the basic paradigm of constitutional review relies on the image of the court as interpreting the fundamental text. Some of the powers described above, such as evaluating the constitutionality of political parties or states of emergency, fit this scheme. Others, such as deciding disputes that arise in the context of elections, are more akin to pure ad-hoc dispute resolution such as found in Weber's image of kadi justice.

One can array these ancillary powers on a spectrum, from those that rather clearly involve judicial lawmaking (such as proposing legislation and articulating the standards which make a political party unconstitutional) to those that involve relatively pure forms of dispute resolution (such as impeachment and electoral disputes) where lawmaking is at a minimum. The function of judicial review itself lies strongly toward the lawmaking end of the spectrum; at the other end of the spectrum are cases in which the court is resolving ad-hoc disputes without even referring to the constitutional text. We will take the powers in this order.

Proposing Legislation

The first power grows rather directly out of the lawmaking functions of review described above. Courts engaged in constitutional dialogues are sometimes characterized as acting as a kind of negative legislator, constraining the legislature and bounding its actions rather than positively making rules. (This formulation goes back directly to Kelsen, who explicitly designed the Austrian Constitutional Court with this conception in mind.) The distinction between negative legislation and positive is really rather formal, and turns only on who has the power of initial proposal. For once a proposal is made, a decision restricting that proposal has as much substantive impact as the initial proposal. Indeed, this very aspect of negative legislation is highlighted in scholarly accounts of separation of power games, where the key term is whether or not an institution provides a "veto gate" on new legislation. The power of the veto gate is really a negative lawmaking power.

The slight distinction between negative and positive legislation breaks down completely when the court has the power to hold legislative *omissions* unconstitutional. In this type of review, well-developed in Germany and copied by constitutional courts in countries as diverse as Hungary, Slovakia, Slovenia, South Korea and Taiwan, the court can set a deadline by which the legislature must act to correct an omission. The court can even suggest specific language that would pass constitutional muster. Statutes then passed in response to court proposals become the basis for another round of review.[19]

It is not much of a jump from this type of review to explicitly allowing the constitutional court to propose legislation, either within a designated area of competence or more generally. Yet it is quite rare that constitutional courts are explicitly given the power to propose legislation: Russia is the only new democracy considered that provides this power. Some state courts in the United States have the power to promulgate the rules of evidence, but proposing norms outside the narrow confines of the judicial function is nearly unheard of. In part, this may result from the separation of powers formalism that sees courts as passive interpreters rather than lawmakers. Where courts have *explicit* norm-proposing power, they can no longer draw on the imagery, identified by Shapiro, of being neutral appliers of pre-existing norms. Their very "court-ness" would be called into question were they allowed to propose general law directly, rather than indirectly as they already do. As a normative matter, it is interesting to speculate whether expanding explicit lawmaking power would really be so deleterious, but that consideration is beyond the scope of this paper.

Supervising Political Parties

It is not infrequent that constitutional courts are given the task of supervising political parties alleged to have unconstitutional programs in polities that take an aggressive stance toward safeguarding democracy (Fox and Nolte 1995). The fountainhead of this kind of supervision is that required by Article 21(2) of the German Basic Law, banning parties that oppose the "free democratic basic order" (Kommers 1997, 200). This gave rise to two famous cases familiar to comparativists wherein the German constitutional court banned unconstitutional parties.[20]

The power to regulate political parties has been widely copied in the post-socialist context and given rise to some of the most dramatic decisions there, including the famous decision of the first Russian court to ban the communist party (Epstein and Knight 2001; Ahdieh 1997; Sharlet 1993), and a prominent decision in Bulgaria to ban a Macedonian-nationalist party.[21] The actual scope of the court's power varies from evaluating party programs to actual behavior. For example, in Macedonia, the court's action is limited to evaluating the statute and programs of political parties to ensure that they are not directed against the constitutional order, designed to encourage ethnic hatred, or inviting military aggression. The German Basic Law regulates both programs and activities of political parties.

The power has also been copied in East Asia. During the democratic transition on Taiwan, the power of declaring political parties unconstitutional was transferred to the Council of Grand Justices (the *de facto* constitutional court of the Republic of China), away from the executive branch that had used the power to threaten advocates of Taiwan independence during the period of one-party rule. Interestingly, although the Council exercises abstract constitutional review power generally, it is only called a constitutional court when it sits to evaluate the programs of political parties.

Giving this power to constitutional courts highlights the small-c constitutional nature of electoral and political party law. Though political party and electoral law are not elaborated in detail in most constitutions, in a very real sense these rules *constitute* the polity. Because of this quasi-constitutional nature, it is logical that the supreme guardian of constitutionality would also have a supervisory role over them. The constitutional court can also draw on the image of neutrality to make what is in fact a major policy decision defining the outer limits of political discourse. Constitutional courts evaluating political parties are really meta-policymakers; they determine the policy about who can make policy.

Indeed, this ancillary power deviates only very slightly from the ordinary functions of judicial review of legislation and administrative action, and simply moves the evaluation forward in the political process. Abstract pre-promulgation review examines proposed laws for their potential impact; policing the programs of political parties can be seen as another form of abstract review that prevents some policies from even being proposed in the first place. This function draws on the recognition that political parties are indeed important elements of a democratic political system, and can be agents of violating constitutional rights just as government can.

Furthermore, as in judicial review, the court is basing its decision on a reading of the foundational text, though in practice it is often up to the court to provide substance to such concepts as the "free democratic basic order." Although this exercise in interpretation may be less textually grounded than the conventional exercise of constitutional review, it is still ultimately an exercise in interpretation.

Impeachment

Another important power of constitutional courts is to adjudicate impeachment hearings of a chief executive or other high official, typically as part of a process involving indictment by a legislative body.[22] This was the most common ancillary power in our survey of post-socialist courts. In terms of the political functions of courts, the obvious immediate analogue to impeachment is social control. A political figure has committed a criminal act or a willful violation of the constitution (the actual formulation of the predicate act varies). The court must determine whether or not a violation has occurred or if it warrants removal from office, sometimes by reference to the constitutional text. In the quasi-criminal context of presidential impeachment, the legislature becomes the prosecutor, and the president the defendant. The constitution becomes the criminal statute to which the court refers.

In fact the analogy is incomplete. The character of impeachment in most constitutional schemes is better understood as a variant of the conflict resolution function that is at the heart of judicial review. This is because impeachment hearings are unlikely to occur unless there is an institutional and political conflict between parliament and the executive. To illustrate, contrast the probabilities of a successful indictment of a chief executive when a single disciplined political party controls the legislature and presidency as compared with a situation of divided government. The president in the former scheme may be able to get away with crimes and misdemeanors that would be impeachable in the latter situation.

Impeachment cases thus presuppose political conflict, and the court becomes a neutral triadic figure to adjudicate between the two antagonists. Recall that the fundamental problem of this type of dispute resolution is to convince the loser to comply. There is no higher authority over the president and legislature that can enforce decisions; enforcement depends on the voluntary performance of the parties. The legislature wants the president out; the president wants to stay. The decision of the court must be self-fulfilling, in the sense that no centralized enforcement is typically needed.

In these circumstances, the primary role of the court is not actually to determine facts or evaluate a standard, but simply to provide an answer to help the parties resolve their dispute. Its role does not depend on the image of court-ness so much as its presence as a neutral party on the same constitutional plane. The criminal analogy is crucial for designating the constitutional court as the relevant third party among all possible third parties, but in fact the criminal analogy is misleading in terms of the political function at work.

When two parties are in a dispute and no external enforcer can impose sanctions on them, the parties are in one variant of a situation game theorists describe as a coordination problem. Coordination problems occur when two parties must decide what course of action to take based on their expectation of what action the other will take, and two potential equilibria exist. The paradigm illustration is two cars in a state of nature that must decide which side of the street to drive on. If both choose the same side of the street ("right" or "left"), they will pass each other on the road safely, but if they choose alternate sides, the two will find themselves in a head-on collision. The parties here need to coordinate their actions, and the key will be what they expect the other party to do. Even if the two parties cannot communicate directly, one way to coordinate actions is for a third party to signal to the players to drive on the appropriate side. Thus, if one driver observes a third party say to the other driver to drive on the left, the first driver may believe that the second driver is likely to follow the instruction, and the third-party's signal can become self-enforcing even if they have no power to sanction the driver.

Many situations in dispute resolution involve similar coordination problems. We will return to this kind of problem further in the next section, which concerns ad-hoc election disputes. For now, it is worth pointing out that the natural instinct to give the impeachment power to the constitutional court ensures that it may be called on to resolve monumental political crises.

Electoral Disputes

Another role for constitutional courts is supervising elections or elections authorities.[23] Referenda are supervised by constitutional courts in Italy, Portugal, Armenia, and many other countries. The *Conseil Constitutionnel* can supervise the legality of elections for the president or legislature, and referenda, as do many of the constitutional courts listed on Table 1. This ancillary power differs from all the previous ones in that there is frequently not even a formal link between the dispute and the text of the constitution. Rather, this jurisdiction is basically one of ad-hoc dispute resolution on a case-by-case basis.

I want to illustrate this point by discussing recent prominent electoral decisions by two very different constitutional courts, the Constitutional Court of Thailand and the United States Supreme Court.[24] The Constitutional Court of Thailand, set up after the return to civilian rule after five years of military control, was given the power of supervising the decisions of the new NCCC. Corruption has been an endemic issue in Thailand, and the 1997 Constitution was designed to ensure clean politics. The NCCC collects reports on assets from politicians and senior bureaucrats to ensure that there are no mysterious increases during the time they are in public service. Those who fail to report assets can be barred from office, subject to approval from the new Constitutional Court.

The most prominent cases that have come before the Thai Constitutional Court to date are those involving scrutiny of politicians. In one case, the Minister of Interior was found to have deliberately submitted a false statement of his assets to the NCCC. The Constitutional Court unanimously confirmed the report of the NCCC, leading to a five-year ban from office for the prominent politician.[25] A higher profile case arose in January 2001, when Thaksin Shinawatra, the billionaire-turned-politician who was the leading candidate for Prime Minister in the upcoming election, was found by the NCCC to have filed a false asset report, the Constitutional Court was put in a difficult position. Thaksin's Thai Rak Thai party subsequently won the elections. In a divided decision that has been described as confused, the Court found that the false report had not been filed deliberately, and thereby allowed Thaksin to take the post of Prime Minister.

Criticism of the rationales of courts in these cases is common precisely because there is a conflict between the image of the court as neutral body basing a decision on pre-existing norms and the social logic of the coordination problem at hand. *Bush v. Gore*[26] is perhaps the paradigm here. In facts recounted extensively elsewhere, the court intervened in a partisan election that had produced a statistical tie. The dispute involved a constitutional scheme described previously described as a train wreck waiting to happen (Levinson 2002; Amar 1998). The court's decision has been widely criticized as poorly reasoned, legally flawed, and unnecessary (Dershowitz 2001; Gillman 2001; *cf.* Posner 2001).

Bush v. Gore is widely viewed as the most political of political decisions. As suggested by the double entendre of the title of Howard Gillman's *The Votes that Counted* (2001), the Court's closely divided vote substituted for the votes of the electorate. The chief difference between an electorate of 100 million and an electorate of nine is that in the latter there are no ties. What could be more activist or political?

From the functional point of view, however, the decision looks quite different. For *Bush v. Gore* is a paradigm case of pure dispute resolution. Two parties come before the court. Both prefer a resolution of some kind to continuing uncertainty. Like Weber's kadi under the tree, the court was certainly not engaged in lawmaking of a real kind, as its own limiting assertions on the implications of its equal protection analysis made clear.[28] Nor was the court carrying out regime policies to exercise social control. There was no regime to serve—and that was of course the issue in the case.

Rather the court was a neutral third resolving a coordination problem among the parties. Here we see the basic social logic of dispute resolution at its apex.

I want to illustrate this with a further detour into game theory because I think it will help illuminate the function of the court in these kinds of disputes. The above description of coordination problems concerned "pure" coordination: Neither driver really cares which side of the road he or she drives on as long as he avoids the accident. The game in election disputes like *Bush v. Gore* is more akin to that of "chicken," famous from the scene in the James Dean movie where two cars drive headfirst at each other to see who will be the first to swerve. Each party would prefer to play the aggressive strategy and refuse to swerve, but if both follow this first best strategy, they will wind up in the collectively worst outcome of a head-on collision. The task for each party is to convincingly demonstrate that he will not swerve, thereby inducing the other party to swerve. To analogize to *Bush v. Gore*, there is only one Presidency with two claimants. Each party prefers that he be the one to occupy the office. However, the most important thing is that some sort of resolution occur. The costs to the constitutional order of continuing to fight exceed the costs of being the "loser." The trick is to figure out who will play the role of "loser" and back down from the confrontation. Left to their own devices, the parties will not be able to coordinate their roles. Each will try to express resolve to induce the other party to back down (Ginsburg and McAdams 2004).

The role of a constitutional court here is to point to one or the other contender and identify him as the "winner." Once a court identifies one party as a winner, the decision may become a self-enforcing focal point. Gore's perception of the likelihood of Bush's backing down changed as soon as the Supreme Court announced its decision. Whereas before the decision, Gore seemed to have a legitimate claim on the Presidency and might have expected Bush to accede, after the decision Bush was unlikely to do so. Gore could have stayed on—but the chances of Bush ever adopting the "swerve" strategy were greatly reduced.

Note that this interpretation of electoral disputes as a game of chicken suggests that the Supreme Court can play a function independent of the quality of any particular justification that it offers. The Supreme Court could have simply flipped a coin to decide *Bush v. Gore* to play this crucial function: Had the court simply pointed to Bush as the random winner, Gore would still have had to readjust his views as to the likelihood of Bush backing down. The particular reasoning offered, flawed as it was, was not the point. Regardless of its rationale, the court decision became focal for the two parties in seeking to coordinate their strategies.[29]

Because any external source can provide a focal point in these kind of disputes, there is no reason that a *constitutional* court must inherently exercise this ancillary power. In many constitutional schemes, the role of the constitutional court is limited to certain types of electoral disputes. For example, in Albania, disputes over local government elections go to the ordinary courts while disputes over parliamentary elections go to the constitutional court. Nevertheless, the constitutional court can be a convenient third party to turn to in constitutional design, in part because it, like other courts, draws on the imagery of a neutral dispute resolver.

Tensions Between Lawmaking and Dispute Resolution

So far we have moved on a spectrum all the way from the high-profile function of lawmaking in constitutional review toward simple dispute resolution in ad-hoc impeachment cases and electoral disputes. We have thus come a long way from the conventional emphasis on the lawmaking function of courts. The image we are left with is of a court that is an ad-hoc decision-maker, akin to Weber's *kadi* under the tree or Shapiro's Papuan with many pigs. The constitutional court helps powerful actors resolve coordination problems, and the particular justifications offered are of little import.

Of course, one important feature of constitutional schemes is that everyone is a repeat player. If we adopt as a hypothesis that courts seek to enhance their power and influence over time, then we must assume the court acts strategically not only in particular cases, as emphasized by Epstein and Knight (1998; 2001), but across different policy areas and cases calling on the exercise of different types of powers. The court is a strategic actor over time, and hence will encounter a sequence of cases of various types.

Here we see a tension emerge between the simple dispute resolution role and the lawmaking function of an actor with policy preferences. For the dispute resolver's neutrality with regard to a particular outcome may be compromised when the court needs to take long-term institutional considerations into account. The Court may not care, as an ideal matter, whether Bush or Gore wins the election, but in fact each justice has real preferences about the ultimate direction of the court in the next presidential term, and may thus have preferences about which candidate should be, for example, appointing new justices. More importantly, the Court must be mindful of its own institutional position. Creating an angry loser, one which by definition has sufficient power to be a force in national politics, may mean creating a permanent enemy.

This may lead courts in such circumstances to act rather more cautiously than they appear to. In the Thai example, the Court may have sought to avoid a fight with an incoming political majority with strong support. In a dispute unfolding as this volume went to press, the Ukrainian Supreme Court required a new election in a disputed presidential contest—but at least some analysts believed that it did so only after the major political forces had reached a consensus that a new election was the appropriate course.

Constitutional designers have quite consciously given courts the wide array of powers described in this chapter. They have done so in part because the global success of judicial review has given constitutional courts a reputation as effective institutions. Constitutional review creates a kind of stock of capital that designers seek to draw on to help resolve impasses in the political system, such as occur in impeachment and election disputes. The risk is that as they are drawn into *explicitly* political conflicts, courts risk drawing down this stock of capital. This risk is no doubt particularly acute in new democracies.

In the context of ordinary dispute resolution, we have long been told that much of the structure and image of adjudication are designed to deal with the problem of the appearance of bias toward the winner of the dispute (Shapiro 1981a). Appeals play this function, as do judges' reliance on the image of applying pre-existing neutral principles. Many of these techniques are unavailable to constitutional courts. There is no higher court to appeal to; and oftentimes the very rationale for designating a special constitutional court is a recognition of the fact that the function is in part political in nature, rather than technical and legal. All constitutional courts have, in the end, is the constitutional text and the notion that founding principles are dictating decisions. In the end, then, the image of judicial review is central to their political success, even when in practice constitutional courts are exercising a wider array of powers.

The dangers and tradeoffs are illustrated in the well-known story of the first Russian Constitutional Court in the Communist Party Case of 1992. The Russian Court, created in the late Gorbachev period, was seen to be a central embodiment of the rule of law and the "new" Russia. Its primary role emerged as mediating disputes between the parliament and president. When Boris Yeltsin, in a series of decrees after the 1991 coup attempt, disbanded the Communist party and seized its property and assets,[30] the communists challenged the decrees as exceeding presidential power. This prompted a cross-petition by opponents of the Communist Party who invoked the

Court's ancillary power to determine the party's legality and constitutional status. The two petitions were joined by the chairman of the Court, Valery Zorkin, bringing together genuinely legal issues with deeply political ones.[31]

The Court was faced with a difficult situation. It could uphold the president's actions, even though he did not follow the relevant legal procedures for banning political associations; or it could strike them and side with the anti-constitutional Communists who had supported the coup. Neither option appeared particularly attractive. Thus caught, the Court attempted to split the difference by finding a mediate solution. In a decision published on November 30, 1992, the Court upheld Yeltsin's decrees against the organs of the national Communist Party of the Soviet Union, but not against its local bodies. This decision provoked disappointment on all sides, and failed to resolve the governmental crisis. Court Chairman Zorkin then sought to negotiate a compromise document between Yeltsin and the parliament. This constitutional compromise marked the deep involvement of the Court, and Zorkin in particular, in the realm of pure politics as opposed to law. The image of the court as a neutral, technical body devoted to the law was dashed. When Yeltsin dispensed with the compromise and announced a decree granting himself emergency powers in March 1993, the Court issued an opinion declaring the actions unconstitutional, even before the decree was issued.[32] Within months, Yeltsin dissolved the parliament and suspended the Court's operation.[33] It was not reconvened until February 1995, with reduced powers.[34] In particular, it lost the ancillary powers to declare parties unconstitutional and issue an advisory option on the impeachment of the president.

The Russian story illustrates the dilemma of courts exercising ancillary powers. Oddly, it was ancillary powers and the extension of the court's chairman into an explicitly political role, rather than lawmaking, that led to the demise of the first Russian Constitutional Court. To the extent that they rely on the dispute resolution logic of all triadic third parties, ancillary powers can facilitate resolution of major political conflicts and coordination problems. But the further the court gets away from its paradigm task of review based on interpretation of a fundamental text, it may find itself acting in a fashion that undermines its own legitimacy. Furthermore, the need to act strategically over a long series of cases that call on various powers of the court means that sometimes "pure" dispute resolution will be compromised by political expediency. Ancillary powers, then, are some, but only some, of the tools the court must use to build up its political role over time.

Conclusion

The recent weight of comparative constitutional scholarship has focused nearly exclusively on the power of constitutional review. As a result, the dominant image of courts is that of lawmaker, creating rules through dialogues with political branches. When one examines the full array of powers explicitly granted and utilized by constitutional courts, however, a somewhat different picture emerges. The ancillary functions highlight how constitutional courts operate as triadic figures, drawing on the basic social logic of courts identified by Shapiro.

This mix of "court-like" features and quasi-legislative features is neither surprising nor inherently problematic. Like other features of modern mixed government, the notion of "pure" governmental functions implicit in separation of powers formalism remains a fantasy. "Executive" administrative agencies adjudicate cases and write rules; legislatures hold hearings and pass private bills; and courts both make law and resolve disputes.

Nevertheless, it is worth sounding a note of caution. The urge to transfer new functions to successful institutions is an understandable one for constitutional designers. The prestige of constitutional courts in general, their reputation for neutrality, and their reliance on political legitimacy as the primary mechanism for enforcement of their decisions, creates an incentive to give them complex political problems to resolve. There is, however, a risk that constitutional courts will be drawn into inherently unwinnable zero-sum conflicts, which require deft maneuvering and skillful action. In new democracies, at least, it is not obvious that the courts themselves will always be up to the task.

Notes

[1] On correction as a key determinant of discretion see Cooter and Ginsburg (1996).

[2] I recognize that these powers are only "ancillary" if one considers judicial review to be the central function of constitutional courts.

[3] Luis Lopez Guerra, *Conflict Resolution in Federal and Regional Systems*, Venice Commission paper CDL-JU 24, 21 February 2002, available at Hwww.venice.coe.int/docs/2002H. The distinct nature of conflict resolution is evident in constitutions that have special procedures for resolving conflicts of competence. See, e.g., Constitution of Austria, art. 138c; Basic Law of Germany, arts. 93.3 and 93.4; Constitution of Spain, arts. 161.1 and 161.2. Occasionally, provisions for multiple lawmakers are utilized in constitutional text with regard to specific territories as a means of ensuring their acquiescence to central authority. In Finland, for example, the Supreme Court can determine conflicts between the central state and the Aland Islands. The Bosnia-Herzegovina constitutional text similarly gives the Court competence to resolve disputes between the two geographic entities. Some constitutions have special procedures for resolving conflicts of competence. Austrian Constitution, art 138c, German Basic Law, arts 93.3 and 93.4, Constitution of Spain, arts. 161.1 and 161.2.

[4] 198 U.S. 45 (1905).

[5] See e.g., Constitution of Bosnia/Herzegovina (1995), Constitution of the Chechen Republic (1992) art. 65; Constitutional Court Act of Russia, art. 9.

[6] See, e.g., Constitution of the Republic of China, as amended (1997); Basic Law of Germany (1949), art. 21(2); Constitution of Bulgaria (1991), article 149(5).

[7] See, e.g., Constitution of Bulgaria (1991), art. 149(8); Constitution of Hungary (1949), art. 31(a); Constitution of Mongolia (1992), art. 35(1); Basic Law of Germany (1949), art. 61.

[8] See, e.g., Constitution of France (1958), art. 58-60, Basic Law of Germany (1949), art. 41(2); Constitution of Lithuania (1992), art 105(3)(1).

[9] See Rules Enabling Act, 28 U.S.C. § 2072 (1994); Pfander (2001).

[10] 28 U.S.C. § 591.

[11] art. 93.

[12] Ludwikowski (1993). The Constitution was passed in 1995 without these provisions.

[13] Constitution of South Africa (1997), art. 144.

[14] Constitution of Armenia (1999), art. 83.

[15] Constitution of Thailand (1997), § 180.

[16] Constitution of Thailand (1997), § 219.

[17] Constitution of Thailand (1997), § 142 (referring to §§ 137 and 139).

[18] Constitution of Thailand (1997), § 47 para. 3.

[19] The use of deadlines in this type of review is slightly at odds with the rule of law imagery underlying constitutional court power. The court finds that legislation violates the constitution, but lets it stand for a designated period. Those affected by the legislation will be treated as constitutionally bound one day, and not bound a day later after the deadline. Clearly this type of system is a pragmatic recognition of the dialogue phenomenon.

20   Kommers 1997 at 217–24. These were the *Socialist Reich Party Case*, 2 BverfGE 1 (1952), concerning a neo-nazi party and the *Communist Party Case*, 5 BverfGE 85 (1956).

21   BBC Monitoring Service, 29 Feb., 2000.

22   A related role is to determine disqualification of legislators. See, e.g., Constitution of Bulgaria (1991), art. 72.

23   Sometimes this is an appeals jurisdiction, as in Hungary where the court rules on appeals from the National Electoral Commission on the legality of particular questions subject to referenda.

24   As this chapter was going to press a high profile dispute was unfolding in the Ukraine in which the country's supreme court over-turned a disputed election.

25   Constitutional Court Decision 31/2543 (2000).

26   531 U.S. 98 (2000).

27   531 U.S. 98 (2000).

28   *Bush v. Gore*, 121 U.S. at 109 ("Our consideration is limited to the present circumstances, for the problem of equal protection in election processes generally presents many complexities.").

29   I should state that I am not offering a defense of *Bush v. Gore* (cf. Posner 2001). I am not at all convinced, as Richard Posner seems to be, that the consequences of continued indecision would necessarily be grave. The Court was not the only source of a focal point. Indeed, one of the important features of self-enforcing focal points is that they can come from *many* external sources—anything that can change expectations about what the other party will do can become a focal point. My argument is not a normative one, but rather a functional attempt to understand why the decision worked as a positive matter. Viewing *Bush v. Gore* as a coordination problem may in part explain why it is that the court's legitimacy as an institution was affected only very slightly by the decision (Kritzer 2001; Clayton 2002, 80).

30   Decree No. 79 of 23 August 1991; Decree No. 90 of 24 August 1991; and Decree No. 169 of 6 November 1991.

31   The legal grounds of the case were complicated, and better elaborated elsewhere. Suffice it to say that the case featured some bizarre arguments, such as when Yeltsin's team argued that the decree to ban a political association was legal under a 1932 Stalinist decree that permitted the executive to undertake such action. *See generally* AHDIEH 1997.

32   In fact, the decree never materialized. The Court thus issued an advisory opinion.

33   Decree No. 1400 of 21 September 1993 and No. 1612 of 7 October 1993.

34   Ahdieh, 1997, 149; Pashin 1994.

9.

The Internationalization
of Economic Review of Legislation:
Non-Judicial Legalization?

Bronwen Morgan

Introduction

This chapter documents an emerging trend at the intersection of national and international lawmaking: the economic review of legislation. This trend demonstrates that a systematic, institutionalized set of practices constraining discretion by rule need not necessarily be judicial in nature. In today's globalizing spaces, where territorially based legal rules are decreasingly likely to have the "last word," economic rationality is an increasingly powerful constraint upon discretion, particularly legislative discretion. I aim to show here that the most recent developments in economic review of legislation are a species of legality, and in that sense institutionalize an emergent "rule of economics" that shares interesting characteristics with the rule of law.

My approach is comparative, though not in the usual sense of the term. In essence, I compare the functions of courts with those of certain other non-judicial reviewing institutions, with an eye to similarities in the underlying *institutional architecture*. The point of the comparison is to expand our understanding of what is encompassed by legal phenomena. Hence my main argument: that the expanding trajectory of the economic review of legislation represents a species of *non-judicial legalization*. To make this argument, I draw in part on a logic of analogy that is familiar to a legally trained scholar. But I also draw on work in political studies of courts. An appreciation of the political incentives that motivate and constrain legal actors has helped scholars (perhaps paradoxically) to account for what is in fact most *distinctively legal*. This chapter shows how this logic can be reversed to cast new light on the production of economic regulatory legislation; specifically, to recharacterize its traditionally political nature as increasingly legal, albeit non-judicially so. Just as an appreciation of judicial decision making as political policymaking at its core illuminates key features of legality (e.g., the neutrality of office and the nature of judicial reasoning), so an appreciation of certain economic policymaking procedures as a form of legality casts fresh light on key features of those regimes (e.g., their reliance on technocratic forms of rationality, their insulation from politics).

In the first part of the paper, I build the theoretical framework for giving content to "non-judicial legality." The second and third parts of the paper will work through detailed empirical illustrations at a national and international level, with relatively more emphasis in Part II on analogical logic and in Part III on the political incentives shaping the trajectory of the "rule of economics."

I.

Recent work in both law and political science suggests the importance of paying attention to the development and spread of the economic review of legislation. Economic review of legislation encompasses any set of institutions and processes that embed regulatory review mechanisms on a systematic basis into the every-day routines of governmental policymaking, such that a particular form of economic rationality becomes part of the taken-for-granted ways of policymaking. For example, under the reforms introduced by the Australian government explored in Part II of this paper, government requires the application of a public benefit test to justify the maintenance of any public policy that prima facie restricts competition. Policies for which a public benefit cannot be demonstrated must be repealed or modified so that they do not reduce competition. This principle of regulatory reform is institutionalized as a *general mechanism of governance,* not confined to one-off efforts to reform particular policy sectors, but instantiated as a generally applicable, sector-neutral and continuously applied technique of regulatory reform.

These review regimes in effect adjudicate the economic policymaking functions of government. I want to situate them at the intersection of two trends observed from different disciplinary standpoints, converging from opposite directions: the judicialization of politics on the one hand and the increasing importance of non-judicial mechanisms of accountability on the other. While from some perspectives, the domain of politics is increasingly populated by more and more courts and judges, at the same time the legal domain—especially from the viewpoint of those who write on regulation—is more and more a world of institutions other than courts or judges, both public and private. My contention is that these observational trajectories are not incompatible but rather, intersect at a site of non-judicial legality: increasingly legalized politics without courts or judges of non-judicial legality. The conceptual tools underlying my argument are grounded upon Martin Shapiro's analytical approach, and his work will bridge the two bodies of literature I first present.

Judicialization

For some time now, commentators have noted the increasing extent to which judicial decisions and institutions shape and constrain politics, at least in Organization for Economic Co-operation and Development (OECD) countries. Colin Scott, for example, argues that juridification "describes a process by which relations hitherto governed by other values and expectations come to be subjected to legal values and rules" (Scott 1998, 19). Alec Stone Sweet argues that judicialization occurs when "judges routinely intervene in legislative processes, [by] establishing limits on lawmaking behavior, reconfiguring policymaking environments, even drafting the precise terms of legislation" (Stone Sweet 2000, 1). A trajectory of judicialization has both behavioral and normative consequences: Not only do the pronouncements of judges and courts "come to shape how individuals interact with each other," but they also "develop authority over the normative structure in place in any given community" (Stone Sweet 2000, 13).

Judicialization as a trajectory is most readily observable in relation to human rights. "Fundamental rights", particularly those of political minorities, were the catalyst for building both international and national institutions in the aftermath of the Second World War. As one prominent comparative commentator notes,

> Judicial review was introduced in Europe after the Nazi-Fascist era shook the faith of Europeans in the legislature, making them reconsider the possibility of giving the judiciary the power to check the legislature's respect for the fundamental rights of the people. (Cappelletti 1989, 118)

Economic policymaking has typically been relatively less judicialized than issues bearing upon fundamental rights. Most countries have preferred to shape economic policy via a dialogue between government and bureaucracy, subject to such legislative constraints as the institutional context dictates. Bureaucratic consensualism dominates the policymaking process: Courts are monitors of the later implementation of such policy, rather than architects. The United States is an exception in this regard, and there is a wealth of literature on the excessive juridification of U.S. regulatory politics (e.g., Kagan 2001; Moran 2002; Stewart 1988). But even within the exceptional US, economic policymaking has traditionally received at least more constitutional deference from the courts than legislative initiatives affecting fundamental rights.

The relative immunity of economic policymaking from judicialization has undergone a distinct shift in recent years. Linkages between economic policymaking, regulatory reform and legal processes have intensified. Sometimes this is merely an intensification of the relative involvement of courts and judges in the implementation of economic policies, particularly when they are delivered via regulatory agencies. For example, utilities sectors have become increasingly juridified as policymaking in those sectors is shaped and delivered by independent regulatory agencies (Scott 1998, 20; Heritier and Leonor 2001). The main factor here, as Colin Scott argues, is liberalization.

> Liberalization has had the effect of multiplying the number of players participating in each sector (both regulatory and commercial) and tended to threaten the consensual, bureaucratic models of provision and regulation which carried over from the era of public ownership. Increasingly, these more numerous players are seeking to test their rights and obligations against the legal framework of each sector. (Scott 1998, 20)

While courts have always been a source of general (i.e., non-sector-specific) legal constraints on specific *implementation* decisions, non-sector-specific legal constraints also increasingly apply at a *policymaking* stage. One important source of such constraints are trade regimes such as the World Trade Organization (WTO) or the internal market project of the European Union (EU), which are regularly analyzed in terms of the growing "judicialization" of their trajectories (Dillon 2001; McGinnis and Movsesian 2000; Stone Sweet 2000; Weatherill 2000). More diffusely, financial institutions involved in funding development, particularly in countries undergoing a transition from socialist to market economies, have emphasized the importance of establishing the "rule of law" not so much as a safeguard against oppressing minority groups, but as a precondition for effective economic performance (Buscaglia 1998; Sunstein 1988). Where those guiding the reform of countries in transition might once have focused principally on institutions such as independent central banks, now their energies are directed to the production of judicial regimes and legal systems that secure credible and predictable property rights. Judicialization seems, increasingly, just as critical to the promotion of economic development as to the protection of human rights, and not simply as a constitutive framework for market exchange, but also as the arbiter of the balance between competing values struck by economic policies.

Non-judicial Review

An important part of the story of regulatory politics in recent years, then, is the growing presence of judicialization. Another important strand, however, is increasing interest in non-judicial forms of review. The point here is that just as domains of activity that used to be purely political are being invaded by the ever-pervasive presence of law, so too also is scholarship identifying institutions that are outside a narrow conception of the legal (courts and judges) but that nonetheless may serve analogous functions. In law, regulation scholars strongly influenced by socio-legal perspectives have perhaps been most inclined to range beyond legal institutions narrowly conceived (Campbell and Picciotto 2002; Freeman 2000; Scott 2000; Vincent-Jones 2000). Common research foci of scholars who posit ostensibly non-legal institutions as crucial agents in a legal field include the conditions under which effective compliance is secured, the role of private and non-governmental actors in regulatory spaces, or the workings of independent regulatory agencies or quasi-governmental organizations. One particularly interesting focus in these forays beyond the domains of courts and judges is that of non-judicial review.

Non-judicial review has been noted in a range of policy areas, encompassing economic policymaking and fundamental rights. In relation to the carrying out of governmental functions generally, across a wide range of policy areas, Hood et al.'s exploration of bureaucratic regulation within government in effect takes note of a form of non-judicial review, whose general features are specified as "oversight of bureaucracies by other public agencies operating at arm's length from the direct line of command, the overseers being endowed with some sort of official authority over their charges" (Hood et al. 2000, 284). In regulatory arenas that affect economic policymaking, prescriptions for the delegation of dispute resolution and even policymaking to politically insulated independent agencies, also a form of non-judicial review, are pervasive (Spiller 1998). Even in relation to fundamental rights, typically an area more readily delegated to courts and judges, a burgeoning interest in non-judicial forms of review is apparent. In particular, scholars are noting with interest the "hybrid" forms of review of fundamental rights institutionalized in New Zealand and the United Kingdom (UK), which give a prominent *but not decisive* role to courts and judges in reviewing governmental action bearing upon rights, supplementing the contribution of these legal actors with mandated inter-institutional dialogues with more purely political actors (Gardbaum 2001; Tushnet 2001). Mark Tushnet goes as far as to cast the actions of these more purely political actors (such as U.S. Senators debating points of order raised by constitutional questions) as forms of non-judicial review per se, even without a dimension of dialogue with courts and judges.

Interestingly, the underlying implication of the goal served by non-judicial review is rather different as between economic policymaking and fundamental rights. In respect of the latter, the participation of non-judicial institutions in review of fundamental rights is thought to *"reinject matters of principle* back into legislative...debates" (Gardbaum 2001) (emphasis added), whereas the more common focus in matters of economic policymaking is the notion that a kind of a-normative, technical neutrality is secured by the participation of institutions of non-judicial review. However, common to both those visions is an idea of neutrality or disinterestedness. This is most explicitly captured by Tushnet. What makes non-judicial review different from "pure politics" is, he argues, that the actors carrying it out possess incentives that push them in the direction of offering interpretations that are not substantially less disinterested than the interpretations offered by judges (Tushnet 2001). What matters here is a "professional and bureaucratic interest in providing disinterested...interpretation" (Tushnet 2001, 3–4). Such an incentive may be secured by a blend of ideological commitment and bureaucratic mission vested in non-judicial governmental actors possessing some institutionally secured independence.

It is important to realize that disinterestedness may not *necessarily* require that the actors performing judicial review do so with reference to some stable substantive set of knowledge (whether that be scientific expertise, "principled" theories of human rights, or objective economic expertise). A more sparse account of what is important in this account of judicial review would focus simply on the institutional relationships between the reviewers and the reviewees. Guillermo O'Donnell captures this well in explaining his conception of horizontal accountability:

> [A]nother dimension of accountability, which I call 'horizontal'...means the controls that state agencies are suppose to exercise over other state agencies....The basic idea is that formal institutions have well-defined, legally established

boundaries that delimit the proper exercise of their authority, and that there are state agencies empowered to control and redress trespasses of these boundaries by any official or agency (...) (O'Donnell 1997, 185)

This ultimately is the essence of non-judicial review that I am interested in highlighting here. Though he could be describing the functions of courts and judges, the quotation could also encompass the functions of a variety of non-judicial governmental institutions. Notice that despite this capaciousness, O'Donnell still sees all forms of horizontal accountability as an expression of something fundamentally belonging in the legal domain: "[horizontal accountability] is an often overlooked *expression of the rule of law* in one of the areas where it is hardest to implant, i.e., over state agents, especially high-ranking officials" (O'Donnell 1997, 185) (emphasis added). This links to the final step in building a theoretical framework for discussing the importance of the economic review of legislation: the notion that non-judicial review is a manifestation of legalization. That is, judicialization is only one species of a more basic genre: The legal domain encompasses a wider range of institutions than courts and judges. This is most easily grasped by observing, not actors and institutions, but an underlying social logic. What marks a domain out as legal is a distinctive and observable texture to a set of social practices, rather than the participation of a specified set of actors and institutions. Once the underlying social logic is exposed, its applicability to the economic review of legislation is more readily established.

Legalization

I stated earlier that international financial institutions have recently come to see judicial institutions as equally critical to effective economic policymaking as independent central banks. I noted that as part of the trajectory of judicialization, but I want to emphasize now that it should not be taken to imply a contrast between independent central banks and judicialization. Rather, my argument emphasizes the commonalities between such institutions. What, in generalizable terms, is at stake when a policymaking process is subjected to a trajectory of judicialization?

Most crucially, a trajectory of judicialization involves significant delegation of decision making power to an arms-length, neutral and independent institution. Shapiro's characteristically terse analysis in *Courts* exposes the triadic logic that underlies the position of courts as dispute-resolution institutions (Shapiro 1981a). As he summarizes it in a more recent publication:

> If a conflict arises between two persons and they cannot resolve it themselves, then in all cultures and societies it is logical for those two persons to call upon a third to assist in its resolution...The triad contains a basic tension. To the extent that the triadic figure appears to intervene in favor of one of the two disputants and against the other, the perception of the situation will shift from the fairest to features of processes that tend otherwise to be identified as political the most unfair of configurations: two against one. Therefore the principal characteristics of all triadic conflict resolvers will be determined by the need to avoid the perception of two against one, for only then can they rely on their basic social logic. (Shapiro and Stone Sweet 2002, 211)

Where triadic institutions are relatively highly formalized, two devices are especially important in preventing perceptions of "two against one": office and rules (Shapiro and Stone Sweet 2002, 212). More specifically, the personal neutrality of the judge, and the resolution of the dispute by reference to a pre-existing decision rule expressed in general terms, together ensure that the triadic logic is maintained.

This pared-back perspective on the social logic underlying judicial institutions is an approach that challenges too bright a distinction between courts and other governmental organs, or between judges and other official policymakers. It emphasizes the political nature of legal institutions, their *governance* function as conflict resolvers, while still capturing their distinctiveness—albeit in terms more general and abstracted than the presence of judges or courts. Other institutions and personnel within the modern state may, from this perspective, carry out analogous functions if they display analogous social logic.

The notion that legality as a phenomenon may extend beyond courts and judges has since begun to spread within political science. In particular, a group of international relations scholars recently proposed the concept of legalization as an analytic device that has the capacity to capture a broad variety of ways in which "law and politics are intertwined across a wide range of institutional forms" (Goldstein et al. 2001, ix). Importantly, the institutional spectrum of phenomena captured by legalization extends well beyond courts and tribunals. Goldstein and her colleagues define legalization in such a way that casts a wider net than courts and tribunals. They focus on three criteria: obligation, precision and delegation:

> [H]ighly legalized institutions are those in which rules are obligatory on parties...,in which rules are precise (or can be made precise through the exercise of delegated

authority), and in which authority to interpret and apply the rules has been delegated to third parties acting under the constraint of rules. (Goldstein 2001, 34)

The third criterion echoes Shapiro's emphasis on the importance of interpretation by an arms-length third party. Indeed, the other two criteria, obligation and precision, can also be linked to the underlying social logic of the triad, that is to say, to preventing any perception of two-against-one. The more precisely a pre-existing rule specifies the outcome of particular modes of conduct, and the more such outcomes are imposed as a matter of obligation, the more constraints are placed on the personal preferences of the third party enforcer of precise obligations. Consequently, when a decision favors one or other party, as it must to some extent inevitably do, it will be all the less perceived as two-against-one, but rather as driven by precise guidance applied by a neutral office-holder. To summarize, then, the underlying social logic of judicialization, the triangulation of conflict, also characterizes legalization, since interactions shaped by obligatory, precise, arms-length applied rules, will minimize perceptions that raw power has determined the outcome.

In Part II, I discuss a regime established in Australia in the 1990s to review economic legislation and point to the key features that mark it as a form of legalization, albeit not one which involves courts, judges or quasi-judicial panels. Once legalization is explicitly delinked from courts and judges, a range of different forms become imaginable. Consider an elaboration by Goldstein and her colleagues on the nature of a legalized policymaking process, and imagine an array of different referents.

Legal processes involve a discourse framed in terms of reason, interpretation, technical knowledge, and argument, often followed by deliberation and judgment by impartial parties. Different actors have access to the process, and they are constrained to make arguments different from those they would make in a nonlegal context. Legal decisions, too, must be based on reasons applicable to all similarly situated litigants, not merely the parties to the immediate disputes. (Goldstein et al. 2001, 35)

For a legal audience, a court is the most ready referent of the above description. One might think, for example, of the process of justifying regulatory action to courts under administrative law. But what would we make of a requirement to justify regulatory policy before an economists' commission appointed with relative independence of tenure, as Australia requires? Or a dialogue between specialized units in the executive branch and bipartisan parliamentary committees as to whether regulatory reform proposals retain the "necessary protection" against harm required by the public interest, an innovation the UK recently implemented in its Regulatory Reform Act 2001? Are these developments instances of legalization? Part II argues that, at least in relation to the Australian case, the answer is yes.

II.

The focus of this section is the detail of Australia's regime for reviewing economic legislation, which subjected its economic policymaking processes at both state and federal level to the disciplines of non-judicial legality. In what follows, I describe different aspects of the regime in such a way as to highlight the three core features of delegation, precision and obligation that were identified in Part I as crucial to a trajectory of non-judicial legality (see also Morgan 2003). I do so first in relation to the institutional design of the Australian regime for economic review of legislation, and second in relation to key aspects of its implementation patterns. The regime may not possess these characteristics in the same way that judicial regimes do, but they are sufficiently present, I argue, to constitute at least a species of *incipient* legality.

Precision, Obligation and Delegation in Design

In April 1995, to vociferous political credit-claiming and media fanfare, the Commonwealth (federal) and all Australian state governments signed a triad of intergovernmental agreements known as National Competition Policy (NCP). Although limited aspects of NCP are embodied in "mirror legislation" (i.e., statutes passed in identical terms by the six states, two territories and federal government) the main outlines of the reforms are recorded in *intergovernmental compacts*, the legal status of which is not entirely clear. In form, they resemble most closely international treaties, but the parties are sub-units of one domestic state, rather than distinct national states. The Competition Principles Agreement (CPA) is the intergovernmental compact that puts in place the overall regime, imposing pro-competitive disciplines not on individual or corporate behavior, but on public rulemaking and policymaking processes. The CPA applies to rules that are made either formally through legislative processes, or by an accretion of policy decisions that treat government entities differently from private entities. It requires the application of a public benefit test to justify the maintenance of any public policy that prima facie restricts competition.

Policies for which a public benefit cannot be demonstrated must be repealed or modified so that they do not reduce competition. This is required in clearly stated terms drafted as a legal agreement typically is. What follows is the core clause (5, slightly edited) of the CPA:

> 5(1) The guiding principle is that legislation (including Acts, enactments, Ordinances or regulations) should not restrict competition unless it can be demonstrated that:
> a. the benefits of the restriction to the community as a whole outweigh the costs; and b. the objectives of the legislation can only be achieved by restricting competition....
> (3) Subject to subclause (4) each Party will develop a timetable by June 1996 for the review, and where appropriate, reform of all existing legislation that restricts competition by the year 2000....
> (5) Each Party will require proposals for new legislation that restricts competition to be accompanied by evidence that the legislation is consistent with the principle set out in subclause (1).

The agreement applies not only on a continuing basis to new rules and programs coming into force after April 1995, but also, on a rolling basis over five years, to the totality of *existing* rules and programs across all levels of government. Its scope is ambitious in the extreme: More than 1,700 pieces of legislation were initially listed for review and all new legislation is subject to the regime. [1] While the legal status of intergovernmental compacts in Australia is not entirely clear, as I noted above, the obligatory nature of the commitments was a core assumption of the political debates predating the signing of the agreements. Moreover a novel enforcement mechanism intensifies the obligatory nature of the reform regime by linking compliance to substantial competition payments. The agreement provided for the payment of some Aus$16 billion between 1995 and 2000, and the payments have since been extended on a continuing basis. Receipt of the money, however, is conditional on satisfying a newly created national independent agency—the National Competition Council (NCC)—on an annual basis that "effective implementation" of the NCP reforms is taking place.

The existence of this newly created independent agency is an important facet of the delegation embedded in the institutional design of the regime. The NCC is a statutory independent agency that holds primary responsibility for technical oversight of compliance with the CPA. [2] The NCC is a statutory independent agency made up of five private sector appointees from business backgrounds and supported by 20–23 staff, most of whom are economists but some of whom are lawyers. The council is appointed for a three-year term, by vote of all the states and territories, from a list approved by the (non-voting) federal government—it thus, represents a national perspective. The NCC makes annual assessments of the rate of progress of each jurisdiction in legislation review, and evaluates the justifications advanced by each state for retaining their regulatory programs. These assessments are public documents and do not need to be cleared by the government of the day, and it is upon them that the payment of the annual competition payments depends. Although the Commonwealth Treasurer formally authorizes the payment or non-payment of the competition payments, the NCC makes the final recommendation, in practice dispositive, as to whether any financial penalties for unsatisfactory compliance are to be levied.

There is, therefore, at the core of the review regime, a national oversight institution insulated from electoral pressures. But further, more complex versions of delegation exist in the layers below the NCC, within the confines of the federal and state governments. Here, separate executive units and independent agencies within government monitor and enforce the application of the criteria governing economic review of legislation. For example, in the federal government, technical oversight of compliance with the CPA has been entrusted to the Office of Regulation Review, a unit employing fifteen professional economists and one lawyer, and located in the independent statutory body now known as the Productivity Commission. The Productivity Commission, set up to promote micro-economic reform, has considerable insulation from the political process. Three particularly important facets of this are the statutory basis for the agency's powers, the five-year tenure of the Chairman (election cycles are every three years) and the ability to publish sensitive policy recommendations, inquiries and reports without government clearance.

State governments, in contrast, exhibited a preference for retaining more direct political control over the agenda-setting stage and subsequent oversight. This was reflected in the governmental location of NCP officials. For example, Victoria, under the auspices of the right-wing Kennett government, established a National Competition Policy Unit in the Treasury with a staff of between three or four economists. The Treasury location of oversight and control placed decisive power in officials who were, albeit not completely politically insulated, nonetheless, at one remove from the much more direct lobbying by affected interest groups that characterized policy departments. Moreover, the Victorian NCP Unit made strenuous efforts to ensure that legislative review at policy department level used independent review structures and arms-length economically qualified consultants, an approach that ensured a type of delegation in reform design at departmental level as well as that of oversight (Interview 2001a).

Delegation did, however, vary with the color of political control. New South Wales, under a minority Labor government, chose to retain relatively greater political input into the agenda-setting and oversight process, and secured this with a relatively decentralized institutional configuration. The government created a Regulatory Review and Intergovernmental Affairs Unit, employing between three and four staff (all economists) and based in the Cabinet Office, and reporting directly to the Premier. With this direct line to final political decisions, the Unit had considerable power to annotate and thus influence review recommendations. But the Unit's senior officials saw their role as facilitator of a change in bureaucratic culture from the inside, rather than as a policing gatekeeper of externally imposed criteria (Interview 2001b). Thus, review was decentralized to a large extent, allowing departments and their relevant Ministers to make initial agenda-setting choices without the constraint of centrally set guidelines, and to have final decisions on the constitution of review teams. There was less emphasis on "independence from politics" (meaning usually, Ministers and the stakeholders exerting influence through Ministers), and therefore, a lower intensity of delegation in the sense relevant to legality.

Despite these and other variations in the level of insulation from politics (see generally Morgan 2003) the more general point about incipient legality holds across the spectra of political variation observed. The key position of the NCC—the oversight institution most highly insulated from politics—is critical. NCC's relatively strong insulation *combined with its fiscal enforcement powers* cast an insulating shadow over the other constituents of the oversight network, at least at the level of day-to-day operating principles. Thus, even where NCP units were part of political decision making environments, as with the states, the professional orientation of their staff members as economists facilitated "common understandings, good relationships and a general consensus on the main aims [of the regime]" (Interview 2001c). These shared commitments had space to operate relatively autonomously of the political pressures placed on the state NCP oversight decision-makers due to the triangulating impact of NCC on the incentive structure. Because the "external, independent" judgment of the politically insulated NCC would impact the state budget, the NCP units could insist on holding departments and politicians to courses of actions that they might otherwise resist. As a result, what emerged was a relatively politically insulated network of central agency officials, in a context of semi-autonomous institutional structures.

Also very important to a persuasive account of this development, as one of incipient legality, are key aspects of how the reforms were implemented.

In the next section, I discuss three important aspects of implementation that bolster the precision, obligatory nature and delegative aspects of the regime instituting economic review of legislation.

Precision, Obligation and Delegation in Implementation

The nub of this section is that written interpretative guidance regarding the implementation of the CPA catalyzed a pattern of routinized dialogue amongst a network of central agency officials, all of whom shared professional commitments to the tenets of economic rationality. The combined effects of these aspects of implementing the review regime was to create a texture of incipient legality, albeit one that was sometimes fragile. Precision, obligation and delegation weave in and out of the effects of the implementation narrative.

Written Guidance. The precision of legislative review under the CPA was considerably fleshed out as the regime was implemented by participating governments. Although the "guiding principle" stated in Clause 5(1) (above) may seem broadly worded, it was implemented at member jurisdiction level by detailed documents providing "interpretive guidance." Such guidelines were, in time, relied upon by all the central agency units overseeing the Australian economic legislation review regime. The   greater   precision thereby acquired facilitated a pattern of enforcement that lent obligatory weight to the reform program. For example, in Victoria, all those departmental officials in charge of reviews carried out under the CPA had to obtain signed consent by the NCP unit at three separate stages: when terms of reference were set and a review team constituted, when a draft report came in, and when final recommendations were made. In giving or refusing such consent, the Unit referred to the detailed centrally approved guidelines. The Unit, therefore, retained considerable policy control at the same time as it performed the gate-keeping function of ensuring technical compliance with the reforms (Interview 2001a).

The various central agency guidelines all shared a conceptual template reflecting the shared professional commitments of the network of central agency officials, commitments flowing from training in neoclassical economics. This shared commitment made it possible for officials from different jurisdictions within Australia to establish connections and conduct informal dialogues as the reform program unfolded, thereby building up a fund of experience that enhanced predictability. Victoria, for example, stated in its instruction manual:

> Each of the steps [taken in assessing legislation to determine if it comes within the review agenda] involves the application of economic concepts. It would therefore be advisable when assessing compliance with this guideline to obtain suitable economic advice. Such advice may be obtained from internal departmental resources, specialist bodies such as the Office of Regulation Reform (ORR) or economic consultants with expertise in microeconomic reform. (Victorian Government 1995)

From the perspective of those central agency officials with key interpretive power, the aim of the reform program was to require policymakers to think in terms of market competition as the first option for solving social problems. The goal was to alter common sense intuitions about what justified policy, rather than to generate sophisticated cost-benefit modeling of precise quantitative costs. As one official said,

> We want departments to think about the objective of regulation in terms of market failure, to think through the problem from an economic perspective rather than from a heavily quantitative basis. Questions like 'what is the market failure justification? Or what is the legitimate social policy objective?' are more important than numbers, costs or benefits. (Interview 2001c, 3)

Taking Words Seriously. One important implication of this altered "common sense" in the context of the production of economic regulation was a particular interpretive stance with which the network of central agency officials infused their common commitments to the spirit of economic rationality. That stance, to quote one of the officials, was one of "taking words seriously" (Interview 2001c, 3). Another official commented that at times the text of the intergovernmental agreements seemed to have acquired the status of being the object of quasi-biblical exegesis (Interview 2001d, 3). More broadly, interviews supported the notion that building bureaucratic compliance around highly specific reliance on the meaning of particular phrases, in the context of the shared professional norms of the key officials, was an important technique for securing the kind of insulation from direct political influence I have been emphasizing as constitutive of "incipient legality" (Interview 2001c, 3, 9; Interview 2001a)

Two examples illustrate this stance vividly, both illustrating debates that commonly emerge in forums of judicial legality, but are here also importantly shaped by the commitment to economic rationality. Both examples relate to the precise meaning of the key obligation imposed by the Competition Principles—the guiding principle of Clause 5(1) that legislation "should not restrict competition unless it can be demonstrated that…the benefits of the restriction to the community as a whole outweigh the costs and…the objectives of the legislation can only be achieved by restricting competition." The first example of "taking words seriously" concerns how the network of central agency officials expended significant energy debating and establishing the precise onus of proof implied by this wording. The second example is how, later in the life of the reforms, a careful, strategic, and highly legalistic change in the weight of this guiding principle was secured by amending the intergovernmental agreements at a juncture of political crisis.

First, we will consider the notion that the agreements created an "onus of proof," and more specifically one *against* regulatory intervention. Broad as the guiding principle of giving primacy to competitiveness goals in regulatory policymaking may seem, sharp debates took place within the bureaucracy regarding the precise onus of proof implied by the wording. Was the purpose of the guiding principle to create a presumption against a decision to intervene politically into the economy, especially via command-and-control regulation? Many of those implementing the reform program were committed to this interpretation. The general rules of the review regime may not *preclude* a decision to regulate, they argued, but they are intended to discourage it. For example, the NCC insisted from its very first assessment of progress in implementing regulation that under Clause Five, unless actual empirical evidence was provided in support of government intervention, the *presumption* would be against government intervention (National Competition Council 1996). In the federal government, Office of Regulation Review (ORR) personnel were strongly committed to the notion that the most important facet of the CPA involved its challenge to the status quo through the establishment of a burden of proof that militated in favor of change (Interview 1997a). Absent an "adequate" case in favor of regulatory intervention, deregulation would be the presumptive solution.

Government intervention of any sort, therefore, required a threshold justification that had to be framed in precise terms of addressing a market failure. Furthermore, redressing the failure should only involve government intervention if absolutely necessary. "A command-and-control regulatory approach should be the last option. Economically they are the least efficient and may impose significant costs on the community" (Council of Australian Governments 1997, 24). Or, as the guidelines commissioned by the Victorian government insisted, "market failure is a necessary but not sufficient ground for government intervention" (Victorian Government 1995, point 5 of step 3). That is, *government* failure had to be disproved as well as market failure proved.

Some officials disagreed with this interpretation of a substantive onus of proof—notably those in New South Wales, the least politically insulated of all those in the network. But even their alternative interpretative stance was redolent of legality. They stressed that the guiding principle had no substantive import but rather imposed a formal rationality on regulatory policymaking decisions. As one official argued, "At its heart, the NCP program is not about economic rationalism gone mad, but about a culture of transparency and reasoned justification in economic policy" (Interview 2001b, 7). This reflects a type of due process discourse familiar from judicial legality.

The echo of judicial legality is intensified when we note a development that occurred later in the life of the Australian regime. It touches not only upon due process concerns, but also upon the legitimate scope for reasoned justification of policies by regulating governments: both matters at the heart of judicial review. In November 2000, five years into the reform program, political hostility to the National Competition Policy ran high, especially in states with a high proportion of rural population who had been hard hit by the unbundling of cross-subsidies in essential services. At a closed meeting of heads of governments, some states came close to withdrawing from the intergovernmental agreements, but were mollified by the introduction of "several measures to clarify and fine-tune implementation arrangements for NCP" (Coalition of Australian Governments 2000, 4). One of these measures related to the oversight role of the NCC and had the effect of intensifying the incipient legality of its institutional nature. By way of letters sent to the heads of participating jurisdictions, the intergovernmental compacts were in effect amended by adding the following clause:

> In assessing whether the threshold requirement of Clause 5 has been achieved, the NCC should consider whether the conclusion reached in the report is within a range of outcomes that could reasonably be reached based on the information available to a properly constituted review process. Within the range of outcomes that could reasonably be reached, it is a matter for Government to determine what policy is in the public interest. (Coalition of Australian Governments 2000, attachment)

This clause in effect tries to soften the impact of the "onus of proof" insisted upon in earlier patterns of implementation. It does so by introducing the notion of a "range of outcomes that could reasonably be reached" by reviewing bodies. This eases the bite of the regime, loosening the weight of the assumed onus in favor of competition. Under the amended standard of assessment, even if there is a policy alternative available to a department or government that is less restrictive of competition, the last word on whether that choice is overall in the public interest is explicitly given back to the government, rather than the NCC. There is, in other words, no "right answer" divinable by the NCC but a range of possible answers, all of which are justifiable under the aegis of the regime. Thus, the amending clause lessens the constraint imposed on regulatory policymaking by that regime.[3]

This "refinement" of the CPA is analogous to the way in which judicial review constrains public decision making. Indeed, the precise phrasing of the amendment was, according to some officials, inspired by the logic of judicial review (Interview 2001b, 6). Like a court, the NCC insists that it does not set policy, but merely requires public justification in terms of a neutral rationality. Though this does constrain political choice, it does not direct it to specific ends. It leaves instead a zone of flexibility, within which a range of justifiable regulatory policy choices is feasible. Subsequent uncertainty over whether that zone of flexibility entitles the NCC to take a "hard look" at the rigor and logic of evidence presented is also a familiar theme from judicial review.

An Impartial Network of Officials? These two examples regarding the energy and effort expended on debating the precise wording of the commitments made under Australian review of economic legislation are only part of the story of showing how implementation patterns reinforce non-judicial legality. An even more important aspect of the shared professional commitments of the network of central agency officials concerns the substantive import of economic rationality. What I want to focus on here is not so much concrete policy impact (see Morgan 2003, chaps. 4 and 5), but rather the way these commitments contribute to an ethic of disinterestedness. Such an ethic is a critical aspect of triangulated delegation: that core logic of legality that involves reliance on an arms-length third party for conflict resolution. What is important here is that the delegation is impartial. While quasi-obligatory precisely worded obligations assist in constructing an impartial arena by imposing a background discipline of "rule," there is inevitably interpretive slippage (and thus, a reappearance of discretion) in the day-to-day practices of implementation. The substantive rationality that animates interpretive discretion must therefore crucially be perceived as impartial, if actors affected by the review regime are to be convinced of its evenhandedness. In the context of the growth of economic review of legislation, as illustrated by the Australian regime, that rationality is an economic one, and core to its claim of disinterestedness are assumptions embedded in public choice approaches to regulation.

A public choice perspective on regulatory politics is one that emphasizes technocratic expertise, particularly that derived from specialist economic knowledge, and seeks to insulate economic policymaking choices from democratic politics, based on a set of assumptions about regulatory legislation. The most important assumption is that much of what passes for democratic political choice is distorted by the influence of special interest groups. Winners and losers of binding political decisions are typically asymmetrically distributed, it is argued, such that political decisions with concentrated costs and diffuse benefits will be intensely resisted by those groups suffering the concentrated cost. As a corollary, political decision making will tend to skew towards choices that award concentrated benefits to certain groups at the price of diffusely distributed costs. In the public choice schema, most regulatory legislation is precisely this: the product of a democratic process distorted by concentrated interest groups who arrogate "rent" to their benefit by means of securing protectionist legislation (Stigler 1971).

The design of the legislative review component of National Competition Policy in Australia did not entirely eliminate the political role of democratically elected officials in having the "last word" on regulatory policy choice. Rather, it imposed an additional hurdle (a market-centered net benefit test) that constrained those choices, and built institutions and incentives that come close to creating an actual veto point in the political process. This design sought to insulate regulatory policy choice not from politics *per se*, but from a certain kind of politics—that which reflects the disproportionate influence of concentrated interest groups. Politicians can ultimately choose to retain or create new regulatory policies that do not pass the market-centered public interest test as interpreted by the NCC, but in doing so, they must both sacrifice considerable fiscal resources and expose themselves to public criticism. The rationale of the reforms is that these disincentives will facilitate political decisions that reflect the "true" general interest of the (diffuse) public, and not the sectional interests of a powerful or disproportionately affected few. As the NCC stated,

> Governments should be congratulated for their continued commitment to the NCP reform program...This reflects a commitment to good government in the interests of all Australian, rather than the pursuit of narrow, short-term political interests. (NCC 2001, vi)

This is increasingly presented as not simply a discipline that serves efficiency values, but also as one that enhances political legitimation. The argument here is that the constraints of processes like this review regime are put in place on behalf of the unrepresented, unorganized taxpayer or consumer. The underlying logic is that due to collective action problems, diffuse and unorganized groups such as taxpayers and consumers are effectively suffering "taxation without representation" when regulatory policies are implemented by governments (Lindseth 2002; Poiares Maduro 2000; McGinnis and Movsesian 2000). Regimes that institutionalize economic review of legislation thus, "represent" a set of otherwise silenced interests, placing a political gloss on the economic perspective. The link between this approach to regulatory politics and impartiality is vividly captured—with an explicit link to notions of legality—in an Australian senior Treasury official's comment.

> There is a constitutional function for Treasury which is relatively independent of the government of the day…that doesn't mean that we pursue our agenda independently of the government of the day…[but] I believe that my thoughts and actions stem from that set of stimuli [which make up the independent constitutional function] rather than from the government per se, although they are tempered by the policy program of the government. (Campbell and Halligan 1992, 24)

This comment captures the essence of the view powerful in public choice theory, that economic rationality places a constraint on politics and by so doing serves the "true" public interest. The institutional design of National Competition Policy, with its oversight function given to an independent federal agency, intensifies the relevance of this view. And examples of this public choice perspective pervade, not only the documentary history of the National Competition Policy reforms, but also interviews with key officials (e.g., Interview 1997a; Interview 2001d; NCC 2001; ORR n.d).

"Purified politics" is strained of factionalism and rendered transparent by the application of economic rationality at arms-length from the political process and constrained by norms of due process. Justification in accordance with the terms of economic rationality was, in the Australian program, obligatory under the terms of intergovernmental compacts the words of which were taken seriously, and the precision of which was hard-fought for, by key implementing officials. The network of these officials, though iterated dialogue and technical cooperation over time, built around written guidelines centrally enforced in a context of shared professional commitments, all came together to create a background constraint for regulatory decision making. That constraint imposes the discipline of economic rationality upon legislative discretion via a rule-based institutionalization that amounts, as I have argued here, to a clear instance of incipient non-judicial legality.

III.

Now clearly, assumptions of the kind that typify a public choice perspective on regulation are politically controversial. Indeed, that is the reason for the question mark I placed at the end of the last subheading, which was intended to keep open the *disinterested* nature of the substantive commitments animating the review regime. For the institutional design that infuses the economic review of legislation with a combination of precision, obligation and delegation reminiscent of legality is of course the result of politically motivated choices. That has been relatively obscured in my discussion so far, for my exposition of the Australian regime primarily relied on analogical logic, implicit in my use of Shapiro's triadic logic to expand our conception of what might be described by the notion of legality. But to stop there would not do full justice to the Shapiro style of exposing the underlying social logic of developments. That exposure depends crucially on an appreciation of the political incentive structure facing actors who wish to institutionalize economic review of legislation. I want to explore this briefly by pointing to the growing intensification of economic review of legislation at the international level. The reason for moving to the international level in this last section of the essay is to illustrate that the patterns of political conflict underpinning the social logic of non-judicial legality have a much wider salience than the Australian case alone might suggest. As a bridge to discussing developments at the international level, I briefly point to the political stakes in Australia, their implications for its regime of economic review of legislation thus far, and their link to similar political battles at the international level.

The political stakes in Australia can be briefly illustrated by referring back to my earlier discussion of the amendment to the intergovernmental agreements that constituted the regime of economic review of legislation. Over time in Australia, as National Competition Policy gradually bit harder, considerable political backlash developed against it, driven by a perception, whether accurate or not, that it epitomized an ideologically driven neo-liberal agenda that intensified inequality and diluted non-economic dimensions of policymaking. More generally, the conflicts arising around regimes that review economic legislation tend to be ones between the collective welfare benefits of increased economic productivity, and social values such as community cohesion, ecological integrity and redistributive equity. In the Australian case, political elites had in effect a dual strategy for managing the conflict over how to allocate the costs of reform: temporary buy-out of the immediate losers, combined with a more technocratically managed adjustment of the institutional balance between political discretion and the constraints of "rule-by-economics."

The first aspect of this strategy was embedded in an openly political debate about adjustment assistance. This was partly a matter of monetary compensation for disproportionately affected groups, but also of providing services that would "help people feel more optimistic about their ability to adapt in a world where ongoing change is a part of life, and perhaps most important of all, to ensure that people do not feel that they have been forgotten or discarded by the rest of the community" (Samuels 2001, 13). The second aspect was the amendment process already discussed in Part II: a highly legalistic adjustment in very precise terms of the formal obligations and responsibilities of the arms-length institution (the NCC) delegated with the responsibility of imposing the discipline of economic rationality upon legislative discretion.

There are two important points about this dual strategy of managing the substantive political stakes underpinning economic review of legislation. The first is that it effectively *entrenches* non-judicial legality by tempering its immediate political costs, but simultaneously intensifying the commitment to its deeper institutionalization at a more systemic level. Secondly, that entrenchment creates a potential legitimacy crisis for the institution monitoring the review regimes: in the Australian case, the National Competition Council (NCC). The terms in which the NCC's legitimacy was attacked resonate (not accidentally in my view) with arguments over the legitimate role of judicial institutions in monitoring political decisions. When the NCC in its second tranche assessment in July 1999 recommended that Queensland lose AUS$113 million of competition payments for its refusal to drop a dam proposal and to deregulate dairy milk prices, the Queensland Premier called in the national press for the NCC to be abolished, and the Queensland Treasurer remonstrated:

> The NCC has fundamentally exceeded its legitimate role and responsibilities, as provided for under the [intergovernmental] agreements. Inappropriately, the Council has sought…to 'second guess' the outcomes of public benefit tests. Effectively, the NCC is an umpire which is seeking to determine the outcome of the game, rather than just enforcing the rules. (Hamill 1999)

The conflict over the legitimacy of NCC oversight is structurally similar to the legitimacy conundrum that judicial review proper throws up. It is embedded in the issue of where lies the legitimate "last word" on balancing non-economic benefit and productive efficiency: the technical assessment performed in the review itself (and shaped by the terms of economic rationality), or politicians making a strategic electoral calculus?

The question of what kind of institutions decide such trade-offs has salience far beyond the borders of Australia. For in the broader international forum, political conflicts over the social costs of prioritizing economic efficiency and competitiveness are very similar to those that underpin the evolution of the Australian regime. To some extent, the distributive issues they raise are increasingly framed in terms of social and economic rights rather than (as has tended to happen at national levels) in terms of welfare state provision or developmental goals.[4] But the pages of the *New Left Review* in recent years are just one place where the political stakes of "globalization" are increasingly presented as part of a narrative that has substantive continuity with earlier nation-state level conflicts over the limits of the welfare or developmental state. The question for this paper is: why would key actors at either the national or the international level have incentives to manage such conflicts via the medium of non-judicial legalization?

Otherwise put, this question asks why and who would wish to constrain legislative discretion in regulatory policymaking by rule, and in particular, by a rule-of-economics? Obviously, answers will depend on specific contexts, but broadly speaking one might argue that legislative discretion to enact regulatory policy in small economies such as Australia's has in practice narrowed in proportion with the increasing integration of a global economy that imposes a capital cost upon policies perceived as market-distorting in terms of their beyond-the-border effects. Given the tension between reduced legislative discretion and continuing internal pressures for redistributive and protective regulatory policies, political elites benefit from institutionalizing a system that justifies a reduced use of pro-regulatory legislative discretion on principled, technocratic grounds. First, this will dampen political conflict, or at least reduce the scope of issues over which it could arise. Second, since the rules on which such regimes are based are grounded in economic theories which lay strong claim to maximize general welfare in the medium to long term, this protects the political elites from charges of bad faith (though only up to a point, since these economic rationales are strongly contested in contemporary political arenas).

Now at an international level, the incentives laid out above might be thought less relevant, at least for major economic actors such as the United States and the EU, who arguably maintain much more capacity for policy maneuver in the global economy. But there are two reasons why even very powerful economic actors in the global economy might still agree to a set of rule-based constraints on their domestic legislative discretion. The first is that, iterated reciprocity in respecting a rule-of-economics as between economic actors of roughly equal power is the situation most likely to maximize general economic welfare in the way that that theory predicts it should. Thus it is probably no accident that the EU and the United States[5] are both committed to the WTO system of rule-based constraint of legislative discretion vis-à-vis trade effects. It is also notable that initiatives such as the Transatlantic Business Dialogue make even denser that commitment as between its two most economically powerful members. Secondly, the kinds of politically sensitive redistributive issues that led to political backlash in Australia are even more intensely felt in an international setting between North and South. Analogously to the Australian dynamic, at least some of this political conflict can be tempered by funneling it through a technocratic rule-based lens. Witness how discussions of the costs suffered by those with structurally asymmetrical access to the review regime (i.e., the least developed countries) gravitate to discussions of technical assistance as solutions to the problem (Shaffer 2003): The response is markedly similar to the Australian strategy of providing adjustment assistance while embedding the systemic institutionalization of the rule-of-economics itself even more firmly into the day-to-day operating practices of legislatures across the globe.

What remains in the closing section of this part is to briefly point to three actual instances of emerging regimes for reviewing economic legislation in an international context. The point of setting them out is to illustrate the institutional variation that is possible within a general trajectory of non-judicial legalization, particularly regarding the regime monitor to whom the power of economic review is delegated. The three variations are: independent bureaucratic agency, quasi-judicial review, and peer review.

The first of the three possibilities surveyed here is to use independent bureaucratic monitoring agencies: a choice already evidenced by the Australian regime. Beyond Australia, a wide range of countries at different levels of economic development are increasingly putting in places institutions to monitor the quality of economic regulatory legislation. The OECD has codified these practices into what it calls an "international quality standard" on the production of government regulation (OECD 1995), and by 1999, four years after the initial promulgation of this OECD

Recommendation, twenty-four OECD countries were using regulatory impact analysis to guide their regulatory policy decision making process, compared to only three in 1980 (Jacobs 1999). Moreover, fourteen of these countries had established specific units and personnel in central bureaucracies to monitor and support the new routines (Deighton-Smith 1997, 33).

Most of these regimes review economic legislation according to rule-based criteria of reasonable precision, but for the most part—and in contrast to Australia—the substantive focus of the criteria are cost-benefit and cost-effectiveness ones. However, a number of other developments make it likely that these criteria will, in the medium term, either incorporate or be effectively superseded by criteria that seek to maximize both competition and international trade flows. Competition and trade-focused review criteria will likely bite much more decisively into the scope of legislative discretion that national-level governments could expect to exercise over economic regulatory legislation. Their looming salience arises as a result of mooted intersections between national-level regimes that institutionalize economic review of legislation and the rules governing international trade.

The OECD is a particularly enthusiastic supporter of such linkages. In a recent paper, it comments,

> As trade barriers at the border fall through successive trade negotiations, it is increasingly evident that domestic regulation may represent a significant source of residual trade barriers. Current national regulatory systems were developed when the nation-state was seen as the primary economic unit; with the increased importance of the global economy today, regulatory reform may be necessary to ensure that the expected benefits of globalization are realized and that the different national systems do not become barriers to international trade and investment. (OECD 2000)

The OECD does not provide any *international institution* with delegated power to monitor the linkage between domestic regulatory reform and international trade regimes. The WTO however, with its Dispute Settlement Understanding utilizing quasi-judicial panels, is potentially poised to do just that. Even to date, the process of challenging or justifying economic policies that impact on cross-border trade before a panel of the WTO has brought "[m]atters which were once the sole purview of regulators at the state level [to]...now squarely on the international agenda" (Paton 2003, 2). Article VI of the General Agreement on Trade in Services (GATS), in the process of being negotiated at this writing, would extend the compass of rule-based constraints upon domestic legislative discretion much wider, and would do so in a context where the crucial delegate of monitoring power was not only internationally constituted, but also quasi-judicial in nature. Article VI requires domestic regulations, *whether or not they discriminate between foreign or domestic actors,* to meet one particularly significant criterion among others,[6] that of being "no more burdensome than necessary." It is not yet clear just how this would be filled out, but the current range of possibilities includes at least three: compliance with pro-competitive principles, compliance with proportionality tests, or a requirement to choose the regulatory option that is "least restrictive to trade" (Gould 2002). Whatever the details, the substantive constraint on domestic legislative discretion is clearly potentially significant. Interestingly, the range of alternative interpretations includes not just an imposition of economic rationality, but also the more judicially inflected suggestion of a proportionality test. This reflects the quasi-judicial nature of the panels that pass judgment on the worthiness of a government's underlying objectives in deciding whether the regulatory means they have chosen to implement economic policy are too restrictive. Such a means of monitoring "rule-by-economics" in the intersection between domestic regulatory reform and international trade regimes will make the former enforceable from above, in ways that echo the importance of fiscal incentives in the Australian regime for its ultimate leverage on policymaking.

Peer review is the final institutional option worth noting. It differs from the ones thus far surveyed in two principal ways: It is notably more political and it is horizontally monitored. Oversight is still delegated, but to peers rather than independent technocratic institutions, and only temporarily. In the WTO's Trade Policy Review Process, for example, an extensive pre-prepared report on a particular country's level of compliance with trade obligations is produced at regular intervals by WTO-employed economists, and subsequently discussed in an open forum with the aid of independent commentators (Braithwaite and Drahos 2000, 209). While this process does not at present have any particular formal sanctions attached to it, the "public shaming" effect it has may function as a hook for the imposition of economic review of legislation within national borders (Interview 2001e). There is potential here for trade regimes to act as an enforcement tool for domestic regimes of economic review of legislation, or at least to leverage both their initial introduction and ongoing compliance.

Peer review mechanisms for linking domestic regulatory reform and international trade objectives, however, involve a more diluted form of delegated monitoring than the autonomous bureaucratic or quasi-judicial forms noted above, for they depend more upon persuasion than upon obligation and coercion. To characterize it as non-judicial legality may be to push the boundaries of that notion too far. But its *differences* from the "core" instances of non-judicial or indeed even judicial legality matter, for they mean that the political stakes underlying the imposition of regimes of economic review would be managed very differently. In other words, institutional choice in such regimes is likely to reflect in important ways the incentive structure driving the desire for (and desirability of) such regimes. In the conclusion, I touch on this while also summing up the overall argument.

Conclusion

This chapter has used a political perspective on law and courts to explore the social logic underlying regulatory review mechanisms relying on economic rationality, and their systematic interjection into the every-day routines of governmental policymaking. It has situated this development at the intersection of an increasing legalization of politics and a growing reliance on non-judicial mechanisms of accountability. This intersection is a site of *non-judicial legality.* Just as constitutions place extra-political constraints on the lawmaking process, so too Australia's regime for the economic review of legislation under its National Competition Policy placed a different kind of extra-political constraint on lawmaking. That constraint institutionalized skepticism about the efficacy of command-and-control regulation and the positive social benefits flowing from such regulation. It did so by subjecting legislative discretion to the rule-based constraints of economic rationality, thereby imposing a kind of "rule-of-economics."

Over time, the Australian review regime has not only "come to shape how individuals interact with each other" in economic policymaking fora, but has also "develop[ed] authority over the normative structure in place" (Stone Sweet 2000, 13), at least within the community of central agency officials who shared a certain blend of ideological commitment and bureaucratic mission that gave them a "professional and bureaucratic interest in providing disinterested...interpretation" (Tushnet 2001, 3–4). It has increasingly placed well-defined, mandatory boundaries upon the exercise of regulatory policymaking power, and "empowered state agencies to control and redress trespasses of these boundaries" (O'Donnell 1997, 185) thus, institutionalizing one of the forms of horizontal accountability that O'Donnell argues is crucial to establishing the rule of law. Like legal processes more traditionally conceived, non-judicial legality as applied to the review of economic legislation in Australia "involve[d] a discourse framed in terms of reason, interpretation, technical knowledge, and argument...[and was] followed by deliberation and judgment by impartial parties...based on reasons applicable to all similarly situated [policymakers]" (Goldstein et al. 2001, 35).

This proto-institutionalization of the rule-of-economics is increasingly mirrored at international levels, driven in part by strategic linkages between international trade rules and domestic regulatory reform procedures. One reason for dwelling in some detail on the Australian regime in the middle part of this chapter was that Australia's experience may very well influence the future trajectory of the "rule-of-economics." The Trade Policy Review Process in the WTO was modeled on procedures developed by the Australian Productivity Commission (then the Industry Commission), and the Trade Policy Review Body was initially staffed by some key former members of that Commission (Interview 2001e). The more recent reforms embedded in the National Competition Policy and explored in Part II of this chapter have already attracted considerable interest from countries as diverse as Canada, Germany and Mexico,[7] as well as industrializing countries in the Pacific Rim. And the OECD may play a role in promoting the Australian model as an international exemplar. The OECD's prominent support for regulatory review regimes has been driven primarily by a small but influential key network of some five or six advocates, including two Australians (Interview 1997b; Interview 1997c). That influence could be crucial, since the OECD, as what one commentator has called "the single most important builder of business regulatory epistemic communities," (Braithwaite and Drahos 2000, 29) is an important player in setting international agendas (Salzman 2000). Already the OECD refers in its promotion of regulatory review regimes to the detailed guidelines developed by Victoria (Center for International Economics 1999) in implementing the Competition Principles Agreement (Interview 2001e), suggesting the salience of this regime for broader international developments.

In both Australia and in the international context, the future direction of this trajectory of non-judicial legality remains highly uncertain. Its institutionalization is yet fragile and its authority over the normative structure of economic policymaking is highly contested. Although interactions shaped by obligatory, precise, arms-length applied rules go some way towards minimizing any perception that raw power has determined the outcome, the perception of disinterested triangulation of conflict in the case of the economic review of legislation is a fragile one to maintain. The Australian experience has shown the difficulty of incorporating redistributive goals, and more broadly a sense of social cohesion and community, into the justificatory structure of its review regime. This is arguably a concomitant of the choice to delegate important portions of the interpretive power shaping regulatory policymaking decisions to arms-length actors who will dispose of them with technical precision in ways that mute their discretionary and value-laden dimensions. Although this muting is arguably part of the appeal for political elites of non-judicial legality, it can nonetheless, also be seen as a politically salient weakness, particularly in the international context. Trade-offs between non-economic benefit and productive efficiency do not have easy metrics: They involve incommensurabilities and painful compromises whose costs and benefits often have a degree of arbitrariness. Such arbitrariness might be borne in the context of a nationally bounded community where the government of the day possesses sufficiently effective discretion to create a safety-net for those who lose out. But increasingly, such discretion is constrained by the dictates of a rule-bound monitoring system that operates at arms-length from national governments and that imposes a rule-of-economics upon their regulatory decisions. Though institutional choices still remain open in this respect, it is clear that the triadic logic of (non-judicial) legality will provide a provocative axis around which to measure the variegated future developments of the review of economic legislation.

Notes

1   The CPA had two general methods for excluding legislation from review, but both required positive arguments to be made, so it is valid to say the scope included all legislation. *Exemption* required a department to demonstrate that the legislation had either been recently or currently under review, or that it was not cost-effective to review it. *Exclusion* required a substantive argument that the legislation had no relevance to issues of market competitiveness.

2   NCC was not the sole national oversight body. The Council of Australian Governments, a federal network of senior government representatives advised by a secretariat of senior bureaucrats (the Committee on Regulatory Reform), was responsible for overall policy direction and the forward work program of NCC. However, the implementation of the regime of economic review of legislation fell very largely to the remit of the NCC.

3   The NCC's response to this amendment provides even more evidence of an approach redolent of legality. Essentially, the NCC, while conceding that there might well be less constraint on specific outcomes under the amended approach, exploited the potential for a tightening of constraints on *process*. They noted that the wider feasibility in permissible outcomes is conditioned on the existence of "information available to a properly constituted review process," and indicated that the notion of "proper constitution" of review processes was intended to bear heavy interpretive weight. The NCC's guidelines for the June 2001 "third tranche assessment" of competition payments stressed three consequences of the requirement for proper constitution: transparency, independence and "analytical rigour" (NCC 2001, 5.2; see also Morgan 2003). Interviews with officials (Interview 1997a; Interview 2001c, 7–8) fleshed this out as requiring that the search for the least restrictive solution in regulatory policy choice involve publicly available reasoning undertaken by persons without a direct material interest in the outcomes.

4   For example, the "trade and..." debate is increasingly focused (Alston 2002; Cottier 2002; Petersmann 2000) on the question of whether the WTO is an appropriate forum for resolving the question of how much competing weight to give environmental or human rights claims that may conflict with the rules that open up trade in order to maximise global economic productivity.

5   The United States commitment to the international trading regime through the WTO is presently looking increasingly fragile, but I will assume for the purposes of this paper that this is temporary.

6   The other criteria are that regulation be objective, transparent, and administered in a reasonable, objective, and impartial manner.

7   All three of these countries have sent officials on investigatory visits to Australia in this regard (Ranald 1995; Interview 2001d).

10.

Law, Courts and Politics

Martin Shapiro

The study of comparative law is shared by a number of disciplines, among them law and political science. As practiced by lawyer-scholars comparative law has long since reached the classificatory stage at which charts of the various legal components of each "family" of law, Anglo-American, civil law, etc. have been produced. Beyond these classifications, lawyers have produced numbers of essentially pragmatic studies that look for particularly successful legal doctrines or procedures in one legal system and propose and hypothetically test their adoption by another. There have also been some attempts at grand general theories such as Hans Kelsen's (1945), and a few more specifically comparative ones, but with the distinguished exception of Mirjan R. Damaska's (1986), very few that generate testable hypotheses. Most lawyer scholarship is content to note differences and correspondences between particular pieces of law in particular jurisdictions and suggest selective transfers or, as in much European Union (EU) oriented studies, suggest principles or cores under which national variations could be subsumed.

Political science has done far less. Not simply its law segment, but political science in general has divided itself into American, comparative, international and public law segments. Essentially what that really meant is that political scientists who studied the United States were in one camp and those who studied the politics of any other particular nation were placed in another. Those in the comparative camp were not really engaged in comparison and, more importantly, even when comparativists actually began to compare, on the one hand, they were forbidden to use the U.S. as one of their phenomena for comparison and, on the other, forbidden to know anything about the law and courts of any country or countries. Precisely because it was its own sub-field of political science, "public law" might have combined the study of U.S. and foreign law, but for a very long time it actually acted as a subsidiary of American politics. Students of international politics were licensed to study international law, but during the long cold war there was none to speak of. International relations political scientists were fairly well placed to deal with the new concern for globalization of nearly everything except law. Public law political scientists were not even at sea when confronted by globalization given that most of them could only get abroad as far as Hawaii and Alaska. Until very recently there was almost no comparative law in political science. Henry Abraham's *Judicial Process* (1993) had provided fledgling political scientists with an entry into foreign law that almost none of them took. The quantitative movement attempted a kind of Gutman scaling around the world, but alas most of the world will not cooperate by providing the necessary judicial voting data. And Walter Murphy and Joseph Tanenhaus (1977) provided a case book for an undergraduate course in comparative constitutional law which did not actually get taught because no one had the training to teach it. Donald Kommers (1977) and a few others did admirable but isolated studies of the constitutional law of some foreign countries. Even if there had been some comparative law, it would have been solely comparative constitutional law, because political scientists didn't seem able to interest themselves in any law other than constitutional.

For someone who took Ph.D. exams in public law, and was required to know little more than the hundred leading Supreme Court constitutional decisions and the clichés of judicial activism versus judicial self-restraint by the U.S. Supreme Court when exercising constitutional judicial review, this volume is very frightening. It seems to suggest to both fledgling lawyer scholars and political science students in the law sub-field that they are now compelled to know a lot more than they used to.

First of all, lawyer scholars must know a lot of political science. There is no official law and political science movement as there is a law and economics movement. That is not because there is little political science in law, but because some fields of law, notably constitutional and administrative, have so internalized political science modes of analysis and findings that they have become intrinsically law and politics fields. Even the titles and certainly the substance of the constitutional law studies of such dominant academic lawyers as Bickel (1962), Black (1960), Choper (1980), Ely (1980), Ackerman (1991), and Tushnet (1999) bear evidence to this evolution. In administrative law, one need only look at the table of contents of the latest edition of the most conventional of the case books, Gellhorn and Byse, (Strauss et al. 2000) to note the ever increasing ratio of non case materials and how much of that material sounds in political as opposed to narrowly legal analysis. In this volume, Paul Craig and Carol Harlow are lawyers and a number of other contributors are lawyers and Ph.D.s. One would be hard put to differentiate their concerns and modes of analysis from those of the political scientists in the volume. Law in general and judicial review in particular play a part in Craig's study, and it is framed in terms of constitutionalism. Yet, Craig's central concern is the building of administrative, that is political, institutions and particularly the network of relationships being built up between the bureaucracies of the member states and that of the European Union (EU). When he does arrive at the European Court of Justice (ECJ) in his detailed study of Community Agricultural Policy (CAP), it is to show the ECJ adjusting the complex political relationship between the Commission and the Member States, one that Americans would tend to call a relationship of cooperative federalism of the sort described in Shep Melnick's contribution to this volume.

Harlow is an administrative lawyer but one who has devoted much of her career to the interface between the private and the public sector rather than to administrative law as a purely internal set of rules for bureaucratic behavior. And here she chooses as her topic "governance," a topic that is of central concern to political science. Her main themes are administrative law on the one hand and democracy on the other. If there were recognized law and political science as there is law and economics, this would be it.

Both the Craig and Harlow papers also show interesting developments in comparative law as practiced by academic lawyers. Harlow's treatment is comparative, ranging over the experience of particular countries and EU. And it is not presented at the static level of classification or comparative anatomy but at a dynamic level of comparative physiology in which the concern is with common causes and common effects across a range of polities. The very substance of Craig's paper, shared management between member states and the Union, belies the division between domestic and foreign law. Even English legal scholars who wished to devote themselves solely to English law, as so many American legal scholars have to American law, would, as Craig shows, now necessarily become involved in law foreign in order to understand law domestic.

Three contributors to the volume represent more explicitly and formally the growth of the "law and..." movement. Javier Couso, Bronwen Morgan and Tom Ginsburg hold Ph.D.s from the Jurisprudence and Social Policy Program at Berkeley and teach on law faculties. All three are involved in law and political science and law and social science more generally. Ginsburg's work here is explicitly comparative and treats the United States as one of the data points in the comparison. Along this dimension it moves beyond the old American-Comparative division of political science while also being linked to the older political science in concerning itself exclusively with constitutional courts. As comparative law it does proceed at the level of classification of samenesses among and differences between legal regimes. But it seeks to use the classification effort as the basis for more dynamic analyses and for the testing of general theoretical propositions about the political role of courts.

Couso's paper goes to the fundamental concern with political legitimacy that is central to political science. It is explicitly comparative in terms of Latin America. One of its concerns is with constitutional courts, but more basically it is concerned with the broader topic of the dynamics of judicial independence. As with Ginsburg, the goal is not the cataloguing of similarities and differences but comparison as a method or technique of deriving and testing cause and effect hypotheses about law, courts and politics.

In a fit of ill temper, I once wrote that political scientists specializing in law and courts ought to move on to any law other than constitutional, any court other than the U.S. Supreme Court, and any country other than the U.S. Morgan's paper goes several steps beyond. It is comparative and international, and about all sorts of law other than constitutional, but it is also about legalization that is not necessarily linked to judicialization. It is closely linked to both Craig's and Harlow's in its concern, not simply for the litigational aspects, but for the whole range of legal and political relationships governing regulatory and management regimes. Morgan's work, both in subject and method, is also linked to the several extended studies of another contributor to this volume, R. Shep Melnick. For in those works Melnick (1983, 1994) is concerned with "everyday" rather than elevated constitutional areas of law, and with judge made law as only one aspect, and often not the most important aspect, of complex regulatory and management regimes in which many kinds of law and many kinds of politics intersect.

Melnick, Howard Gillman and Alec Stone Sweet are the more or less pure political scientists in this volume although here again there is evidence of the sub rosa law and political science movement with Gillman and Stone Sweet now holding joint appointments in their universities' law schools. Of them, Melnick has been a leading figure in the move of the public law subfield outward, upward and downward from the old preoccupation with the Constitutional Supreme Court, but has remained essentially concerned with American politics. Gillman is a leading spokesman of the "new institutionalism" in the study of law and courts, concerned to break out of narrow pluralist models of politics to an appreciation of the role of ideas, values, and aspirations in law and politics. He has remained largely concerned with American politics. Trained in comparative and international politics, Stone Sweet represents other dimensions of the new institutionalism. In their papers here Stone Sweet, Morgan, Craig and Harlow are all concerned not only with comparative studies of national legal regimes but with the study of transnational legal regimes as is Ginsburg in other of his work (Ginsburg and McAdams 2004). Stone Sweet's paper does concentrate on judicialization as opposed to the Morgan and Craig focus on non-judicialized transnational legalization and Harlow's major concern with democratization through legislative bodies. Stone Sweet is concerned with comparison as a mode for developing explanatory theory. Trained as an Americanist, Robert Kagan has shifted much of his interest to comparative work based on ideas and analysis developed in his American studies and concentrated not on judges alone but on the broad politico-legal movement he calls adversarial legalism which entails the study of interest groups, lawyers and the legislative and electoral processes (Kagan 2002). In the light of all this, what are political science students preparing for the Ph.D. qualifying exam in the "public law" or law and courts subfield or the young law professor alive to the "law and..." movements to do?

One quick answer suggested by this volume is "learn everything." Another quick answer is, "Despair." The right answer is, as usual, do as much as a reasonable human being can do in a reasonable amount of time. Beyond that, however, a general road map can be indicated.

First, any student of law, whatever "ands" may be attached, still must begin with law. Particularly for academic lawyers engaged in "law and..." work, it is too easy to forget how much standard legal technique, discourse, and practice in the broad sense is almost unconsciously packed into their enterprise. For them, however, it does not matter that they forget. Consciously or unconsciously they will exploit their training. Whom it is important for is those who do not have that training. The excessive concentration of political scientists on constitutional law is a bad thing for a lot of reasons, but the most important reasons may be that constitutional law is one of the least law-like of all the areas of law and constitutional courts are the least court-like. Lawyers are major players in the politics of law. The new institutionalism tells us that the way political players think, the discourse they employ, are important explanatory variables (Jacob et al. 1996). The newer political science tells us that many areas of non-constitutional law like regulatory and administrative law and even such "lawyer's law" areas as tort and contract are major policy making domains. This volume, among many others, shows that these domains are now, not only national, but transnational. Moreover, even if we limit our focus to "judicialization" or courts as political institutions, most of what most courts do lies within standard legal discourse and practice. The elephant cannot be described solely by reference to its constitutional trunk—or more realistically—left hind knee. Having passed through a useful stage of unmasking the political in the legal, students of law and politics must pay at least enough attention to the legal in the legal to be able to see the game as the players see it. The trick is to understand and give sufficient causal weight to interior legal perspectives while sustaining an exterior perspective. A little tort or contract or family law would be good for anyone, particularly one trying to construct general explanatory theories about courts or law and courts.

Secondly, at this point it seems very unwise for students of law and politics to limit at least their initial preparatory studies to one country. Transnational legal developments are now sufficient that even one solely concerned with a single country will have to grapple with their impact on that country. Comparison as a technique for building and testing empirical legal theory is sufficiently promising that novices ought not to debar themselves from its use even if they truly are only interested in their own country. As this volume shows, someone intent on the American federalism described by Melnick would be foolish indeed to know nothing of the EU described by Stone Sweet. Comparison should be seen as a method rather than comparative as a synonym for foreign. Thus, the move of many political science departments to subsume public law under American politics, particularly for hiring purposes, runs counter to the scholarly developments reflected in this and many other volumes. At worst, it leads to a department whose law and courts scholarship will be truncated and out of date. At best it leads back to the old situation of Americanists who are forbidden to use the comparative method and comparativists who are authorized to compare all countries except the United States. Paradoxically it is the preservation of the old fashioned arrangement of a separate public law field that would now make an organizational space for the new approaches to law and politics illustrated in this volume.

Thirdly, this volume is, I believe, indicative of something of the mix we ought to be pursuing. In spite of our recent fascination with judicialization of politics, and its undoubted real world importance, this volume indicates that non-judicialized law is important politically and worthy of study. Both Morgan's and Craig's contributions point toward legal texts and practices that may have significant political impact quite apart from or even in the absence of litigation. Melnick's major works show that courts are sometimes major, sometimes minor and sometimes non-players in public policymaking and implementation. Much triadic conflict resolution of significance is done by subnational and transnational entities that are not or are not quite courts. Thus, some students of law and politics should concentrate on courts. Others should not. And there should be much concern for long, multi-stage, multi-player lawmaking and implementation sequences. There are a lot of forests out there.

A similar point can be made about constitutional law and courts. The startling explosion of constitutional judicial review around the world has recently led both political science and law specialists in American constitutional law to turn their attention to foreign climes (to join those few who had been long engaged in non-U.S. constitutional law). The growth in comparative constitutional law, illustrated in this volume by the work of Couso and Ginsburg and, indeed, Stone Sweet, and Craig, is surely not to be denigrated simply because American political science has concentrated too much on constitutional law. Constitutional law is, no doubt, the most political of all law. It is the U.S. Supreme Court's constitutional decisions that make it of such central concern to students of American politics. Gillman's major work illustrates nicely the value of constitutional law—Supreme Court studies for the development of the new institutionalism.

Again, what is pernicious is not the choice of individual scholars as to what they wish to study, but curricular choices. Law schools hardly need worry that all their faculty will be constitutional law scholars. But political science departments that insist that American constitutional law must be taught, and that any other law courses are mere icing on the cake, do exert enormous distorting pressure on the choices of specialization young political science scholars make. In all honesty I must still tell my graduate students that if they choose to know nothing about anything other than U.S. constitutional law, they can get political science jobs and that if they know everything about all other law everywhere else and nothing about constitutional law in the U.S., they probably cannot. That undergraduates hold the quite incorrect belief that they "need" a U.S. constitutional law course to get into law school is no excuse. That they believe that they need that course rather than a course on tort law or a course called "legal process" or some such is the result not the cause of political science departments offering the course and staffing themselves as if it had to be offered.

Similarly while "judicialization" is not the only thing to be studied, it certainly ought to be studied (Shapiro and Stone Sweet 2002; Hirschl 2004). Kagen has been a central figure in such studies (Kagan 2001). Stone Sweet (1992; 2000) has been particularly concerned with the explosion of constitutional judicial review at the national level in Europe and more recently, as in the paper presented here, with the ECJ. The ECJ is of particular interest to comparativists for a number of reasons. All of the continental states that have moved to constitutional judicial review have followed the Kelsenian model, that is established a separate constitutional court while, in theory, denying constitutional review powers to their regular courts. The ECJ breaks from this pattern. It is a court of general jurisdiction exercising constitutional review powers alongside its jurisdiction to hear cases arising under Union legislation. Thus, its existence means that Europeans are confronted by two rival models of constitutional review. Both as a court of general jurisdiction and as a court much concerned with federalism, the ECJ is more comparable to the U.S. Supreme Court than it is to other European constitutional courts. Comparisons of the ECJ to the Supreme Court fit neatly into the growing body of "trans-Atlantic" comparative studies. The ECJ, like the French constitutional court and the British courts, inhabited an initial position in which there was no formal constitutional bill of rights and then, like them, has more or less invented its own constitutional rights. In the British and EU settings, formal bill of rights texts have subsequently been generated. In Israel and France, they have not. The opportunities for comparison are obvious. Finally the ECJ and the European Court of Human Rights are relatively successful transnational courts following a long historical period in which international courts were relatively unsuccessful. These two European successes have been followed by the creation of the transnational World Trade Organization and the North Atlantic Free Trade Agreement (NAFTA) tribunals and then by the new international war crimes court. Thus, study of the ECJ anchors new comparative studies of transnational courts.

The end result is that the study of judicialization has moved from being a sub-specialty of American law and politics to an area of study that demands of its participants knowledge that spreads across fields conventionally labeled in political science as American, comparative and international politics.

It ought to be noted, however, that comparative judicialization studies have been dogged by one unfortunate misunderstanding. Generally speaking in the English speaking world prosecutors are members of the executive branch while in continental Europe they are judges. Thus, American-European discussions of the merits and evils of "judicial activism" or "judicialization of politics" often flow past one another without quite coming head to head. While the growth of constitutional judicial review in Europe leaves Americans and Europeans on the same judicialization page, quite often Europeans complaining about or applauding judicial activism or politically unaccountable judiciaries are really talking about prosecutors when Americans think they are talking about judges. For instance, American defenders of judicial activism are wont to point out that judicial powers are severely limited because judges can only react to problems brought to them by litigants while, of course, no such limitation exists for continental prosecutors. Similarly, prosecutorial discretion is openly and formally acknowledged in the United States and rendered politically accountable through the election or political appointment of prosecutors. Although an obvious reality, on the continent such discretion is formally denied and prosecutors insulated from political control. The failure to meet these differences head on has been a particularly distressing feature of the debate over the new international war crimes court with Europeans accusing Americans of fearing at the international level the very judicial activism that flourishes in the United States, while Americans were really far more concerned with the new international institutions' potential for pro-active and entirely non-responsible prosecutors than with the possible decisions of judges on the bench. The need for more comparative prosecutor studies is clear.

If this volume strikes a useful rough balance between constitutional—non-constitutional and judicial—non-judicial studies, it may be viewed as not having paid sufficient attention to individual or human right. All of the contributors at one point or another in their scholarship concentrated on rights but none of them happen to do so here, although rights implication are pretty clear in any study of constitutional courts, judicialization or even non-judicial legalization. Two great quasi-religious movements swept the world in the latter half of the twentieth century, environmentalism and rights. (Can we ever forget the do trees have rights debate?) The explosion of constitutional judicial review in Europe was fueled in part by rights concerns also clearly manifested in the European Convention on Human Rights. Bills of rights became a part of most postwar European constitutions and, in many, individuals were given direct access to constitutional courts to protect their rights. In France, the initial failure to write a constitutional bill of rights was cured by judicial discovery of one by constitutional interpretation. In the United Kingdom, a long-term push for a written constitution was motivated in part by rights concerns culminating in a Charter of Rights. In the EU, the ECJ also found individual rights in the Treaties by implication and its interpretative initiative has been followed up by the major push toward a Bill of Rights in the new draft constitution. Immigration has become a central legal concern of the EU member states and much of that concern is expressed in rights terms.

In the United States we are, of course, familiar with the Warren Court's multi-faceted rights campaign which has actually been confirmed and extended by the Burger Court albeit with a few retreats. An enormous range of persons and groups vie with one another to achieve the politically powerful label "rights" for their particular interest. That is a central theme of Gillman's contribution and a crucial part of the story told here by Couso. This rights talk has been globalized and produced such new institutions as the international war crimes court.

The global flourishing of rights discourse has, however, revealed one basic, unresolved tension. The older notion of rights is essentially individualistic and negative. Rights are reserves of individual autonomy against intervention by the state, as in the famous U.S. First Amendment: "Congress shall make no law..." Negative rights may be designated for judicial enforcement relatively easily because such rights review involves courts only in striking down particular government actions rather than commanding other parts of government to initiate new policies. Such negative rights conceptions have, particularly in the age of the positive state, been subject to the sleeping under bridges critique. Precisely because of the appeal of rights, it is useful for those seeking greater social and economic equality to translate their goals into rights, but rights as claims to positive government services and benefits via proclamations of rights to subsistence, housing, medical care, education and so on. Such claims are a major aspect of what Kagan has called "adversarial legalism" (Kagan 2002). These social and economic rights can be instituted by legislation creating "entitlements." If, however, these statutory entitlements can be ratcheted up to constitutional rights, they can be better protected against subsequent legislative retrenchment and be employed as priority claims to further government assistance. If these positive rights can not only be constitutionalized but placed within the realm of judicial review, then judges can not only intervene negatively to veto legislative and administrative cutbacks of entitlements but order legislative or administrative increases in entitlement expenditure or even initiation of new entitlements.

The postwar failure of France to adopt a constitutional bill of rights is attributable less to the traditional French hostility to judicial review as such than to a left-right deadlock over whether to incorporate social (ist), positive or only bourgeois rights in the new constitution. The enormous popularity of the Hungarian Constitutional Court rested in part on its invocation of positive constitutional rights to thwart International Monetary Fund (IMF) demands that government benefits be cut back. In the United States, which traditionally concentrated on negative rights, the Supreme Court did switch right to counsel from the negative to the positive column, used the equal protection clause to demand certain positive state action to remedy past discrimination and the cruel and unusual punishment clause to mandate positive government provision of better living conditions for prison inmates. There was, indeed, a highly sophisticated, self-conscious drive by left-wing lawyers and other activists to constitutionalize welfare entitlements as judicially enforceable rights, but it met with relatively little success. Indeed the "conservatism" of the Burger and Rehnquist Courts lies far less in what they have done about negative rights than in their confirmation of the Warren Court's refusal to be pushed further down the positive rights path.

Yet, it is this path that is likely to be of crucial interest in the immediate future to students of constitutional judicial review and law and courts more generally and particularly to those pursuing comparative analysis. If the religion of rights has enjoyed a global surge, another religion, socialism, has been in dramatic decline. Faith in government ownership of the means of production and central economic planning to achieve high levels of material prosperity has dramatically declined. But that decline is not equivalent to a resurgence of faith in free markets. It is now approaching cliché that this fall from socialism results not in free markets but highly regulated ones and not in individual economic autonomy but continued allegiance to the welfare state. It is also clear to all that a host of interacting dynamics from the globalization of markets to advances in medical science and changing age demographics have imposed significant budgetary constraints on government funded welfare. How much regulation of markets and how much constraint on welfare are the central questions of domestic politics on both sides of the Atlantic.

The right has made some attempt to resist regulation by reconstitutionalizing property rights, both in the United States and Europe, and usually more as federalism than as substantive property rights claims. It has enjoyed only marginal success. Far more crucial has been the attempt of the left to constitutionalize welfare rights.

It has become a commonplace of recent constitutional theory that those political forces dominant at a time of new constitution writing will favor judicial independence and constitutional judicial review *if* they fear that their current political dominance will be lost in the future. Such forces are willing to submit their own powers to judicial constitutional constraint in return for the assurance that their opponents will be subjected to the same constraints when they come to power in the future. Those interested in promoting statutory welfare entitlements, subject to legislative retrenchment precisely because they are statutory, into constitutional rights are playing the same game. Constitutionalizing welfare entitlements is an obvious strategy in the many European and other states in which the left and right are closely balanced electorally and frequently alternate in control of government. More generally, all the industrialized states with relatively ambitious social benefits are facing what appear to be relatively long term financial constraints and pressures to reduce such benefits, particularly pension and medical benefits where costs are rising rapidly during a period of slow economic growth and correspondingly sluggish tax revenues. A principal barrier to the transformation of economic entitlements into judicially protected constitutional rights is the awkwardness for democracy involved in authorizing non elected judiciaries to order legislatures to enact new benefits statutes and levy new taxes to pay for them. This awkwardness is partially avoided where the legislature has already enacted the benefits and courts need only order them not to cut entitlements. It is not simply a matter of avoiding the spectacle of courts making the choices among competing interests necessary when drafting new welfare legislation. Judicial commands not to cut are going to be delivered to legislatures which are under great electoral pressure not to cut. They will gladly obey judicial orders not to cut and gratefully transfer responsibility to the courts for any economic damage the failure to cut causes.

Moreover, where courts are engaged in reviewing cuts in benefits, they may enjoy the comfort of a soft form of review. They need not proclaim as a constitutional matter that existing levels of benefits may never be cut but only that they may not be cut so far as to vitiate the basic rights involved and/or that the burden of proof is on the legislature to justify cuts. In these areas, balancing least means and proportionality doctrine, which the courts have already developed for negative rights, is clearly applicable and allows for much give and take between the legislative and judicial governors.

Thus, a constitutionalizing strategy is particularly attractive for industrialized states that wish to have their cake and eat it too in the global marketplace. Either by domestic constitution, transnational constitution (the EU) or global treaty, the entrenchment of welfare benefits and other social and labor "rights" accomplished in tandem with the institution of free trade tends to benefit rich states while protecting them against competition from low labor cost states. In this arena welfare rights discourse becomes the basis for either exporting the competitive disadvantage of high worker benefits to other states or barring imports from states that refuse to accept the export.

Here, the growth of global networks of welfare advocates provides strong and apparently democratic pressures in favor of judicialization. Indeed welfare advocates thwarted politically in their own states can now see movement to the transnational or international arena as a way of end-running domestic opposition. The EU is now experiencing just such an alliance of rich, high benefit states and transnational welfare networks in the drafting of the social rights provisions of its new constitution.

In short, in an era in which they are faced with massive demonstrations of its failures, proponents of socialism can no longer be socialists and former socialists face the prospect of alternation in office with capitalists. The maintenance of welfare benefits becomes the centerpiece of the political agenda of the left, and the constitutionalizing and judicializing of those benefits an attractive strategy for pursuing that agenda.

Law and politics scholars, therefore, as they move beyond their previously excessive preoccupation with constitutional judicial review ought to remain aware of the continued, indeed the increasing, salience of that variety of law and politics. And those who continue to specialize in the study of constitutional judicial review ought not to be frozen into the old American story of property rights being replaced by civil rights as the centerpiece of constitutional review. For all the pressing concerns about genocide, war crimes and discrimination against minorities, economic rights, of workers more often than owners, are again coming to center stage in constitutional law.

So the political science field of law and courts studies has been greatly expanded "outward" to other nations than the United States and to transnational polities and "downward" from the Supreme Court to trial and intermediate appellate courts, arbitration and various other "access to justice" extra-judicial arrangements and the bar. It continues to be concerned with rights and constitutional law continues as a vital center of concern while now concerning itself with many other areas of law as well. And not only the rights but the federalism aspects of constitutional law remain important as R. Shep Melnick's second contribution here clearly shows. There has also been movement in a number of other major directions.

By the 1950s, the standard pluralist vision of politics focused on interests and interest groups acting upon and through legal-political processes to achieve benefits or advantages. The vision largely looked down a one-way street with interests acting upon politics rather than vice versa. Interests were the input, political processes such as legislatures, courts and bureaucracies the through-put, and public policies the output. Of course, even in the 1950s, it was recognized that groups could be the product of legislation as well as legislation the product of groups. If government legislated a benefit, such as a farm subsidy or pension scheme, it would be creating an interest in the preservation and expansion of that benefit around which new interest groups would be organized or existing ones strengthened. Although widely recognized, this impact of law upon groups was treated as a kind of addendum to the standard input/output models.

Today, however, the words constitute and constitutive are constantly with us. Legislative, administrative and judicial lawmaking and even potential lawmaking are seen not only as avenues of interest group driven law making, but as constitutive of interest groups, individual political identities and ideologies. For instance, groups may come into existence and define themselves in response to new opportunities to litigate to further their interests created by new legislation. Or existing groups may be further energized and their energies redirected by new litigational opportunities. Individuals may redefine their own interests and affiliations or very natures to correspond to legally created categories such as "handicapped," "disabled," "sexually harassed" or "tribal." Students of law and courts ought to be just as concerned with how law constitutes interests as with how interests constitute law. New or newly emphasized feedback loops proliferate on the old input-output models. The constitutive potential of law for political mobilization and personal redefinition come center stage as does the entrepreneurial role of lawyers and lobbyists in creating the interests they seek to represent (McCann 1986; 1994).

Another way of expressing this shift in scholarly attention is to say that the law and society movement, which long concentrated on how society changed law, is increasingly concerned with how law constitutes society. The long struggles of the Third World, and more recently of the fragments of the former Soviet empire and of China, to reconstruct not only their governments but their economies and even their basic social structures, focus attention on law as an instrument for constituting new political, economic and social arrangements. In spite of its many failures, in one guise or another the law and development movement continues to flourish as Couso's contribution to this volume indicates. Free-market proponents and human rights advocates become bedfellows propounding the rule of law as one of the foundations for human flourishing.

When the study of law and courts was limited largely to the United States, a relatively well developed and stable society and economy, individual self-identification as citizens of a functioning state could be more or less assumed. Attention largely could be devoted to the how, where, what, when and why of marginal changes in law. As we move to the study of law and courts in political spaces where these foundations are weak, crumbling or non-existent, our attention naturally turns to how law and courts may contribute to constituting society and economy as well as to law and courts as reflections of them.

Another redirection from the simpler pluralist interest model has been a renewed concern for values and ideas along with interests seen as naked preferences. Here again the political relevance of these phenomena were not entirely neglected by the old pluralism. Law and courts scholars in particular had been vividly aware that some of the lobbying and litigating groups of concern to them, like the ACLU. and the Legal Defense Fund of the NAACP were in pursuit of more or less universal values rather than particular economic self-interests or pursued self-interest through appeals to broader values. Nonetheless, the constant talk of law and politics as interest group competition tended to emphasize particular self-interest and obscure the political and legal energies of commitment to broader values, ideas and ideals.

Indeed, a kind of general model emerged in which political and legal victory was predicted for groups with relatively great political resources in pursuit of public policies with concentrated benefits and diffuse costs. Law and politics came to be seen not even as a grand contest between interest groups but as a game in which each interest group took its turn at bat hoping to raid the general public treasury in behalf of its own particular special interest. Those groups with the biggest bats would win the most.

Things happened in the real world, however, that undermined our faith in the view that in a democracy concentrated benefits diffuse costs were always winners and diffuse or general or public benefits, concentrated costs were always the loser. The decisions of the Warren Court on rights of accused showed a concentrated benefits diffuse costs win but by a group with almost no resources. Its reapportionment decisions entailed concentrated costs and concentrated benefits if viewed as a transfer of voting power from rural areas and central cities to suburbs or concentrated costs and general benefits if viewed as reducing rural voting power in favor of one person one vote— voting equality for all. The desegregation decisions can be viewed as concentrated costs and concentrated benefits, costs to white segregationists, benefits to African Americans or, as in reapportionment, costs concentrated on segregationists and benefit to the general value of equality. And here again, a group with relatively weak resources seemed to win.

Even more dramatic was the Congressional scene where in the 1960s, 1970s and 1980s a considerable number of civil rights, health, safety, consumer protection and environmental laws were enacted. Of course there were interest groups active in behalf of these measures, but nearly all entailed wins for legislative proposals entailing general or diffuse or public interest or universal benefits and relatively highly concentrated costs. Indeed the interest groups that pushed these measures seemed to win precisely because they could channel very widely and relatively strongly held general public sentiments in favor of such general values as racial equality, health and safety and environmental protection, win against very well financed politically powerful special interests and win by portraying the struggle as one between the public interest and special interests.

Even if one prefers, as I do, a purely descriptive as opposed to normative study of law and politics, all of law and politics cannot be crammed into a narrowly pluralist vision of competing organized interest groups. Even the idea of interest groups has been modified by notions of networks and epistemic communities that are more about shared ideas than shared naked self-interests. And as Harlow notes "governance" implies an interpenetration not only of private and public actors but of aspirations. Ultimately, even a "realist" perspective must take account of the normative aspects of law and politics because those aspects are among the real causes and effects of law and politics whether expressed in the "internal" discourse of law, national political and legal cultures or universal belief systems. It may be that comparative law as a discipline has been peculiarly deficient in this regard. Certainly in all comparative work, last resort explanations in terms of political or legal "culture" have been viewed with the suspicion that culture is invoked when all else that the investigator can imagine fails. Yet whether there are or are not national legal cultures or "families" of law, no one doubts that humanly perceived "oughts" have something to do with human achieved "ises." Ideas and interests go hand in hand in law and politics. And so the already much overburdened student of law and politics must take on the normative side of political and legal theory as well as everything else on his plate if for no other reason than that such norms interact with what happens, or, if you like, are a crucial part of the "is."

Reality has forced us to concede that widely shared values, ideas and ideologies as well as particularized economic interests play an important part in American politics and no doubt the politics of other democratic states (Shapiro 1988a). Whether or not courts are more open to such value appeals than are legislatures or administrators and political executives is one of the questions on our research agenda. Thanks to the work of the quantitative behaviorists we have had confirmation for some time that the political and economic preferences of judges greatly influence their decisions (Baum 1997). That same quantitative work indicates that these judicial preferences are far less a reflection of the particular economic self-interests of individual judges than of their commitments to general values. Above and beyond this particular set of findings for the judiciary, however, we are now fairly certain that law more generally is the product not only of the accommodation of selfish economic interests but of the accommodation of those interests to more generally held public values and the translation of both values and interests into government action through the existing stock of policy ideas and technical knowledge. Thus, beyond counting the particular preferences of judges, the student of law and courts must take account of the movements of ideas and values in society.

If students of law and courts must now take account of general values and ideas, it must follow that they must take account of legal values and ideas. Since the birth of sociological jurisprudence, a considerable amount of time and effort has been taken to overcome the conventional view that law and politics were separate. Of course no one ever denied that statutory law was, and indeed was supposed to be, the product of politics. Once enacted and in the hands of judges, however, politics was supposed to disappear. The application and interpretation, even the making, of law by judges was supposed to be the product of legal reasoning as opposed to political preference. In opposition to this view students of law and politics have tried to show that many judicial decisions involve choices among alternative legal outcomes and in making those choices judges engage in the same kind of interest balancing and pursuit of preferences as do legislators and administrators, subject to pressures, constraints, opportunities and expectations comparable to those experienced by legislators and administrators and embedded in the same political regimes as other government officers. The critical legal studies equation of law with politics merely echoed the work of law and courts political scientists. The shock value of critical legal studies came not from new ideas but from its Trojan horse position within the walls of the legal academy rather than from an outside, and thus necessarily benighted, discipline.

Law and courts political scientists never denied that there were a number of different roles and institutions in politics, that popes and presidents, while both politicians, were not expected to, and in fact did not, act in exactly the same ways, nor did Congressmen and judges. Yet precisely because their work developed in reaction to the conventional rigorous separation of (judicial) law and politics, political scientists tended to emphasize the politics of law and politics when describing the judiciary. Today we are more open to recognizing that just as when a group of physicists do politics their tribal culture of physics strongly influences their choices, so when a group of lawyer judges does politics their choices too are influenced by the specialized body of knowledge that defines them as lawyers or by their legal culture or received legal values transmitted by legal education and embedded in legal practices. If values and ideas play a part in all politics, then legal values and ideas play a part in judicial politics.

The so-called new institutionalism in the social sciences has a number of strands. One, or perhaps it is better to say two, of those strands are reflected in the ambiguity of the word "institution" itself. In the more rigorous version common among sociologists, an institution is a set of habitually observed rules or values that prescribe, constrain and define a set of habitual behaviors or practices. Private property is an institution, as is the medical profession, the legislative process and elections. In the more common usage, often employed by political scientists, institutions are established organizations. Congress and the Presidency are American political institutions. San Quentin Penitentiary and the Los Angeles public schools are government institutions on which courts sometimes impose "institutional remedies." Courts are political institutions in this latter sense. We are more and more reminded now that courts are also institutions in the sociological sense, that is they are congeries of rules or values that define distinctive practices which the institutional actors are expected to pursue (see Stone Sweet, Sandholtz and Fligstein 2001). Of course some of the values and expectations that define courts are the general political values of the political regime of which a particular court is a part. But some are distinctively legal or judicial, deviation from which leads to a denial that the deviators are really judges and their organization really a court. Current concerns for judicial independence (Russell and O'Brien 2001) reflect this attention to the "institutionalization" of courts, not merely in the sense of the creation of a recognizably distinct organization or set of offices but in the sense of an accepted set of values, rules and expectations distinguishing courts from other segments of the political regime. The new institutionalism is in part new because it emphasizes that although courts are political institutions, different political institutions are defined by somewhat differing sets of values, rules, expectations and practices.

At one extreme of this reemphasis of the legal is the legal sociology of Nichlass Luhmann with its notion of law as autopoetic, that is as developing over time through its own internal dynamics rather than as a mere reflection of broad social and political developments (Teubner and Febbrajo 1992). If legal practitioners, including judges and legal academics do have a somewhat autonomous intellectual or epistemic community or communications network and consequently a somewhat autonomous dynamic of ideological development, then certainly one factor in explaining the evolution of judicial policy choices over time is the internal tendencies of legal thinking and doing over time. For instance I have argued that one factor in the development of a very activist judicial review of administrative regulation has been the internal tendency of the legal community to seek to cabin executive discretion by procedural rules although also at play is a far broader political urge to render government decision making participatory and transparent (Shapiro 1988).

Judicial lawmaking by American courts has been the central focus of law and politics studies. Quite obviously such lawmaking at least purported to rest on a practice of *stare decisis* or precedent. Quantitative studies of Supreme Court and other judicial decision making confirmed earlier realist assertions that *stare decisis* did not dictate single correct judicial answers to the legal questions posed in litigation but instead offered judges a range of choices. Nonetheless, if court decisions were not treated by judges themselves as announcing rules to be followed in future cases, thus at least constraining or limiting their future choices, then judicial lawmaking itself would dissolve into a series of completely arbitrary and unpredictable, case-by-case public policy choices. Such a dissolution would effectively sabotage the institutional viability of courts and indeed that of the political regime itself if that regime sought to rule by law rather than arbitrary exercises of power. If the citizenry cannot predict with reasonable accuracy what the future outcomes of judicial applications of law will be, they will not resort to courts and, more importantly, will not conduct their affairs in accordance with predictions of what behavior courts would deem lawful and unlawful if asked. Without predictable enforcement, law ceases to be an effective restraint on conduct. Without predictable outcomes, courts cease to be effective means of law enforcement and thus lose their usefulness to political regimes that choose to rule by law. Thus, even legal regimes that deny judicial law making and/or deny the practice of *stare decisis* in reality either do treat past judicial decisions a constraints on future ones and/or create alternative modes of creating judicial predictability while allowing for change over time, such as systems of authoritative legal commentary.

This central feature of the dynamics of judicial practice could hardly be ignored entirely by students of law and politics who focused on Anglo-American courts which not only purported to operate on the basis of *stare decisis* but in many instances purported to follow a "common law" that consisted of rules laid down in earlier court judgments.

Even for social scientists dedicated to their favorite theories, it is difficult to deny all significance to the massive central mode of discourse employed by the political actors being observed. Anglo-American lawyers spent much time and enormous amounts of their own and clients' money learning, speaking and writing the language of precedent. Predictability clearly was a central necessity of any effective government by law. Thus, while denying that *stare decisis* eliminated judicial policy choices, political scientists studying courts were driven to admit that Anglo-American judges operated in a web of precedential constraints or boundaries on their policy choices or had to satisfy expectations that a considerable degree of predictability must be a characteristic of their policy choices, predictability that could be achieved only if judges treated their own past decisions as building blocks of their future ones.

Conventional legal scholarship might treat precedent oriented legal discourse as a unique form of "legal reasoning" which set courts off from "the political branches." As noted earlier, political science expended considerable effort on showing that *stare decisis* was not a unique mode of decision making but merely a sub-species of incremental decision making which the March and Simon-Lindblom school of administration-bureaucracy scholars had found to be characteristic of all collective policy decision making. *Stare decisis* did not separate courts from politics. Rather incremental decision making was common to all forms of political decision making including judicial decision making (Shapiro 1968).

One of the central strains of the new institutionalism is its emphasis on "path dependency," on the notion that where you will be next is highly dependent on where you were last. Judicial studies necessarily was so involved with judicial incrementalism. Incremental decision theory is the old name or forerunner of path dependency theory. While on the one hand path dependency is an intellectual boon to all social scientists seeking to predict, under the name of precedent it is an institutional necessity of judges embedded in political regimes seeking to rule by law. Judicial studies had arrived at path dependency before the new institutionalism announced that it was new.

In the broader sense, the new preoccupation with path dependency is expressed in a renewed interest in political history among political scientists. This new swing toward history intersects the historical approaches to constitutional law that had long been practiced by conventional "public law" scholars both in political science departments and law schools. Among the contributors to this volume, Howard Gillman's (1993) work most clearly illustrates this intersection. If we say that institutions are important, we are saying that rules or expectations or organizational arrangements both persist over time and play a significant part in the political decisions and actions taken at any and every time. Institutionalists, however, can hardly deny that over time change occurs. And I suppose few post-Marxist institutionalists insist that current choices are not choices at all but wholly determined by history. Gillman's longer term historical studies and the shorter term policy histories of R. Shep Melnick and others are stories of immediate choices constrained by long-term institutions whether institutions are defined as persistent organizations or persistent rules and values.

These studies also involve another aspect of path dependency. Today's policy choices are incremental not only in the sense of being constrained by institutions that persist over time but also constrained by the substance of policy choices made in the past (Levin and Shapiro 2004). There is some Humpty Dumpty in politics but also many Jack-built houses. A socialist government may nationalize the banks, but they will still act like banks. A subsequent government may privatize them, but, at least in the short term, typically will maintain a major or even controlling stock ownership. That deregulation necessarily entails re-regulation is by now a familiar story. Thus, students of judicial politics, like students of all other kinds of politics today, must become, among all the other things they must become, students of public policy. Perhaps they need not make normative commitments as to what policies are good and what policies are not. They cannot hope to reach high levels of technical expertise in each of the policy areas that courts must handle. If, however, current judicial policy choices depend in part on the intersection of established institutions and past policies, then students of courts must know something not only of institutional history but of policy history as well, still another daunting task.

Yet another complex of approaches and techniques associated with the new institutionalism and of compelling contemporary interest to students of law, courts and politics is the law and economics, rational or public choice, positive political theory set of concerns. Like some other aspects of the new institutionalism, some aspects of the application of economic analysis to law and courts, and politics more generally, does not seem particularly new. The so-called economic theory of legislation, for instance, seems little more than old pluralist theory dressed in new language. In both, legislation is seen as the product of group struggle in the legislature and of temporary winning coalitions coalescing to pass particular laws. Both point out the grave risk that legislation will benefit those special interests enjoying the greatest political resources at the expense of the public interest. Both highlight the potential for capture by the groups regulated of regulatory legislation and regulatory agencies. Both point out that precisely because of their coalitional origins, statutes may embody several, even contradictory purposes and/or paper over differences within the coalition by general or vague language that defers real policy decision to the implementation stage. And both note that precisely for these reasons, subsequent judicial policy intervention will be more or less successful depending on the unity of purpose and persistence over time of the winning coalition or the lack thereof. Putting all this in the language of rents and deviations from efficiency and diagrams of decision points may assist us in thinking more clearly but is hardly new.

In some ways economic or rationality approaches to law and courts would appear to be fundamentally at odds with "institutionalism" itself. If everyone is everywhere and always in pursuit of their self-interest and all political decisions are searches for Paretan optimality, then neither institutions or history should matter much. Indeed, they should merely be the reflections of and record of past rational decisions with no necessary influence on current ones. The market begins anew every day and would be no fun or agony if past prices determined future ones.

The new institutionalism aspect of law and economics or rational choice is the realization that the rules, practices and agreed sequencings of the decision making routines employed by rationally self-interested makers of collective public choices tend to advantage some participants over others. Thus, procedural rules and institutions both in the sense of accepted rules of the game and accepted organizational decision making channels will partially determine policy outcomes. That, of course, was the gist of the pioneering March and Olsen (1984) piece on the new institutionalism, and is reflected very much in Stone Sweet's contribution to this volume. Such understandings lead to a reintegration of politics and policy studies and to wholistic institutional studies. If the rules and institutions of the whole policy making sequence partially determine policy outcomes, and you are interested in policy outcomes, then it makes little sense to study only courts, or only Congress or only bureaucracies. The influential McNollgast (McCubbins, Noll and Weingast 1990) pieces, arguing that Congress seeks to determine policy outcomes by setting the procedural rules for administrative agency decision making and the opportunities for judicial review, warn political scientists who specialize in the study of courts that too much attention ought not to be paid to the courts alone.

Of course, to assert that all are in pursuit of their rational self-interests is not to assert that politics or law are fully and consistently rational or that efficient outcomes will necessarily or automatically occur. Much of law and economics studies are concerned with strategic behavior, uncertainty, incomplete contracting, principal-agent problems, market failures and so on. As Stone Sweet's and several other contributions to this volume (see also Shapiro and Stone Sweet 2002) indicate, this newer vocabulary must now be mastered, for instance by constitutional, administrative and international law scholars like Couso concerned with such traditional concepts as sovereignty and due process and all of those generally concerned with the development of legal and judicial institutions over time (see, e.g., Roth 1999; Sterett 1997). One editor of this volume, Tom Ginsburg, has been one of a number of scholars applying law and economics approaches to problems of "constitutional design" and identifying the political conditions contributing to successful constitutionalism and judicial review (Ginsburg 2003).

One of the reasons Ph.D.s take so long and J.D.s do not is that implicit in the Ph.D. qualifying examination system is the command "know everything" while the course by course law school examinations demand only that the student know what has been taught in particular courses. The "everything" for the law and courts or public law field of political science has expanded along a great many dimensions in the last fifty years. Participants in the law, courts and endeavor should be aware that all these things are within their domain, and that having learned some segments of them as a student will facilitate movement on to others in later scholarly life. Each participant in this volume, some very close still to their student days, has found him or herself moving onward from the knowledge bases conveyed to them in their education. It is to be hoped that this volume will help others do the same.

Bibliography

Abraham, Henry. 1993. *The Judicial Process: An Introductory Analysis of the Courts of the United States, England and France*, 6th ed. New York: Oxford University Press.

———. 1999. *Justices, Presidents and Senators*. Boston: Rowman and Littlefield Publishers.

Ackerman, Bruce. 1991. *We the People*. Cambridge, MA: Harvard University Press.

Adelman, Jeremy. 1999a. *Republic of Capital: Buenos Aires and the Legal Transformation of the Atlantic World*. Stanford: Stanford University Press.

———. 1999b. *Colonial Legacies: The Problem of Persistence in Latin American History*. New York and London: Routledge.

Adelman, Jeremy and Miguel Angel Centeno. 1997. Between Liberalism and Neo-liberalism: Law's Dilemma in Latin America. Paper Presented at the American Bar Foundation Conference. New Challenges for the Rule of Law: Lawyers, Internationalization, and the Social Construction of Legal Rules, Santa Barbara, California.

ACIR. 1993. *Federal Regulation of State and Local Governments: The Mixed Record of the 1980s*. Washington, DC: Advisory Commission on Intergovernmental Relations.

Ahdieh, Robert. 1997. *Russia's Constitutional Revolution: Constitutional Structure, Legal Consciousness & the Emergence of Constitutionalism from Below, 1985–1995*. University Park, PA: Pennsylvania State University Press.

Akehurst, Michael. 1981. The Application of General Principles of Law by the Court of Justice of the European Communities. *British Yearbook of International Law* 52:29.

Alston, Philip. 2002. Resisting the Merger and Acquisition of Human Rights by Trade Law: A Reply to Petersmann. *European Journal of International Law* 13:815–44.

Alter, Karen. 2003. *Establishing the Supremacy of European Law: The Making of an International Rule of Law in Europe*. Oxford: Oxford University Press.

Alter, Karen and Sophie Meunier-Aitshalia. 1994. Judicial Politics in the European Community: European Integration and the Pathbreaking Cassis de Dijon Decision. *Comparative Political Studies* 26(4):535–61.

Aman, Jr., Alfred. 1997. Administrative Law for a New Century. In *The Province of Administrative Law*, ed. M. Taggart. Oxford: Hart Publishing.

———. 2002. Globalization, Democracy and the Need for a New Administrative Law. *UCLA Law Review* 49:1687.

Amar, Akhil Reed. 1998. A Constitutional Accident Waiting to Happen. In *Constitutional Stupidities, Constitutional Tragedies*, eds. William N. Eskridge and Sanford Levinson, 61–66. New York: New York University Press.

Armstrong, Kenneth A. 2002. Rediscovering Civil Society: The European Union and the White Paper on Governance. *European Law Journal* 8:102.

Atiyah, P.S. and Robert S. Summers. 1987. *Form and Substance in Anglo-American Law: A Comparative Study of Legal Reasoning, Legal Theory, and Legal Institutions*. Oxford: Clarendon Press.

Aucoin, Peter. 1990. Administrative Reform in Public Management…Principles, Paradoxes and Pendulums. *Governance* 3(2):115–37.

Aylwin, Patricio. 1998. *El Reencuentro de los Demócratas*. Santiago: Grupo Zeta.

Ayres, Ian and John Braithwaite. 1992. *Responsive Regulation: Transcending the Deregulation Debate*. New York: Oxford University Press.

Bankowski, Zenon and Emilios Christodoulidis. 1998. The European Union as an Essentially Contestable Project. *European Law Journal* 4:341.

Barnes, Jeb. 2004. *Overruled? Legislative Overrides, Pluralism, and Contemporary Court-Congress Relations.* Stanford: Stanford University Press.

Barrow, Deborah J., Gary Zuk, and Gerard S. Gryski. 1996. *The Federal Judiciary and Institutional Change.* Ann Arbor: University of Michigan Press.

Barrows, Chester L. 1941. *William M. Evarts: Lawyer, Diplomat, Statesman.* Chapel Hill: University of North Carolina Press.

Bauer, Michael W. 2002. The EU 'Partnership Principle:' Still A Sustainable Governance Device Across Multiple Administrative Arenas? *Public Administration* 80:769.

Baum, Lawrence. 1997. *The Puzzle of Judicial Behavior.* Ann Arbor: University of Michigan Press.

Bengoetxea, Joxeramon. 2003. The Scope for Discretion, Coherence, and Citizenship. In *Judicial Discretion in European Perspective*, ed. O. Wiklund, 48–74. Stockholm: Kluwer Law International.

Bensel, Richard Franklin. 1990. *Yankee Leviathan: The Origins of Central State Authority in America, 1859–1877.* New York: Cambridge University Press.

———. 2000. *The Political Economy of American Industrialization, 1877–1900.* New York: Cambridge University Press.

Berk, Gerald. 1994. *Alternative Tracks: The Constitution of American Industrial Order, 1865–1917.* Baltimore: Johns Hopkins University Press.

Berlin, Dominique. 1992. Interactions between the Lawmaker and the Judiciary within the EC. *Legal Issues of European Integration* 1992 (2):17–48.

Bickel, Alexander. 1962. *The Least Dangerous Branch: The Supreme Court at the Bar of Politics.* New York: Bobbs-Merrill.

Black, Charles. 1960. *The People and the Court.* New York: Macmillan.

Black, Julia. 2000. Critical Reflections on Regulation. *Australian Journal of Legal Philosophy* 27:1.

Blankenburg, Erhard. 1994. The Infrastructure for Avoiding Civil Litigation: Comparing Cultures of Legal Behavior in the Netherlands and West Germany. *Law and Society Review* 28:789–808.

Borchard, Edwin. 1917. *Guide to the Law and the Legal Literature of Argentina, Brazil and Chile.* Washington, DC: Library of Congres.

Bradley, Kieran St. Clair. 1999. Institutional Aspects of Comitology: Scenes from the Cutting Room Floor. In *EU Committees: Social Regulation, Law and Politics*, eds. Christian Joerges and Ellen Vos. 71–93. Oxford: Hart Publishing.

Brahm, Enrique. 1999. *Propiedad sin Libertad: Chile 1925–1973.* Santiago: Ediciones Universidad de los Andes.

Braithwaite, J. and P. Drahos. 2000. Global Business Regulation. New York: Cambridge University Press.

Bravo, Joaquín Rodriguez. 1888. *Estudios Constitucionales.* Santiago de Chile: Imprenta Victoria.

Buchanan, James, Roger D. Congleton and Joe Oppenheimer. 1998. *Politics by Principle, Not Interest: Toward Nondiscriminatory Democracy.* New York: Cambridge University Press.

Burke, Thomas. 2002. *Lawyers, Lawsuits, and Legal Rights: The Battle over Litigation in American Society.* Berkeley: University of California Press.

Burley, Anne-Marie and Walter Mattli. 1993. Europe before the Court: A Political Theory of Legal Integration. *International Organization* 47:41–76.

Buscaglia, Edgardo. 1998. Obstacles to Judicial Reform in Latin America. In *Justice Delayed: Judicial Reform in Latin America*, eds. E. Jarquin and F. Carrillo. Washington, DC: Inter-American Development Bank.

Bybee, Keith. 1998. *Mistaken Identity: The Supreme Court and the Politics of Minority Representation*. Princeton, NJ: Princeton University Press.

Campbell, Colin and John Halligan. 1992. *Political Leadership in an Age of Constraint: The Australian Experience*. Pittsburgh: University of Pittsburgh Press.

Campbell, David and Sol Picciotto, eds. 2002. *New Directions in Regulatory Theory*. Oxford: Blackwell Publishers.

Cappelletti, Mauro. 1989. *Judicial Process in Comparative Perspective*. Oxford: Oxford University Press.

Cappelletti, Mauro, Monica Seccombe and Joseph Weiler, eds. 1986. *Integration through Law: Europe and the American Federal Experience. Vol. 1: Methods, Tools and Institutions*. Berlin, Germany: De Gruyter.

Carrasco Albano, Manuel. 1858. *Comentarios Sobre la Constitución Politica de 1833.* Valparaiso: Imprenta y Libreira del Mercurio.

Castiglione, Dario. 1996. The Political Theory of the Constitution. *Political Studies* 44:417.

Casto, William R. 1997. *Oliver Ellsworth and the Creation of the Federal Republic*. New York: Second Circuit Committee on History and Commemorative Events.

Center for International Economics. 1999. *Guidelines for National Competition Policy Legislation Reviews*. http://www.intecon.com.au.

Chemerinsky, Erwin. 1999. *Federal Jurisdiction*, 3rd ed. New York: Aspen.

Chiti, Edoardo. 2000. The Emergence of a Community Administration: The Case of Agencies. *Common Market Law Review* 37:309.

Choper, Jesse. 1980. *Judicial Review and the National Political Process*. Chicago: University of Chicago Press.

Cichowski, Rachel A. 1998. Integrating the Environment: The European Court and the Construction of Supranational Policy. *Journal of European Public Policy* 5(3):387–405.

———. 2001. Judicial Rule-making and the Institutionalization of EU Sex Equality Policy. In *The Institutionalization of Europe*, eds. A. Stone Sweet, W. Sandholtz and N. Fligstein, 113–36. Oxford: Oxford University Press.

Clayton, Cornell. 1998. The Supreme Court and Political Jurisprudence: New and Old Institutionalisms. In *Supreme Court Decision-making*, eds. Cornell Clayton and Howard Gillman, 15–41. Chicago: University of Chicago Press.

———. 2002. The Supply and Demand Sides of Judicial Policymaking (Or Why Be So Positive About the Judicialization of Politics?). *Law and Contemporary Problems* 65:69–86.

Clayton, Cornell and Howard Gillman, eds. 1998. *Supreme Court Decision-making.* Chicago: University of Chicago Press.

Coalition of Australian Governments. 2000. Communique. On file with author B. Morgan.

Collier, Jane Fishburne. 1973. *Law and Social Change in Zinacantan*. Stanford, CA: Stanford University Press.

Collier, Simon. 1995. *A History of Chile: 1808–1994*. New York: Cambridge University Press.

Collins, Michael G. 1986. The Unhappy History of Federal Questions Removal. *Iowa Law Review* 71 (March):717–73.

Committee of Independent Experts. 1999. *First Report on Allegations Regarding Fraud, Mismanagement and Nepotism in the European Commission*, Brussels. March 15.

———. 1999. *Second Report on Reform of the Commission, Analysis of Current Practice and Proposals for tackling Mismanagement, Irregularities and Fraud*, Brussels. September 10.

Conlan, Timothy. 1998. *From New Federalism to Devolution: Twenty-Five Years of Intergovernmental Reform*. Washington: Brookings.

Cooter, Robert and Tom Ginsburg. 1996. Comparative Judicial Discretion: An Empirical Test of Economic Models. *International Review of Law and Economics* 16:295.

———. 1998. Division of Powers in the European Union Constitution. In *The New Palgrave Dictionary of Law and Economics*, ed. Peter Newman, New York: Stockton Press.

Coppalli, Richard. 1979. *Rights and Remedies Under Federal Grants* . Washington: BNA.

Correa, Jorge. 1999. La Cenicienta se Queda en la Fiesta. El Poder Judicial Chileno en la Decada de los 90. In *El Modelo Chileno. Democracia y Desarrollo en los Noventa*, eds. Paul Drake and Ivan Jaksic. 281–315. Santiago, Chile: LOM Ediciones.

Cottier, T. 2002. Trade and Human Rights: A Relationship to Discover. *Journal of International Economic Law* 5:111–32.

Council of Australian Governments. 1997. Principles and Guidelines for National Standard Setting and Regulatory Action by Ministerial Councils and Standard-Setting Bodies. On file with author B. Morgan.

Council Regulation. 1988. 2052/88 on Structural Funding OJ L185/9 (15 July 1988).

Cover, Robert M. 1975. *Justice Accused: Antislavery and the Judicial Process*. New Haven, CT: Yale University Press.

Craig, Paul. 1993. *Francovich*, Remedies and the Scope of Damages Liability. *Law Quarterly Review* 109: 595.

———. 2000. The Fall and Renewal of the Commission: Accountability, Contract and Administrative Organization. *European Law Journal* 6:98.

Craig, Paul, and Grainne de Burca. 1998. *EU Law*. Oxford: Oxford University Press.

Cyert, Richard M. and James G. March. 1963. *A Behavioral Theory of the Firm*. Englewood Cliffs, NJ: Prentice Hall.

Dahl, Robert A. 1957. Decision-Making in a Democracy: The Supreme Court as a National Policy-Maker. *Journal of Public Law* 6:279–95.

Dakolias, Maria. 1995. A Strategy for Judicial Reform: The Experience in Latin America. *Virginia Journal of International Law*, 36:167.

Damaska, Mirjan. 1986. *The Faces of Justice and State Authority. A Comparative Approach to the Legal Process*. New Haven, CT: Yale University Press.

Davies, Gareth. 2002. The Great Society after Johnson: The Case of Bilingual Education. *Journal of American History* 88:4

Davis, Kenneth Culp. 1976. *Discretionary Justice: A Preliminary Inquiry*. Urbana: University of Illinois.

De Burca, Gráinne. 1993. The Principle of Proportionality and Its Applications in EC Law. *Yearbook of European Law* 13:105–50.

De Figueiredo, John M. and Emerson H. Tiller. 1996. Congressional Control of the Courts: A Theoretical and Empirical Analysis of Expansion of the Federal Judiciary. *The Journal of Law and Economics* 39 (October):435–60.

De Ramón, Armando. 1989. La Justicia Chilena Entre 1875 y 1924. In *Cuadernos de Análisis Jurídicos.*Santiago, Chile: Editorial de la Universidad Diego Portales.

Debbasch, Charles. 1976. *Institutions et droit administratifs.* Paris, France: PUF.

Dehousse, Renaud. 1994. *La Cour de Justice des Communautés Européennes.* Paris, France: Montchrestien.

———. 1999. Towards a Regulation of Transnational Governance? Citizen's Rights and the Reform of Comitology Procedures. In *EU Committees: Social Regulation, Law and Politics.* eds. Christian Joerges and Ellen Vos. Oxford: Hart Publishing.

———. 2002. Misfits: EU Law and the Transformation of European Governance. In *Good Governance in Europe's Integrated Market*, 216–24, eds. Christian Joerges and Renaud Dehousse. Oxford: Oxford University Press.

Deighton-Smith, Rex. 1997. The Machinery of Regulatory Reform. The OECD Observer. June/July.

Dershowitz, Alan. 2001. *Supreme Injustice: How the High Court Hijacked the Election.* New York: Oxford University Press.

Derthick, Martha. 1990. *Agency Under Stress: The Social Security Administration in American Government.* Washington, DC: Brookings Institution.

Derthick, Martha and Paul Quirk. 1985. *The Politics of Deregulation.* Washington, DC: Brookings Institution.

———. 2001. *Keeping the Compound Republic: Essays on American Federalism.* Washington, DC: Brookings Press.

Devins, Neal. 1996. *Shaping Constitutional Values.* Baltimore: Johns Hopkins University Press.

———. 2002. The Federalism-Rights Nexus: Explaining Why Senate Democrats Tolerate Rehnquist Court Decision Making But Not the Rehnquist Court. *University of Colorado Law Review* 73:1307.

Diez-Picazo, 2002. What Does It Mean to Be a State Within the European Union? 12 *Rivista Italiana di Diritto Pubblico Comunitario* 12:651.

Dillon, Sara. 2001. *International Trade and Economic Law and the European Union*, Oxford: Hart Publishing.

Dinan, John. 2002. Congressional Responses to the Rehnquist Court's Federalism Decisions. *Publius* 32:1.

———. 2003. The Consequences of the Rehnquist Court's Federalism Decisions. Paper Presented at the Midwestern Political Science Association, Chicago, IL.

Dodson, Michael and Donald Jackson. 2001. Judicial Independence and Instability in Central America. In *Judicial Independence in the Age of Democracy. Critical Perspectives from Around the World*, eds. Peter Russell and David M O'Brien 251–72. Charlottesville and London: University of Virginia Press.

Eckstein, Harry. 1975. Case Studies and Theory in Political Science. In *Handbook of Political Science*, eds. F. Greenstein and N. Polsby, vii. Reading: Addison-Wesley.

Eisenberg, Theodore. 1981. *Civil Rights Legislation: Cases and Materials.* Charlottesville, VA: Michie.

Ellickson, Robert C. 1991. *Order Without Law: How Neighbors Settle Disputes.* Cambridge, MA: Harvard University Press.

Ellis, Evelyn, ed. 1999. *The Principle of Proportionality in the Laws of Europe.* Oxford: Hart Publishing.

Elster, Jon and Rune Slagstad, eds. 1988. *Constitutionalism and Democracy*. New York: Cambridge University Press.

Ely, John Hart. 1980. *Democracy and Distrust: A Theory of Judicial Review*. Cambridge, MA: Harvard University Press.

Empel, Martin Van. 1992. The 1992 Programme: Interaction Between Legislator And Judiciary. *Legal Issues of European Integration* 1992(2):1–16.

Epp, Charles. 1998. *The Rights Revolution: Lawyers, Activists and Supreme Courts in Comparative Perspective*. Chicago, IL: University of Chicago Press.

Epstein, Lee and Jack Knight. 1998. *The Choices Justices Make*. Washington, DC: CQ Press.

Epstein, Lee, Jack Knight and Olga Shvetsova. 2001. The Role of Constitutional Courts in the Establishment and Maintenance of Democratic Systems of Government. *Law and Society Review* 35(1):117–64.

Epstein, Lee, Jeffrey A. Segal, Harold Spaeth, and Thomas G. Walker. 1994. *The Supreme Court Compendium: Data, Decisions, and Developments*. Washington, DC: Congressional Quarterly.

Eskridge, William. 1994. *Dynamic Statutory Interpretation*. Cambridge, MA: Harvard University Press.

Eule, Julian. 1982. Laying the Dormant Commerce Clause to Rest. *Yale Law Journal* 91:425.

European Commission. 2000. Reforming the Commission.

———. 2001. *White Paper on European Governance* (WPG) (COM(2001) 428), OJ C287.

———. 2003. Report from the Commission on European Governance.

Everson, Michelle. 1995. Independent Agencies: Hierarchy Beaters. *European Law Journal* 1:180.

———. 1998. Administering Europe? *Journal of Common Market Studies* 36:195.

Fairman, Charles. 1987. *Reconstruction and Reunion, 1864–88*. New York: Macmillan.

Ferejohn, John A. and Barry R. Weingast. 1992. A Positive Theory of Statutory Interpretation. *International Review of Law and Economics* 12: 263.

Fesler, James and Donald Kettl. 1996. *The Politics of the Administrative Process*, 2nd ed. New York: Chatham House.

Fisher, Louis. 1985. Judicial Misjudgments about the Law Making Process: The Legislative Veto Cases. *Public Administration Review* 45:705.

———. 1988. *Constitutional Dialogues: Interpretation as Political Process*. Princeton: Princeton University Press.

Fiss, Owen. 1993. The Right Degree of Independence. In *Transition to Democracy in Latin America: The Role of the Judiciary*, ed. Irwin Stotzky. Boulder: Westview Press.

Fligstein, Neil. 2001. *The Architecture of Markets: An Economic Sociology of Twenty-First-Century Capitalist Societies*. Princeton: Princeton University Press.

Fligstein, Neil and Iona Mara Drita. 1996. How to Make a Market: Reflections on the European Union's Single Market Program. *American Journal of Sociology*, 102(1):1–33.

Fligstein, Neil and Alec Stone Sweet. 2002. Of Polities and Markets: An Institutionalist Account of European Integration. *American Journal of Sociology*, 107(5):1206–43.

Follesdal, Andreas. 2003. The Political Theory of the White Paper on Governance: Hidden and Fascinating. *European Public Law* 9:73.

Foner, Eric. 1988. *Reconstruction: America's Unfinished Revolution, 1863–1877*. New York: Harper and Row.

Fox, Greg and Georg Nolte. 1995. Intolerant Democracies. *Harvard International Law Journal* 36:1–70.

Frankfurter, Felix and James M. Landis. 1928. *The Business of the Supreme Court: A Study in the Federal Judicial System.* New York: Macmillan.

Freedom House. 2002. *Freedom in the World 2001–2002.* New York: Transaction Publishers.

Freeman, Jody. 1997. Collaborative Governance in the Administrative State. *UCLA Law Review* 45:1.

———. 2000. Private Parties, Public Functions and the New Administrative Law. *Administrative Law Review* 52:513.

Freeman, Jody. 2000. The Private Role in Public Governance. *New York University Law Review* 75:543.

Freyer, Tony Allan. 1978. The Federal Courts, Localism, and the National Economy, 1865–1900. *Business History Review* 53(Autumn): 343–63.

———. 1979. *Forums of Order: The Federal Courts and Business in American History.* Greenwich, CT: JAI Press.

Friedman, Barry. 1998. The History of the Countermajoritarian Difficulty, Part One: The Road to Judicial Supremacy. *New York University Law Review* 73(May): 333–433.

———. 2001. The History of the Countermajoritarian Difficulty, Part Three: The Lesson of Lochner. *New York University Law Review* 76(Nov.):1383–1455.

Friedman, Lawrence M. 1985. *Total Justice.* New York: Russell Sage Foundation.

Fritz, Christian G. 1991. *Federal Justice in California: The Court of Ogden Hoffman, 1851–1891.* Lincoln, NE and London: University of Nebraska Press.

Fruhling, Hugo. 1984. *Law in Society: Social Transformation and the Crisis of law in Chile, 1830–1970.* Ph.D. diss., Harvard University School of Law.

Galanter, Marc. 1992. Law Abounding: Legalization Around the North Atlantic. *Modern Law Review* 55:1.

Gardbaum, S. 2001. The New Commonwealth Model of Constitutionalism. *American Journal of Comparative Law* 49:707–60.

Garrett, Geoffrey. 1992. International Cooperation and Institutional Choice: The EC's Internal Market. *International Organization.* 46(2):533–60.

———. 1995. The Politics of Legal Integration in the European Union. *International Organization* 49(1):171–81.

George, Alexander. 1979. Case Studies and Theory Development: The Method of Structured, Focused Comparison. In *Diplomacy: New Approaches in History, Theory, and Policy*, ed. P. Lauren. New York: Free Press.

George, S. and I. Bache. 2001. *Politics in the European Union.* Oxford: Oxford University Press.

Gerstenberg, Oliver. 2002. Unraveling Government through Gouvernance sans Frontiers. *Oxford Journal of Legal Studies* 22:563.

Gibson, Charles. 1964. *The Aztecs Under Spanish Rule: A History of the Indians of the Valley of Mexico.* Stanford: Stanford University Press.

Gillman, Howard. 1993. *The Constitution Besieged: The Rise and Demise of Lochner Era Police Powers Jurisprudence.* Durham and London: Duke University Press.

———. 1998. The Court as an Idea, Not a Building (Or a Game): Interpretive Institutionalism and the Analysis of Supreme Court Decision-Making. In *Supreme Court Decision-Making*, eds. Gillman and Clayton, 65–87. Lawrence, KS: University Press of Kansas.

———. 2001. *The Votes That Counted: How the Court Decided the 2000 Presidential Election.* Chicago: University of Chicago Press.

————. 2004. Martin Shapiro and the Movement from "Old" to "New" Institutionalist Studies in Public Law Scholarship. *Annual Review of Political Science* 7: 363–82.

Gillman, Howard and Cornell Clayton. 1998a. *The Supreme Court in American Politics: New Institutionalist Interpretations*. Lawrence, KS: University Press of Kansas.

————. 1998b. Beyond Judicial Attitudes: Institutional Approaches to Supreme Court Decision Making. In *Supreme Court Decision-making*, eds. Cornell Clayton and Howard Gillman, 1–13. Chicago: University of Chicago Press.

Ginsburg, Tom. 2002. Economic Analysis and the Design of Constitutional Courts. *Theoretical Inquiries in Law* 3:49–85.

————. 2003. *Judicial Review in New Democracies: Constitutional Courts in Asian Cases*. New York: Cambridge University Press.

Ginsburg, Tom and Richard McAdams. 2004. Adjudicating in Anarchy: An Expressive Theory of International Dispute Resolution. *William and Mary Law Review* 45:1229–1302.

Goldstein, Judith, Miles Kahler et al., eds. 2001. *Legalization and World Politics*. Cambridge: MIT Press.

Goldstein, Leslie. 2001. *Constituting Federal Sovereignty: The European Union in Comparative Context*. Baltimore: Johns Hopkins University Press.

Gómez, Gastón. 1999. El Recurso de Inaplicabilidad. *Informes de Investigación del Centro de Investigación Jurídica de la Facultad de Derecho*. Santiago: Universidad Diego Portales.

Góngora, Mario. 1975. *Studies in the Colonial History of Spanish America*. New York: Cambridge University Press.

Gordon, Robert W. 1983. Legal Thought and Legal Practice in the Age of American Enterprise, 1870–1920. In *Professions and Professional Ideologies in America*, ed. Gerald L. Geison. Chapel Hill: University of North Carolina Press.

Gormley, Laurence. 1985. *Prohibiting Restrictions on Trade within the EEC*. North Holland, The Netherlands: Elsevier-TMC Asser Instituut.

Gould, Ellen. 2002. Transatlantic Consumer Dialogue, Background paper on Trade in Services. http://www.tacd.org.

Graber, Mark A. 1993. The Non-Majoritarian Difficulty: Legislative Deference to the Judiciary. *Studies in American Political Development* 7:35–73.

————. 1998a. Establishing Judicial Review? Schooner Peggy and the Early Marshall Court. *Political Research Quarterly* 51(March):21–39.

————. 1998b. Federalist or Friends of Adams: The Marshall Court and Party Politics. *Studies in American Political Development* 12:209.

————. 1999. The Problematic Establishment of Judicial Review. In *The Supreme Court in American Politics: New Institutionalist Interpretations*, eds. Howard Gillman and Cornell Clayton. Lawrence, KS: University Press of Kansas.

Grant, W. 1997. *The Common Agricultural Policy*. London: MacMillan.

Greve, Michael. 1999. *Real Federalism: Why It Matters, How It Could Happen*. Washington, DC: AEI.

————. 2004. Preemption in the Rehnquist Court. Unpublished paper.

Griffin, Stephen M. 1996. *American Constitutionalism: From Theory to Politics*. Princeton, NJ: Princeton University Press.

Guerra, José Guillermo. 1929. *La Constitución de 1925*. Santiago, Chile: Anales de la Universidad de Chile.

Guild, Elspeth. 1998. The Constitutional Consequences of Lawmaking in the Third Pillar of the European Union. In *Lawmaking in the European Union*, eds. Paul Craig and Carol Harlow, Dordrecht: Kluwer Law International.

Haas, Ernst B. 1958. *The Uniting of Europe: Political, Social, and Economic Forces, 1950–1957*. Stanford, CA: Stanford University Press.

———. 1961. International Integration: The European and the Universal Process. *International Organization* 15(3):366–92.

———. 2001. Does Constructivism Subsume Neo-Functionalism? In *The Social Construction of Europe*, ed. T. Christiansen et al., London: Sage.

Haines, Charles Grove. 1932. *The American Doctrine of Judicial Supremacy*. Berkeley: University of California Press.

Hall, Kermit L. 1973. The Taney Court in the Second Party System: The Congressional Response to Federal Judicial Reform. Ph.D. diss., University of Minnesota.

———. 1975. The Civil War as a Crucible for Nationalizing the Lower Federal Courts. *Prologue* 7(Fall):177–86.

———. 1976. Social Backgrounds and Judicial Recruitment: A Nineteenth-Century Perspective on the Lower Federal Judiciary. *Western Political Quarterly* 29:243.

Halperin-Donghi, Tulio. *El Espejo de la Historia. Problemas Argentinos y Perspectivas Latinoamericanas*, Buenos Aires: Editorial Sudamericana.

Halpern, Stephen. 1995. *On the Limits of the Law: The Ironic Legacy of Title VI of the Civil Rights Act*. Baltimore, MD: Johns Hopkins University Press.

Hamill, David. 1999. Why the National Competition Council Should Be Abolished. http://www.onlineopinion.com.au/July99/Hamill.htm.

Harding, Christopher. 1992. Who Goes to Court in Europe? An Analysis of Litigation against the European Community. *European Law Review* 17: 105.

Harlow, Carol. 1992. Towards a Theory of Standing for the European Court of Justice. *Yearbook of European Law* 12:213.

———. 2002a. *Accountability in the European Union*. Oxford: Oxford University Press.

———. 2002b. Public Law and Popular Justice. *Modern Law Review* 63:1.

Harriet, Fernando Campos. 1963. *Historia Constitucional de Chile*. Santiago de Chile: Editorial Jurídica de Chile.

Hart, H. L. A. 1994. *The Concept of Law*. Oxford: Clarendon.

Heritier, Adrienne and Moral Soriano Leonor. 2001. Differentiating and Linking Politics and Adjudication: the Example of European Electricity Policy. SSRN Electronic Paper Collection. http://papers.ssrn.com/sol3/papers.cfm?abstract_id=299443.

Hilbink, Lisa. 1999a. La Actuación del Poder Judicial Chileno en los años 90. In *El Modelo Chileno.Democracia y Desarrollo en los Noventa*, eds. Paul Drake and Iván Yaksic, 317–37. Santiago: LOM Ediciones.

Hilbink, Lisa. 1999b. *Legalism Against Democracy: The Political Role of the Judiciary in Chile, 1964–1994*. Ph.D. diss., University of California, San Diego.

Hirschl, Ran. 2000. The Political Origins of Judicial Empowerment Through Constitutionalization: Lessons From Four Constitutional Revolutions. *Law and Social Inquiry* 25(Winter):91–148.

———. 2004. *Toward Juristocracy: The Origins and Consequences of the New Constitutionalism*. Cambridge, MA: Harvard University Press.

Hix, Simon. 1999. *The Political System of the European Union*. Basingstoke: Macmillan.

Hodess, Robin, ed. 2003. *The Global Corruption Report*. Berlin: Transparency International.

Hodson, Dermot and Imelda Maher. 2001. The Open Method as a New Mode of Governance. *Journal of Common Market Studies* 39:719.

Holmes, Stephen. 1995. *Passions and Constraint. On the Theory of Liberal Democracy.* Chicago: University of Chicago Press.

Hood, C., O. James et al. 2000. Regulation of Government: Has It Increased, Is It Increasing, Should It be Diminished? *Public Administration* 78: 283–304.

Horowitz, Donald. 1976. *The Courts and Social Policy.* Washington, DC: Brookings.

Horwitz, Morton J. 1982. The History of the Public/Private Distinction. *University of Pennsylvania Law Review* 130: 1423–28.

Huber, John and Charles Shipan. 2000. The Costs of Control: Legislators, Agencies, and Transaction Costs. *Legislative Studies Quarterly* 25(1):25–42.

Huneeus, Jorge. 1880. *La Constitución Ante el Congreso.* Santiago, Chile: Imprenta de los Tiempos.

Hyman, Harold M. and William M. Wiecek. 1982. *Equal Justice Under Law: Constitutional Development, 1835–1875.* New York: Harper and Row.

Interview. 1997a. Senior Official A, Office of Regulation Review, Productivity Commission, Canberra, 15 February 1997.

Interview. 1997b. Victor Perton, Member of Parliament of Victoria, Chairman of Scrutiny of Acts and Regulation Committee, 29 January 1997.

Interview. 1997c. 'Terry Downing, Senior Policy Officer, NSW Cabinet Office, 7 February 1997.

Interview. 2001a. Senior Official B and Senior Official C, Department of Treasury and Finance, Victorian Government, 2 April 2001.

Interview. 2001b. Senior Official D and Senior Official E, New South Wales Department of the Premier and Cabinet, 9 March 2001.

Interview. 2001c. Senior Official F, National Competition Council of Australia, 3 April 2001.

Interview. 2001d. Fred Hilmer, Chairman of Fairfax Ltd and Former Chairman of the National Competition Policy Review, 9 April 2001.

Interview. 2001e. John Braithwaite, Professor of Law, Research School of Social Sciences, Australian National University, 16 December 2001.

Jachtenfuchs, Markus. 2001. The Governance Approach to European Integration. *Journal of Common Market Studies* 39:245.

Jackson, Robert H. 1941. *The Struggle for Judicial Supremacy: A Study of a Crisis in American Power Politics.* New York: Vintage Books.

Jacob, Herbert et al. 1996. *Courts, Law and Politics in Comparative Perspective.* New Haven, CT: Yale University Press.

Jacobs, Clyde E. 1954. *Law Writers and the Courts: The Influence of Thomas M. Cooley, Christopher G. Tiedeman, and John F. Dillon Upon American Constitutional Law.* Berkeley, CA: University of California Press.

Jacobs, S. 1999. The Second Generation of Regulatory Reforms. Paper Presented at the IMF Conference on the Second Generation Reforms, available at http://www1.oecd.org/subject/regreform/speeches/.

Jaksic, Iván. 2001. *Andrés Bello: Scholarship and Nation-Building in Nineteenth-Century Latin America.* New York: Cambridge University Press.

Jarkín, Edmundo and Fernando Carrillo, eds. 1998. *Justice Delayed: Judicial Reform in Latin America.* Washington, DC: Inter-American Development Bank.

Jarvis, Malcolm. 1998. *The Application of EC Law by National Courts*. Oxford: Oxford University Press.

Joerges, Christian and Renaud Dehousse, eds. 2002. *Good Governance in Europe's Integrated Market*, Oxford: Oxford University Press.

Kadelbach, Stefan. 2002. European Administrative Law and the Law of a Europeanized Administration. In Christian Joerges and Renaud Dehousse. 2002. *Good Governance in Europe's Integrated Market*, eds. 167–206. Oxford: Oxford University Press.

Kagan, Robert A. 1995. What Socio-Legal Scholars Should Do When There Is Too Much Law to Study. *Journal of Law and Society* 22: 140–48.

———. 1997. Should Europe Worry About Adversarial Legalism? *Oxford Journal of Legal Studies* 17: 165–83.

———. 2001. *Adversarial Legalism: The American Way of Law*. Cambridge: Harvard University Press.

Kagan, Robert A., Bryant Garth and Austin Sarat. 2002. Facilitating and Domesticating Change: Democracy, Capitalism, and Law's Double Role in the Twentieth Century. In *Looking Back at Laws Century*, eds. Austin Sarat, Bryant Garth, and Robert A. Kagan, Ithaca, NY: Cornell University Press.

Kagan, Robert and Lee Axelrad. 2000. *Regulatory Encounters: Multinational Corporations and American Adversarial Legalism*. Berkeley: University of California Press.

Katzmann, Robert. 1986. *Institutional Disability: The Saga of Transportation Policy for the Disabled*. Washington: Brookings.

Kaufman, Herbert. 1981. *The Administrative Behavior of Federal Bureau Chiefs*. Washington, DC: Brookings.

Keck, Thomas. 2002. Activism and Restraint on the Rehnquist Court: Timing, Sequence, and Conjuncture in Constitutional Development. *Polity* 35(Fall): 121–52.

Kelemen, R. Daniel and Eric Sibbitt. 2004. The Globalization of American Law. *International Organization* 58:103–36.

Keller, Morton. 1977. *Affairs of State: Public Life in Late Nineteenth Century America*. Cambridge: Belknap Press.

Kelsen, Hans. 1945. *General Theory of Law and State*. New Haven, CT: Yale University Press.

Kickert, Walter. 1993. Complexity, Governance and Dynamics: Conceptual Explorations of Network Management. In *Modern Governance: New Government-Society Interactions*, ed. Jan Kooiman, 275. London: Sage.

Kilpatrick, C. 2000. The Future of Remedies in Europe. In *The Future of Remedies in Europe*, ed. C. Kilpatrick, et al., 1–34. Oxford: Hart Publishing.

Kilroy, Bernadette A. 1996. Member State Control or Judicial Independence? The Integrative Role of the European Court of Justice, 1958–1994. Unpublished manuscript.

Klarman, Michael J. 1996. Rethinking the Civil Rights and Civil Liberties Revolutions. *Virginia Law Review* 82(Feb.):1–67.

———. 2001. How Great Were the 'Great' Marshall Court Decisions? *Virginia Law Review* 87(Oct.):1111.

Knight, Jack and Lee Epstein. 1996. On the Struggle for Judicial Supremacy. *Law and Society Review* 30:87–120.

Koelbe, Thomas. 1995. The New Institutionalism in Political Science and Sociology. *Comparative Politics* 27:231–43.

Kommers, Donald. 1997. *Constitutional Jurisprudence of The Federal Republic of Germany* 2nd ed. Durham, NC: Duke University Press.

Kriegel, Blandine. 1995. *The State and the Rule of Law*. Princeton, NJ: Princeton University Press.

Krislov, Samuel and Daniel Kirslov. 1996. Separating Powers and Compounding Interests. In *Courts and the Political Process: Jack Peltason's Contributions to Political Science.* Ed. Austin Ranney, 69–98. Berkeley: Institute of Governmental Studies Press.

Kritzer, Herbert M. 1996. Courts, Justice, and Politics in England. In *Courts, Law and Politics in Comparative Perspective*, ed. Herbert Jacob et al., 81–176. New Haven, CT: Yale University Press.

———. 2001. Into the Electoral Waters: The Impact of Bush v. Gore on Public Perceptions and Knowledge of the Supreme Court. *Judicature* 84:32.

———. 2003. Martin Shapiro: Anticipating the New Institutionalism. In *The Pioneers of Judicial Behavior*, ed. Nancy Maveety, Ann Arbor: University of Michigan Press.

Kutler, Stanley I. 1968. *Judicial Power and Reconstruction Politics*. Chicago and London: University of Chicago Press.

Ladeur, Karl-Heinz. 1997. Towards a Legal Theory of Supranationality—The Validity of the Network Concept. *European Law Journal* 3: 33.

Laffan, Brigid. 1997. From Policy Entrepreneur to Policy Manager: The Challenge Facing the EC. *Journal of European Public Policy* 4: 422.

Lanza, Stephen. 2000. The Liberalization of Article III Standing: The Supreme Court's Ill-Considered Endorsement of Citizen Suites in Friends of the Earth v. Laidlaw Environmental Services, Inc. *Administrative Law Review* 52:1447.

Larkins, Christopher. 1996. Judicial Independence and Democratization. *American Journal of Comparative Law* 4: 605.

Lee, Maria and Carolyn Abbot. 2003. The Usual Suspects? Public Participation Under the Aarhus Convention. *Modern Law Review* 66:80.

Leftwich, Adrian. 1993. Governance, Democracy and Development in the Third World. *Third World Quarterly* 14:605.

Lenaerts, Koen. 1990. Constitutionalism and the Many Faces of Federalism. *American Journal of Comparative Law* 38:205–64.

Lenaerts, Koen and J. Vanhamme. 1997. Procedural Rights of Private Parties in the Community Administrative Process. *Common Market Law Review* 34:531.

Lenaerts, Koen and Amaryllis Verhoeven. 2002. Institutional Balance as a Guarantee for Democracy in EU Governance. In *Good Governance in Europe's Integrated Market*, eds. Christian Joerges and Renaud Dehousse, 78–85. Oxford: Oxford University Press.

Levin, Martin A. and Martin Shapiro, eds. 2004. *Transatlantic Policymaking in an Age of Austerity*. Washington, D. C.: Georgetown University Press.

Levinson, Sanford. 2002. Bush v. Gore *and the French Revolution*. Law and Contemporary Problems 65:7.

Lindblom, Charles. 1959. The Science of 'Muddling Through'. *Public Administration Review* 19: 79–88.

Lindseth, Peter. 1996. Comparing Administrative States: Susan Rose-Ackerman and the Limits of Public Law in Germany and the United States. *Columbia J. of International Law* 2: 589.

———. 1999. Democratic Legitimacy and the Administrative Character of Supranationalism: The Example of the European Community. *Columbia Law Review* 99: 628.

———. 2002. Delegation Is Dead—Long Live Delegation: Managing the Democratic Disconnect in the European Market Polity. In *Good Governance in Europe's Integrated Market*, eds. Joerges and Dehousse, Oxford: Oxford University Press.

Loader, Ian. 2000. Plural Policing and Democratic Governance. *Social and Legal Studies* 9: 323.

Lorenz, Werner. 1964. General Principles of Law: Their Elaboration in the Court of Justice of the European Communities. *American Journal of Comparative Law* 13:1.

Loveman, Brian. 1993. *The Constitution of Tyranny: Regimes of Exception in Spanish America*. Pittsburgh: University of Pittsburgh Press.

Ludwikowski, Rett R. 1993. Constitution Making in the Countries of Former Soviet Dominance: Current Developments. *Georgia Journal of International and Comparative Law* 23:155.

MacCormick, Neil. 1978. *Legal Reasoning and Legal Theory*. Oxford: Clarendon.

———. 1993. Beyond the Sovereign State. *Modern Law Review* 56:1.

———. 1999. *Questioning Sovereignty, Law, State and Nation in the European Commonwealth*. Oxford: University Press.

Macrory, Richard and Sharon Turner. 2002. Participatory Rights, Transboundary Environmental Governance and EC Law. *Common Market Law Review* 39: 489.

Majone, Giandomenico. 1994. The Rise of the Regulatory State in Europe. *W. European Politics* 17: 77.

———, ed. 1996. *Regulating Europe*. London: Macmillan.

———. 2001. Two Logics of Delegation: Agency and Fiduciary Relations in EU Governance. *European Union Politics* 2(1): 103–22.

Mancini, G. Federico 1991. The Making of a Constitution for Europe. In *The New European Community*, eds. R. Keohane and S. Hoffman, 177–94. Boulder, CO: Westview.

Mancini, G. Federico and David T. Keeling, 1994. Democracy and the European Court of Justice. *Modern Law Review* 57:175.

_____. 1995. Language, Culture and Politics in the Life of the ECJ. *Columbia Journal of European Law* 1: 392.

March, James G. and Olsen, Johan P. 1984. The New Institutionalism: Organizational Factors in Political Life. *American Political Science Review* 78: 734–49.

Marcus, Maeva, ed. 1992. *Origins of the Federal Judiciary: Essays on the Judiciary Act of 1789*. New York and Oxford: Oxford University Press.

Mattli, Walter. 1999. *The Logic of Regional Integration*. New York: Cambridge University Press.

McCann, Michael. 1986. *Taking Reform Seriously: Perspectives on Public Interest Liberalism*. Ithaca, NY: Cornell University Press.

———. 1994. *Rights at Work: Pay Equity Reform and the Politics of Legal Mobilization*. Chicago: University of Chicago Press.

McCown, Margaret and Alec Stone Sweet. 2002. *Dataset on European Court of Justice Citation Practices in Preliminary Reference Rulings, 1961–1998*. Nuffield College, Oxford.

McCubbins, Matthew, Robert Noll and Barry Weingast. 1987. Administrative Procedure as Instruments of Political Control. *Journal of Law, Economics, and Organization* 3:243–77.

———. 1990. Positive and Normative Models of Due Process: As Integrative Approach to Administrative Procedures. *Journal of Law, Economics and Organizations* 6:307–30.

McCurdy, Charles W. 1978. American Law and the Marketing Structure of the Large Corporation, 1875–1890. *Journal of Economic History* 38(Sept.): 631–49.

McGinnis, J. and M. Movsesian. 2000. The World Trade Constitution: Reinforcing Democracy Through Trade. *Harvard Law Review* 114: 511–605.

McMahon, J. 2000. *Law of the Common Agricultural Policy*. Essex: Longman.

Melnick, R. Shep. 1983. *Regulation and the Courts: The Case of the Clean Air Act.* Washington DC: Brookings Institution.

————. 1985. The Politics of Partnership. *Public Administration Review* 45.

————. 1992. Pollution Deadlines and the Coalition for Failure. In *Environmental Politics: Public Costs, Private Rewards*, eds. M. Greve and F. Smith. New York: Greenwood.

————. 1994. *Between the Lines: Interpreting Welfare Rights*. Washington DC: Brookings Institution.

Merryman, John Henry. 1984. *The Civil Law Tradition: An Introduction to the legal Systems of Western Europe and Latin America.* Stanford: Stanford University Press.

Metcalfe, Les. 1996. The European Commission as a Network Organization. *Publius* 26(4): 43.

Milgrom, Paul and John Roberts. 1992. *Economics, Organization and Management.* Englewood Cliffs, NJ: Prentice-Hall International.

Miller, J. G. 2000. The Standing of Citizens to Enforce against Violations of Environmental Statutes in the United States. *Journal of Environmental Law* 12:370.

Miller, Jonathan M. 1994. Informe de la Comision de Juristas Internacionales Sobre la Administracion de Justicia en Peru. Lima, Peru: Instituto de Defensa Legal.

————. 2000. Evaluating the Argentine Supreme Court Under Presidents Alfonsín and Menem (1983–1999). *Southwestern Journal of Law and Trade in the Americas* 7(Fall):369.

Moe, Terry. 1987. An Assessment of the Positive Theory of Congressional Dominance. *Legislative Studies Quarterly* 12(4): 475–520.

————. 1990. Political Institutions: The Neglected Side of the Story. *Journal of Law, Economics, and Organization* 6(1): 213–53.

Moran, Michael. 2002. Understanding the Regulatory State. *British Journal of Political Science* 32: 391–413.

Moravscik, Andrew. 1991. Negotiating the Single European Act: National interests and Conventional Statecraft in the European Community. *International Organization* 45: 19–56.

————. 1993. Preferences and Power in the European Community: A Liberal Intergovernmentalist Approach. *Journal of Common Market Studies* 31:473.

————. 1995. Liberal Intergovernmentalism and Integration: A Rejoinder, *Journal of Common Market Studies* 33(4): 611–28.

————. 1998. *The Choice for Europe: Social Purpose and State Power from Massina to Maastricht.* Ithaca, NY: Cornell University Press.

Morgan, Bronwen. 2003. *Social Citizenship in the Shadow of Competition: the Bureaucratic Politics of Regulatory Justification.* Aldershot, UK: Ashgate Press.

Morse, Richard. 1954. Towards a Theory of Spanish American Government. *Journal of the History of Ideas* 15.

Mortelmans, Kamiel. 1991. Article 30 of the EEC Treaty and Legislation Relating to Market Circumstances: Time to Consider a New Definition? *Common Market Law Review* 28: 115.

Moustafa, Tamir. 2003. Law versus the State: The Judicialization of Politics in Egypt. *Law and Social Inquiry*. 28: 883–930.

Murphy, Walter. 1964. *Elements of Judicial Strategy*. Chicago: University of Chicago Press.

Murphy, Walter and Joseph Tanenhaus. 1977. *Comparative Constitutional Law: Cases and Commentaries*. New York: St. Martin's Press.

Myers, Gustavus. 1918. *History of the Supreme Court of the United States*. Chicago: Charles H. Kerr.

National Competition Council. 1996. Considering the Public Interest under National Compeition Policy. Canberra: Australian Government Publishing Service.

————. 2001. *Framework for the Third Tranche Assessment of Government's Progress with Implementing National Competition Policy and Related Reforms*. Ausinfo, Canberra: Australian Government Publishing Service.

Nehl, Hanns-Peter. 1998. *Principles of Administrative Law*. Oxford: Hart Publishing.

Nivola, Pietro. 2002. *Tense Commandments: Federal Prescriptions and City Problems*. Washington, DC: Brookings Institution.

Noonan, Jr., John T. 2002. *Narrowing the Nation's Power: The Supreme Court Sides with the States*. Berkeley: University of California Press.

North, Douglass R. 1990. *Institutions, Institutional Change, and Economic Performance*. New York: Cambridge University Press.

Nugent, Neill. 1999. *The Government and Politics of the European Union, 4th ed.* London: MacMillan.

————. 2001. *The European Commission*. New York: Palgrave.

O'Brien, David M. 2000. *Storm Center: The Supreme Court in American Politics* 5th ed. New York: W.W. Norton.

Oakeshott, Michael Joseph. 1951. *Political Education*. Cambridge: Bowes and Bowes.

————. 1962. The Rule of Law. *Rationalism in Politics and other Essays*. London: Methuen.

Öberg, Perola. 2002. Does Administrative Corporatism Promote Trust and Deliberation? *Governance* 15: 455.

O'Donnell, G. 1997. *Counterpoints: Selected Essays on Authoritarianism and Democratization*. South Bend: Notre Dame University Press.

Office of Regulation Review (ORR). N.D. Guidelines for Identifying Priorities for Portfolio Review Programs and Bodies to Undertake Reviews and Publis Consultations. On file with author B. Morgan.

Oliver, Peter. 1996. *Free Movement of Goods in the European Community*. London: Sweet and Maxwell.

Olson, Mancur. 1993. Dictatorship, Democracy, and Development. *American Political Science Review* 87(Sept.): 567–76.

Organization for Economic Co-Operation and Development (OECD). 1995. *Recommendation of the Council of the OECD on Improving the Quality of Government Regulation*. Paris: PUMA.

Organization for Economic Co-Operation and Development (OECD). 2000. *Trade and Regulatory Reform: Insights from the OECD Country Reviews and Other Analyses*. http://www.olis.oecd.org/olis/2000doc.nsf/linkto/td-tc-wp(2000)21-final or http://www1.oecd.org/ech/docs/reg.htm.

Osborne, David and Ted Gaebler. 1992. *Reinventing Government*. New York: Addison Wesley.

Pásara, Luis, ed. 2003. *Justicia y Sociedad Civil. El Papel de la Sociedad Civil en la Reforma Judicial: Estudios de Casos en Argentina, Chile, Colombia y Perú*. Santiago: Centro de Estudios de Justicia de las Américas.

Pashin, Sergy. 1994. A Second Edition of the Constitutional Court. *East European Constitutional Review* 82(3):3.

Paton, Paul. 2003. Legal Services and the GATS: Norms as Barriers to Trade. Paper Presented at the Annual Meeting of the Law and Society Association, Pittsburgh (June).

Paul, Arnold M. 1960. *Conservative Crisis and the Rule of Law: Attitudes of Bar and Bench, 1888–1895*. Ithaca, NY: Cornell University Press.

Peña, Carlos. 1994. Hacia una Caracterización del Ethos Legal. In *Evolución de la Cultura Jurídica Chilena*, ed. Agustín Squella. Santiago, Chile: Corporación de promoción Universitaria.

———. 1996. *Práctica Constitucional y Derechos Fundamentales*. Santiago, Chile: Corporación Nacional de Reparación y Reconciliación.

Peretti, Terri Jennings. 1999. *In Defense of a Political Court*. Princeton, NJ: Princeton University Press.

Perry H.W. 1991. *Deciding to Decide: Agenda Setting in the United States Supreme Court*. Cambridge, MA: Harvard University Press.

Perry, J. H. 1990. *The Spanish Seaborne Empire*. Berkeley: University of California Press.

Petersmann, E-U. 2000. From 'Negative' to 'Positive' Integration in the WTO: Time for 'Mainstreaming Human Rights' into WTO Law? *Common Market Law Review* 37:1363–82.

Pfander, James. 2001. Marbury, Original Jurisdiction, and the Supreme Court's Supervisory Powers. *Columbia Law Review* 101: 1515.

Picciotto, Sol. 2002. Reconceptualizing Regulation in the Era of Globalisation. *Journal of Law and Society* 29:1.

Pierson, Paul. 1998. The Path to European Integration: A Historical-Institutionalist Analysis. In *European Integration and Supranational Governance*, eds. W. Sandholtz and A. Stone Sweet, 27–58. Oxford: Oxford University Press.

Poiares Maduro, Miguel. 1998. *We, the Court: The European Court of Justice and the European Economic Constitution*. Oxford: Hart Publishing.

———. 2000. Europe and the Constitution: What If This Is as Good as It Gets? In *European Constitutionalism beyond the State*, eds. J. Weiler and M. Wind. New York: Cambridge University Press.

Pollack, Mark. 1998. Engines of Integration? Supranational Autonomy and Influence in the EU. In *European Integration and Supranational Governance*, eds. W. Sandholtz and A. Stone Sweet, 217–49. Oxford: Oxford University Press.

Posner, Richard. 2001. *Breaking the Deadlock: The 2000 Presidential Election, The Constitution, and the Courts*. Princeton: Princeton University Press.

Powell, Walter and Paul Dimaggio. 1991. *The New Institutionalism in Organizational Analysis*. Chicago: University of Chicago Press.

Presser, Stephen B. 1982. *Studies in the History of the United States Courts of the Third Circuit*. Washington, DC: Government Printing Office.

Prillaman, William C. 2000. *The Judiciary and Democratic Decay in Latin America*. Westport, CT and London: Praeger.

Purcell, Edward A., Jr. 1992. *Litigation and Inequality: Federal Diversity Jurisdiction in Industrial America, 1870–1958*. New York and Oxford: Oxford University Press.

———. 1999. Reconsidering the Frankfurterian Paradigm: Reflections on Histories of Lower Federal Courts [Review Essay on Frankfurter and Landis' *The Business of the Supreme Court*]. *Law and Social Inquiry* 24(Summer):679–750.

———. 2000. *Brandeis and the Progressive Constitution: Erie, the Judicial Power, and the Politics of the Federal Courts in Twentieth-Century America.* New Haven, CT: Yale University Press.

Ramseyer, J. Mark. 1994. The Puzzling (In) Dependence of Courts: A Comparative Approach. *Journal of Legal Studies* 23(June):721–47.

Ranald, P. 1995. National Competition Policy. *Journal of Australian Political Economy* 36:1–25.

Rawlings, Richard. 1993. The Eurolaw Game: Some Deductions from a Saga. *Journal of Law and Society* 20(3):309–40.

Redish, Martin and Shane Nugent. 1987. The Dormant Commerce Clause and the Constitutional Balance of Federalism. *Duke Law Journal* 1987:569.

Reynolds, Glenn and Brannon Denning. 2000. Lower Court Readings of Lopez, or What If the Supreme Court Held a Constitutional Revolution and Nobody Came? *Wisconsin Law Review* 2000:369.

Rhodes, R. 1994. The Hollowing Out of the State: The Changing Nature of the Public Service in Britain. *Political Quarterly* 65:138.

———. 1996. The New Governance: Governing Without Government. *Political Studies* 44:652.

———. 1997. *Understanding Governance.* Buckingham: Open University Press.

Richards. 1996. An Outside Watchdog Is the Best Security. *The Age.* November 23.

Rieger, E. 2000. The Common Agricultural Policy, Politics against Markets. In *Policy-Making in the European Union* 4th ed., eds. H. Wallace and W. Wallace. Oxford: Oxford University Press.

Roldán, Alcibíades. 1913. *Elementos de Derecho Constitucional de Chile.* Santiago de Chile: Encuadernación Barcelona.

Rose-Ackerman, Susan. 1995. *Controlling Environmental Policy: The Limits of Public Law in Germany and the United States.* New Haven, CT: Yale University Press.

———. 1999. *Corruption and Government.* New York: Cambridge University Press.

Rosenberg, Gerald. 1991. *The Hollow Hope: Can Courts Bring About Social Change?* Chicago: University of Chicago Press.

Rosenn, Keith. 1987. The Protection of Judicial Independence in Latin America. *University of Miami Inter-American Law Review* 19:1–35.

Ross, William G. 1994. *A Muted Fury: Populists, Progressives, and Labor Unions Confront the Courts, 1890–1937.* Princeton, NJ: Princeton University Press.

Roth, Brad. 1999. *Governmental Illegitimacy in International Law.* Oxford: Clarendon Press.

Russell, Peter. 2001. Toward a General Theory of Judicial Independence. In *Judicial Independence in the Age of Democracy. Critical Perspectives from Around the World,* eds. Peter Russell and David M O'Brien 1–24. Charlottesville and London: University of Virginia Press.

Russell, Peter and David M. O'Brien, eds. 2001. *Judicial Independence in the Age of Democracy. Critical Perspectives from Around the World.* Charlottesville and London: University of Virginia Press.

Sáez García, Felipe. 1998. The Nature of Judicial Reform in Latin America and Some Strategic Considerations. *American University International Law Review* 13:1267.

Salzman, James. 2000. Labour Rights, Globalization and Institutions: The Role and Influence of the Organization for Economic Cooperation and Development. *Michigan Journal of International Law* 21:769–848.

Samuels, G. (2001) Remarks made at Conference on Regulatory Reform Management, August 2001. Sydney: Australia. Unpublished Manuscript.

Sandholtz, Wayne and Alec Stone Sweet, eds. 1998. *European Integration and Supranational Governance*. Oxford: Oxford University Press.

Sandholtz, Wayne and John Zysman. 1989. 1992: Recasting the European Bargain. *World Politics*. 42(1): 95–128.

Sandler Ross and David Schoenbrod. 2003. *Democracy by Decree: What Happens When Courts Run Government*. New Haven: Yale University Press.

Sartor, Giovanni. 1994. A Formal Model of Legal Argumentation. *Ratio Juris* 7:212-26.

Schepel, Harm. 1998. Legal Pluralism in the European Union. In *Europe's Other: European Law Between Modernity and Postmodernity*, eds. Peter Fitzpatrick and James Henry Bergeron, 56. Aldershot: Ashgate.

Schmitter, Philippe. 1979. Still the Century of Corporatism? In *Trends Toward Corporatist Intermediation*, eds. Philippe Schmitter and Gerhard Lehmbruck. Beverly Hills: Sage.

Schor, Miguel. 1999. The Rule of Law and Democratic Consolidation in Latin America. Unpublished manuscript.

Schwartz, Gary. 1991. Product Liability and Medical Malpractice in Comparative Context. In *The Liability Maze*, eds. Peter Huber and Robert Litan. Washington, DC: Brookings Institute.

Schwarze, Jurgen. 1993. Developing Principles of European Administrative Law. *Public Law* 1993:229.

Scott, Colin. 1998. The Juridification of Relations in the UK Utility Sector. In *Commercial Regulation and Judicial Review*, eds. Julia Black, P. Muchlinkski and P.Walker. Oxford: Hart Publishing.

———. 2000. Accountability in the Regulatory State. *Journal of Law and Society* 27:38–60.

———. 2001. Analysing Regulatory Space: Fragmented Resources and Institutional Design. *Public Law*. 2001:283–305

Scott, Joanne and David Trubek. 2002. Mind the Gap: Law and New Approaches to Governance in the European Union. *European Law Journal* 8:1–18.

Segal, Jeffrey A. 1997. Separation of Powers Games in the Positive Theory of Law and the Courts. *American Political Science Review*. 91:28–44.

Segal, Jeffrey A. and Harold J. Spaeth. 1993. *The Supreme Court and the Attitudinal Model*. New York: Cambridge University Press.

Shaffer, Gregory. 2003. Making the WTO Dispute Settlement System Work for Developing Countries: Some Proactive Developing Country Strategies. Paper Presented at the Annual Meeting of the Law and Society Association, Pittsburgh.

Shapiro, Ian, ed. 1994. *The Rule of Law. Nomos XXXVI*. New York: New York University Press.

Shapiro, Martin. 1961. Morals and the Courts: The Reluctant Crusades. *Minnesota Law Review* 45:897.

———. 1963a. Judicial Modesty: Down With the Old!—And Up With the New? *UCLA Law Review* 10:533–60.

———. 1963b. The Supreme Court and Constitutional Adjudication: Of Politics and Neutral Principles. *George Washington Law Review* 31:587–606.

————. 1964a. *Law and Politics on the Supreme Court.* New York: Free Press.

————. 1964b. Political Jurisprudence. *Kentucky Law Journal* 52:294

————. 1966. *Freedom of Speech: The Supreme Court and Judicial Review.* Englewood Cliffs, NJ: Prentice-Hall.

————. 1968. *Supreme Court and Administrative Agencies.* New York: Free Press.

————. 1969. *The Supreme Court and Public Policy.* Glenview, IL: Scott, Foresman.

————. 1970. Decentralized Decision making in the Law of Torts. In *Political Decision making,* ed. S. Ulmer,. New York: Van Nostrand.

————. 1971. Obscenity Law: A Public Policy Analysis. *Journal of Public Law* 20:503.

————. 1972. Toward a Theory of *Stare Decisis. Journal of Legal Studies* 1:125.

————. 1975. Courts. In *Handbook of Political Science,* eds. F. Greenstein and N. Polsby. Reading, MA: Addison-Wesley.

————. 1980. Comparative Law and Comparative Politics. *University of Southern California Law Review* 53:301.

————. 1981a. *Courts. A Comparative and Political Analysis.* Chicago and London: University of Chicago Press.

————. 1981b. The Presidency and the Federal Courts. In *Politics and the Oval Office,* ed. Arnold Meltsner. San Francisco, CA: Institute for Contemporary Studies.

————. 1983a. Fathers and Sons: The Court, the Commentators, and the Search for Values. In *The Burger Court: The Counter-Revolution that Wasn't,* ed. Vincent Blasi, New Haven, CT: Yale University Press.

————. 1983b. Recent Developments in Political Jurisprudence. *Western Political Quarterly* 36:

————. 1985. Gerrymandering, Unfairness and the Supreme Court. *UCLA Law Review* 33:227–56.

————. 1988a. Of Interests and Values: The New Politics and the New Political Science. In *The New Politics of Public Policy,* eds. Landy, Marc K. and Martin A. Levin. Baltimore: The Johns Hopkins University Press.

————. 1988b. Prudence and Rationality Under the Constitution. In *The Constitution and the Regulation of Society,* eds. Gary Bryner and Dennis Thompson. Provo, UT: Brigham Young University Press

————. 1988c. *Who Guards the Guardians? Judicial Control of Administration.* Athens: University of Georgia Press

————. 1989a. Morality and the Politics of Judging. *Tulane Law Review* 63:1555.

————. 1989b. Political Jurisprudence, Public Law, and Post-Consequentialist Ethics: Comments on Professors Barber and Smith. *Studies in American Political Development* 3:88.

————. 1991. Law and Courts. In *Political Science: State of the Discipline II,* ed. Ada Finifter. Washington, DC: American Political Science Association.

————. 1992a. Federalism, Free Movement, and the Regulation-Averse Entrepreneur. In *North American and Comparative Federalism,* ed. Harry Scheiber. Berkeley: Institute of Governmental Studies Press.

————. 1992b. The European Court of Justice. In *Euro-Politics,* ed. A. Sbragia,123. Washington, DC: Brookings Institution.

————. 1992c The Giving Reasons Requirement. *University of Chicago Legal Forum.* 1992:179–220.

————. 1993. The Globalization of Law. *Indiana Journal of Global Legal Studies* 1:37.

————. 1994. Judges as Liars. *Harvard Journal of Law and Public Policy* 17:155.

————. 1997. The Problems of Independent Agencies in the United States and European Union. *Journal of European Public Policy* 4:276.

————. 1998. The European Court of Justice: Of Institutions and Democracy. *Israel Law Review* 32:3.

————. 1999a. The European Court of Justice. In *The Evolution of EU Law*, eds., Paul P. Craig and Gráinne De Burca. Oxford: Oxford University Press.

————. 1999b. The Success of Judicial Review. In *Constitutional Dialogues in Comparative Perspective*, eds. Sally Kenny, William Reisinger, and John Reitz. London: Macmillan; New York: St Martin's Press.

————. 2001a. The Institutionalization of European Administrative Space. In *The Institutionalization of Europe*, eds. W. Sandholtz, A. Stone Sweet, and N. Fligstein. Oxford: Oxford University Press.

————. 2001b. Administrative Law Unbounded: Reflections on Government and Governance. *Indiana Journal of Global Legal Studies* 8:369.

Shapiro, Martin and Alec Stone Sweet, eds. 1994. Special Issue: The New Constitutional Politics in Europe. *Comparative Political Studies* 26(4).

————. 2002. *On Law, Politics and Judicialization*. Oxford: Oxford University Press.

Sharlet, Robert. 1993. Chief Justice as Judicial Politician, *East European Constitutional Review* 2:37.

Silverstein, Gordon. 2003. Globalization and the Rule of Law: 'A Machine that Runs of Itself?' *International Journal of Constitutional Law* 1:427–45.

Simon, Herbert. 1976. *Administrative Behavior*. 3rd ed. New York: Free Press.

Skowronek, Stephen. 1982. *Building a New American State: The Expansion of National Administrative Capacities, 1877–1920*. New York: Cambridge University Press.

Slaughter, Anne-Marie, Alec Stone Sweet and Joseph Weiler, eds. 1998. *The European Courts and National Courts—Doctrine and Jurisprudences*. Oxford: Hart Publishing.

Smith, Rogers. 1988. Political Jurisprudence, the "New Institutionalism," and the Future of Public Law. *American Political Science Review* 82: 89.

Snyder, Francis. 1990. *New Directions in European Community Law*. London: Weidenfeld.

————. 1993. The Effectiveness of European Community Law: Institutions, Processes, Tools and Techniques. *Modern Law Review* 56:19.

————. 1994. Soft Law and Institutional Practice in the European Community. In *The Construction of Europe, Essays in Honour of Emile Noel*, ed. S. Martin. Dordrecht: Kluwer.

Spiller, Pablo. 1998. Regulatory Agencies and the Courts. In *The New Palgrave Dictionary of Economics and the La*, ed. Peter Newman, 263–66. New York: Stockton Press.

Stampp, Kenneth M. 1967. *The Era of Reconstruction, 1865–1877*. New York: Random House.

Stein, Eric. 1981. Lawyers, Judges, and the Making of a Transnational Constitution. *American Journal of International Law* 75(1):1–27.

Stein, Peter. 1980. *Legal Evolution: The Story of an Idea*. New York: Cambridge University Press.

Steiner, Josephine. 1992. Drawing the Line: Uses and Abuses of Article 30 EEC. *Common Market Law Review* 29:749.

Steinmo, Sven et al., eds. 1992. *Structuring Politics: Historical Institutionalism in Comparative Analysis*. New York: Cambridge University Press.

Sterett, Susan. 1997. *Creating Constitutionalism?* Ann Arbor: University of Michigan Press.

Stewart, Richard B. 1975. The Reformation of American Administrative Law. *Harvard Law Review* 88:1667.

———. 1988. Regulation and the Crisis of Liberalization in the United States. In *Law as an Instrument of Economic Policy: Comparative and Critical Approaches*, ed. Terence Daintith, 79–133. Berlin: de Gruyter.

Stigler. 1971. The Theory of Economic Regulation. Bell Journal of Economics and Management Science 2(1):21.

Stone Sweet, Alec. 1990. The Birth and Development of Abstract Review: Constitutional Courts and Policy-Making in Western Europe. *Policy Studies Journal* 19: 81–95.

———. 1992. *The Birth of Judicial Politics in France*. Oxford: Oxford University Press.

———. 1994. What Is a Supranational Constitution?: An Essay in International Relations Theory. *Review of Politics* 56(Summer):441–74.

———. 1995. Complex Coordinate Construction in France and Germany. In *The Global Expansion of Judicial Power*, eds. Neal Tate and Thorsten Vallinder, 205–29. New York: New York University Press.

———. 1999. Judicialization and the Construction of Governance. *Comparative Political Studies* 32:147–84.

———. 2000. *Governing with Judges: Constitutional Politics in Europe*. Oxford: Oxford University Press.

———. 2002. Constitutional Courts and Parliamentary Democracy. *West European Politics* 25(1):77–100.

———. 2004. *The Judicial Construction of Europe*. Oxford: Oxford University Press.

Stone Sweet, Alec and James Caporaso. 1998. La Cour européenne et l'intégration. *Revue Française de Science Politique* 48(2):195–244.

Stone Sweet, Alec and Margaret McCown. 2003. Discretion and Precedent in European Law. In *Judicial Discretion in European Perspective*, ed. O. Wiklund, 85–115. Stockholm: Kluwer Law International.

Stone Sweet, Alec and Thomas Brunell. 1998a. Constructing a Supranational Constitution: Dispute Resolution and Governance in the European Community. *American Political Science Review* 92(March):63–81.

———. 1998b. The European Court and the National Courts: A Statistical Analysis of Preliminary References, 1961–95. *Journal of European Public Policy* 5(1):66–97.

———. 2000. The European Court, National Judges and Legal Integration: A Researcher's Guide to the Data Base on Prelimnary References in European Law, 1958–98. *European Law Journal.* 6: 117–27.

Stone Sweet, Alec, Wayne Sandholtz and Neil Fligstein, eds. 2001. *The Institutionalization of Europe*. Oxford: Oxford University Press.

Stone, Deborah. 1984. *The Disabled State*. Philadelphia: Temple University Press.

Strauss, Peter et al. 2000. *Gellhorn and Byse's Administrative Law*. 10th ed. Westbury, NY: Foundation Press.

Sullivan, Kathleen M. 1992. Foreword: The Justices of Rules and Standards. *Harvard Law Review* 106:22.

Sunkin, Maurice. 1994. Judicialization of Politics in the United Kingdom. *International Political Science Review* 15:125.

Sunstein, Cass. 1988. Constitutions and Democracy: An Epilogue. In *Constitutionalism and Democracy*, eds. J. Elster and R. Slagstad. New York: Cambridge University Press.

————. 1992. What's Standing After *Lujan?* Of Citizen Suits, 'Injuries', and Article III. *Michigan Law Review* 91:163.

Tallberg, Jonas. 2002. Delegation to Supranational Institutions: Why, How, and With What Consequences? *West European Politics* 25(1):23–46.

Tanase, Takao. 1990. The Management of Disputes: Automobile Accident Compensation in Japan. *Law and Society Review* 24:651.

Tate, C. Neal and Torbjorn Vallinder, eds. 1995. *The Global Expansion of Judicial Power.* New York: New York University Press.

Taylor, Serge. 1984. *Making Bureaucracies Think.* Stanford University Press.

Teubner, Gunther, ed. 1987. *Juridification of Social Spheres.* Berlin: Walter de Gruyter.

————. 2000. Contracting World: The Many Autonomies of Private Law. *Social and Legal Studies* 9:399.

Teubner, Gunther and Sergio Febbrajo, eds. 1992. State, Law and Economy as Autopoetic Systems. *European Yearbook of the Sociology of Law.* Milan: Giuffre.

Thatcher, Mark, and Alec Stone Sweet, eds. 2002. Special Issue: The Politics of Delegation: Non-Majoritarian Institutions in Europe. *West European Politics* 25(1).

Thayer, James Bradley. 1893. The Origin and Scope of the American Doctrine of Constitutional Law. *Harvard Law Review* 7:129.

Theodissiou, Maria. 2002. An Analysis of the Recent Response of the Community to Non-compliance with Court of Justice Judgements: Article 228(2) EC. *European Law Review* 25:41.

Tridimas, T. 1999. Proportionality in Community Law: Searching for the Appropriate Standard of Scrutiny. In *The Principle of Proportionality in the Laws of Europe*, ed. E. Ellis. Oxford: Hart Publishing.

Truman, David. 1951. *The Governmental Process.* New York: Knopf.

Tsebelis, George. 1995. Decision-Making in Political Systems: Veto Players in Presidentialism, Parliamentarism, Multiculturalism, and Multipartyism. *British Journal of Political Science* 25:289–325.

Tushnet, Mark. 1999. *Taking the Constitution Away From the Courts.* Princeton, NJ: Princeton University Press.

Twiss, Benjamin R. 1942. *Lawyers and the Constitution: How Laissez Faire Came to the Supreme Court.* Westport, CT: Greenwood Press.

Upham, Frank. 1987. *Law and Social Change in Postwar Japan.* Cambridge: Harvard University Press.

Usher, J. 1988. *Legal Aspects of Agriculture in the European Community.* Oxford: Oxford University Press.

Verner, Joel. 1984. The Independence of Supreme Courts in Latin America: A Review of the Literature. *Journal of Latin American Studies* 16:463.

Victorian Government. 1995. National Competition Policy: Steps to Assist Agencies in Complying with the Guidelines for the Application of the Competition Test to New Legislative Proposals. Melbourne: Victorian Government Publishing Service.

Vincent-Jones, Peter. 2000. Contractual Governance: Institutional and Organizational Analysis. *Oxford Journal of Legal Studies* 20:317–51.

Vogel, Steven. 1996. *Freer Markets, More Rules.* Ithaca, NY: Cornell University Press.

Voigt, Stefan and Eli M. Salzberger. 2002. Choosing Not to Choose: When Politicians Choose to Delegate Powers. *Kyklos* 55(May).

Walker, David. 2000. *The Rebirth of Federalism.* New York: Chatham House.

Walker, Neil. 2002. Policing and the Supranational Polity *Policy and Society* 12:307.

Ward, Dr., Angela. 2000. *Judicial Review and the Rights of Private Parties in EC Law*. Oxford: Oxford University Press.

Warren, Charles. 1913. Legislative and Judicial Attacks on the Supreme Court of the United States—A History of the Twenty-fifth Section of the Judiciary Act. *American Law Review* 47:1–34, 161–89.

Weatherill, S. 2000. New Strategies for Managing the EC's Internal Market. *Current Legal Problems* 53:595–619.

Weaver, Kent. 1986. The Politics of Blame Avoidance. *Journal of Public Policy* 6(4):371-98.

Weber, Max. 1958. *The Protestant Ethic and the Spirit of Capitalism*. Trans. Talcott Parsons. New York: Scribners.

Wechsler, Herbert. 1954. The Political Safeguards of Federalism: The Role of the States in the Composition and Selection of the National Government. *Columbia Law Review* 54:543.

Weiler, Joseph H.H. 1981. The Community System: The Dual Character of Supranationalism. *Yearbook of European Law* 1:268–306.

———. 1991. The Transformation of Europe. *Yale Law Journal* 100:2043.

———. 1993. Journey to an Unknown Destination: A Retrospective and Prospective of the European Court of Justice in the Arena of Political Integration. *Journal of Common Market Studies* 31:417.

———. 1997. The European Union belongs to its Citizens: Three Immodest Proposals. *European Law Review* 22:150.

———. 1998. The Constitution of the Common Marketplace: Text and Context in the Evolution of the Free Movement of Goods. In *The Evolution of EU Law*, eds. P. Craig and G. De Burca, 349–76. Oxford: Oxford University Press.

———. 1999. *The Constitution of Europe: 'Do the New Clothes Have an Emperor?' and Other Essays on European Integration*. New York: Cambridge University Press.

Weingast, Barry. 1993. Constitutions as Governance Structures: The Political Foundations of Secure Markets. *Journal of Institutional and Theoretical Economics* 149:286–311.

———. 1997. The Political Foundations of Democracy and the Rule of Law. *American Political Science Review* 91(June):245–63.

Westin, Alan. 1953. The Supreme Court, the Populist Movement, and the Campaign of 1896. *Journal of Politics* 15(Feb.):3–41.

Wheeler, Russell R. 1992. *Origins of the Elements of Federal Courts Governance*. Washington, DC: Federal Judicial Center.

White, Eric L. 1989. In Search of the Limits to Article 30 of the EEC Treaty. *Common Market Law Review* 26:235–80.

Whittington, Keith E. 1999. *Constitutional Construction: Divided Powers and Constitutional Meaning*. Cambridge: Harvard University Press.

———. 2000. Once More into the Breach: Post-Behavioralist Approaches to Judicial Politics, *Law and Social Inquiry* 25:601–34.

———. 2003. Legislative Sanctions and the Strategic Environment of Judicial Review, *International Journal of Constitutional Law* 1:446–74.

Widner, Jennifer. 2001. *Building the Rule of Law*. New York: W.W. Norton.

Wiecek, William M. 1969. The Reconstruction of Federal Judicial Power. *American Journal of Legal History* 13:333–59.

Wiegand, Wolfgang. 1996. Americanization of Law: Reception or Convergence? In *Legal Culture and the Legal Profession*, eds. Lawrence M. Friedman and Harry N. Scheiber,. Boulder, CO: Westview Press.

Wildavsky, Aaron. 1964. *Politics of the Budgetary Process*. Boston: Little Brown.

Wilson, James Q. 1989. *Bureaucracy*. New York: Basic Books.

———. 1994. Can the Bureaucracy be Deregulated? In *Deregulating the Public Service*, ed. John DiIulio. Washington, DC: Brookings Institution.

Wincott, Daniel. 1984. Does the European Union Pervert Democracy? Questions of Democracy in New Constitutionalist Thought on the Future of Europe. *European Law Journal* 4:411.

Woodward, C. Vann. 1966. *Reunion and Reaction: The Compromise of 1877 and the End of Reconstruction*. Boston: Little, Brown.

Ziamou, Theodora. 2001. *Rulemaking, Participation and the Limits of Public Law in the USA and Europe*. Aldershot: Ashgate.

Ziller, Jacques. 2001. European Models of Government: Towards a Patchwork with Missing Pieces. *Parliamentary Affairs* 54:102.

Contributors

Javier Couso is Professor at Diego Portales University in Santiago, Chile. He holds a Ph.D. from the Jurisprudence and Social Policy Program at Berkeley.

Paul Craig is Professor of English Law, St. John's College, Oxford, and a leading authority on European Law.

Howard Gillman is Chair and Professor of Political Science at the University of Southern California. He has authored and edited several books on law and courts, including *Supreme Court Decision-making: New Institutionalist Approaches* (Chicago 1999).

Tom Ginsburg is Associate Professor of Law and Political Science at the University of Illinois, Urbana-Champaign. His book *Judicial Review in New Democracies* won the 2004 C. Herman Pritchett Prize from the American Political Science Association.

Carol Harlow is Emeritus Professor of Law at the London School of Economics and Political Science, where she has worked since 1976, holding the Chair of Public Law until 2000. She writes on public law, including the public law of the European Union, and comparative administrative law, with special reference to France. She is the author of several books, including *Law and Administration,* written jointly with colleague Richard Rawlings, and most recently *Accountability in the European Union* (Oxford, 2003).

Robert A. Kagan is Professor of Law and Political Science and Director of the Center for Law and Society at the University of California at Berkeley. He is the author of *Adversarial Legalism: the American Way of Law* (Harvard, 2002).

R. Shep Melnick is Thomas P. O'Neill, Jr. Professor in the Political Science Department at Boston College, and the author of several books, including *Regulation and the Courts: The Case of the Clean Air Act* (Brookings, 2003).

Bronwen Morgan is the Harold Woods Research Fellow at Wadham College and Center for Socio-Legal Studies, University of Oxford, England, and author of *Social Citizenship in the Shadow of Competition: The Bureaucratic Politics of Regulatory Justification* (Ashgate, 2003).

Martin Shapiro is the James W. and Isabel Coffroth Professor of Law at the University of California, Berkeley.

Alec Stone Sweet is Leitner Professor of Law, Politics, and International Studies at Yale Law School.

TEACHING TEXTS IN LAW AND POLITICS

David Schultz, *General Editor*

The new series Teaching Texts in Law and Politics is devoted to textbooks that explore the multidimensional and multidisciplinary areas of law and politics. Special emphasis will be given to textbooks written for the undergraduate classroom. Subject matters to be addressed in this series include, but will not be limited to: constitutional law; civil rights and liberties issues; law, race, gender, and gender orientation studies; law and ethics; women and the law; judicial behavior and decision-making; legal theory; comparative legal systems; criminal justice; courts and the political process; and other topics on the law and the political process that would be of interest to undergraduate curriculum and education. Submission of single-author and collaborative studies, as well as collections of essays are invited.

Authors wishing to have works considered for this series should contact:

> Peter Lang Publishing
> Acquisitions Department
> 275 Seventh Avenue, 28th floor
> New York, New York 10001

To order other books in this series, please contact our Customer Service Department at:

> 800-770-LANG (within the U.S.)
> (212) 647-7706 (outside the U.S.)
> (212) 647-7707 FAX

or browse online by series at:

> WWW.PETERLANGUSA.COM